Statistical Techniques in Geographical Analysis

Statistical Techniques in Geographical Analysis

Third Edition

- **Dennis Wheeler**
- **Gareth Shaw**
- **Stewart Barr**

 David Fulton Publishers

David Fulton Publishers Ltd
The Chiswick Centre, 414 Chiswick High Road, London W4 5TF

www.fultonpublishers.co.uk

First published in 1985 by John Wiley and Sons
Second edition 1994

This edition published in Great Britain in 2004 by David Fulton Publishers

10 9 8 7 6 5 4 3 2 1

Note: The right of Dennis Wheeler, Gareth Shaw and Stewart Barr to be identified as the authors of this work has been asserted by them in accordance with the Copyright, Designs and Patents Act 1988.

David Fulton Publishers is a division of Granada Learning Limited, part of ITV plc.

British Library Cataloguing in Publication Data
A catalogue record for this book is available from the British Library.

ISBN 1 84312 176 X

Typeset by RefineCatch Limited, Bungay, Suffolk
Printed and bound in Great Britain

Contents

Preface to the third edition

The preface to the second edition of this book indicated the developments in computing that had taken place since the first edition, and the need to embrace those changes in a new text. Ten years later the evolutionary process continues. The second edition took into account the rapid growth in PCs and the decline of the mainframe computer. This new edition is prompted by further changes of which the switch from DOS-based to Windows-based, menu-driven forms of SPSS and MINITAB is the most important. A second change has been increased availability of data in digital form from websites or via CD-ROMs. These now form a far more important part of data gathering than has hitherto been the case. All such advances are welcome, and this new edition of *Statistical Techniques in Geographical Analysis* endeavours to recognise the changes that have taken place over the last decade. What have not changed are, of course, the statistical procedures themselves. But even they are not immune to changes in popularity. For this reason we have removed a large part, but by no means all, of the material dealing with non-linear regression, and included a new chapter on cluster analysis. The layout of the book is also new; gone are the DOS screen copies, to be replaced by the more readily comprehensible Windows-type displays. We have also taken advantage of new technology to include for the first time a CD-ROM that contains the data sets used in the worked examples together with other hopefully useful material.

We would like to thank both Minitab Inc. and SPSS plc for their support and for the provision of the latest editions of their software. We trust that they approve of the way in which we have employed their products, and that the readers – teachers and students alike – find this to be a text that guides them into a new century of computing and geographical analysis.

Dr Dennis Wheeler
School of Health, Natural and Social Sciences
University of Sunderland

Professor Gareth Shaw and Dr Stewart Barr
Geography Department
University of Exeter

Acknowledgements

The authors would like to take the opportunity to thank those who have contributed to this third edition. Many of the diagrams were prepared by the cartography team of the Geography Department at the University of Exeter. Ian Whyte of Minitab Inc. provided pre-release copies of MINITAB v.14. Terry Marsh (Centre for Ecology and Hydrology, Wallingford) offered useful guidance on the National River Flow Archive. The files with discharge data for the rivers Clyde and Tees were downloaded from the Archive, but the Natural Environmental Research Council (NERC), the Environment Agency, the Scottish Environment Protection Agency and the Rivers Agency (NI) accept no liability for any loss or damage, cost or claims arising directly or indirectly from their use. The statistics included in the CD-ROM files COUNTY.MTW and COUNTY.SAV are Crown Copyright material and are reproduced with the permission of the Controller of Her Majesty's Stationery Office. The authors also acknowledge the assistance of the UK Met Office and Hadley Centre from whose website the data files DURHAM.TXT and HadCET_act.TXT were obtained and with whose permission they are reproduced here. These data are also Crown Copyright material. Appendix VII of critical values of the Kruskal-Wallis statistic is reprinted by kind permission of the American Statistical Association. Appendices VIII and IX are reproduced from *Statistical Tables*, by H. R. Neave by kind permission of Taylor & Francis Books Ltd. Appendix X(a) and (b) are reprinted by kind permission of Professor A. Abrahamse (formerly of the Erasmus University of Rotterdam), and originally appeared in his text *On the Theory and Application of the General Linear Model* published by the University of Rotterdam Press. The environmental survey data used in Chapter 7, section 15 was also used in the preparation of Barr, S., Gilg, A. W. and Ford, N. J. (2003) 'Who are the environmentalists? Part 1: environmentalism in Britain today', *Town and Country Planning* **72**(6), 185–6 and kindly provided by the authors. Our thanks also go to Tracey Alcock of David Fulton Publishers for her help and patience in the preparation of this book.

Minitab Inc. and SPSS plc have both contributed to the preparation of this text. For more information on their products, the following websites should be consulted:

http://www.minitab.com

and

http://www.spss.com

1

Introduction

1.1 Introduction

STATISTICAL METHODS ARE NOW an accepted, indeed expected, part of a geographer's training, and most higher education programmes will include some elements of this important area of study. Regrettably, for many students this can be a painful and sometimes unrewarding encounter. Problems may arise from a lack of any comprehensive background in numerical analysis; a problem too often compounded by a seemingly bewildering notational system of unfamiliar Greek symbols. Further problems arise from the disillusion that many undergraduates find when courses and texts venture no further than univariate or bivariate methods, yet it is all too apparent that many geographical issues are multivariate in character, with the result that statistical training may not match geographical insight or analytical ambition.

These difficulties are not new, and have been recognised by a generation of geography teachers. Efforts to overcome them have met with mixed success, and over the last ten years or so another element has entered the equation. Widely available and powerful statistics software offer undoubted advantages, but must be used with caution, and make yet more, and not less, apparent the need to coach students in the theory and understanding of statistical methods. The temptation to use highly sophisticated and perhaps inappropriate techniques on indiscriminately large data sets is a regrettable consequence of the electronic age, but one that needs to be resisted. The value of any computational exercise is wholly undermined if the user has an uncertain grasp of the data requirements, principles and possible pitfalls of their chosen method of analysis.

With this background in mind, the authors have designed a book that embraces three themes. The first of these is the statistical methods themselves, the second is their application using computational software, and the third is the identification of data sources and management of those data. We draw these strands together by introducing a wide range of statistical procedures, each amplified by worked examples using the MINITAB and SPSS (Statistics Package for the Social Sciences) systems. It was decided to adopt both systems as in doing so we included the packages used by over 70 per cent of university geography departments. The range of methods covered should be sufficiently varied to satisfy the needs of an even greater proportion of undergraduate and postgraduate students and their teachers. In any such text, however, only a selection of a truly vast array of methods can be covered. In this the authors were guided principally by an examination of the methods most widely used in published geographical research works. We cannot, and have not attempted to, replicate the encyclopaedic statistics manuals of which S. Siegal's (1956) *Nonparametric Statistics for the Behavioral Sciences* is such a splendid example. Neither have we attempted to embrace the full range of options and alternatives in the SPSS and MINITAB systems. Again we have offered what is likely to be most necessary for students at undergraduate and early postgraduate level. Here, however, the excellent 'on-line' Help Guides of both systems could, and should, be consulted where there are any doubts or the reader wishes to investigate in greater depth what these two remarkable software packages have to offer.

The CD-ROM that comes with this book contains data files in MINITAB and SPSS formats for the worked examples, and provides ample opportunity to practise immediately with the methods as they are introduced. Although similar in so many respects, SPSS and MINITAB differ in the way in which test results are presented and in the range of output statistics that are available. These differences become more marked as this text progresses to the more sophisticated procedures. In all cases we have attempted to provide the alternative with which students are likely to be most at ease. Only occasionally can we provide text-based examples of the application of both systems to one method. In those many cases where MINITAB or SPSS have been used alone, the CD that accompanies the text will provide examples of the alternative system's procedures, using screen displays and some text. By this means those with access to only one of SPSS or MINITAB will not be at a disadvantage. Almost all the methods introduced can be executed in either SPSS or MINITAB. There are, however, a small number that cannot be performed by the standard software, and one or two that are not available on older versions.

The layout of the book is deliberately progressive, from the simpler to the more advanced methods and from the univariate and descriptive to the multivariate, more analytical approach. The chapters should not, however, be seen in isolation. We have tried to emphasise the continuity as one progresses from one theme to another, and to strike a balance between indispensable theory and necessary practice. Many geography students enrol on a degree programme without having pursued the study of mathematics beyond the age of 15 or 16 and approach statistics with some apprehension. With this problem foreseen, we have included a chapter that reviews the more common algebraic and mathematical principles with which the user should be familiar. As with the statistical procedures, it is not intended to be an exhaustive review, but covers the essential points from which students can move on with greater confidence. Because of the near-universal reliance on software packages, it might be thought that such arithmetic knowledge would serve little purpose. This is not the case, and it remains fundamental if the execution of the techniques is to be correctly undertaken, and the results understood! Indeed, students are often surprised to find that the level of mathematical competence required to perform manually some of the statistical analysis is not demanding. Addition, subtraction, multiplication, division and the use of squares, square roots and logarithms meet most needs. Statistics is, however, characterised by the repetitive nature of the arithmetic, with long columns of numbers to be treated. Although tedious to the researcher, this of course, is the great virtue of electronic computers, which can perform these simple tasks with imagination-defying speed. Nevertheless, it is valuable for students to perform some of the simpler statistical procedures manually, and the inclusion of details of software applications must not be taken as an invitation for their use in all cases.

The authors have assumed that students are generally familiar with the MS Windows operating system, and we have concentrated on the specific requirements of the two software systems, both of which are used in their most recent Windows-based versions. Inevitably therefore, some sections are devoted to the more mechanical tasks of running the software but, even here, we need to know the nature of the methods in order that appropriate options can be chosen from the wide range presented by the programs. Use is made wherever possible of screen images to show how the instructions are given to the computer. These were prepared using MINITAB v.14 and SPSS v.11, but they apply to the most recent Windows-generation versions of these two systems.

The question of data collection and gathering has also been considered. The growing availability of on-line data sources, of downloadable files and CD-ROMs has prompted a veritable revolution in this field. Most certainly, some areas of geography are better served than others in this respect, but we have drawn attention to the more important of the UK-base websites. Again, however, the list is not fully comprehensive, neither can it be in an area that is developing as quickly as this one.

As far as it can be, this book is designed therefore to be a self-contained guide that gives methodological instruction, offers guidance with computational procedures and directs geographers to data sources. In respect of theory and practice, and of the range of methods and their applications we hope that we have struck a helpful balance that encourages and does not daunt the reader.

1.2 The CD-ROM

The inclusion of the CD is designed to complement and not replace the textbook. It includes additional guidance notes in PDF format, together with copies of all the data files used in the worked examples. Much can be learned from simply investigating the system with different instructions and utilising different options. With this in mind, one particularly large data file, which covers observations for 35 socio-economic variables for the 46 English counties has been included. Only a few of its constituent variables

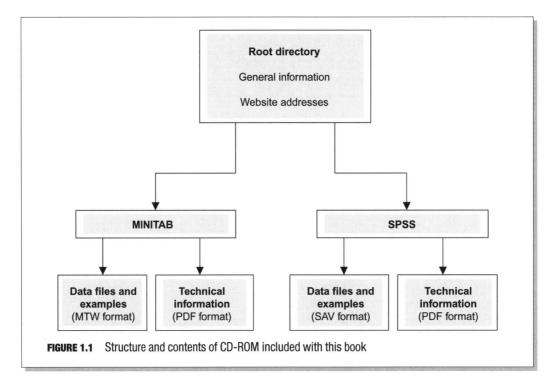

FIGURE 1.1 Structure and contents of CD-ROM included with this book

have been used, mostly in Chapters 9 and 10, and students and teachers are invited to investigate this data set and the software at their leisure.

Each data file is set up in both MINITAB and SPSS formats so that they can be called up directly into the appropriate system with further manipulation. The reader will see that the root directory of the CD is partitioned into MINITAB and SPSS subdirectories for just this purpose (Figure 1.1). Also included under the different techniques headings are PDF files with additional worked examples in both systems to cover those many cases where text limitation prevent duplication of procedures using both MINITAB and SPSS. These PDF files require Adobe Acrobat reader, and this software can be downloaded free of charge from the website whose URL is given in the root directory of the CD. You need only click on the address for the connection to be made through the world wide web (www).

The root directory also provides the URLs of the various website sources that are used in the text. This list is, it must be noted, highly selective, and it is not offered as a comprehensive review of all such sources.

1.3 Conventions and layout

In order to facilitate use of the book, we have adopted a number of conventions and approaches to the layout of the text. Wherever possible, screen displays of examples are used to guide the reader. Limitations on space prevent, however, every stage from being illustrated in this fashion, although the CD provides more scope for this aspect of the presentation. A number of conventions have also been adopted to make the text easier to follow:

1 **Bold text items**: many references are made to key words and button names on the pull down menus and in the dialogue boxes. To highlight their importance and clarify the text all such instructional items are printed in bold. Where successive instructions are required these are indicated by use of the > symbol. For example, to open an existing MINITAB data file, the instructions would be indicated thus: **File > Open Worksheet**. The first item is the header on the pull down menu, and the second is the required option from the list presented. In many cases there will be longer sequences of options. Such commands usually produce a dialogue box. If specific buttons in the dialogue boxes such as **OK, Continue, Options** etc. are required to be clicked, they are similarly printed in bold.

2 *Italicised text items*: where specific technical terms are used that are not part of the software's command or instructional vocabulary, they are printed in italics on their first appearance in the text, but thereafter in Roman form.

3 UPPER CASE TEXT ITEMS: where reference is made to data files written on the CD, the file names are given in upper case, non-bold, text. The file formats, e.g. SAV or MTW are also in upper case.

2

An introduction to mathematical statistics and computer applications

2.1 Introduction

THE AIM OF THIS chapter is not to educate the reader in all or even many of the branches of mathematics or aspects of computing, but rather to provide a brief introduction to the arithmetic and computational procedures used in the following chapters. We have assumed a basic level of numeracy, and a general familiarity with the MS Windows' operating system, but nothing more than this. Those who have pursued a course in mathematics at 'A' level or equivalent grades elsewhere may feel confident in skipping the first six sections of this chapter, though all would benefit from the introductory sections that describe the two statistics packages adopted in this book for the execution of the analytical methods described in the following chapters.

Geography students, many of whom embark on their degree levels studies with a generally 'arts' background, are rarely at ease when handling quantitative data, the successful analysis of which is not so much a question of mathematical ability as of confidence and clear thinking. All too often students allow themselves to be intimidated by the vocabulary and algebraic shorthand of statistical methods, and some do not recover from the trauma of their initial encounters with this important branch of their chosen discipline. This need not be the case. In reality many of the equations used by statisticians are surprisingly simple, and involve only the irksome repetition of the basic arithmetic procedures of addition, subtraction, multiplication or division. Only rarely do they provide challenging mathematical enterprises. Perhaps it is the abundant use of Greek symbols or the wealth of subscripts that prompts uncertainty in the minds of many students. But whatever the cause, this chapter demonstrates that such fears are groundless. When the syntax of statistical algebra becomes familiar, many of the difficulties disappear. Furthermore, and as will become clear, a great deal of arithmetic drudgery can be left to the computer; though this is certainly not to suggest that the mathematical principles on which they operate can be overlooked – quite the opposite, they need to be clearly understood in order that sense can be made of the results that appear on the screen or from the printer. Finally, the facility offered by both SPSS and MINITAB for the arithmetic transformation and manipulation of raw data requires that the user has at least a working familiarity with the principles that govern such operations.

2.2 Arithmetic procedures

A common problem when using statistical equations arises from misunderstanding of the sequence in which different arithmetic procedures are carried out. Although such procedures may be individually correct, when not executed in the proper order they will lead to an incorrect answer. A simple example will clarify this point. Unless otherwise specified, multiplication and division must always precede addition and subtraction. Thus in the expression $2.5 + 17.2 \times 3.1$, it is the multiplication of 17.2 by 3.1 that must be executed first. Only then can 2.5 be added to this product, to give the answer 55.82. Had the 2.5 been first added to 17.2 and the result multiplied by 3.1 we would have arrived at the (incorrect) answer of 61.07. By the same convention, divisions also precede additions and subtractions, so that $4.7/2.1 - 2.0$ gives $2.238 - 2.0 = 0.238$, whereas $4.7/0.1 = 47.0$ would be incorrect. Within strings of successive additions and subtractions or of multiplications and divisions alone the order of execution is immaterial, hence $3.2 \times 1.1 \times 7.0/2.0$ would yield 12.32 irrespective of the order in which the operations were executed. Care, however, is needed when successive subtractions are indicated. For example $17 - 2 - 1$ has the answer 14 and not 16 as the last two items are $- 2 - 1$ (which is -3), and not $2 - 1$. In such cases difficulties are avoided by proceeding from left to right. This problem does not, of course, arise with successive additions.

Should any change in the conventional order of precedence be required, it is indicated by the use of brackets. Going back to $2.5 + 17.2 \times 3.1$; had we wished to add the first two items and only then multiply by 3.1 the expression would have been written as $(2.5 + 17.2) \times 3.1$. The instructions within such brackets must always be executed before moving to those instructions that lie outside. This is an important principle and one that should be clearly understood as it has particular importance for many of the equations that appear in this, and other, texts.

Powers and floating point format

There are, however, further conventions to be respected. Powers and indices, as operational indicators, take precedence over addition, subtraction, multiplication and division. For example:

$$2 \times 4^3 = 2 \times 64 = 128 \text{ and is not } 8^3 = 512$$

Notice that, especially with powers, failure to follow the correct order of precedence can lead to large errors in the final answer. Should that order need to be changed brackets will again be used to denote the required sequence of execution. A common example in statistical analysis is the need to square the difference between two quantities, say 7·2 and 2·4. It would be incorrect to express this as $7·2 - 2·4^2$ because, as we have seen, the squaring would be carried out before the subtraction. The expression should read $(7·2 - 2·4)^2$. Now the subtraction is completed first, and only then is the result squared.

$$(7·2 - 2·4)^2 = 4·8^2 = 23·04$$

Where several pairs of brackets are used in an expression, the operations within the innermost are executed first, working then outwards to the surrounding bracket pairs. It is sometimes helpful to distinguish the order by using rounded and square brackets, but the brackets must always be in matched pairs. For example:

$$[2(3·2 + 4·0)]^2 = [2(7·2)]^2 = 14·4^2 = 207·36$$

but

$$[2(3·2 + 4·0]^2) \text{ is incorrect.}$$

The executable instructions $=, -, \times$ and $/$ (or $\div$), together with indices provide the basis of nearly all of the equations used in this book. The first four instructions should provide no difficulty, but the use of indices or powers requires further elaboration.

At the most elementary level indices and powers indicate repetitive multiplication so that:

$$2^2 = 2 \times 2 = 4$$

or

$$4·2^4 = 4·2 \times 4·2 \times 4·2 \times 4·2 = 311·17$$

Indices are therefore a useful shorthand without which lengthy arithmetic descriptions would be required. The expression 10^7 is easier to understand, and less likely to be misread, than its full version (10,000,000). This index format is a facility widely used by computers to avoid presenting long sequences of digits when referring to very large or to very small numbers. Most machines will not display numbers more than eight digits in length in their standard form. Numbers greater than 99,999,999 or less than 0·0000001 are commonly presented in *floating point* format. It is important that this system of numbers is well understood before using either SPSS or MINITAB, both of which employ it. For example a calculation might yield the result 611,280,800. This is will be displayed on a screen or printer as 6·1128 08 or as 6·1128 E08. In both cases the numbers should be understood to be $6·1128 \times 10^8$ in which the power to which 10 has been raised indicates the number of places that the decimal point has to be moved (in this case to the right) in order to arrive at the full number. Remember that to multiply any number by 100 (which is 10^2) is to move the decimal point two places to the right. Thus $2·5 \times 10^2$ becomes 250·0.

The floating point convention applies also to small numbers, but their explanation requires a brief discussion of negative indices. In the same way as 2^2 is executable, so too are expressions such as 2^{-3} or $3 \cdot 6^{-3}$. Negative indices are best understood by remembering that they change their sign if their reciprocals are used, i.e. if the expression is placed 'below the line' with 1 above. Thus,

$$2^{-2} = 1/2^2 = 1/4 = 0 \cdot 25$$

and

$$3 \cdot 6^{-3} = 1/3 \cdot 6^3 = 1/46 \cdot 66 = 0 \cdot 0214$$

Notice that the use of negative indices with positive numbers can never yield a negative answer. We can now see how floating point formats can be used to present small quantities.

Computer output might give the number $7 \cdot 4 - 08$ or $7 \cdot 4 \text{ E}{-}08$, both of which represent the quantity $7 \cdot 4 \times 10^{-8}$, which can be rewritten as $7 \cdot 4 \times 1/10^8$. When expanded this expression becomes the much more unwieldy $7 \cdot 4 \times 0 \cdot 00000001$ or $0 \cdot 000000074$. The negative index now indicates how many places the decimal point must be moved, but to the left. The final quantities thereby becoming smaller as the index becomes larger.

There is, however, a price to be paid for the convenience of floating point numbers. If the quantity 611,280,800 is given as $6 \cdot 1128 \text{ E}08$ then the expansion to its 'standard' form will give only 611,280,000, implying an apparent rounding error of 800 although the computer will internally retain the correct figure. Clearly, such errors are relatively small, but computer users should be aware of them.

Attention can now be turned to the question of fractional indices. Integer (whole number) indices should offer few problems, but fractional terms are less simple. How should $4^{2 \cdot 3}$ or $7^{1 \cdot 5}$ be evaluated? From the practical point of view, many pocket calculators can evaluate these numbers and, as the following section demonstrates, logarithms can be used to solve the problem.

Table 2.1 summarises the contrasting results of using positive and negative fractional indices. Note should be made of the fact that $1 \cdot 0$ raised to any power remains $1 \cdot 0$, while any number raised to the power $0 \cdot 0$ is, by convention, taken as $1 \cdot 0$. The following points should also be noted as guiding principles when numbers are raised to various powers:

- positive indices greater than $1 \cdot 0$ will increase the final quantity

- positive indices less than $1 \cdot 0$ will decrease the final quantity, but can never yield a value of less than $1 \cdot 0$

- negative indices of any magnitude greater than $1 \cdot 0$ can only yield answers of less than $1 \cdot 0$

- for numbers between $1 \cdot 0$ and zero any positive index can only yield a result that is itself between $1 \cdot 0$ and zero. The result can only exceed $1 \cdot 0$ if a negative index is used.

TABLE 2.1 Numerical equivalents of power terms

Expression	Result	Expression	Result
9^2	81·0	9^{-2}	0·0123
9^1	9·0	9^{-1}	0·1111
$9^{0.8}$	5·799	$9^{-0.8}$	0·1724
$9^{0.5}$	3·0	$9^{-0.5}$	0·3333
$9^{0.2}$	1·552	$9^{-0.2}$	0·6444
9^0	1·0	$9^{-0.1}$	0·8027

The reader should be aware of the various means by which the instructions for a square root can be given. Most will already know that $\sqrt{X}$ indicates the square root of X. But fractional indices can also be used to the same effect. Both $X^{0.5}$ and $X^{\frac{1}{2}}$ indicate that the square root is required.

This brief review can be concluded by stating the three 'laws' of operations with indices:

- powers may be added for multiplication from a common base

  $X^m \times X^n = X^{m+n}$, e.g. $3^3 \times 3^2 = 3^5 = 243$

- powers may be subtracted for division from a common base

  $X^m / X^n = X^{m-n}$, e.g. $3^3 / 3^2 = 3^{3-2} = 3^1 = 3$

- powers may be multiplied when they appear in sequence

  $(X^m)^n = X^{m \times n}$, e.g. $(3^3)^2 = 3^{3 \times 2} = 3^6 = 729$

2.3 Logarithms

Any number on the 'arithmetic' scale that is greater than zero can be expressed by its counterpart on the logarithmic scale. The advantages of such re-expressions are many, some will appear later in the book, meanwhile it is only the basic principles that require attention.

The reader will need to be familiar with the two most frequently used logarithmic systems – the natural logarithms (denoted by ln or $\log_e$) and the common logarithms (denoted by $\log_{10}$). The latter are the simpler to comprehend, and the more widely employed. Table 2.2 summarises some of the more well known features of logarithmic numbers, and shows how arithmetic and logarithmic terms are related.

TABLE 2.2 Common logarithmic equivalents of numbers greater than 1·0

Number	Log	Number	Log	Number	Log	Number	Log
1·0	0	3·0	0·4771	5·0	0·6989	7·0	0·8451
10·0	1·0	30·0	1·4771	50·0	1·6989	70·0	1·8451
100·0	2·0	300·0	2·4771	500·0	2·6989	700·0	2·8451
1000·0	3·0	3000·0	3·4771	5000·0	3·6989	7000·0	3·8451

Table 2.2 demonstrates also the relationship between common logarithms and their 'base' of 10. In mathematical terms, the common logarithm of a number is the power to which 10 (the base) has to be raised to obtain that number. The previous section dealt with the use of indices, and here is an example of those principles at work. Thus:

$$10^2 = 100 \text{ so that } \log_{10}100 = 2\cdot0$$

and

$$10^{1\cdot6989} = 50 \text{ so that } \log_{10}50 = 1\cdot6989$$

No logarithmic system permits logs to made from negative numbers, but there are numbers – those between 1·0 and zero – that are expressed by negative logarithms. Table 2.3 shows how numbers less than 1·0 relate to their logarithmic equivalents.

From Table 2.3 it can be seen that there can be no log of zero, and that increasingly small fractions are expressed by increasingly larger negative logarithms. The relationship that links such fractions with the common logarithms is again determined by the power to which 10 must be raised to produce that number. Thus:

$$10^{-1} = 0\cdot1 \text{ so that } \log_{10}0\cdot1 = -1\cdot0$$

and

$$10^{-0\cdot301} = 0\cdot5 \text{ so that } \log_{10}0\cdot5 = -0\cdot301$$

Those students who are familiar with the published tables of logarithms will have noted that while Table 2.2 conforms to their expectations with regard to the logarithmic equivalents of given numbers, Table 2.3 does not. This difference arises because

TABLE 2.3 Common logarithmic equivalents of numbers less than 1·0

Number	Log	Number	Log	Number	Log
0·1	−1·0	0·3	−0·5229	0·5	−0·301
0·01	−2·0	0·03	−1·5229	0·05	−1·301
0·001	−3·0	0·003	−2·5229	0·005	−2·301

published logarithmic tables use the 'bar' system when dealing with numbers of less than 1·0. Under this convention the log of, for example, 0·3 would be $\bar{1}$·4771 and not, as in Table 2.3, –0·5229. In the same fashion, the log of 0·03 would be $\bar{2}$·4771 and not –1·5229. The connection between the two systems is made clear if we write the 'bar' notation in its full form. Thus, $\bar{1}$·4771 should be expressed as –1 + 0·4771, which is of course –0·5229. Publishers of mathematical tables find the 'bar' system useful because it avoids the need to print two sets of log tables, one for numbers greater than 1·0, and another for numbers less than 1·0. Computers are, however, unable to work with this convention.

Antilogging is the process by which logs are converted back to their arithmetic equivalents. The common antilog of 2·0, for example, is 100·0. If the base of the logarithmic system, in the current case 10, is raised to the power indicated by the logarithm, the result is the antilog. For example, if we have a logarithm of 0·4771, its antilogarithm can be found from $10^{0.4771}$, which is 3·0.

Logarithms have many advantages for statistical analyses, as will be shown later. They can also be used to solve problems involving powers; lengthy multiplications and divisions are also made easier when numbers are expressed in their logarithmic forms. These points are conveniently summarised and illustrated by the two following 'laws' of logarithmic operations.

The first law of logarithms

When multiplying two numbers we may instead add their respective logarithms; the antilog of the result being the required answer. For example, the product of 28·47 × 39·23, can be found as follows:

$$\log_{10}28\text{·}47 = 1\text{·}4544 \text{ and } \log_{10}39\text{·}23 = 1\text{·}5936$$

but

$$\log_{10}(28\text{·}47 \times 39\text{·}23) = \log_{10}28\text{·}47 + \log_{10}39\text{·}23$$

from which we establish that the common log of the product is:

$$1\text{·}4544 + 1\text{·}5936 = 3\text{·}048$$

But this quantity is itself in logarithmic form, and must be antilogged in order to give the final answer. In this case the antilog of 3·048 is $10^{3.048}$, which is 1116·86.

Divisions are performed in a similar fashion, but by subtraction. Thus the result of 28·47/39·23 can be found by subtracting the two logarithms:

$$1\text{·}4544 - 1\text{·}5936 = -0\text{·}1392$$

Again this is in logarithmic form, and the antilog is given by $10^{-0.1392}$, which gives the final answer 0·7257.

The general algebraic expressions of these laws can be written as:

$$a \times b = \text{antilog}(\log_{10}a + \log_{10}b)$$

and

$$a/b = \text{antilog}(\log_{10}a - \log_{10}b)$$

The second law of logarithms

The value of a number raised to any power can be found by multiplying the log of that number by the (unlogged) power term, and then antilogging the resulting product. For example, $3.67^{1.89}$ can be evaluated as follows:

$$(\log_{10}3.67) \times 1.89 = 0.5647 \times 1.89 = 1.0673$$

the antilog of which is 11.673.

Negative powers can be dealt with in a similar fashion and $3.67^{-1.89}$ would be evaluated as follows:

$$0.5647 \times (-1.89) = -1.0673$$

the antilog of which is 0.0856.

This operation can be expressed algebraically as:

$$a^b = \text{antilog}(\log_{10}a \times b)$$

The examples used to illustrate these laws are simple, but the principles that they illustrate will be found to be useful in the more practical settings found in later chapters.

Natural logarithms

Attention can now be turned to the second of the major logarithmic systems, the so called natural logarithms. Common logs have 10 as their base, but natural logarithms have as their base $2.71828 \ldots$ a quantity designated by the symbol e, and having a number of properties that go beyond the scope of this book. The natural logarithm of $2.71828 \ldots$ is, thus, 1.0. The natural log of a number is the power to which e must be raised to obtain that number. A range of equivalents are listed in Table 2.4. All of the rules demonstrated for common logs apply equally to their natural counterparts. For example, $3.67^{1.89}$ would, using natural logarithms, be evaluated from:

$$(\log_e 3.67) \times 1.89 = 1.3002 \times 1.89 = 2.457$$

Again this is a logarithm, the natural antilog of which is 11.67.

As with common logarithms, the process of antilogging is that of raising the logarithm base (e in this case) to the power specified by the log itself. For example, the natural antilog of 2.457 is found from:

$$e^{2.457} = 11.67$$

TABLE 2.4 Some numbers and their natural logarithms

Number	Number as an exponent of e	Natural log
1	e^0	0
2·71828 . . .	e^1	1
5·0	$e^{1·609}$	1·609
7·3891	e^2	2
10·0	$e^{2·303}$	2·303
20·0855	e^3	3·0
1·6487	$e^{0·5}$	0·5

To avoid any confusion we shall henceforth adopt the convention of denoting common logs by the term 'log' and natural logs by '*ln*'. Conversion between the two systems is easy as

$$log(x) = ln(x) \times 0·4343$$

and

$$ln(x) = log(x) \times 2·303$$

2.4 Statistical procedures

Thus far attention has focused on arithmetic and mathematical operations. There is, however, a further notation common in statistical methods that employs what appears to be a bewildering wealth of subscripts and Greek symbols. In reality such symbols are merely a shorthand for a number of mathematical tasks, few of which go further than those outlined in the preceding pages.

One of the most frequently encountered of these instructional symbols is the Greek letter Σ (capital sigma). No numerical quantity is associated with this symbol; it is an operational instruction that indicates the necessity of adding together the values of the variable that it precedes. That variable might, for example, be daily rainfall at some given location, which could be denoted by the term X (or indeed any other letter). The instruction to add the series of rainfall readings would appear as ΣX. In the same way ΣY would indicate the necessity of adding together the individual items that constitute the variable denoted by Y.

A more comprehensive form of this expression may be used to indicate how long the data series might be, or what part of the series is to be added. If a data set contained the daily rainfall readings for a particular site, the instruction to calculate the annual total would be given by:

$$T = \sum_{i=1}^{365} X_i$$

where T = the annual rainfall total and X is the variable list that includes all the individual daily readings. The subscript i indicates that, in this case, items 1 to 365 should be added. Table 2.5 indicates how i, X and Σ are connected if the total rainfall for a week is required.

The total number of observations in a data set or, more correctly in the context of statistics, sample, are not usually known in advance and the term n is conventionally employed to denote that quantity. This allows a more general summation instruction to be written:

$$\sum_{i=1}^{n} X_i$$

Such general instructions appear frequently when using the different methods of statistical analysis. Furthermore, instructions need not be restricted to beginning at the first item of the list (where $i = 1$). Thus, for example, if only the 10th to the 20th members of a list need to be added, this could be expressed by:

$$\sum_{i=10}^{20} X_i$$

One subscript only (in the above cases i) is used when observations are limited to single lists, or vectors, no matter how long they might be. If, however, the sample consists of rows and columns of data, i.e. it is in the form of a matrix, then double subscripts

TABLE 2.5 The index notation in statistical analysis, taking the example of a week's daily rainfall totals

Sequence number (i)	Numerical value
1	$X_i = X_1 = 10\cdot2$
2	$X_i = X_2 = 11\cdot2$
3	$X_i = X_3 = 0\cdot0$
4	$X_i = X_4 = 1\cdot3$
5	$X_i = X_5 = 0\cdot5$
6	$X_i = X_6 = 3\cdot4$
7	$X_i = X_7 = 2\cdot1$

Weekly rainfall (T) = $\displaystyle\sum_{i=1}^{7} X_i$ = $10\cdot2 + 11\cdot2 + 0\cdot0 + 1\cdot3 + 0\cdot5 + 3\cdot4 + 2\cdot1 = 28\cdot7$ mm

a) Vector

i = 1	X_1
i = 2	X_2
i = 3	X_3
i = 4	X_4
i = 5	X_5

b) Matrix

	j = 1	j = 2	j = 3	j = 4	j = 5
i = 1	$X_{1.1}$	$X_{1.2}$	$X_{1.3}$	$X_{1.4}$	$X_{1.5}$
i = 2	$X_{2.1}$	$X_{2.2}$	$X_{2.3}$	$X_{2.4}$	$X_{2.5}$
i = 3	$X_{3.1}$	$X_{3.2}$	$X_{3.3}$	$X_{3.4}$	$X_{3.5}$
i = 4	$X_{4.1}$	$X_{4.2}$	$X_{4.3}$	$X_{4.4}$	$X_{4.5}$
i = 5	$X_{5.1}$	$X_{5.2}$	$X_{5.3}$	$X_{5.4}$	$X_{5.5}$

FIGURE 2.1 Graphical representation of vector and matrix subscripts

are needed so that individual items can be identified by reference to their row and column number. The difference in the manner in which vectors and matrices are described can be illustrated by a simple example. The seven day set of rainfall observations used in the earlier example form a vector, and represent the conditions at one specific site. If, however, rainfall data have been recorded at five different sites over the same period of time the results can be presented in the form of a matrix in which each day corresponds to a row and each column to a site (see Figure 2.1). The rainfall on day two at site three might be expressed as item $X_{2,3}$ in the matrix. The rainfall on day five and site four would be expressed as item $X_{5,4}$. In neither case are the actual rainfall totals given, and only their location in the matrix is indicated. If we wanted to specify that the sum of all daily rainfalls over all sites (T) were needed, the instruction would be written as:

$$T = \sum_{i=1}^{r} \sum_{j=1}^{k} X_{ij}$$

where X indicates the variable (in this case daily rainfall totals), i the row number and j the column number. In this case note that all row elements for all columns are specified for inclusion up to the maximum r and k, which in this example are 5 and 5 respectively.

The need to add successive items in a vector or matrix is commonplace in statistics, but the system of notation can be developed to indicate more useful outcomes. The arithmetic mean or average of a data sum is the sum of all its items divided by the number of items (see Chapter 4). This can be expressed as follows:

$$\bar{X} = \frac{\sum_{i=1}^{n} X_i}{n}$$

where $\bar{X}$ = the mean, and n = the number of observations in the sample. The 'bar' over the symbol representing the variable in question (X in this example) indicates that the mean of the sample of observations is required. It is a convention in statistical methods and must not be confused with the bar notation used in published log tables as described above. In this case the sub and superscripts $i = 1$ and n have been retained. To simplify matters they will not be included from this point onwards unless circumstances dictate their retention for clarification.

Because Σ is an operational instruction, it is important to establish where it stands in the order of precedence for arithmetic procedures. The use of brackets, or the position of the sign in the equation will usually make the position clear. In the example of the mean, the placing of the sigma sign and variable designator above the line indicates that the summation is completed first, and only then is the total divided by the sample size (n). Indices take precedence over summations however, and the instruction ΣX^2 indicates that the individual items are squared and those squares are then summed. Table 2.6 summarises such conventions and illustrates how brackets may be needed to impose a different sequence of procedures.

A final example, but one which occurs many times in statistics, is the need to square a set of differences, sum them and then divide by the total number of observations. Most often this appears in the form of differences from the mean of the data set. The mean is calculated beforehand ($\bar{X}$), then subtracted from each of the individual observations (X) in turn. The differences are squared, then summed and then divided by the sample size (n) to give the desired quantity (s). Such a sequence of operations would be indicated by the equation:

$$s = \frac{\sum (X - \bar{X})^2}{n}$$

TABLE 2.6   Conventions for the execution of mathematical statements using the summation sign

Instruction	Sequence of execution	
ΣX^2	1. Square all Xs	2. Sum the squares
$(\Sigma X)^2$	1. Sum all Xs	2. Square the sum
ΣXY	1. Multiply all paired values of X and Y	2. Sum the products[1]
$3(\Sigma X)$	1. Sum all Xs	2. Multiply the sum by 3·0
$3[\Sigma(X-1)]$	1. Subtract 1·0 from each X	2. Sum all subtractions
	3. Multiply the sum by 3·0	
$\displaystyle\sum \frac{(X-Y)^2}{25}$	1. Subtract each Y from its corresponding X	2. Square all differences
	3. Divide all the squares by 25	4. Sum all the quotients

[1] To be wholly unambiguous, this instruction should be written as $\Sigma(XY)$, but is conventionally written as above, and will be presented as such in later chapters.

Had we wished, however, to square the sum of the difference rather than sum the squares of the differences, an additional pair of outer brackets would have been needed, thus:

$$s = \frac{\left[\sum (X - \bar{X})\right]^2}{n}$$

2.5 Graphs of statistical data

Graphs, maps and diagrams can all help geographers to describe and to understand the information with which they are working. In later chapters we will be dealing with procedures that summarise in the form of graphed lines and curves the relationship between pairs of variables (see Chapters 9 and 10 in particular). Such lines and curves are often derived from simple algebraic equations.

Equations can be used to summarise the co-behaviour of two variables that are thought to be related; the changes in one influencing changes in the other. For example, it is well known that rainfall over many parts of the world increases with altitude, or that population density decreases with distance from a city centre. The equations that can summarise and describe these relationships can be plotted by computer or by hand on a sheet of graph paper. Chapter 9 will introduce the nature of such equations and their derivation from 'real' data, but the principles on which they are based can be introduced at this stage by taking some simple examples.

The equation of a straight line

The equation $Y = a + bX$ can be plotted as a straight line. The terms Y and X might be geographic variables such as rainfall (Y) and altitude (X), while the terms a and b are constants, and have values that are fixed for any particular data set. They quantify the link between X and Y. The individual values of X will be different, and by substituting those different values into the equation a corresponding series of estimates of Y can be made. The variable Y is, therefore, said to be dependent upon a, b and X. Section 9.2 will demonstrate how, for any given case, the values of a and b can be estimated, but for the moment let us assume that $a = 5 \cdot 0$ and $b = 1 \cdot 5$. Remember that these two quantities are now fixed for the purposes of this example. If we now substitute a series of values for X into the equation, it will produce the results shown in Table 2.7. The graphical expression of these results is shown in Figure 2.2. By convention, X is plotted along the horizontal axis (the ordinate), and Y on the vertical axis (the abscissa).

The effect of selecting other values for a and b are also shown in Table 2.7 and Figure 2.2. Larger values for b lead to steeper lines, while larger values for a move the origin of the line upwards on the abscissa. It should also be noted that the point at which the line crosses the Y axis is the value of the expression when X is zero, and is determined by the value of a. Although not shown here, both a and b can have negative

TABLE 2.7 Straight line data obtained by successive substitutions of X in different forms of the equation $Y = a + bX$

Value of X	$Y = 5{\cdot}0 + 1{\cdot}5X$	$Y = 5{\cdot}0 + 2{\cdot}5X$	$Y = 2{\cdot}0 + 1{\cdot}5X$
0·0	$Y = 5{\cdot}0 + 0{\cdot}0 = 5{\cdot}0$	$Y = 5{\cdot}0 + 0{\cdot}0 = 5{\cdot}0$	$Y = 2{\cdot}0 + 0{\cdot}0 = 2{\cdot}0$
2·0	$Y = 5{\cdot}0 + 3{\cdot}0 = 8{\cdot}0$	$Y = 5{\cdot}0 + 5{\cdot}0 = 10{\cdot}0$	$Y = 2{\cdot}0 + 3{\cdot}0 = 5{\cdot}0$
4·0	$Y = 5{\cdot}0 + 6{\cdot}0 = 11{\cdot}0$	$Y = 5{\cdot}0 + 10{\cdot}0 = 15{\cdot}0$	$Y = 2{\cdot}0 + 6{\cdot}0 = 8{\cdot}0$
6·0	$Y = 5{\cdot}0 + 9{\cdot}0 = 14{\cdot}0$	$Y = 5{\cdot}0 + 15{\cdot}0 = 20{\cdot}0$	$Y = 2{\cdot}0 + 9{\cdot}0 = 11{\cdot}0$
8·0	$Y = 5{\cdot}0 + 12{\cdot}0 = 17{\cdot}0$	$Y = 5{\cdot}0 + 20{\cdot}0 = 25{\cdot}0$	$Y = 2{\cdot}0 + 12{\cdot}0 = 14{\cdot}0$
10·0	$Y = 5{\cdot}0 + 15{\cdot}0 = 20{\cdot}0$	$Y = 5{\cdot}0 + 25{\cdot}0 = 30{\cdot}0$	$Y = 2{\cdot}0 + 15{\cdot}0 = 17{\cdot}0$
12·0	$Y = 5{\cdot}0 + 18{\cdot}0 = 23{\cdot}0$	$Y = 5{\cdot}0 + 30{\cdot}0 = 35{\cdot}0$	$Y = 2{\cdot}0 + 18{\cdot}0 = 20{\cdot}0$

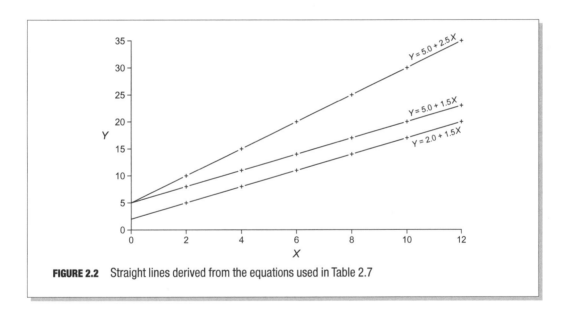

FIGURE 2.2 Straight lines derived from the equations used in Table 2.7

values. In the former case the line crosses the Y axis at some point below the X axis intersection, while negative values for b give lines that slope downwards from left to right denoting decreases of Y with increases in X.

The equation for a curve

The equation for a straight line differs only in respect of the quantities attributed to its various components (a, b and X). There are, on the other hand, a very large number of equations which when plotted will describe a curve of one form or another. We will examine only the most elementary of these. Consider an expression such as $Y = aX^b$. This is similar to the linear model cited above; it has two constants and one X term, but on plotting it will yield a curve. Depending upon the values chosen for the two constants, the character of the curve can vary. In Table 2.8 we have taken three different sets of constants. The plots from these three equations are presented in Figure 2.3. Because X is now raised to the power b it produces a curved rather than a straight line (remember that X^b is evaluated before multiplication by a). But there are differences between them that can be summarised thus:

TABLE 2.8 Curved lines derived by successive substitution of X in the different equations of the general form $Y = aX^b$

Value of X	$Y = 60X^{0.3}$	$Y = 0.3X^3$	$Y = 30X^{-2}$
0·5	48·72	0·038	120·0
1	60·0	0·30	30·0
2	73·8	2·4	7·50
3	83·4	8·1	3·33
4	90·9	19·2	1·87
5	97·2	37·5	1·20
6	102·7	64·8	0·83
7	107·5	102·9	0·61

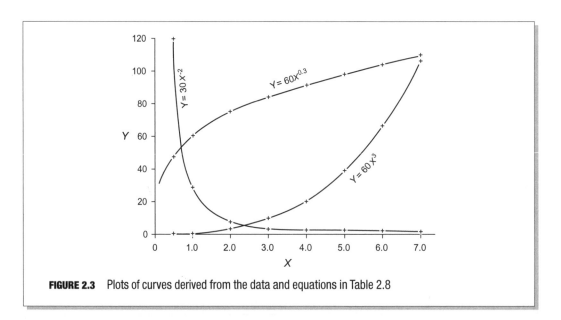

FIGURE 2.3 Plots of curves derived from the data and equations in Table 2.8

- when the power is positive and greater than 1·0, Y increases with X, and the curve is concave-upwards.

- when the power is positive but less than 1·0 Y also increases with X, but the curve is convex-upwards.

- when the power is negative, Y decreases with X and the curve is concave-upwards.

The degree of curvature is dictated by the b term, and is greater for larger values. The value of a determines the general location of the curve on the co-ordinate system. In the linear model above the line had to pass through the point where $X = 0·0$ and $Y = a$, but this curve must pass through the point where $X = 1·0$ and $Y = a$. In order to understand this remember from section 2.2 that 1·0 raised to any power is 1·0. Hence, for example, whenever $X = 1·0$, it remains 1·0 irrespective of the power to which it is raised, and Y must, therefore, be $a \times 1·0$ at that point.

Many other forms of curve are possible, such as $Y = 1/X$ or $Y = a + X^b$. Furthermore, not all equations need be restricted to just two constants, and so-called *polynomial* expressions can often be used such as $Y = a + bx + cX^2$. All, however, can be plotted in much the same way as those above. The principle requirement is to have values for the various constants, after which substitutions of X will provide estimates of Y.

We can conclude with one last, but important, group of curves: the so-called logarithmic curves. The simplest have the form of $Y = a + b \log X$. Table 2.9 and Figure 2.4 show how such curves can be calculated and plotted. Notice how the slope of the curve changes with the sign of the product $b \times \log X$, and that X has to be logged before multiplication by b. Values of Y increase with X if b is positive, but decrease with increasing X if it is negative.

TABLE 2.9 The results of successive substitutions of X in two logarithmic equations

Value of X	$Y = 2·0 + 1·5 \log X$	$Y = 5·0 - 1·5 \log X$
0·5	$Y = 2·0 + 1·5 \times -0·301 = 1·549$	$Y = 5·0 - 1·5 \times -0·301 = 5·451$
1·0	$Y = 2·0 + 1·5 \times 0·0 = 2·0$	$Y = 5·0 - 1·5 \times 0·0 = 5·0$
5·0	$Y = 2·0 + 1·5 \times 0·699 = 2·949$	$Y = 5·0 - 1·5 \times 0·699 = 3·951$
10·0	$Y = 2·0 + 1·5 \times 1·0 = 3·5$	$Y = 5·0 - 1·5 \times 1·0 = 3·5$
20·0	$Y = 2·0 + 1·5 \times 1·301 = 3·952$	$Y = 5·0 - 1·5 \times 1·301 = 3·049$
40·0	$Y = 2·0 + 1·5 \times 1·602 = 4·403$	$Y = 5·0 - 1·5 \times 1·602 = 2·597$
60·0	$Y = 2·0 + 1·5 \times 1·778 = 4·667$	$Y = 5·0 - 1·5 \times 1·778 = 2·335$
80·0	$Y = 2·0 + 1·5 \times 1·903 = 4·855$	$Y = 5·0 - 1·5 \times 1·903 = 2·146$
100·0	$Y = 2·0 + 1·5 \times 2·0 = 5·0$	$Y = 5·0 - 1·5 \times 2·0 = 2·0$

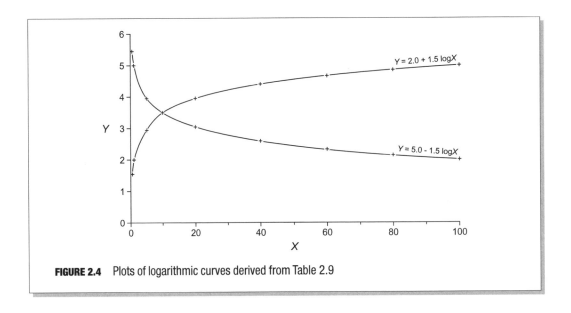

FIGURE 2.4 Plots of logarithmic curves derived from Table 2.9

Logarithmic curves are an unusual case insofar as specially prepared graph paper is available which allows us, in effect, to plot logged data without first calculating those logged values. Semilogarithmic graph paper has uniform and regular increments along one of its axes. The other, however, has a logarithmic scale on which the numbers are plotted but separated by distances along the axis that represent their log equivalents. Figure 2.5 shows the data from Table 2.9, but now plotted on semilogarithmic graph paper. In effect we are plotting the logs of X without having them transformed into logs. A significant feature of this form of data treatment is that the data now plot as straight lines.

Although not displayed here, graphs can be produced with logarithmic scales on both axes. It should also be noted that logarithmic axes range over a number of 'cycles'. In Figure 2.5, the X axis has two cycles because it covers the ranges 1 to 10 and 10 to 100 which are represented on the logarithmic scales by 0 to 1 and 1 to 2. But three, even, four cycles might be covered if the number range is great enough. For example, three cycle plots might cover the range 0·1 to 1, 1 to 10 and 10 to 100 (in logarithmic terms −1 to 0, 0 to 1 and 1 to 2).

2.6 Mathematical symbols

Some mathematical symbols and constants will already be familiar to the reader. The universal constant π (pi) has a value of 3·14159 . . ., and is used in equations to describe properties of circles and spheres. Another such universal constant is e, the base of natural logarithms, which always has the value of 2·7128. . . . Both will reappear in later chapters, but at all times they assume the same values, and do not differ from case to case.

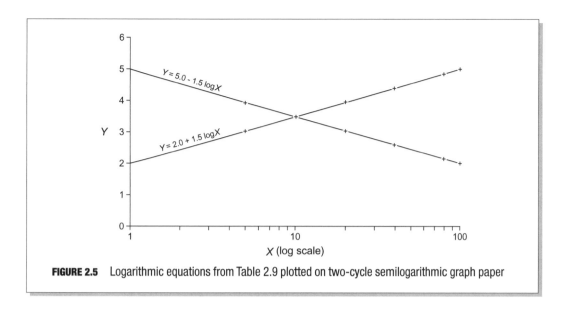

FIGURE 2.5 Logarithmic equations from Table 2.9 plotted on two-cycle semilogarithmic graph paper

Some mathematical symbols may be less familiar. The *factorial* sign (!) has no numerical equivalent and, as with + or –, it is an instruction not unlike the Σ sign. It can appear only following integer (whole number) quantities, and it instructs the reader to multiply together all whole numbers from 1 upwards to the number indicated. Thus:

$$4! = 1 \times 2 \times 3 \times 4 = 24$$

Some care is needed when the factorial sign is encountered, and the following examples show its order of precedence:

$$5! + 2! = 120 + 2 = 122 \text{ and cannot be treated as } 7! \text{ (which gives 5040)}$$
$$5! \times 3! = 120 \times 6 \text{ and does not equate to } 15! \text{ (which gives } 1 \cdot 307 \times 10^{12})$$

However, the expression $(6 - 3)!$ must be treated as $3!$ as the operation within the brackets take precedence over the factorial.

Another instructional sign is that for the *modulus*. This is given by a pair of vertical lines. They are not brackets, but indicate that the sign of the operation indicated between them is to be ignored and taken to be positive. For example, the result of $|2 - 4|$ is to be taken as 2, and not as –2.

The plus/minus sign (±) indicates that the numbers either side of it must be both added *and* subtracted, having the effect of giving two answers. For example,

$$64 \pm 2\cdot5 = 66\cdot5 \text{ and } 61\cdot5$$

The 'greater than' (>) and 'lesser than' (<) signs will also be encountered in later chapters. They are a useful shorthand and might appear as follows:

$$X > Y \text{ means that } X \text{ is greater than } Y$$

and

$Z < X$ means that Z is less than X

2.7 Using computers for statistical analysis

The computer revolution has greatly assisted those who wish to undertake all forms of statistical analysis, and the Windows-based platform now offers the most effective means with which to analyse large datasets. There are a number of statistical packages that provide both basic and advanced statistical analysis, but of these the two market leaders in geography are MINITAB and SPSS (Statistics Package for the Social Sciences). These offer slightly different platforms and each has their relative merits and drawbacks. Users may find that certain statistical procedures may be preferred in one or other of the programs. However, these differences may often be aesthetic rather than technical, and be more focused on the types of display or graphics offered and the potential for file management and manipulation. Both packages are offered in student format, which means they are accessible to most individuals within secondary and higher education at a reasonable price. Almost all of the statistics that are covered in this text are offered by both packages and the choice is dependent more on the outputs you wish to derive rather than the ease of operation. At the time of writing, the versions the authors refer to are MINITAB Release 14 and SPSS Version 11. The packages vary in two principal respects. First, command syntax and windows operations are different, though not wholly dissimilar. Second, the outputs from the two systems vary in detail, layout and the compatibility with other Windows' programs such as MS Word and MS Excel. Looking to the future meanwhile, there may be small presentational changes during the life of this book as newer versions of both packages come onto the market. They are unlikely, however, to be fundamental to the operation of the programs, and the procedures that are described in the following chapters will continue to hold good for some time to come.

In the case of both MINITAB and of SPSS applications the authors have assumed that the reader is familiar with general file handling and directory structures in MS Windows, and that he or she can call up or save files to specific directories, and navigate their way around the system. No specific references will be made, therefore, to how these basic operations are performed, and the focus is exclusively with the operation of the two statistical packages.

2.8 Data and file management with MINITAB

MINITAB has two main windows, the **Data window** and the **Session window** (Figure 2.6). They appear on the same screen display, the Session window occupying the upper half of the screen, and the Data window the lower.

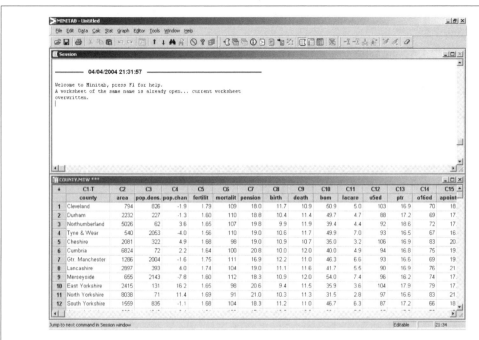

FIGURE 2.6 The standard window display in MINITAB, showing the Session window (upper half) and Data window (lower half)

All numeric and text data are stored in the Data window, which behaves as a spreadsheet, with all commands and results displayed in the Session window. Their positions can be adjusted easily by using the conventional Windows' icons at the top right of each frame, enabling you to close the window or maximise its size. Individual windows can also be resized by simply hovering the mouse over the frame edge and by clicking and dragging.

Getting started in MINITAB is relatively straightforward. Data can be typed in at the Data window. Alternatively files can be called up using the **File > Open Worksheet** commands. If the files are already in MINITAB workfile format (*.MTW), they will load in immediately, but other formats may require some processing before they can be used – more advanced aspects of this are discussed in sections 3.7 and 3.8. Alternatively, data can be 'copied-and-pasted' from Excel or similar spreadsheets. The commands **File > New > Minitab project** are useful if the system is to be cleared and new data are imported for a wholly new project. The system is closed by the commands **File > Exit**.

MINITAB is most easily used through the 'pull down' menus on the tool bar, which call into action the whole range of procedures and options. As an alternative it is possible to use *command syntax*, which has to be activated by using the **Editor > Enable Commands** procedure from menu toolbar. This aspect of MINITAB, by which coded instructions are typed in at the Session window, is not explored in this book. The more easily accessible top menu bar will, however, offer unlimited access to the statistics and methods that are available on the system. The majority of these are under the **Stat** menu. The other menus offer a range of options:

- **File:** data management for opening or saving data files or graphs and for specifying printing options
- **Edit:** basic copying, pasting and selecting options
- **Data:** editing the content of data windows, manipulating data (coding and ranking) and editing rows and columns
- **Calc:** arithmetic operations for changing the data, e.g. to percentages
- **Graph:** for producing graphs and diagrams
- **Editor:** for finding and replacing data
- **Tools:** using non-MINITAB programs to edit and examine outputs
- **Windows:** formatting windows and navigation between windows
- **Help:** searching for help and MINITAB tutorials.

There may be further choices from secondary options generated by the system after selection of the primary menu but, in most cases, dialogue boxes will appear into which instructions have to be entered. In any of those procedures in which data are manipulated for either analysis, for summary or for presentation in graphical form, you will need to indicate which variables in any data set are to be used. The method by which this is done is explained in the specific examples in the following chapters. The precise nature of the dialogue boxes differ from method to method but, in general, there will be a space into which the names of the variables to be analysed, graphed or otherwise studied need to be inserted. The same dialogue box will provide a list of all variables in the current data file. By double clicking on the variables to be used, the system transfers them to the appropriate part of the dialogue box. An example is given in Figure 2.7 in which we have used the command sequence **Stat > Basic Statistics > Display Descriptive Statistics** to instruct MINITAB to produce a table of summary statistics for the two variables birth rate ('birth') and unemployment rates ('unemploy') from a much larger set of socio-economic measures for English counties held in the file COUNTY.MTW (a copy is provided on the CD). The precise function and purpose of this option is discussed in Chapter 4, but the Figure shows how, after double clicking, the variables are automatically transferred into the **Variables** box from the main list. It must, however, be emphasised that this is only one example, and the layout will differ slightly from procedure to procedure.

Notice also that the variables are defined by text names and by the column in which they appear in the form Cx, where x is the column number in question. The results (not shown) are displayed in text format in the Session window, and can be directly copied and pasted into MS Word or other documents by highlighting them and clicking on the copy icon in the toolbar.

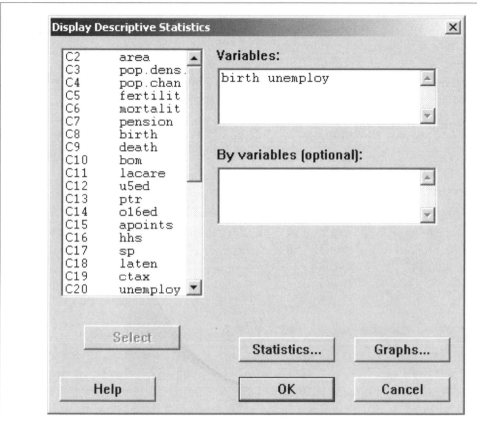

FIGURE 2.7 Typical dialogue box in MINITAB showing the result of indicating which variables in a data set ('birth' and 'unemploy' in this example) are to be analysed

The raw data can be pasted in from elsewhere, for example from an Excel file, or typed at the keyboard. Be sure, however, to place the variable identifiers in the grey row above row 1 in the spreadsheet matrix of cells. If no column (variable) names are given, MINITAB defaults to denoting them as C1 (for column 1), C2 (for column 2) etc. Any text data, as opposed to numeric data, will be signified in MINITAB by a 'T' after the relevant column number (e.g. C2-T). Accordingly, no statistical procedures can be undertaken on these text data. In addition to being typed at the keyboard and being pasted from Excel, data can also be imported from other sources such as a website. These options are more complex, and are dealt with in Chapter 3.

The Data view window can also be used to supply additional information. For example, where a number of individual data points or observations need to be allocated to specific classes or groups, they can be identified in MINITAB according to number codes provided by the user (see section 7.11 for an application of this useful principle) in which, for example, items to go into group 1 are coded as 1, group 2 as 2 etc. Thus, 1 above might be an observation to go into a group of observations for SE England data, 2 for N England etc. The group allocation codes, one for each case (row), are entered in one of the free columns in the spreadsheet. Unlike SPSS, MINITAB does not have a function for attaching a key word or descriptor for the code numbers and you will need to keep a separate list of what each of them means. Otherwise data management in MINITAB is a relatively straightforward matter and, as noted above, the Data window can be regarded as similar to a conventional spreadsheet.

To save any new data for future use you need only specify **File > Save Current Worksheet As**. The subsequent dialogue box (Figure 2.8) will allow you to name the data file and store it in your directory structure. All such files can be identified by the format subscript *.MTW. These MTW files can be called up in later sessions with the commands **File > Open worksheet**. MINITAB also has a notable number of possible graphical outputs. These can be saved as image files using the commands **File > Save Graph As**. These files are saved in the format *.MGF. Furthermore, the complete text output to the Session window (this may be lengthy on major sessions) can be saved for later use

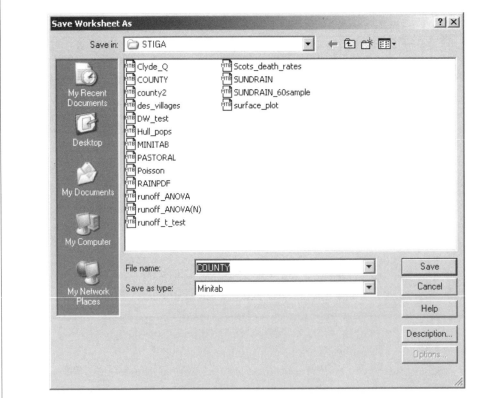

FIGURE 2.8 Windows' style dialogue box used to provide instructions for saving a MINITAB 'workfile' of data. Similar boxes are used for saving other types of output, and for opening files

by instructing MINITAB with **File > Save Project As**. A Windows' dialogue box will enable you to name this file and save it anywhere on your system. It will be stored with the format *.MPJ. In this form it can be recalled to later MINITAB sessions using the commands **File > Open Project**. You can use the dialogue box to navigate to your file storage point. Upon its recall, the 'project' file is sent to the Session window and, usefully, the associated data file is simultaneously brought up on the Data window ready for further analysis.

To obtain further guidance in MINITAB, you can use the **Help** menu command. The **Help** facility is extremely valuable and offers a wide range of information on both technical and statistical questions. By selecting **Help > Help**, the window in Figure 2.9 is generated. You can search for keywords on the left hand side, or request more information about menu commands in the main section of the window. There is an integrated **Stat Guide** that guides the user through particular procedures and there are also five **Tutorials**, which are logically presented from basic data interpretation to experimental design. By clicking on **MINITAB on the Web**, your browser will be directed to the MINITAB website where updates and information can be obtained. In all cases, searching this mechanism will provide you with the information you need – MINITAB's Help mechanism is both easy to navigate and detailed.

Specific information on the icons and their command features are provided on the CD that accompanies this book, along with an introduction to importing and saving data files and preparing data for analysis.

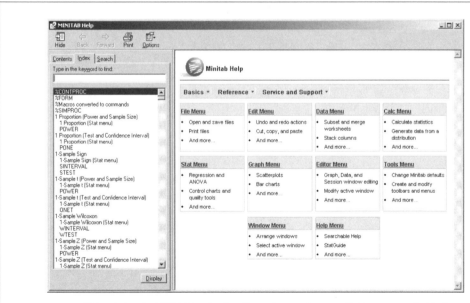

FIGURE 2.9 Help window in MINITAB indicating the various options available as a scrolled index (left window) or in review sections (right window)

2.9 Data and file management with SPSS

SPSS has a different interface to MINITAB. The initial window, known as **Data View**, stores data in columns (Figure 2.10) and performs the same spreadsheet-like function as the Data window in MINITAB but SPSS differs in providing an additional worksheet that has detailed information regarding the variables. This is the **Variable View** window (Figure 2.11). The information on the Variable View window includes the following, all of which have a default setting, but can be redefined by the user.

- **Name** – the variable's name for use in the SPSS output. The default is VAR001, VAR002 etc. but the user-defined names are possible.

- **Type** – indicates if it is numeric or text data. This defaults to **numeric** and if a **string** (text) variable is needed the allocation will have to be changed.

- **Width** – is the maximum number of characters in the variable name.

- **Decimal** – the number of decimal places after the point. The default is 2.

- **Label** – the full name of the variable. This does not appear on the output.

- **Values** – these are the coding of any categorical definitions, e.g. the names of groups otherwise defined by numbers.

- **Missing** – information on missing values and their treatment.

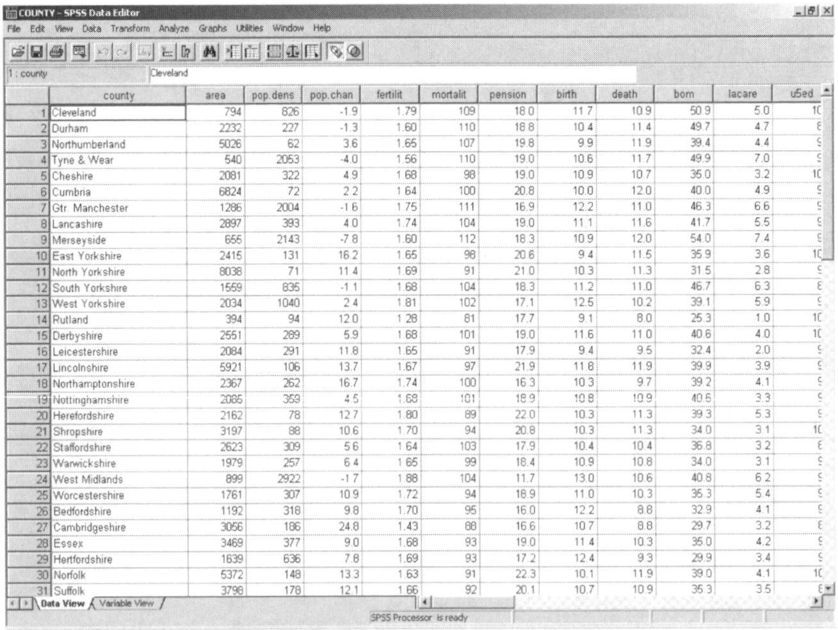

FIGURE 2.10   A typical Data View window in SPSS. The data are arranged by column-based variables

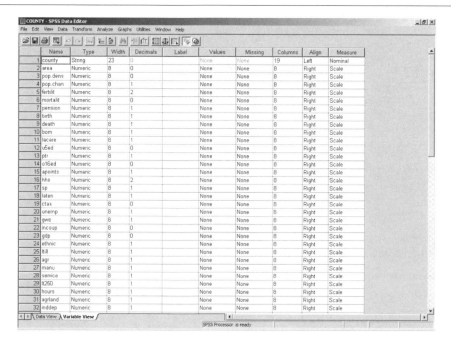

FIGURE 2.11 **Variable View** window in SPSS indicating information on each of the variables in Figure 2.10. Notice the tabs in the lower left hand of the window that allow the user to move between **Data View** and **Variable View** mode

- **Columns** – the number of columns used to display the variable name.

- **Align** – alignment in the Data View cells.

- **Measure** – the data's scale of measurement, which can be **Scale, Ordinal** or **Nominal** (see also Chapter 4).

To switch from Data View to Variable View mode, you need only click the appropriate tab on the lower left hand of the window (see Figures 2.10 and 11).

The pull-down menu options do not differ between these two SPSS worksheets. The major difference between them is that Data View provides a display of the data, while the Variable View provides information about all of the different attributes of each variable and how they are presented on the screen and output. It is therefore important to complete this sheet correctly. This includes, for example, the type of measurement used, the number of decimal places to which numerical quantities are recorded and whether there are missing cases. The Variable View worksheet can also be used to append information on category code numbers. This cannot be done in MINITAB, but SPSS helpfully allows you to define these numbers attaching a text description to each by using the **Values** column. Thus we can stipulate, for example, that sub-group 1 represents observations from, for example, 'SE England'; 2 from 'N England' etc. These

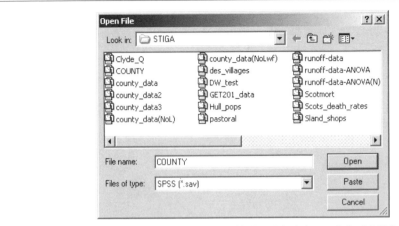

FIGURE 2.12 Dialogue box for opening files in SPSS. The default format is for *.SAV, but this can be changed using the **Files of type** box

descriptions appear in the output, often making it more understandable and without the need for repeated reference to the definition of individual category code numbers. The information and definitions in the Variable View window can be changed at any stage in the SPSS session, and you can also import additional data and variables.

Data can be introduced into SPSS by typing from the keyboard directly into the Data View window. If SPSS format (*.SAV) files are to be used, they can be called up using the command **File > Open > Data** and using the windows-type dialogue box (Figure 2.12) to locate the required file. Copying-and-pasting from Excel spreadsheets is also easily accomplished. The command sequence **File > New > Data** will clear the Data View window of old data in preparation for any new data to be introduced. To save any data you need to be in Data or Variable View mode and use the commands **File > Save As**. This will bring up the dialogue box in Figure 2.13. In common with all MINITAB and SPSS dialogue boxes, they are in Windows' format, and you can navigate to the directory in which you want the data file to be held. Type the name and click on the **OK** button. By default the data file is then saved in *.SAV format which allows it to be called up directly into any future SPSS run using the key instruction **File > Open > Data** noted above.

Calculations and many of the statistical procedures using SPSS are undertaken by going to the **Analyze** menu at the top of either the Data View or Output Viewer. All of these initial options will result in a dialogue box, usually offering a range of further options with which the procedure can be refined and directed. As with MINITAB, there are further items on the toolbar, and these can be activated from either the Data and Variable View modes:

- **File:** data management, file management, opening and saving files and printing data
- **Edit:** cutting, copying and pasting data

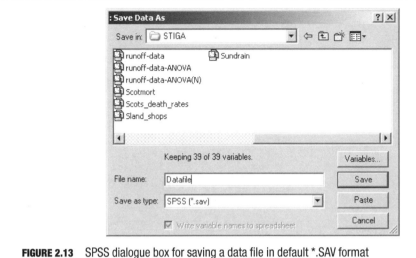

FIGURE 2.13   SPSS dialogue box for saving a data file in default *.SAV format

- **View:** selecting toolbars that you wish to use and switching between the Data and Variable Views

- **Data:** data manipulation and selection of cases and variables within the Data View

- **Transform:** arithmetic calculations, coding and ranking data

- **Graphs:** use this menu to select and prepare a range of graphs

- **Utilities:** information on files and coding of data

- **Window:** switching between SPSS windows

- **Help:** a range of options, including tutorials and general searches.

Most importantly, the user needs to indicate which variables in any data set are to be analysed. This is accomplished in SPSS by a method that is not wholly dissimilar to that in MINITAB (section 2.8 above). As noted, all instructions for data analysis will provide a dialogue box in which all the variables in the current data set are listed. The desired variables are, one by one, highlighted and transferred into the appropriate analysis box by clicking the arrow button shown in Figure 2.14. In this example two variables have been selected for analysis (birth rate and unemployment) from the data file COUNTY.SAV. The SPSS instructions to produce this dialogue box were **Analyze > Descriptive Statistics > Descriptives** (this produces a summary of the two variables). Although the precise layout of the dialogue box will differ between procedures, the system is broadly similar in all cases. To remove any variable from the selection list, click on it, the arrow button 'reverses', which can then be clicked to put the variable back into the general list. Readers might like to experiment with this key procedure using the file COUNTY.SAV on the CD.

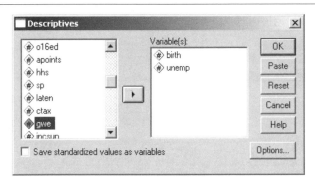

FIGURE 2.14   Typical SPSS dialogue box, showing the arrow button with which selected variables from the list on the left are transferred to the **Variable(s)** box for analysis

When you undertake any operation in SPSS there will be some form of output, which nearly always appears in a new window called the **Output Viewer**. This is completely separate from the Data and Variable Views and has different menu options, and it should be noted that there are some procedures that can only be accessed when in Data or Variable View mode. You can move between one and the other using the options under the **Windows** pull down menu. An example of the Output Viewer is given in Figure 2.15 showing some tabulated and graphical output (the tabled results were produced by the dialogue box instructions in Figure 2.14).

The SPSS Viewer mode presents the results on the right-hand side of the screen (Figure 2.15), but, helpfully where a session may have required many different forms and stages of analysis, the left-hand side of the screen shows a record of what has been done and allows the user to go back quickly to any earlier output by clicking on that item. Unless saved this output will be lost when the SPSS session is closed. Fortunately, these viewer files can be saved using the instructions **File > Save As** (but you must be in SPSS Viewer mode to carry out this particular task). A dialogue box will appear in standard Windows' format in which you can specify the file name and where you want it to be stored (it is, by default, held as an *.SPO file). This will save all the output for that session and it can be called up in the same format at any later time. This file may be lengthy, and as a useful alternative you can right-click the mouse button on the individual output graphs or tables, a menu will appear and you can copy and paste that particular item to most word processing packages. Saving output can be very useful in report writing, and it avoids the need to rerun your analysis and gives a permanent record of your findings.

2.10 General issues when using MINITAB and SPSS

Computer packages make data analysis using statistics relatively simple and fast. However, what is gained in the ease of computation should not mean a subsequent loss

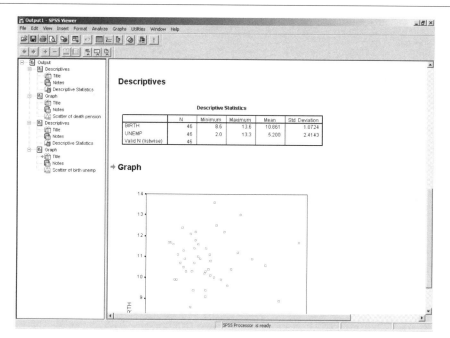

FIGURE 2.15 Output viewer window in SPSS showing a typical summary table of statistics (requested in Figure 2.14) and a simple scatter diagram. The left-hand window allows the user to navigate back through the list of tasks undertaken in that session

in the understanding of the statistical theories that underlie these procedures. It would be folly simply to press buttons and interpret the outputs without reference to the statistical assumptions and requirements that are outlined for the procedures introduced in the following chapters. SPSS permits you to assign different scales of measurement to your variables. You will find that these scales of measurement inevitably dictate which statistical procedures can be undertaken using any particular data set. Some procedures are suitable for categorical data, others for numerical data such as rainfall figures or population levels. However, despite labelling your data and variables in SPSS Variable View, the system will provide no warnings if you attempt to use a procedure that is not valid for those data. Always remember that when you use computers for analysis, you are in charge, not the machine. The computer package is merely a tool for computing statistical tests effectively. Whether you have chosen the right procedure is your prerogative, not the machine's. The following chapters will guide you through a wide range of procedures and methods, at the conclusion of which you should be confident in managing the analysis of all forms of geographical data.

Geographical sources, data collection and data handling

3.1 Introduction

DATA, IN VARIOUS FORMS, are the raw material with which geographers pursue much of their research. Yet collection, acquisition and, even, availability of data can pose problems in themselves. This chapter explores some key issues, and some solutions, associated with data sources. As we shall see, the quality and, in some circumstances, the quantity of our data determines which statistical methods should be used, and it is important that we understand the strengths and weaknesses of our data before we embark on any statistical analysis. This chapter is not, however, intended to be a comprehensive review of sources, but rather an introduction to the main types of data available and the means of collecting them.

The two principal data sources used by geographers are published 'archival' material (in either paper or digital form) and field observations. A further distinction lies between secondary and primary sources (Walford 2002). Secondary sources can be further classified in terms of whether they are spatial or non-spatial in form. In terms of the former, the data traditionally exist in the form of maps, aerial photographs and remote sensing information, the latter from an increasing variety of satellites. A range of texts exist on remote sensing, but Gibson (2000) provides a comprehensive, introductory text while more advanced texts include Lillesand and Kiefer (2000) and Gibson and Power (2000). In both human and physical geography, information from satellites is an important source and, as Aplin (2003) points out, 'an extensive range of detailed data and advanced analytical techniques are available for geographical study' (p. 304).

Traditionally, the map was often the geographer's single means of description, as well as being used to measure the locational properties of objects (Borchert 1987). While such facets are still important, maps are now one of a number of data stores for locational information. One of the most important advances has been the development of *Geographical Information Systems* (GISs). Much of the early demand arose in the USA, with an emphasis on land management, and the refinement of GISs has been strongly related to technological development in computer hardware and software (Maguire 1989). GISs are based on integrated geographical data sets, together with associated hardware and software, which enable large amounts of data to be stored, manipulated and presented – often in cartographic form (Heywood *et al.* 1998). These systems may be classified in two main forms based on how they handle geographical data, namely:

- *vector based* systems in which GISs handle data encoded as vectors using Cartesian grid co-ordinates. These are much used within the context of thematic and topographical information.

- *taster based* type use data encoded in a grid cell format. These are often utilised with remote sensing.

The use of non-spatial data by geographers, as we shall see, covers a wide variety of sources, although many share the characteristics of being readily transferred to a map or even converted into some form of spatial index. Of course, in most cases these sources have not been compiled for geographical purposes and therefore a number of problems arise in their application. These include:

- Many of the spatial units within which the data are collected are unsatisfactory for some types of geographical analysis; usually because they vary significantly in size and shape.

- The release and publication of official data is often limited to specific time intervals, such as every decade for the full UK Census. Such intervals may not be frequent enough for those studies interested in charges over certain time periods.

- The overall accuracy of these sources is outside the geographer's direct control and many may suffer from problems of inaccuracy.

Fieldwork is another major source of information for geographers, and field techniques have become increasingly sophisticated (Clifford and Valentine 2003). It is in the area of field measurement that we can recognise some of the major changes in the processes of data collection. Such measurements can range from the simple enumeration of objects, for example counting numbers of shops in a study of service provision, through to establishing large-scale systematic surveys. In many areas of human geography, such surveys are often associated with assessing attitudes and responses from people, and questionnaire design is an important part of a geographer's training (McLafferty 2003). Similarly, in many branches of physical geography, emphasis is given to the systematic monitoring and collection of data (Goudie 1990; Reid 2003).

The most important impact on data sources, however, is the Internet and the world wide web (www). This has transformed the range and scale of data available to researchers by placing before geographers a wealth of data from a variety of sources. As we are interested in quantitative analysis, we will restrict our discussion to numerical data. In very broad terms, we can recognise three main types of data available on the www. These are:

- Official statistics – these are provided by world wide organisations such as the United Nations (UN) and the World Tourism Organisation, by supra-regional organisations such as the European Union (EU) and by national and local governments.

- Data archives for research work – a good example of this source is the former ESRC Data Archive, now termed the Data Archive at the University of Essex, which represents a major collection of social science data of use to human geographers. A similar role is taken in the USA by the Inter University Consortium for Political and Social Research based at the University of Michigan (Kitchin and Tate 2000). Reference will be made in section 3.6 to similar research-based sources in physical geography.

- Ephemeral, non-official www sites that provide data useful to geographers – these may be provided by individual researchers or non-governmental organisations, but might not be vetted for quality and should be used with caution.

Given the vast range of information available on the www, it is impossible to provide a comprehensive coverage, but we do discuss some key sites later in this chapter.

3.2 Sources in human geography

Given the range of data sets available on the www, along with other important data archives, it is not surprising that a considerable amount of data in human geography is derived from secondary sources. These sources can be subdivided into a number of different types, in terms of their origin, purpose and content. As we have already discussed, a major division is between official and unofficial sources. Many of the statistics issued by international bodies such as the UN tend to be summaries collated from the official statistics of individual countries. This is only partly true of those produced by the EU as increasingly European-wide surveys have been initiated as part of the Europa scheme, the EU's statistical service. Some selected key sources at the international level are listed in Table 3.1. The importance of such data are that they are valuable for comparative studies, although some caution is needed when using summary statistics from different sources as individual countries may have used different methods of classification, and the summary statistics may not have taken such differences into account. An example of such a problem is the definition of 'urban', and the variety of criteria used by national censuses for delimiting urban populations. Attempts to overcome this problem are discussed in a number of UN publications including the UN's *Growth of the World's Urban and Rural Population 1920–2000* (United Nations 1969). Similar problems associated with variations in the classification of industrial activities, as discussed by Smith (1975).

National governments are the main compilers of statistics that are available in a variety of formats including major www sites. This variety is illustrated in the case of the UK (Table 3.2). Initially, many statistics were collected as a by-product of routine administration. However, in advanced economies the collection of statistical

TABLE 3.1 Selected data sources available at an international level

Topics	Worldwide	European Community
General	*UN Statistical Yearbook* (1948–)	*Eurostat* (1968–) General statistics (11 issues/year) data on short-term economic trend statistics (1960–)
Population/social trends	*UN Demographic Yearbook* (1948–)[1]	*Demographic Statistics* (1977–)[4] *Regional Statistics* (1971–)
Agriculture	*UN Yearbook of Food and Agricultural Statistics* (1947–)[2]	*Yearbook of Agricultural Statistics* (1970–) *Agricultural Statistics* six issues/year and annual volume (1959–)
Trade and industry	*UN Yearbook of International Statistics* (1950–) *UN Yearbook of National Account Statistics* (1957–)[3]	*Industrial Statistics*, quarterly (1959–); also a yearbook (1962–) *External Trade Statistics* (1962–)

( ) = date of first publication.

[1] Contains introduction about previous statistics published by League of Nations, 1922–42.

[2] From 1950 onwards, publication issued in two volumes, one covering production and the second, trade and commerce in agriculture.

[3] Gives details of accounts by country, e.g. GNP and distribution of national income.

[4] First edition in 1977 covers statistics for the period 1960–76, and annually thereafter.

TABLE 3.2 Selected official published statistics available for the UK

Topic and source	Frequency of publication	National statistics	Sub-national (by urban area etc.) statistics
1. Population/social			
Census reports	10-yearly	*	*
Housing Statistics (GB)	Quarterly	*	*
Local Housing Statistics (E & W)	Quarterly	*	
Digest of Health Statistics	Annually	*	
2. Production			
Agricultural Statistics	Annually	*	
Census of Production	10-yearly	*	
Business Monitor	Periodically	*	
3. Distribution			
Census of Distribution (1951–71)	10-yearly	*	*
Business Monitor	Periodically	*	
4. Transport			
Passenger Transport	Annually	*	
Highway Statistics	Annually	*	

* Indicates availability.

information is an important part of government planning and greater emphasis is placed on the integration of such data sources. Despite this, many government statistics are not available at either a comparable spatial scale or for the same time periods.

Within the UK, one useful official publication that presents data on a variety of topics at common scales is *Regional Trends* (Central Statistical Office 1971–), which gives information at county level and by reference to standard statistical regions. Other examples of standardisation adopted by official sources in the UK are the standard Industrial Classification and the Registrar General's socio-economic groupings as used in the Census.

A further problem concerns the changing nature of official statistics over time as the way in which some official statistics are collected has changed over the years making statistical comparison more difficult. In order to understand the scale and importance of such changes, it is worthwhile consulting some of the guides to official statistics. A number of these exist, including the *Guide to Official Statistics* (Central Statistical Office 1980), Openshaw's (1995) guide to the UK Census and a review of official social classifications by Rose and O'Reilly (1998).

The task of accessing secondary data, searching it and understanding its coverage has been made easier through the official government sites on the www. Most countries now have such sites, although their quality does vary. We only have space to draw more detailed attention to two such sites for the UK and the USA.

Since the mid-1990s there have been increasingly sophisticated attempts to create comprehensive www sites of official statistics in England and Wales. Currently, the major www site is *National Statistics Online* found at www.statistics.gov.uk. This contains a significant data set organised around key themes (Table 3.3). This source was used to compile the data files COUNTY.MTW and COUNTY.SAV that are used extensively in the following chapters. In addition, it has an internal search engine that allows the user to find specific

TABLE 3.3 Key themes for which data are available on *National Statistics Online* (England and Wales)

Key theme	Specific area
1. Economic data	Agriculture, fishing and forestry
	Commerce, energy and industry
	Economy
	Labour market
2. Population data	Population and migration
3. Society and welfare data	Crime and justice
	Education and training
	Health care
	Social and welfare
4. Society and welfare data	Crime and justice
	Education and training
	Health care
	Social and welfare
5. Environmental data	Natural and built environment
6. Other data	Public sector and other

information. Moreover, it is possible to navigate through a wealth of data at various spatial scales, including postcode level. The user can even call up a series of maps associated with these data, although some information is only available to registered online users.

A similarly comprehensive www site has been constructed for official data in the USA, and can be found at www.fedstats.gov. As Figure 3.1 shows, this has two main access routes, links to statistics and related maps, again at different spatial scales. It links also to over 100 US statistical agencies. Both pathways have useful search engines. It is not necessary to present detailed descriptions of such sites, as the best way of finding out what they contain and can do is to use them. For most data access is free and the sites are well explained.

3.3 Collecting primary data in human geography: questionnaires

There are many ways in which human geographers collect primary data, not all of which involve quantitative information. Indeed, there has been an increasing emphasis on the use of qualitative information collected by focus groups, participant observation

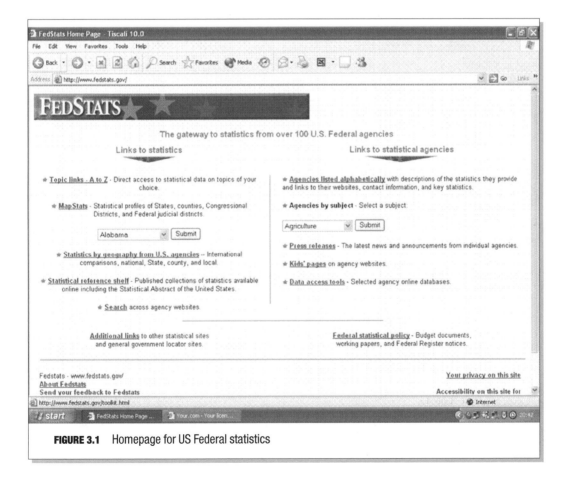

FIGURE 3.1 Homepage for US Federal statistics

and in-depth interviews (Dunn 2000). All these approaches are valuable and provide important insights into many aspects of human geography, however, the questionnaire remains the primary tool for collecting quantitative information.

To be useful, questionnaires require careful planning and preparation, and their effectiveness is largely determined by their design. In human geography, question-naires are used to measure behaviour, perceptions, attitudes and respondent character-istics. Only a brief guide is given here to techniques of questionnaire design, and for more detailed information the reader is directed to specialist texts such as Babbie 2001; Fink and Kosecoff 1999; Fowler 2002; and Oppenheim 1992. The main stages in the questionnaire design process are summarised in Table 3.4. In the first instance, the deci-sions concern the type of information required, the population (in a statistical sense) under consideration and the method of reaching respondents. These problems relate not only to the construction of the questionnaire, but also to matters of data collection and survey design that are outlined in section 3.4.

One of the critical decisions relates to the phrasing of individual questions (Table 3.5). In most questionnaires, it is common to use a variety of questioning depending on the type of information that is required. For example, measures of attitudes and perceptions very often use scaling methods, with respondents being asked to rate various attributes (Table 3.5). There are a number of recognised scaling methods, but the most commonly used are the:

- *Likert Scaling* – this usually requires respondents to indicate a degree of 'agreement' or 'disagreement' with items commonly, but not always, on a five-point scale, i.e. 'agree strongly', 'agree', 'don't know', 'disagree' and 'strongly disagree'.

TABLE 3.4   Stages in the questionnaire design process

1. Initial decisions
  (a) Decide what information is required
  (b) Who are the respondents?
  (c) What method of survey approach will be used?

2. Content of questionnaire
  (d) Which questions are essential?
  (e) Is the question sufficient to generate the required information?
  (f)   Are there any factors that might bias or negate the response to the question?

3. Phrasing and format of questions
  (g) Is the question phrased correctly or could it mislead respondents?
  (h) Can the question be asked best as an open-ended, multiple-choice or dichotomous question?

4. Layout of the questionnaire
  (i)   Are the questions organised in a logical way?
  (j)   Is the questionnaire designed in a manner to avoid confusion?

5. Decision to carry out pilot questionnaire

TABLE 3.5 The main ways of asking questions

A. Types of scaling questions

1. General scaling

Please indicate below the importance of cost in determining your holiday destination.

Not important	Relatively unimportant	Quite important	Very important	Not sure
☐	☐	☐	☐	☐

2. Likert Scale

Please indicate below how much you agree with each statement.

	Strongly agree	Agree	Neither agree nor disagree	Disagree	Strongly disagree
I like to relax on holiday.	☐	☐	☐	☐	☐
I like to be active on holiday.	☐	☐	☐	☐	☐

3. Semantic Differential Scale

This holiday destination is:

Very relaxing . . . . Not very relaxing

B. Ranking questions

Please rank the following reasons for selecting your holiday destination (from 1 = most important):

cost	☐	weather	☐	facilities	☐	safety	☐
culture	☐	other (please state and rate factor)		☐			

C. Contingency questions (closed questions)

Please indicate below your family income

Less than £20,000	☐	£21,000–£30,000	☐	£31,000–£40,000	☐
£41,000–£50,000	☐	over £50,000	☐		

D. General information questions (open-ended)

How many holidays have you taken in the last three years? _____

How would you describe the experience of your last holiday?

_____

■ *Semantic Differential Scaling* – which consists of a set of bipolar adjectives, e.g. 'good-bad', 'strong-weak' that are normally used to measure respondents' attitudes towards particular objects or experiences.

The way in which questions are phrased and designed can condition responses, and a critical problem in the design of questionnaires is measurement error, since differently worded questions on the same topic often produce very different response rates. Noelle-Newman (1970) has illustrated this in a study of women's attitudes to work. In answer to the question 'Would you like to have a job if this were possible?', 81 per cent stated that they would like to work. This compares with only 32 per cent who made the same reply to the question 'Would you prefer to have a job, or do you prefer to do your housework?' The second version of the question is more explicit and produced a very different response. A further critical influence and frequent source of error is associated with the layout of the questionnaire. In general, it is best to keep the initial questions simple and engaging in order to gain the attention of the respondent, and one topic should follow on logically from the next.

3.4 Research design and data sampling

Research design is used here as a term to encompass a number of different organisational stages in the gathering of information. Once we have defined our subject for investigation, the next step is to outline our research aims and objectives, along with the methods used to collect the data with which to test our ideas. It is not our intention to explore the nature of the research question, but rather to focus on the stages in the research design and the practicalities of sampling. In ideal circumstances, the stages in the design of any research project can be viewed as a sequence of logical steps as outlined in Table 3.6. As we have shown in the preceding sections, the principal methods of data collection are associated with the use of secondary sources or primary fieldwork. Measurement techniques will vary considerably within each of these categories, but both share the problem of how much of the 'population' to measure.

Geographers are becoming increasingly involved with this problem of coverage and there are two main ways it can be overcome. The first is by increasing the amount of information available through the large-scale accumulation of data. This may be achieved by the creation of databases, and the IT revolution has certainly stimulated this approach to large-scale data accumulation. The alternative approach is through the use of sampling methods, and it is to these that we now turn.

There are a number of factors that need to be considered in the application and use of samples; these are illustrated in Table 3.7 and summarised as follows.

- The initial step is to specify the *population* and the individuals contained within it.
- The second stage involves developing a *sampling frame*, which locates the individuals within the population (Fowler 2002). Typical sampling frames list all the objects within the population; electoral registers are good examples of this. In many

TABLE 3.6 Stages of research design

1. Define the problem and the type of information required.

2. Select the method of data collection and determine whether secondary or primary data are required, or some combination.

3. Select the technique of measurement – for example, decide whether to use questionnaires, and of what type.

4. Decide whether to measure the total population or a sample and, if the latter, select the appropriate sample strategy (Tables 3.8 and 3.9).

5. Determine the appropriate means of analysing the data.

TABLE 3.7 Stages in the sampling process

Stage	Process
1. Define the population	Defined in terms of (a) units, (b) elements, (c) area, (d) time period
2. Define sampling frame	How the elements of the population can be described
3. Specify sampling unit	Identify units for sampling, e.g. city, streets or households
4. Determine sampling method	Method by which units are to be sampled, e.g. probability or non-probability schemes
5. Determine size of sample	The number of units/individuals to be selected
6. Specify sampling plan and method of collecting data	The operational procedures necessary for selecting the sample data

instances, sampling frames are more difficult to construct. For example, sampling from mobile populations such as passers-by in the street, car traffic or river water all pose problems. Another difficulty is where the statistical population is not known.

■ The third step is to specify the sampling unit or individual, the selection of which depends on the nature of the topic, the sampling frame and the design of the project. For example, in a study of residential mobility our basic sampling unit would ideally be individual households. However, data constraints may force us to work with aggregated census information at the enumeration district or postcode level. Within geography, spatial sampling from maps is obviously of importance and a number of geometrical sampling units may be used, including points, lines or transects and quadrants. Each has its advantages and drawbacks as reviewed in Harvey (1969).

■ The choice of method by which sample units (individuals) are selected represents a critical phase in the sampling process.

A range of sampling methods exist, but an essential distinction can be made between *purposive* or *non-probability sampling*, and *probability sampling*. In the case of non-probability sampling, sample units are mainly selected for economy or convenience, while at the same time hopefully representing the characteristics of the population from which they are drawn. The reliability of these samples depends to a large extent on the skill and knowledge of the researcher, as such they are also termed *judgemental samples* (Kitchin and Tate 2000). As Table 3.8 shows, there are three main types of non-probability samples, ranging from the simple *convenience* sample, where the main criterion is the ease of collection, through to the *quota* sample, where individuals are selected to provide a replica of the population. For example, in a study of consumer behaviour, we may select quota samples based on such controls as age, income and geographical location. These types of non-probability samples are increasingly used in human geography as an easier alternative to probability samples. However, they suffer from two main problems. First, they may fail to secure a representative sample, although quota sampling is better placed

TABLE 3.8 Types of non-probability sampling schemes

Types	Characteristics
Convenience	May just select first group of units from population, e.g. the first 200 consumers to interview in a street
Purposive	Sampling units are selected subjectively by research worker, on the basis of background knowledge
Quota	Selection of sample that is as close as possible to a replica of the population

to do this. While Rice (2003) goes so far as to state 'Non-probability methods [samples] cannot be used to make statistical inferences about a population from which they are drawn' (p. 232). The researcher should always be aware of this limitation, the methodological implications of which are discussed in Chapter 6. Secondly, such methods may make fieldwork more difficult. For example, if quota samples were being used and controlled by six age categories, four income bands and four geographical areas, there would be $6 \times 4 \times 4$ or 96 cells in the sample frame, each of which would require information. A common type of purposive sample is the 'case study'; the typical farm, shopping centre or river for example. The major problem here is the lack of generality and, in addition, how representative it is cannot be guaranteed.

3.5 Methods in probability sampling

Because of the limitations noted above, it is not surprising that probability sampling is often preferred to other approaches. A probability sample is one in which the sampling units or individuals are selected by chance and, moreover, the probability any particular unit being chosen can be assessed. The problem facing the geographer is to determine which of the numerous types of sampling design to select (Table 3.9).

A *random sample* is one in which a predetermined number of units or individuals is selected in such a way that each of them had an equal chance of being chosen. Such a sample could be taken by assigning to each unit in the population a number, use can then be made of random number tables (Appendix XI) to select the sample. For example, suppose that a random sample of five students needs to be taken from a group

TABLE 3.9 Types of probability sampling designs

Design types	Characteristics
Simple random	Assign to each population element a unique number; select sample units by use of random number tables
Systematic	Determine the systematic interval, e.g. every fifth individual; select the first sample unit/individual randomly, and select remaining units according to the interval
Stratified	Determine strata; select from each stratum a random sample of the size dictated by analytical considerations
Cluster	Determine the number of levels of cluster; from each level of cluster select randomly or stratify sample

of 50. We must first list all the students, label the first of them 00, the second 01 and so on. We can then enter the random number tables at any point and read the list, either horizontally or vertically, of successive two-digit numbers. All out-of-bound numbers would have to be ignored, which in this example are 51 to 99, but the first five 'within bound' numbers on the list will indicate the five students to be chosen. It should be noted that random number tables are constructed in such a way that the same procedure can be used to read off, three-, four- – or even more – digit numbers. This method of sampling assumes that there is a degree of homogeneity within the population being sampled. For example, if all our students were male then the random sampling method could be used. However, if we had individuals from both genders in the population and we needed a number from each of them, random sampling is not appropriate as it might not yield a balanced sample in respect of this attribute.

A *systematic sample* is, when correctly applied, a form of random sample. However, instead of predetermining by random numbers which individual to include in the sample, the researcher may decide to include individuals at regular intervals through the population. For example, in a traffic census, the researcher might stop every tenth vehicle. Or, in a shopping survey, a random shopper would be selected as the start point and then every twentieth shopper to pass along the street would be interviewed. If the population is distributed through space, rather than time, we might overlay a regular grid on the map area concerned and then include in our sample all the points or individuals at each grid line intersection. This may, for example, be undertaken for a soil survey of a particular area, with a sample being taken for analysis at each grid intersection point. Such methods are simple and efficient to manage and, in most instances, they will also produce a random sample, provided that its regularity does not coincide with any regularity in the population.

In a *stratified sample*, units or individuals do not have equal chances of being selected, since some strata or sub-groups of the population may be deliberately over-represented in the sample. This is a method that is frequently used by geographers, and it is particularly useful when the situation under study is of an extremely variable nature. For example, in surveys of coastal sedimentary environments with varying proportions of dunes and inter-tidal beaches, or in a study of various tourism businesses as shown in Table 3.10. In the example discussed previously of requiring a representative number of individuals from both genders, the sampling scheme could be structured by gender to produce, say, five from each of those two strata. Such stratified samples have two important advantages. First, they make it possible to sample in proportion to the characteristics of the population and, second, by doing so they render the sample a more faithful representation of the population. The first of these is termed a *proportionate stratified sample*, which contrasts with a *disproportionate stratified sample*. The latter may be used when it is not feasible to sample strata in proportion to their size. In this situation, it is much more efficient to take a random sample of similar size within each stratum and then weight the statistics according to the size of each stratum.

TABLE 3.10   Example of how to select a stratified random sample

The problem is to select a 10 per cent stratified sample of firms from a survey of 100 businesses of different sizes, namely:

Size of firm (number of employees)	Number in stratum	Sample size
Less than 10	40	4
10–50	30	3
51–100	20	2
101 and over	10	1

In this example, we would then proceed to sample randomly from each of the four strata.

A final major type of sampling scheme is *cluster* or *area sampling*, in which the sample is selected in stages or groups. For example, if we were undertaking a survey of national trends in consumer behaviour on 500 households we would, in the first stage, draw a random sample of five districts. Should we want to have a sample of 500, we would then draw a further 100 households at random within each of the five districts. Such cluster sampling might also be combined with a stratified scheme. Cluster sampling may offer the further advantage of being efficient in terms of time. For example, in a survey of agricultural production in a developing country, we could establish the following sampling strategy:

- stage one – select a sample of villages
- stage two – select a sample of landowners within each village
- stage three – take a sample of plots from each sampled landowner to determine agricultural production.

In this way, considerable time is saved by not having to prepare a sampling frame for what could be a potentially large number of individual plots worked by all owners in every village.

Having decided on the sampling frame, the next step is to determine the size of the sample. For most researchers this is a cause of some problems. Sample size will depend on the degree of certainty required compared with the resources available. In this sense there is usually a compromise but, of course, as a general rule the accuracy of a sample increases with sample size (Figure 3.2). However, the relationship is not simple and it is commonly agreed the aim should be directed only towards some generally optimal range (Rice 2003). The question of how large a sample to take is related to the concepts of a sampling distribution and the notions of probability discussed in Chapter 6. At this stage in our discussions, it is sufficient to note two key points related to the practical aspects of sampling, namely:

- the form of the relationship between sample size and accuracy has been calculated for most probability schemes. Thus, for a simple random sample, the relationship is that the sampling error is proportional to the square root of the number of observations.

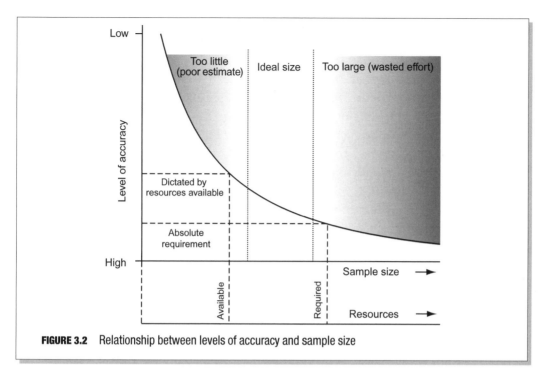

FIGURE 3.2   Relationship between levels of accuracy and sample size

- as such relationships are known, it is possible to calculate the required sample size by specifying the allowable error, the confidence level and the coefficient of variation. Note these issues are discussed fully in Chapter 6.

Finally, attention needs to be focused on the sample size of non-probability samples, which are generally determined on the purely practical grounds of the cost and effort involved in collecting the information. Added to these factors is the important consideration of what the data will be used for and how they will be analysed. For example, if a non-probability sample of the type discussed earlier in this section has been used to obtain respondents in a questionnaire survey, then the sample size may be conditioned by the analysis to be undertaken and the questionnaire structure itself. Let us assume that the questionnaire was designed to explore the influence of gender, age and residence on the fear of crime. We may need certain minimum target figures to assess each main variable, and its sub-groups. As a general rule, we can say that sample size will increase with the number of factors being considered in the survey, so the more factors the greater the sample size. In this case there are only three, but it could be more.

Sampling has been discussed at length in the preceding sections because of its importance in the acquisition of reliable data. Although attention has focused on the applications in human geography, the broader issues of sampling methods apply equally to physical geography. In a similar fashion, the following sections focus on sources in physical geography, but the computational procedures in SPSS and MINITAB that are introduced are, again, applicable to both sub-disciplines.

3.6 Sources in physical geography

For the most part, physical geography lacks the benefits offered to human geographers when it comes to the question of online or documented data sources. There is no counterpart to the CSO (Central Statistical Office) publications and website facilities in terms of either the wide-ranging nature of the data available or its helpful degree of centralisation. This is not, however, to suggest that some areas are not well represented in physical geography, and those of hydrology and climatology offer important possibilities for students searching for statistical information. Some sources provide ready-made, downloadable data files, others offer data in less readily accessible forms, and some measure of manipulation, even number-by-number transcription might be necessary. We will concentrate attention on those sources that currently exist and provide some form of electronic data files. This is not, however, to minimise the importance of printed sources, despite their obvious disadvantages, or to suggest that the list is by any means exhaustive – it isn't – and in this rapidly developing field new websites will be constantly appearing. It must be remembered also that most downloadable data files are not set up with any particular software application in mind. As a result they tend to be in adaptable CSV (comma separated value), XLS (Excel spreadsheet) or TXT (text only) formats. All such formats will require some manipulation before the data can be analysed using either SPSS or MINITAB. This section deals, therefore, not only with the data sources but also demonstrates how downloaded files can be processed for analysis in these packages. Both have options that allow a considerable degree of data file manipulation to bring them into a form that they can accommodate. In some cases, however, some simple text editing in MS Notepad or a similar text editor might be required. The following paragraphs are not claimed to be exhaustive in respect of either sources or of forms of data treatment that might be necessary, but they do include those most likely to be required by students and teachers. Furthermore, although these sections are concerned with sources in physical geography, the same procedures can be applied to similarly formatted data files with human geography statistics.

We will focus on those websites that offer data that are free of charge. There are, however, a number of sources, of which the British Atmospheric Data Centre (BADC) is one of the largest, for which charges are levied. These are not included in the following sections, but anyone interested in this source should go to http://badc.nerc.ac.uk/help/query.html. The UK Met Office, while offering a limited service for free data (see below) can also be approached for more detailed charge-based data provision (http://metoffice.com). Other sources of climatic data are reviewed in section 3.8.

One of the best examples of a source of readily available data is the UK National River Flow Archive (NRFA) (URL: http://www.nwl.ac.uk/ih/nrfa/index.htm), from where daily and summary discharge data for over 200 gauging stations covering the past 20 years can be obtained free of charge. Not only can the data be downloaded, but the site also includes useful background information of each of the stations; this descriptive material allows suitable stations to be selected for particular studies, and assists in data analysis and interpretation. The home page allows the investigator to select the site for which data are required. Selection then opens the web page for that particular gauging station. Data are provided in two forms. Most usefully, the long-term daily series can be downloaded in CSV format. These files include all the daily data available for that station, and you may therefore want to edit the file at a later stage (see below) to include only that time interval in which you have an interest. Each row in the file represents one day, and the columns are ordered by day number in the month, month number, year and discharge. When data are unavailable the row date remains, and is marked with an absence indicator (usually 'M'). A sample file of data for the River Tees (TEES_Q.XLS) of this type can be found on the CD. Taking this as an example, the methods by which all XLS and CSV files are prepared for use in MINITAB and SPSS will now be reviewed and sample data files can be found on the CD.

3.7 Importing CSV and XLS files into SPSS and MINITAB

After requesting the file, it will be downloaded to your computer where it will automatically open in MS Excel, which will then display the data. Using the usual MS conventions you can then store the file on your system, saving it either in either Excel *.CSV or Excel *.XLS formats. These files can be called up for use by either SPSS or MINITAB. In the case of SPSS the **File > Open > Data** command should be used. You should then search for your stored data file in the conventional MS fashion. The SPSS search default is for SPSS (*.SAV) files only, so you will need to request MS Windows, using the **Files of type:** box, to list **All Files (*)**. You should then find it, stored with a file name for the river in question. If you saved your file in Excel *.XLS format, SPSS will recognise it as an Excel file and open the request window in Figure 3.3 in which the file you specified is indicated.

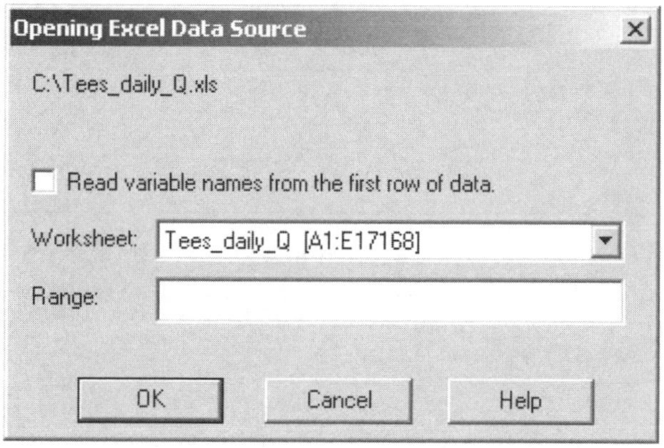

FIGURE 3.3   Request window opened by SPSS before importing Excel files

You will be asked if you want to **Read variable names from the first row of the data**. You should 'untick' this box because the first rows of the NRFA files provide station information and not variable names. Click **OK** and SPSS will open the file in **Data View**, at which point you should delete the first row (or rows) that contains the station text information. You should then go to **Variable View** mode and add for yourself the appropriate column (variable) names for day number, month number, year and discharge.

If, however, you saved your file in Excel *.CSV format, another set of options will be presented using the system's 'Wizard' procedures with which you can convert it into an SPSS-compatible form. Figure 3.4 shows the opening window of this procedure, which appears automatically when a CSV file (a CSV file TEES_Qcsv is available on the CD) is called up and can be easily followed step-by-step through six stages, none of which

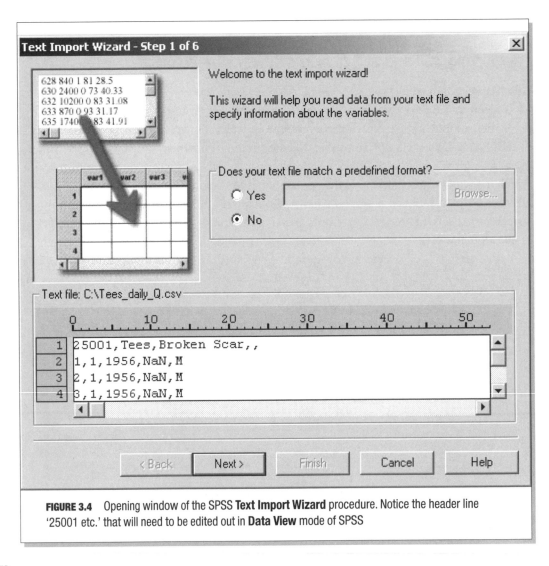

FIGURE 3.4   Opening window of the SPSS **Text Import Wizard** procedure. Notice the header line '25001 etc.' that will need to be edited out in **Data View** mode of SPSS

should require any change from the default options. Usefully, these procedures apply equally to any CSV formatted data file. In most cases these NRFA data files automatically open in Excel. In rare cases depending on your computer's set up, they may not. When this occurs, 'right click' on the **long term csv data file** text item on the web page and activate the **save target as** option. The file can then be stored using standard MS commands.

Students should, however, be alert to an additional change that may have to be made; the discharge data are held in column 4, and if there are any cells with missing data into which alphabetic characters have been inserted to indicate such absences, the system reads this column as a 'string' and not as a numeric variable. To check and correct this go to the SPSS **Variable View** window (see Chapter 2 for general procedures in SPSS and MINITAB). If column 4 is indicated to be a string variable, change it to numeric type. You might also need to reset the number of decimal places allocated to the variable. The data are then ready for processing, and will appear in the **Data View** window in the usual form. You may wish to tidy the modified file by removing superfluous rows or columns, before storing it as an SPSS *.SAV format file for later use.

If the data are stored in an *.XLS format file, they can be called up in MINITAB using the command sequence **File > Open Worksheet**. No additional windows appear, and the data pass immediately into the **Data Screen** window. Once again, however, the introductory line (or lines) of station text will need to be edited out, and the column (variable) names assigned. Using again the file (TEES_Q.XLS), the same problem of data type in column 4 that we found in SPSS will recur in MINITAB. To convert the column from string to numeric form, use the command series **Data > Change Data Type > Text to Numeric**. This will bring up the dialogue box in Figure 3.5 in which you will need to identify the column to be converted (C4 in this case) and a new column into which the numeric data can be placed (C6). Click on **OK**, and the task will be performed. The subsequent MINITAB Session window will list all those alphabetic character entries that cannot be converted, but this warning note can, in most instances, be ignored. At

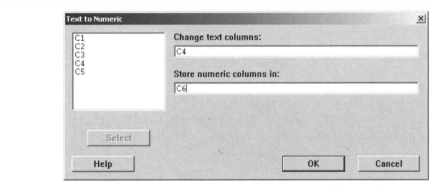

FIGURE 3.5 **Text to Numeric** command box in MINITAB. Both option spaces to the right can contain lists of columns, but they should be in corresponding order

this point any required variable names can be added. As with SPSS, you can now also edit the file and retain only the variables that you require (by deleting unwanted columns) and the data for the particular study period (by deleting unwanted rows). The data can then be processed, and the file saved as a MINITAB work file (*.MTW). You cannot run Excel CSV files in MINITAB, and the files should be saved in XLS format if use by MINITAB is anticipated.

3.8 Importing TXT files into SPSS and MINITAB

Many data sources use the adaptable TXT (text only) format, even though the files contain numbers. The UK Met Office is one such source. Although it offers a relatively limited range of freely available data, these provide for most student and classroom needs. The Met Office site also includes much tabulated data for long-term means of temperature, precipitation, sunshine etc. from a number of British sites. These can be copied and printed from the screen but cannot be downloaded in file form, and the only free downloadable data files are to be found at http://www.metoffice.com/climate/uk/stationdata/index.html. This particular part of the site holds over a century of monthly data for each of ten British weather stations (Armagh, Bradford, Durham, Lerwick, Long Ashton, Oxford, Sheffield, Southampton, Stornoway and Valley). The climatic variables include maximum temperature (tmax), minimum temperature (tmin), precipitation (rain), sunshine (sun), grass minimum temperatures (gmin) and days of snow lying at 0900GMT (snow). The data files can be transferred from this site, and stored in a directory of the user's choice. The data are stored in text (*.TXT) format in which each row corresponds to one month of data; the variables are presented in the order listed above. The files are arranged to run in row sequence through the months and years, both of which are identified by numbers (1 for January, 2 for February and so on). The file can be read in SPSS using the same procedures that we applied to the NRFA files, and require use of the system's text import Wizard option. The first two rows of the **Data View** presentation will contain the column headers, and should be deleted, although for clarity the variable names should then be added in the **Variable View** mode as column identifiers. All columns are, however, imported as string (text) variables, and must be converted to numeric form using **Variable View** to change the **Type** from string to numeric. For ease of comprehension, the field width of the columns can be adjusted to include as many decimal places as necessary. Missing data are denoted by empty cells. A sample TXT file from this source (that for Durham – DURHAM.TXT) is included in the CD and readers are recommended to experiment with transferring it into MINITAB and SPSS.

This form of text file can also be imported into MINITAB, and the layout of such files from this source poses few problems. No adaptations are needed and the commands **File > Open Worksheet** will place the data immediately in the **Data display** window. The column headers are also, usefully picked up and included in MINITAB. Again, however, the data are usually read as string/text variables, and the columns are headed, for example, as **C4-T** – the **T** indicating string variables. As noted previously, conversion to numeric form can be carried out using the command series **Data > Change Data Type > Text to Numeric**, which will bring up the window in Figure 3.5, into which the columns to be converted and columns into which the new data are to be placed are identified.

Long time series climatic data can also be downloaded from the Met Office's research unit at the Hadley Centre. The URL address for access to the files is: http://www. met-office.gov.uk/research/hadleycentre/CR_data/monthly. Among the many files available the most useful are those for the Central England Temperature series (HadCET_act.txt), and the England and Wales precipitation series (HadEWP_act.txt). Both are based on monthly data, the former starts in 1659 and latter in 1772 and both can be directly downloaded. Another source of climatic data that is available free of charge is supported by the Climatic Research Unit (CRU), University of East Anglia. Here can be found downloadable data sets of climatic information that include popular current research themes such as the North Atlantic Oscillation index and Southern Oscillation index (linked to El Niño phenomena). Both are based on monthly data, are regularly brought up-to-date, and go back for well over a century. The Unit's URL address is http://www.cru.uea.ac.uk/ from where you can follow links to the data file pages. There are also hyperlinks to the Hadley Centre data sets. All CRU and Hadley Centre files are stored in text (*.TXT) format. Files from both sources can be used in SPSS using the same procedures described above for CSV and XLS files, although judicious editing of rows and columns, and resetting of string to numeric variables will again be required before analysis can proceed. However, these particular text files, and many other of this type, also have a number of leading lines (usually describing the data) that require careful manipulation before the data can be assimilated in MINITAB and the analysis proceed. In this example we will use the Hadley Centre file HadCET_act.TXT, which contains mean monthly temperatures for Central England from 1659 onwards (it can be found on the CD in the MINITAB sub-directory). The commands **File > Open Worksheet** can be used to call up the file, but it is important to note that when doing so the **Open Worksheet** window's **Files of type** box should specify **Text (*.txt)** and no other formats (Figure 3.6). The **Options** button in the window should be clicked. This will bring up the dialogue box in Figure 3.7. The **Field Definition** should be set to **Free format**, and **Variable Names** to **None**. The problematic introductory lines of text can be avoided by specifying the first line on which the numeric data appear, and you can click on the **Preview** button to check where this row is in the data file. You need only check the **Use Row** option under the **First Row of Data** heading, and enter the appropriate line number. In this example, the data begin on line 8 following some introductory text that is not required. All other options can be left in their default setting. Clicking **OK** and then **Open** will then bring up the data, set out in the form in which it was received, but without the leading text. Column (variable) names will need to be added within MINITAB before the file is stored in *.MTW format and the data processed.

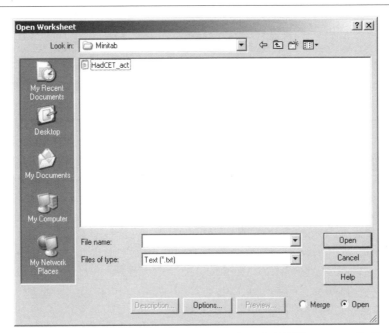

FIGURE 3.6 **Open Worksheet** window in MINITAB, showing how the TXT files are specified in the **Files of type** box. Without this TXT specification the subsequent options (Figure 3.7) are not fully available

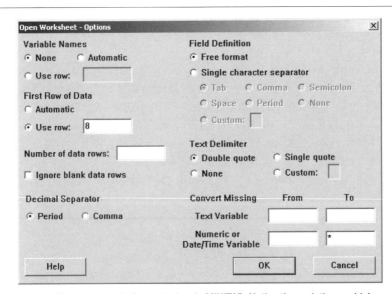

FIGURE 3.7 **Open Worksheet – Options** window in MINITAB. Notice the variations, which are not used in this example but might be required when files from other sources are used, and that **Free format** (when specified) over-rides **Text Delimiter** options

Several other data sites, many based in the USA, also provide free data files. That of the National Oceanographic and Atmospheric Administration (NOAA) has a site dedicated to paleoclimatic data at http://www.ngdc.noaa.gov/paleo/paleo.html from which a very wide range of data is available. Another useful site is operated by the Joint Institute for the Study of the Atmosphere and Ocean (JISAO), which can be found at http://tao.atmos.washington.edu/jisao_sitemap.html. Directions will take you to the data archive section where a large number of files can be downloaded. In most cases these files are in adaptable TXT format, but may require careful pre-processing using SPSS Wizard or MINITAB Open Worksheet Options before they can be used. If either of these fail to adapt the file, MS Notepad or a similar text editor can be called upon (if MS Word is used, be sure to save the file in TXT format). It must not, however, be forgotten that these are only a small sample of the constantly growing, and ever-changing websites that can be called on for data in physical geography.

Measurement and descriptive statistics

4.1 Data characteristics and scales of measurement

MEASUREMENT IS CONCERNED WITH the assignment of values or quantities to particular objects or events. It should be recognised at the outset that measurements exist and are carried out in a variety of forms that reflect the diversity of data used by geographers and the range of phenomena that they study. With this in mind, geographers and other scientists have found it useful to identify four different orders or scales on which data can be measured.

These four scales are summarised in Table 4.1 where they are listed in order of the information and statistical detail that they offer. These characteristics, which are reviewed below, also influence the type of statistical analysis that is appropriate for each scale (see also Table 4.5 and Chapter 7). The four scales can be described as follows.

Nominal scale data

These allow only the classification or naming of observations; numbers, if used at all, are arbitrarily assigned. For example, in a questionnaire survey of consumer behaviour, we may focus on the role of gender and compare male and female shoppers. In this case, we might simply assign '1' to identify males and '2' for females, but the numbers have no arithmetical significance. Another example of nominal scale data is voting habits, in which an individual can be categorised according to the party for which he or she votes, e.g. Conservative, Labour, Liberal Democratic etc.

Ordinal (rank) scale

Ordinal scale data allows the ranking of one observation against another. Thus, we may say that one city is larger than another and proceed to place a number of cities in a rank ordered list. The availability of this type of measurement is important for many of the studies concerning perception and the cognitive components of behaviour, when individuals may be asked to rank particular features. For example, we may ask respondents to select their reason for choosing a particular holiday destination from a list of five options. The reason that is cited most often could be ranked 1, the second most popular

TABLE 4.1 Scales of measurement and their properties

Scale	Characteristics	Measurement
Nominal	Determination of equality; data can be placed in categories only	Discrete
Ordinal	Determination of greater or lesser; data can be ranked	Discrete
Interval	Determination of equality and of intervals and differences. Zero is arbitrary	Continuous
Ratio	Determination of equality, differences and ratios; measurements have a true zero	Continuous

as 2, and so on. Thus there are, as with nominal data, a list of categories, but they can now be placed in an order of importance. Ranks therefore 'order' data by magnitude, but the ranks do not themselves allow the 'statistical distance' between the observations to be measured, merely than one individual ranks higher or lower than another.

Interval scale data

These permit us not only to sort and rank observations but also to establish the magnitude of differences separating each observation. Temperatures represent a good example of this, as not only can we say that one area has a higher mean annual temperature than another, we can also calculate the difference between the two, and the data will tell us not only that one area is warmer than the other (as ranks would do), but that it is warmer by a specified amount. Importantly, interval scale data do not possess an absolute zero. On the Celsius temperature scale 0°C does not, for example, represent the absence of heat. In such systems, the number zero has been arbitrarily attributed to a particular point – in this case the freezing temperature of pure water. In the Fahrenheit scale, that same point is denoted by 32°F. Thus negative and positive numbers do not convey any true sense of absent or missing qualities in the phenomena that they measure. For example 20°F on the Fahrenheit scale is –6·7°C. Notice also that an object with a temperature of 24°C is not one with twice the heat of an object at 12°C. All interval scale data share these important, to some extent limiting, characteristics.

Ratio scale data

This is the highest level of measurement, sharing many features with the interval scale. It differs, however, in having an absolute zero. If we return to our earlier example of city size we could, under the ratio scale, and assuming that we had accurate and reliable data, state not only that one city was larger than another, but also the ratio of the two figures. For example, if one city has a population of one million and another has only 250,000 we can state that not only does the former have 750,000 more people, but that it has four times its population. Rainfall or income are other typical ratio scale variables where zero is not arbitrarily defined, but has a real basis: there is nothing arbitrary about zero rainfall or zero income, for both of which negative values are impossible.

Most geographers frequently use data measured on the interval or ratio scale and for most analytical purposes they can be treated in the same way. The two are sometimes collectively known as *parametric* data. By contrast, information at the nominal and ordinal scales is described as *non-parametric*. A further important distinction can be made between the nominal/ordinal and interval/ratio scales. In the former, the measurements are *discrete*, as observations can be placed only within certain mutually-exclusive classes or categories, for example, male or female, or Conservative or Labour party voter. This is not the case with interval/ratio scale measurements, where observations can occupy any position along the measurement continuum and hence are assessed on what is termed a *continuous* scale. Consider, for example, the difference between measuring the nationality and the income of an individual. In the former case, the attribute places the individual into a clearly defined class, e.g. British, French, German etc. In the case of income, this attribute is a number quantity located at some point along a measured continuum, e.g. £25,680 or £45,742 etc. This contrast is often critical in deciding on the method of analysis to which the data may be subjected.

4.2 Descriptive and inferential statistics

A division needs also to be recognised between *descriptive* and *inferential statistics*. This allows us to distinguish between those approaches that merely describe, in numerical terms, an event or data set, and those that enable us to infer relationships between variables and to test hypotheses.

Descriptive statistics, which are the focus for this chapter, are the simplest way of summarising and presenting data sets, especially relatively large ones. They may take a variety of forms, ranging from the use of simple graphs and frequency tables through to a whole range of spatial measures (see Chapter 13). In making such descriptive summaries, geographers can also speculate more confidently on the character of the data. Inferential statistics are concerned with mathematical probabilities and are characteristic of scientific investigation, which involves a search for principles that have a degree of generality and allow us to explain why things happen. In this type of study the findings are often applied to a wider setting than the cases or samples that were represented in the data. The making of such generalisations from a sample of data and extending them to a population is termed *statistical inference*, and it occupies the attention of most of the following chapters. Inferential methods allow us to make probabilistic statements about the following:

- hypothesis testing – whether a particular supposition is true or false
- the relationship between two or more variables
- the characteristics of the population from which a sample is drawn.

This is not, however, to diminish the role or importance of descriptive statistics that will always be an important preliminary step in most research projects and undertakings.

4.3 Data summaries, tables and graphs

In geography we are often faced with the task of collecting and describing relatively large amounts of data. To illustrate some of the consequent difficulties, let us consider the information collected from the UK Census. Even if we concentrate on a small range of variables, as the official online statistical database illustrates, the total amount of data to be handled is vast. Of course, we can take a sample but, even so, to yield useful results the data must first be summarised and reduced to manageable proportions. Equally, if we had undertaken our own smaller survey, for example a questionnaire of 200 residents, we would still want to form an initial impression of the data by summarising the results.

One of the most useful initial tasks is to construct a frequency table or graph. Table 4.2 shows the breakdown of methods of travel involved in the journey to work in England and Wales; this represents, therefore, an example of a discrete variable at the nominal scale. In this case, each mode of travel provides a discrete category, and each individual can be allocated to one or other of these categories. Notice that, importantly, and typically of nominal scale data, the groups are mutually exclusive and could have been placed in any order without prejudice to the sense of the information.

Table 4.3 illustrates this same process of summarising a data set using a frequency table, but now the exercise is based on a continuous variable on the ratio scale; in this instance perinatal mortality measured in deaths per thousand births. Although the measurement scale is a continuous one, it is important to aggregate the data into classes, as was done here. The perinatal mortality within each county in England and Wales can

TABLE 4.2 Methods of journey to work in England and Wales (*Source*: Office of Population Censuses and Surveys 1984)

Means of travel	Number of people (000s)
Train	80·6
Underground	42·2
Bus	314·2
Motor cycle	61·0
Car – pool driving	82·4
Car – driver	805·5
Car – passenger	165·5
Pedal cycle	79·8
Pedestrian	309·0
Works at home	70·8

TABLE 4.3 Perinatal mortality (deaths/1,000 births) 1987–89 for English and Welsh counties (*Source*: Central Statistical Office 1991)

Class range	Frequency	Percentage	Cumulative percentage
5·25–5·74	1	1·8	1·8
5·75–6·24	0	0·0	1·8
6·25–6·74	2	3·7	5·5
6·75–7·24	4	7·4	12·9
7·25–7·74	3	5·6	18·5
7·75–8·24	13	24·1	42·6
8·25–8·74	10	18·5	61·1
8·75–9·24	9	16·7	77·8
9·25–9·74	6	11·1	88·9
9·75–10·24	3	5·6	94·5
10·25–10·74	2	3·7	98·2
10·75–11·24	1	1·8	100·0

be placed into one, and only one, of the classes shown in Table 4.3. In many situations, geographers prefer to present information in the form of graphs instead of tables. These graphs are commonly one of three different types, the choice of which depends on the nature of the raw data and the requirements of the researcher. The first of these three is the *bar chart*, where the data are in discrete form and the chart summarises the frequency with which individuals fall within each category. The travel to work example above illustrates this form of presentation. On the other hand, where data are in the form of a continuous variable the *histogram* or *ogive* should be used. Histograms and bar charts are, however, similar and the heights of the columns or bars are proportional to the frequency of observations in their respective classes. Figure 4.1 is a bar chart based on the data in Table 4.2. Where discrete nominal classes are portrayed, the bars are usually separated in the graph. They should be plotted as 'touching' bars, only when they depict continuous data that has been arranged into classes. These distinctions will become important in the discussion of SPSS and MINITAB procedures that follow.

Bar chart summaries of nominal data can have their columns rearranged without distorting or misrepresenting the original data set. For example, in Figure 4.1 the bar for bus travellers could be placed anywhere along the graph and there is no intrinsic order in the different forms of travel. Clearly, such reordering cannot be done for data measured on a continuous scale where the number scale dictates the order. While continuous variables can be plotted as histograms, more information can sometimes be revealed by plotting a cumulative frequency curve or ogive where the shape of the curve is determined by the

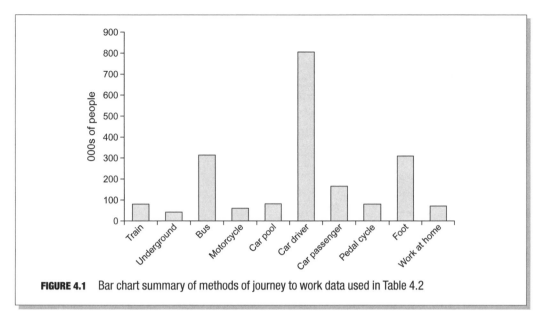

FIGURE 4.1   Bar chart summary of methods of journey to work data used in Table 4.2

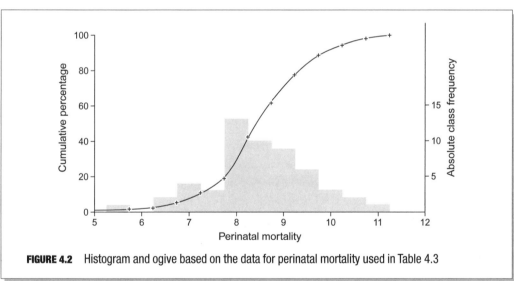

FIGURE 4.2   Histogram and ogive based on the data for perinatal mortality used in Table 4.3

cumulative number of observations through each class. Table 4.3 contains the absolute and cumulative percentages of the raw data from which a histogram and cumulative frequency curve can be plotted (Figure 4.2). It is normal to use cumulative percentages rather than absolute frequencies in such graphs.

Ogives need to be prepared with care. In Figure 4.2 the data are plotted as cumulative percentages 'less than' the upper boundary of each class. As a result, the cumulative percentage points must be plotted at the upper boundary of their respective classes, these points are then connected by a smooth curve or ogive. When passing through classes with greater frequencies of observations, it will be noted that the ogive rises more steeply. When passing through classes with fewer observations, the ogive is less steep. In general, the accuracy of all such plotted curves increases with the number of classes that we can use in their definition.

One important point to consider in the construction of frequency tables and graphs of continuous (interval/ratio scale) data is the selection of class limits and class intervals. The following points should be born in mind:

Class limits – these should be assigned to avoid any ambiguity and to ensure that there is only one possible location for each item. For example, if a continuous variable is being measured, then the system used in Table 4.3 is appropriate, since it leaves no gaps and each observation belongs uniquely to a particular class.

Class intervals – these represent the statistical distance between the upper and lower limits of a class. They should be the same for all classes but may, in exceptional circumstances, vary in size in order to preserve or emphasise some key aspect of the data. For example, in a study of age structure we might group all the over 65s together as those of pensionable age – leaving younger people in, say, ten-year classes. In terms of descriptive statistics, such a strategy may not be a problem, but when dealing with inferential statistics, class intervals need to be identical. A problem lies in deciding on the number of class intervals to be used in the case of a variable measured on the continuous scale. The general advice is that tables should ideally have no less than six, but could have as many as the partitioning of the original data will allow, bearing in mind that smaller class intervals will inevitably limit the frequency of events that fall within them.

In the following examples, the computer systems may automatically make some of these decisions for us, but in every case we can, if we wish, over-ride the computer default option and make our own specifications for class range etc.

4.4 Using MINITAB and SPSS to summarise data in graphs

Both the MINITAB and SPSS packages offer useful means of summarising complex and large data sets in graphical form. The possibilities cover the full range of bar charts, histograms and ogives. All can be produced with relative ease and, as explained in sections 2.8 and 2.9, can be saved as computer files to be used later or pasted into reports and documents.

All of the graph-based outputs in MINITAB and SPSS can, if necessary, be edited further to meet the user's specific requirements, although we will concentrate here on the standard forms of output using the various default options. The most important from the point of view of summarizing the statistical character of data sets are the bar chart, histogram and cumulative frequency curve. In the various examples that follow we will use a dataset related to commuter travel behaviour (you will find these on the CD under

TRAVEL_DATA.MTW (for use in MINITAB) and TRAVEL_DATA.SAV (for use in SPSS)). The data were drawn from 30 individuals and are based on travel to work preferences in 2001. A number of variables were measured relating to the distance travelled to work each day, the mode of transport used, attitudes towards travel and some socio-demographic information, such as age, gender and income. Suppose we were interested in summarising the numbers travelling by different modes of transport. A useful first step would be to plot a bar chart examining the numbers using the different transport modes (in this case simplified to car, bus or train and coded in the file as 1, 2 and 3 respectively). In MINITAB, bar charts are generated by using the commands **Graph > Bar Chart** that produces a dialogue box (Figure 4.3) in which we take the default option of **Simple** to produce a single chart. After **OK** has been clicked, a further dialogue box opens. This box is similar to many others in MINITAB and allows for one or more variables to be specified for processing or analysis. This is done by double clicking over the required variables (see also section 2.8). This transfers the variable names into the **Categorical variables** box, after which **OK** is clicked and the bar chart (Figure 4.4) will be produced. Editing of the chart can be undertaken after the graph has been generated, where double clicking on any part of it will enable you to change various aspects of its presentation such as colour, typeface, shading etc. using the dialogue boxes that appear on the screen. It should be noted that the various graph axes in MINITAB and SPSS will default to the names given to the variables in the data files. If such names do not include the units used in their measurement they will not appear in the graph. Should the user prefer the units to appear, then the editing options will need to be employed to change the axis titles.

The data file TRAVEL_DATA.MTW identifies the mode of transport only by a key number. In this case 1 for a car, 2 for bus and 3 for train. But this key number system may not be convenient, and if we wanted the bar chart to indicate the category more clearly by text name rather than by number we would need to use the **Code** option, for MINITAB to add a text name against each case (row) in the next free column in the Data window. This can be done by using the commands **Data > Code > Numeric to Text**. The dialogue box that appears is shown in Figure 4.5 where we have two options at this point; we can either permanently recode our numeric data to text data, or we can recode the data into a different column. The second of these options is normally preferable given that we might want to undertake further analyses on these original data in due course. We must, as indicated in Figure 4.5, place the variable (described by name or by column number in the form Cx) to be recoded into the **Code data from columns** box and the destination column into the **Into column** box. We then need to specify what text description we wish to attribute to each of our original numeric codes. This can be done sequentially by pairing each original code number with a text name. A new column of text data is then automatically formed, and the **Bar Chart** command can be re-run specifying this new variable, the output from which will now have labelled rather than number code bars.

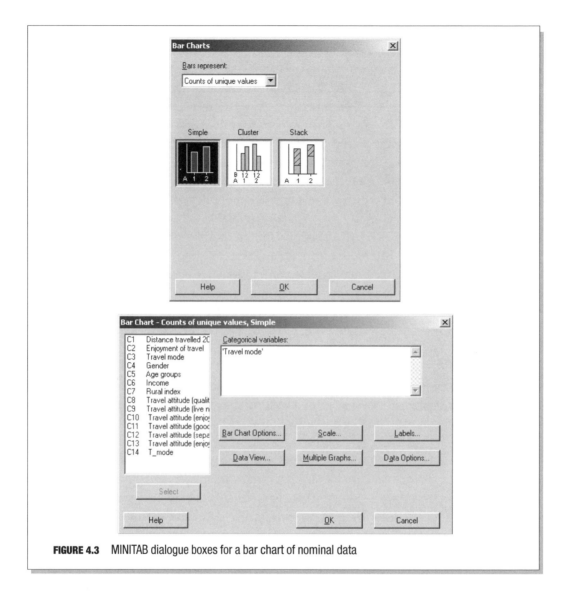

FIGURE 4.3   MINITAB dialogue boxes for a bar chart of nominal data

As noted above, the **Bar Chart** option should be used only where categorical (nominal scale) data are being plotted. Where we are using interval or ratio scale data, there are no intrinsic categories and we must use the **Histogram** option in which the data are grouped into arbitrary, but equal range classes. To demonstrate their use, we can again call on the travel survey data. Suppose that we were interested in examining the distribution of the distance individuals travelled to work each day ('distance travelled 2001'). In MINITAB, we would use the **Graph > Histogram** command sequence. A dialogue box will appear that is similar to that for a bar chart (Figure 4.6). Again we will remain with the default option (**Simple**). The selected variable is transferred for plotting, as it was in the earlier example, by double clicking over the variable name. When **OK** is clicked, the

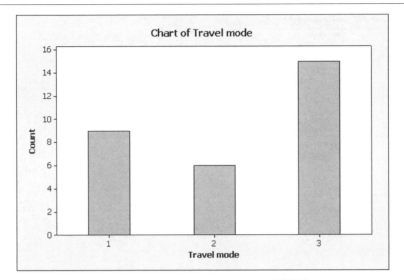

FIGURE 4.4 Bar chart of mode of travel to work data, produced in MINITAB

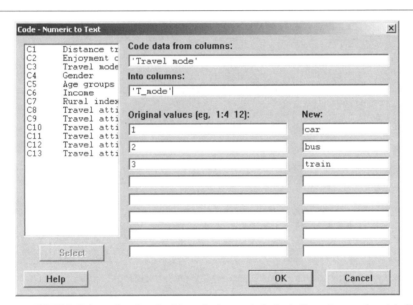

FIGURE 4.5 MINITAB dialogue box for attaching a text name to indicate the category of each individual in a list of nominal data

histogram in Figure 4.7 is created. Notice how, in the histogram case, the continuity of the original data measurements is reflected in the columns being also linked. As with the bar chart, we can edit and modify the graph by double clicking on the histogram and using the option dialogue boxes to change fonts, colour and other attributes.

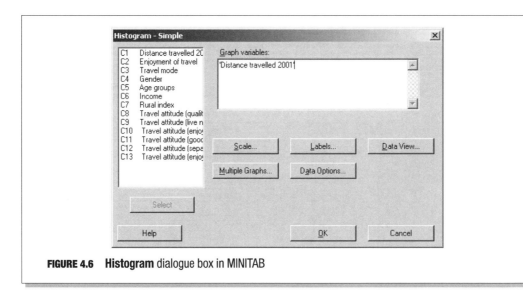

FIGURE 4.6   **Histogram** dialogue box in MINITAB

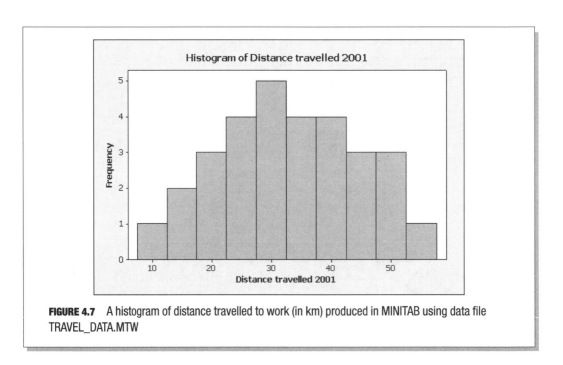

FIGURE 4.7   A histogram of distance travelled to work (in km) produced in MINITAB using data file TRAVEL_DATA.MTW

Finally, we may want to plot the cumulative frequency (ogive) of the data with which we are dealing. This is a variant on the histogram procedure, but requires the commands **Graph >Empirical CDF**. We will select the **Single** graph option once again as only one variable is under study. A dialogue box (not shown but identical to those seen earlier) is then produced, in which the variable to be graphed is selected. Continuing

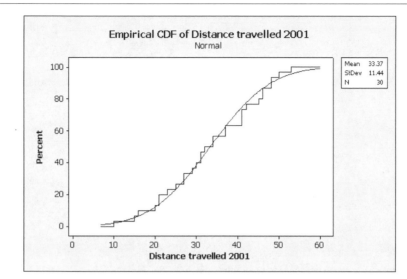

FIGURE 4.8 A cumulative frequency (ogive) plot of the distance travelled to work data produced in MINITAB

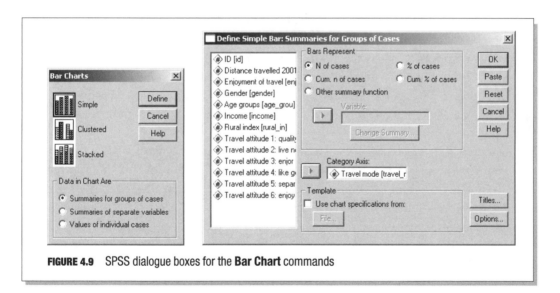

FIGURE 4.9 SPSS dialogue boxes for the **Bar Chart** commands

with the distance to work data, this will produce the ogive in Figure 4.8 in which the percentage of people travelling less than the given distance are plotted, culminating in 100 percent travelling less than the maximum observed distance.

SPSS offers almost identical possibilities and procedures. A bar chart, for example, would be generated by the instructions **Graphs > Bar**. This brings up the window in Figure 4.9. We need select only **Simple** and click on **Define** to bring up the partner

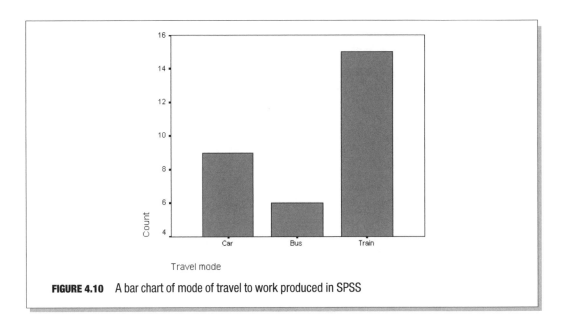

FIGURE 4.10   A bar chart of mode of travel to work produced in SPSS

dialogue box. The variable to be plotted (we can use 'mode of travel' once again) is transferred into the **Category Axis** box by highlighting the variable name in the list, and clicking the 'arrow' button to the immediate left of the box (see also section 2.9). This transfers the variable into the box. Notice that options exist in this dialogue box to plot the bars as numbers or percentages. Cumulative bar charts can also be stipulated at this stage. Click **OK** and the graph (Figure 4.10) will be produced in the **Output Viewer** window. Because the data file has already been coded in Variable View to provide value labels (text names) for the category code numbers, these names appear automatically in this output.

A histogram is produced with equal ease, but by employing the instructions **Graphs > Histogram** the dialogue box (not shown) requires only the transfer of the selected variable into the **Variable** box. Again, and in standard SPSS fashion, this is done by high-lighting the variable and clicking on the arrow button to the left of the box. Click on **OK** and a simple histogram will be produced. If you enter the wrong variable, or want to change the variable already in the box from a previous run, highlight it by clicking over the name; the arrow will now point away from the box, which when clicked will place the variable back in the list to the left.

4.5 Measures of central tendency

It is often useful to summarise data for a single variable as one number. A measure of *central tendency* is such a summary, and there are a number of statistics available to pro-vide this, the choice of which is determined largely by the measurement scale of the data. Three are commonly used: the *mode* (also referred to as the *modal class*), the *median* and the *mean* (often termed the *average*). Each, however, has some specific requirements, and we should note:

- The central tendency of nominal scale data can only be measured using the mode or modal class.
- Ordinal scale data can be described by the mode or the median.
- Interval/ratio scale data are best described using either the median or the mean, although the mode might also be used.

The mode or modal class

This is the class or category in a variable's frequency plot or table that contains the greatest number of individuals or observations. For example, in Figure 4.4 the mode or modal class is group 3 (those who travel to work by train), while in Table 4.3 the modal class is the mortality group in the range 7·75 to 8·24 deaths/1,000 births. Notice, however, that any redefinition of arbitrary classes of interval or ratio scale data can change the frequency of observations that they contain, and the class boundaries in Table 4.3 could easily be redrawn to create a slightly different pattern of frequencies. On the other hand, some data cannot be so easily reclassified and attributes such as race or gender are absolute and not subject to arbitrary definition. In cases where classes can be redrawn, the mode should be used with caution. This tendency to instability when using interval/ratio data can be reduced by using Equation 4.1 to provide an arithmetic (single value) estimate of the mode:

$$\text{Mode} = L + \frac{D_1}{D_1 + D_2} \times i$$

(4.1)

Equation 4.1

D_1 = difference between modal frequency and frequency of next lower class

D_2 = difference between modal frequency and frequency of next higher class interval

L = lower limit of modal class

i = the class interval

There may be situations when two classes are equally dominant, in which case the data are described as *bimodal*. In other cases we may have *multimodal* patterns and little can be stated about the central tendency of the data through use of the mode. Such problems are often associated with small samples and the easiest solution is to increase the sample size if possible. Although the mode is the least reliable measure of central tendency, it remains the only such measure for nominal scale data but can sometimes be of value in characterising interval and ratio scale data.

The median

This is the mid-point of a set of ordinal or interval/ratio scale data, above which lie half the data points or observations, and below which are the other half. To locate the median, the observations need first to be ranked into ascending order and the median is located at the mid-point of this ordered series. For example, if there are an odd number of observations in the data set, say 39, then the median is the 20th in the series as there will be 19 observations above and below this mid-point observation. If there is an even number of observations in the series, say 40, the median is the average of the 20th and 21st observations.

Use of the median allows us to introduce a concept of *percentile values*. In fact, we have already touched on this issue when producing cumulative frequency (ogive) curves. The top end of these curves include 100 per cent of the observations. As we move from the lower end of the curve (0 per cent) to this latter point we progressively include an ever-greater percentage of the observations. The median value is, in reality, the *50th percentile* point in that sequence. Indeed, this value could be estimated graphically by using an ogive such as Figure 4.8 and reading off the point on the X axis that corresponds to the 50 per cent point on the Y axis.

The arithmetic mean

The mean is obtained by adding all observations of a data set, and dividing the sum by the number of observations. This procedure is expressed algebraically in Equation 4.2:

$$\overline{X} = \frac{\Sigma X}{n}$$

(4.2)

Equation 4.2

$\overline{X}$ = mean

ΣX = sum of all values

n = number of observations

In this way each member of the data set contributes towards the mean, and any data set can have only one mean. Furthermore, for the mean to be a reliable estimate of central tendency, the sum of the deviations of each individual data point from its mean should be zero. Thus some observations will be less than the mean, giving a negative difference, while others will be greater than the mean, giving positive differences. The sum of these positive and negative differences should approximate to zero.

It will sometimes be the case that the mean and the median of a data set do not have the same numerical value, although both are measures of central tendency. Such differences are not uncommon and although the mean is the most informative of the measures of central tendency, there are situations (to be discussed below) when data sets may preclude its use and preference should be given to the median.

4.6 Criteria for the selection of mean, median and mode

It should be clear from our previous discussion that the different measures of central tendency are not always directly comparable. For example, the mode is based on the class with the highest frequency, the median the middle position of ranked data and the mean the numerical centrality of the values. The distinction between the median and the mean lies in the fact that the numerical value of all sample observations contributes to the latter, while in the case of the median it is only the order of the observations that determines its location and no account is taken of the statistical distance between the observations. The choice of the most appropriate measure of central tendency depends on a number of criteria, the most important of which is determined by the statistical characteristics or *distribution* of the data.

The distribution of a set of data is something we have already touched upon. The histogram in Figure 4.7 shows the distribution of the 'distance travelled to work' data set, which, although presented as a series of classes, could easily be generalised as a continuous curve. In this figure we have an approximately symmetrical distribution and, under such circumstances, the mean, median and mode will tend to give the same value. If, however, the distribution is *skewed* (lopsided), as in the generalised curves in Figure 4.11, then the equality between the measures disappears. The greater the degree of skewness, the greater the differences between mean, median and mode. Where observations cluster at the lower end of the scale and there is a long 'tail' towards the upper end of the distribution indicating a small number of high values, the distribution is described as *positively skewed*. This is a common feature of geographical data sets, and has the effect of displacing the mean towards the upper end of the distribution as

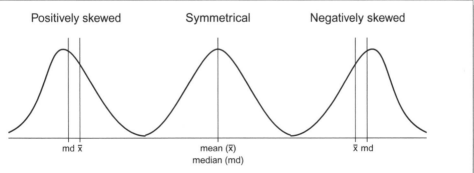

FIGURE 4.11 Idealised curves showing positive-, zero- and negatively-skewed distributions. The positions of the respective hypothetical means ($\bar{X}$) and medians (md) are also shown

the high numbers contribute disproportionately to its final value. In the case of left or *negatively-skewed* data, the mean is displaced to the lower end of the distribution. The mean is not a good indicator of central tendency where data have a skewed distribution as it no longer represents the most frequent or most probable value. The median is less influenced by such extreme behaviour as it is the rank and not the numerical value of those observations that are considered. Whenever our data are skewed it is, therefore, preferable to use the median as its measure of central tendency.

Useful though the measures of central tendency are, they only give us a partial view of the data. They tell us nothing about the variability of the sample – a feature better described as its dispersion.

4.7 Measures of dispersion

In the same way as there are more than one measure of central tendency, so too can we call upon a number of summary statistics to measure the variation or dispersion of data. The utility of each again depends upon the character of the data and their distribution. Importantly, measures of dispersion are only truly applicable to interval/ratio scale data.

The range

The *range* is the difference between the largest and smallest observations in a data set. It measures the dispersion of the data, but only in a simple way that is highly sensitive to individual extremes and overlooks the variability of the remainder of the data.

The inter-quartile range

The *inter-quartile range* partly overcomes the disadvantages of the range by excluding the uppermost and lowermost quarters of the distribution and summarising the variability of the remaining central 50 per cent of the data. It is a direct counterpart to the median that, importantly in this context, is also the 50th percentile of the data set. In order to find the inter-quartile range, we must estimate two further percentile values, those for the 25th and 75th points on the ordered series. These are also known as *quartiles* as they represent points one-quarter (Q_1) and three-quarters (Q_3) of the way along a ranked data series. By convention the data are ranked from lowest to highest, and the first quartile lies towards the lower end of the range and the third quartile towards the upper end (Figure 4.12). The median is, in this context, the second quartile.

The inter-quartile range (IQR in Equation 4.3) is derived from the difference between the third (Q_3) and the first quartile (Q_1), and it measures the numerical range occupied by the central 50 per cent of the observations.

$$IQR = Q_3 - Q_1 \qquad (4.3)$$

There is, in theory, no restriction on the construction of such ranges and, for example, an inter-percentile range could be used simply by taking the 10th and 90th percentiles. But

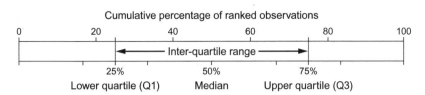

FIGURE 4.12 Diagram showing the position of the median, the first and the third quartiles along a cumulative percentage range of 0 (zero) to 100

the inter-quartile range is generally preferred. However, all such methods are open to the criticism that they exclude a proportion of the data and what is required is a measure that includes all the observations in a data set; a dispersion-based counterpart to the mean.

The variance and the standard deviation

The *variance* and *standard deviation* are measures that take into account all the observations. In statistical terms they are the most comprehensive descriptions of dispersion, since they are given in terms of the average deviation of all observations about the mean. The variance (s^2) is found by using Equation 4.4 in which it is important to obey the order of precedence indicated by the equation (see also section 2.2). In this case, the mean is subtracted from each observation, those deviations are then individually squared and those squared values are then added. Only then is the total divided by n (the sample size).

$$s^2 = \frac{\Sigma(X_i - \overline{X})^2}{n}$$ (4.4)

Equation 4.4

s^2 = variance

X_i = ith value of X

$\overline{X}$ = mean

n = number of observations

In fact the variance (s^2) and the standard deviation (s) are very much the same measure, the latter being the square root of the former so that

$$s = \sqrt{[\frac{\Sigma(X_i - \overline{X})^2}{n}]}$$ (4.5)

The standard deviation is, however, the preferred measure of dispersion of the two. Not only are variance estimates very large, being based on squared deviations from the mean, but the standard deviation, as will be shown in Chapter 6, has some remarkable and very useful probabilistic properties attached to it.

The standard deviation is extremely useful in describing the general characteristics of data. It does, nevertheless, have some limitations and it cannot be used with nominal or ordinal data. Less obviously we should also be cautious where data have a skewed distribution. For the standard deviation to apply equally on both sides of the mean, the distribution should be symmetrical and the positive deviations balanced by the negative. If this is not the case, and the data are skewed, it is better to use the inter-quartile range which is less disturbed by such data irregularities.

The coefficient of variation

The standard deviation is an absolute measure of dispersion, which is of limited use if variables measured on different units are to be compared. The same problem occurs if two samples of the same phenomena, but with different orders of magnitude, are being studied. Under these circumstances, we require a relative measure of dispersion. This can be illustrated by taking the small hypothetical example in Table 4.4, which compares rainfall in two very different areas. Despite the difference in magnitude, both data sets have the same standard deviation. Yet, clearly, a dispersal of 4·23 about a mean of 11·67 is proportionately greater and more significant than the same dispersal about a mean of 61·67.

In this situation we can apply a relative measure of dispersion such as the *coefficient of variation (CV)*. This is calculated by dividing the standard deviation by its respective mean (Equation 4.6).

TABLE 4.4 Estimates of the coefficient of variation to two hypothetical sets of rainfall data

	Weather site 1	Weather site 2
	6	56
	8	58
	10	60
	12	62
	16	66
	18	68
Mean	11·67	61·67
Standard deviation	4·23	4·23
Coefficient of variation (%)	36·2	6·86

$$CV = \frac{s}{\overline{X}} \times 100\%$$ (4.6)

Equation 4.6

CV = coefficient of variation

s = standard deviation of X

$\overline{X}$ = mean of X

The results of such calculations are expressed as percentages, i.e. the standard deviation as a percentage of the mean. If this is applied to the data in Table 4.4, then the coefficient of variation for weather site 1 is 36·2%, compared with 6·86% for site 2. We now have a more appropriate view of the relative deviations about the means of the two samples.

4.8 Other descriptive measures: skewness and kurtosis

We have already seen that some data sets may be particularly skewed and it is useful to have a numerical measure of such skewness. But before doing so these measures can be placed in the wider context of *moments* of the distribution of data. The mean, based only on the data themselves, constitutes the first moment of the distribution. The variance, based on squared deviations about the mean, is the second moment. Skewness and kurtosis estimates form the third and fourth moments and are based respectively on the cubed and fourth power deviation of observations from the mean. All four measure different aspects of the way in which data sets are organised or distributed.

Skewness

This is the degree of asymmetry in a distribution and can be visually assessed from the histogram of the data but more objective measures can be made, most importantly by using Equation 4.7 which gives the *momental skewness* (α_3) of the data.

$$\alpha_3 = \frac{\Sigma(X_i - \overline{X})^3}{n^3}$$ (4.7)

Equation 4.7

X_i = ith value of X

$\overline{X}$ = mean

n = number of observations

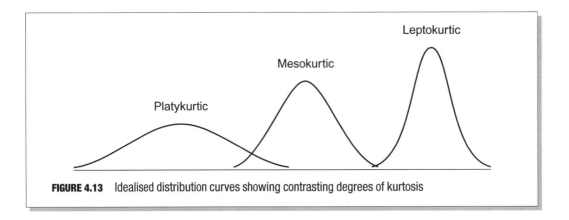

FIGURE 4.13 Idealised distribution curves showing contrasting degrees of kurtosis

The value for a perfectly symmetrical distribution is zero, negative values indicate negative skewness and positive values positive skewness. Such measures of skewness guide us in assessing which measures of central tendency and dispersion should be used. For example, and as noted earlier, means and standard deviations are only useful if the data distribution is not significantly skewed.

Kurtosis

This is the fourth moment of a distribution and indicates the degree of peakedness of a frequency distribution. The normal condition is *mesokurtic* for which the kurtosis value is close to zero. A distribution with a high degree of peakedness (Figure 4.13) is said to be *leptokurtic* and will have a kurtosis value greater than 0·0. A distribution with a low degree of peakedness is *platykurtic* and will have a kurtosis value of less than 0·0.

Both skewness and kurtosis, though not widely used, are potentially valuable statistics, because they:

- can identify highly skewed distributions when the use of means and standard deviations can give misleading estimates of centrality and dispersion;

- allow for the objective comparison of different distributions;

- show how far a distribution deviates from 'normal'. In this context they are important in the application of tests discussed later, which assume certain characteristics to be present in the data set.

4.9 Measures of central tendency and dispersion using MINITAB and SPSS

When dealing with nominal scale data we often need to summarise them by the various categories with which they are measured. Bar charts are one means of accomplishing this and they provide a useful visual impression of the data's main characteristics

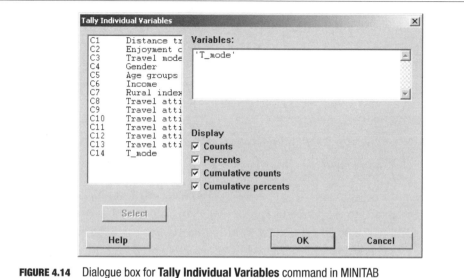

FIGURE 4.14 Dialogue box for **Tally Individual Variables** command in MINITAB

Tally for Discrete Variables: T_mode

T_mode	Count	CumCnt	Percent	CumPct
bus	6	6	20.00	20.00
car	9	15	30.00	50.00
train	15	30	50.00	100.00
N=	30			

FIGURE 4.15 Talley output in MINITAB summarising the 'mode of travel' variable in file TRAVEL_DATA.MTW (see also Figure 4.10)

but we may require more detailed statistics. Suppose that we wanted to examine the different methods of transport in our travel to work survey data in the form of numbers rather than bar charts. In MINITAB, we can make such investigations by using the command **Stat > Tables > Tally Individual Variables**, which brings up the dialogue box in Figure 4.14.

We can select the variables we want to examine and place them into the **Variables** box by double clicking on their titles as described above. In this case we have selected 'T_mode', which is the column in which the text-based category identifiers have been stored following the process described in section 4.4 (this provides a list of categories by name rather than by number). If we tick the appropriate boxes we can choose the attributes in which we are interested, these include such category-based summaries as the raw counts and cumulative counts, and their percentage counterparts. By clicking on **OK** a summary table is generated (Figure 4.15). The various statistics are listed, by rows, for each category in the variable under study. In this example the output is simplified by the request for only one variable to be analysed (we could have included others in the **Variables** box), and by the simple, three-fold categorisation of the variable. The layout is, however, the same for all cases. The modal class and its basic statistical properties can be quickly identified, but information is presented for all classes, and include:

- Count – the number of observations in the category
- CumCnt – the cumulative total count
- Percent – the percentage of observations in each category
- CumPct – the cumulative percentage.

The previous section has indicated the variety and importance of summarising measures of central tendency and dispersion in particular. Generating such descriptive statistics in either of MINITAB or SPSS is relatively straightforward. Focusing again on the data for distance travelled to work (measured in kilometres and therefore a ratio scale variable), we can use MINITAB to generate a wide range of summary statistics. To do this, we use the commands **Stat > Basic Statistics > Display Descriptive Statistics**. In the resulting dialogue box (Figure 4.16) we can select the variables to be analysed by placing them in the **Variables** box. We then click the **Statistics** tab to bring up the statistics dialogue box. A very wide range of summary measures can be generated and those automatically ticked are the default settings, but we can add or remove any of those available. We might choose to examine the mean, standard deviation, minimum, maximum, range, skewness and kurtosis. We need only tick those boxes (uncheck the others), click **OK** and MINITAB will provide the output in Figure 4.17 in the Session window.

There are a number of points that we can make regarding these particular data. First, the mean and median are very similar, indicating a relatively symmetrical distribution, which is also borne out by the histogram in Figure 4.7. The symmetrical nature of the distribution is confirmed by the low skewness statistic (–0·16), indicating that the distribution is not significantly skewed towards either end of the magnitude range. The distribution has, however, a very low kurtosis factor (–0·85), which is well below 0·0 and suggests a platykurtic character. In the light of these general findings, especially the lack of notable skewness, we may conclude that the data properties are such that these measures of central tendency (the mean) and dispersion (standard deviation) are suitable summary statistics, and we do not need to resort to the more robust median and inter-quartile range respectively.

The situation in SPSS is similar to that in MINITAB, and the commands needed are **Analyze > Descriptive Statistics**. At that point, however, two options are available, either **Frequencies** or **Descriptives**. Both of these can be requested to provide the measures of central tendency and dispersion, but we will use **Frequencies**, which creates the dialogue box in Figure 4.18. The required variable is transferred into the **Variable(s)** box by the method described above. The second dialogue box is produced when the **Statistics** button is clicked. Ticking those statistics shown gives the tabled set of results

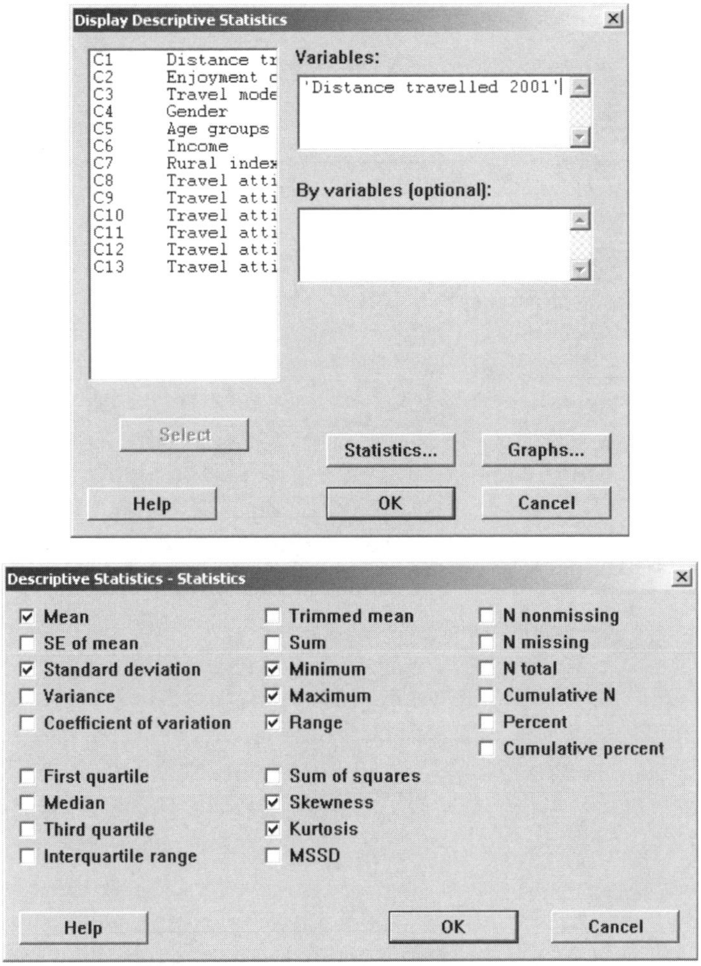

FIGURE 4.16 **Descriptive Statistics** dialogue boxes from MINITAB

in Figure 4.19. The so-called *standard errors* of the skewness and kurtosis measures are automatically produced, but their discussion takes us beyond the scope of this section, and these statistics are introduced in Chapter 6. Notice how the variable label, rather than the abbreviated variable name (see Variable View window for these data) is used to provide the header for the output table in SPSS.

4.10 Conclusions

In this chapter we have restricted our study to the use of descriptive statistics and graphs. These are very useful for summarising and simplifying data sets of all sizes, from the large to the small. But even with such relatively simple methods care must be taken

Descriptive Statistics: Distance travelled 2001

Variable	Mean	StDev	Minimum	Maximum	Range	Skewness	Kurtosis
Distance travell	33.37	11.44	10.00	53.00	43.00	-0.16	-0.85

FIGURE 4.17 Typical MINITAB output for the Descriptive Statistics command

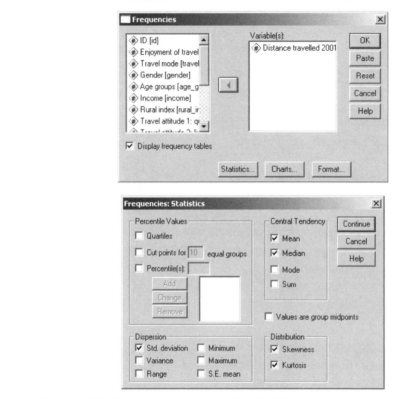

FIGURE 4.18 SPSS dialogue boxes for **Descriptive Statistics**

Statistics

Distance travelled 2001

N	Valid	30
	Missing	0
Mean		33.37
Median		33.00
Std. Deviation		11.436
Skewness		-.163
Std. Error of Skewness		.427
Kurtosis		-.848
Std. Error of Kurtosis		.833

FIGURE 4.19 SPSS output for the Descriptive Statistics option

TABLE 4.5   Scales of measurement and appropriate summary statistics

Data scale	Preferred measure of central tendency	Preferred measure of dispersion
Nominal/ordinal	Mode	None
Interval/ratio (skewed)	Median	Inter-quartile range
Interval/ratio (non-skewed)	Mean	Standard deviation

and the results will not be reliable if applied to unsuitable data. Although both MINITAB and SPSS are sophisticated packages they will not alert the user to such transgressions. Skewed data in particular present a number of problems, the most significant of which is their unsuitability for summarising by the mean and the standard deviation; the median and inter-quartile range are always preferred in such cases. Table 4.5 summarises the general suitability of descriptive statistics in terms of scale of measurement and data character.

5

Probability and probability distributions

5.1 Introduction

PROBABILITY CAN BE DEFINED in both the general and the mathematical senses. We might, for example, say 'it is probable that you will understand this book'. From this we could infer that the reader has a greater chance of understanding the text than of being bewildered by it. But such an expression can be interpreted in only the vaguest of terms, and scientists prefer to use the word in a more rigorous fashion, attaching some numerical value to the probability of an event. This numerical probability can be expressed in either of two ways – on an absolute scale of zero to one, or on a percentage scale of zero to 100. Both are widely used.

It is possible to think of some events to which numerical probability values can be readily attached. Some events – the daily setting of the sun, or gradual erosion of land surfaces – can be thought of being absolutely certain. Such absolute certainties have a probability of 1·0, or 100 per cent. Conversely, for impossible situations the probability is 0·0 or 0 per cent. However, most events are by no means impossible or certain, and the probabilities of their occurrence can be thought of as lying at some point along a probability spectrum between 0·0 and 1·0 (or 0 to 100 per cent). Figure 5.1 illustrates the position for some simple, if non-geographical, events.

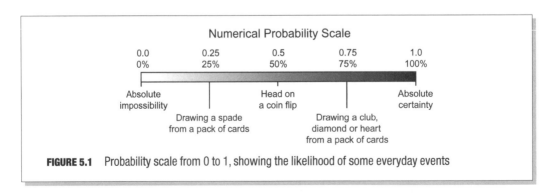

FIGURE 5.1 Probability scale from 0 to 1, showing the likelihood of some everyday events

5.2 Assessment of probability values

Logical reasoning can derive the numerical probabilities of inevitable, of impossible, and of some other events between those extremes, but alternative methods are needed in the less obvious cases. The French mathematician Pierre Simon de Laplace (1749–1827) was the first to define and solve the problem algebraically. If the numerical probability of an event x is denoted by $p(x)$, then:

$$p(x) = n/N \qquad (5.1)$$

Equation 5.1

n = number of ways in which a particular event can be realised

N = total number of possible outcomes (known as the sample space)

To illustrate this important principle, let us consider the problem of drawing one card, at random, from a full pack. There are 52 possible outcomes, hence N (sample space) is 52. Suppose, also, that the specified outcome is a spade card. There are 13 such cards in the deck and, hence, 13 ways in which the specified event can be realised (n). From Equation 5.1 the derived probability (p) of obtaining a spade card is:

$$p(\text{spade}) = 13/52 = 0{\cdot}25 \text{ or } 25 \text{ per cent}$$

Correspondingly, the probability of drawing a card other than a spade – a heart, diamond or club – of which there are 39, is given by:

$$p(\text{non-spade}) = 39/52 = 0{\cdot}75 \text{ or } 75 \text{ per cent}$$

We should, however, note that this derivation of the probability value makes one, very important, assumption – that all 52 cards are equally likely to be drawn. Provided that no duplicate cards are within the deck, this is a realistic assumption. A further point to be noted is that of *complementarity*. Because the result of any draw of a card must be either a spade or a non-spade (no other outcome is possible), the total of the probabilities of the two probabilities must be 1·0.

Another example is provided by the flip of a coin. In this case the sample space provides for only two outcomes, a head or a tail. Each outcome can be realised in only one way. Hence, $n = 1$ and $N = 2$, so that:

$$p(\text{head}) = 1/2 = 0{\cdot}5$$

and

$$p(\text{tail}) = 1/2 = 0{\cdot}5$$

The outcome, if we ignore the vanishingly small probability of the coin landing on its edge, must be one of the above, and their sum must be 1·0.

We may now introduce two new terms, *mutual exclusiveness* and *independence*. Draws of cards and flips of coins produce outcomes that are mutually exclusive. By this we mean that if a head occurs on the flip of a coin then, for that flip, a tail is impossible. If a spade is drawn from a pack of cards, that same draw cannot simultaneously result in a card from any other suit being drawn.

The other important concept is that of independence – simple at this introductory level – but fundamental, and often less obvious, when dealing with 'real world' geographical data. A flip of a coin or the drawing of a card are events that statisticians describe as a *trial*. For these two activities, the succession of outcomes for trials of length greater than 1 (more than one flip of a coin or drawing of a card), form a sequence of independent events. If one of the flips produces a head, then the next flip is neither more nor less likely to produce another head (or tail). This independence applies no matter how many trials might constitute the sequence. Consider, for example, a sequence of ten trials with a coin. If all ten trials yielded a head, unlikely though such a sequence might be, it does not alter the probability of the eleventh flip also producing a head, and it remains at 0·5. Chance, in this context, has no 'memory', and events are independent of one another.

Coins and cards provide clear examples of exclusive and independent events. Very many of the numerical techniques and statistical concepts that follow assume the events they treat to be similarly independent. This is an important assumption, but one not always fulfilled by geographical data, and one whose validity can be difficult to assess. When collecting data we should always be aware of this principal requirement. Questionnaire responses, soil surveys, meteorological observations and many other phenomena provide data in which the constituent observations are not necessarily independent of one another, and our sampling frame (Chapter 3) should take this possibility into account. For example, if we want to know the religious complexion of a community, a questionnaire survey only of people leaving church on a Sunday will be biased because the individuals in the sample are not independent in respect of the interview objectives.

5.3 Probability assessments and the geographer

Laplace's method for estimating probability depends on a complete understanding of the circumstances surrounding the event. Most importantly, this means being able to define both the sample space (N) and the number of ways in which the required event can be realised (n). Such a complete understanding is impossible in most geographical studies, where both N and n may be impossible to define or measure.

Let us consider the notoriously unpredictable weather of the British Isles. Our knowledge of the complex interplay of forces involved in bringing any one day's weather into being is inadequate to allow the Laplace model to be used for determining the probability of rain falling at one place on any one day. Fortunately it is possible to get around this problem by examining the observable consequences of these intricate atmospheric processes, and to determine what are termed *empirical probabilities*. To illustrate how this process might operate, let us consider the probability of rain falling on a day, chosen at random, in March at a single location – in this case Durham City in northern England. An examination of the weather records for the University of Durham's weather observatory shows that over a ten-year period rain had fallen on 196 of the 310 March days. From these two figures we can derive an estimate of the probability of rain on any March day:

$$p(\text{rain}) = 196/310 = 0.63$$

and, logically, the complement of this – a day without rain is:

$$p(\text{dry}) = 1 - 0.63 = 0.37$$

The similarities to the Laplace method are clear: the sample space N becomes the total number of available days (310), while the number of realisations of the event (n) is represented by the number of rain days (196). There are, however, some important differences. The result applies, at best, to only a small area around the weather observatory, the extent of which is governed by local factors of relief. The result also applies only to predictions for days in March. Seasonal variations are barely apparent within the span of one month, and all days can be considered to be equal with respect to the background, long-term climate. Over the year as a whole, on the other hand, this important requirement of equal probability over all days will not be met because of seasonal changes in the 'background' climate. Spring tends to be a relatively dry time of year, and estimates of rain days based on all 12 months would overestimate the probability of March rainfall, but underestimate rainfall probabilities at other, wetter, times of the year. This necessarily restricted application of the empirical method contrasts with the 'universality' of the conclusions using the Laplace method where the probabilities were valid for all trials. We are also assuming that there are no longer term trends or changes in the climate, and that the result of the above procedure applies over all Marches, now and in the future. This may not be the case, and in other situations, such as those in social or economic geography in which short-term changes can be more marked, this assumption is even less realistic.

Lastly, we may return to the question of independence. For the rain day probability estimate to be reliable, we must also be confident that each day is independent of the following or preceding day. If this is not the case, the chance of rain on any one day will be partly determined by what happened on the previous day. The British weather is highly variable from day to day, and the assumption of independence may be correct, but it would require close investigation. In short, this 'empirical' method should be used with caution, but it is one that might be unavoidable in the absence of detailed knowledge of the individual situation.

5.4 Estimating the probabilities of multiple events

We have thus far examined only single events – rainfall on one day, or one draw of a card. Frequently, however, we need to examine compound events. What, for example, is the probability of three days in March all recording some rain? The probabilities of such compound events remain within the range 0 to 1, but they require careful calculation based on the *multiplication law of probabilities*. Let us term a wet day W, and a dry day as D. To find the probability of three wet days in succession we must use this multiplication law. Thus:

$$p(WWW) = 0.63 \times 0.63 \times 0.63 = 0.25$$

The probability of the first two days being wet and the third being dry is found in the same way, by multiplying the probabilities together:

$$p(WWD) = 0.63 \times 0.63 \times 0.37 = 0.147$$

It is important to note that we do not add the probabilities for the individual events. Notice also that we are careful to specify the order in which the events take place – two wet, then one dry day. If order is not important we are presented with a different problem. The arrangement of two wet and one dry day can be accommodated in three ways, with the dry day either first (DWW), second (WDW) or third (WWD) in the sequence. Expressed correctly, we would state that there are three *permutations* of the *combination* of two wet days and one dry day. Should we wish to know the probability of any one of these three permutations occurring (an essentially different situation from that of any one single permutation occurring) we would *add* their individual probabilities so that:

$$p(2W1D) = p(DWW) + p(WDW) + p(WWD)$$

which, because the probability of each of the three permutations must be the same, gives:

$$p(2W1D) = 0.147 + 0.147 + 0.147 = 0.441$$

We would apply the same principle to the specification for one wet and two dry days (1W2D). Again, there are three permutations of this combination – WDD, DWD and DDW – all of which have the same probability. Let us take WDD:

$$p(WDD) = 0.63 \times 0.37 \times 0.37 = 0.086$$

The probability of any one of the permutations is the sum of the three individual probabilities:

TABLE 5.1 Combinations and probabilities for three days of wet (W) and/or dry (D) weather in Durham

Combination	Probability
3W	0·250
2W1D	0·441
1W2D	0·258
3D	0·051
Total	1·0

$$p(1W2D) = p(WDD) + p(DWD) + p(DDW)$$

$$= 0·086 + 0·086 + 0·086 = 0·258$$

To complete the picture we can consider the probability of all three days being dry. As with three wet days, this combination has only one permutation (DDD), so:

$$p(DDD) = 0·37 \times 0·37 \times 0·37 = 0·051$$

These four combinations (WWW, 2W1D, 2D1W and DDD) cover all possible outcomes for three days. They are themselves mutually exclusive, so the addition of their individual probabilities (Table 5.1) gives a total of 1·0 (allowing for marginal rounding errors). Thus, whatever the outcome, it has to be one of the three combinations.

5.5 Histograms and probability

Having considered some of the fundamental concepts in probability, we can now turn to their broader application to geographical statistics. There are few more rewarding areas with which to begin than that of the bar chart and histogram. Both are widely used as descriptive devices representing, as we saw in section 4.3, discrete classes of events or arbitrary classes defined along a measurement continuum. In their simplest forms the bar chart and histogram represent the absolute frequency of events in each class. But the relative frequencies, i.e. the absolute frequencies as proportions of the sample size, can also be plotted. Figure 5.2 is based on the same data as Figure 4.1, but plots the relative frequencies for modes of travel to work.

In the case of Figure 5.2 the data are based on a 10 per cent sample drawn from the UK Census of 1981 (Office of Population Censuses and Surveys 1984), and contained 2,056,840 individuals. Of that number, 805,535 were car drivers as far as 'journey to work' was concerned. The relative proportion of this category was thus 805,535/2,056,840 = 0·39. Such proportions were used to compile Figure 5.2 but serve a more useful purpose because we know that these proportions are also the empirically determined probabilities of randomly selected individuals being from those categories. As a consequence,

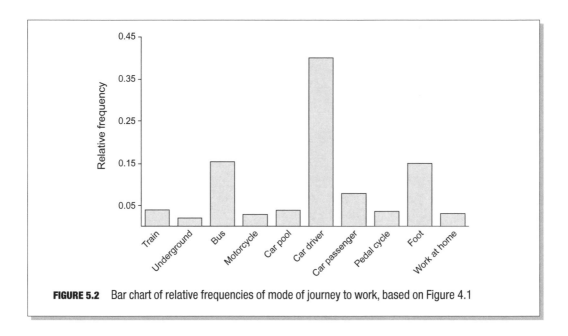

FIGURE 5.2   Bar chart of relative frequencies of mode of journey to work, based on Figure 4.1

there is 0·39 probability that such an individual will drive to work. There is a 0·03 probability that they will walk, a 0·15 probability that they will go by bus, and so on. This line of reasoning can be taken one stage further: if the 10 per cent sample is representative of the UK Census, we can deduce that the derived probabilities apply equally to the whole population.

Such lines of reasoning apply also to data based on discrete classes (as above) and to classes based on the division of a continuum into equal-sized range bands. Both types of categorisation represent mutually exclusive divisions that can be considered to cover all possible outcomes. It is therefore consistent with what has been proposed in section 5.4 that the total of the empirical probabilities (relative proportions) of the classes must add to 1·0, reflecting the absolute certainty that any individual must fall into one, but only one, of the specified classes.

We can now see that the bar chart or histogram represents more than a graphical device. It demonstrates the partitioning of a sample space with a notional total area of 1·0 units. The probabilities of randomly selected individuals falling within any one of the classes, or partition spaces, is proportional to the height of the bar for that class. This sequence of changing probabilities from class to class is known as a *probability distribution*. This concept is of particular importance when dealing with data measured on a continuous scale, and through the vehicle of the histogram we may introduce the idea of the formalised probability distribution – one with consistent distributional characteristics that apply over a wide range of measurable phenomena.

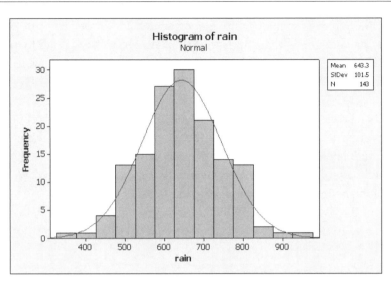

FIGURE 5.3 MINITAB histogram and superimposed normal curve of the distribution of mean annual rainfall for Sunderland, England

5.6 The normal distribution: initial considerations

The concept of the statistical or probability distribution is an important one in many areas of research. The bar chart summarising the journey to work habits of UK residents (Figure 5.2) has a decidedly haphazard appearance in which no regularity can be discerned; a problem made worse by the use of nominal scale data that allow the classes to be shuffled without prejudice to the integrity of the information it contains. But when plotting data classified along a measurement continuum a different picture emerges. The definition of the interval classes can change, but their order cannot, and is determined by the measurement scale – the classes must follow in numerical sequence of the units of the scale. We can use data file SUNDRAIN.MTW on the CD to develop this theme. It contains annual rainfall totals for the northern English city of Sunderland for the period 1860 to 2002. Figure 5.3 was prepared from these data. Using MINITAB, the command route **Graph > Histogram > With Fit** calls up a dialogue box (not shown but see section 4.4) in which the column holding the data needs to be specified to allow the histogram to be generated. The order of classes into which the rainfall range is divided cannot be changed, and the height of each bar represents the frequency of events (annual rainfalls) in that class. More importantly, a degree of regularity is evident in which events close to the mean of 643·3 mm are more frequent, other classes contain less events in approximate proportion to their distance from the mean. The most extreme cases tend to have the lowest frequencies. With 143 observations the histogram presents an approximately symmetrical distribution about the mean that is not uncommon in a wide range of phenomena, although with smaller samples such tendencies to regularity are often less obvious. Data that tend to this characteristically bell-shaped curve are said to follow the *normal distribution*, although the term 'normal' is unfortunate in that there are, as we shall see later in this chapter, other distribution types that are no less 'normal'. The **With Fit** option has instructed MINITAB to fit a perfect, theoretical, normal curve to these data, and it can be seen how closely the histogram approximates to this ideal condition.

Such a tendency to regularity is no academic abstraction, and it reflects some arithmetically definable characteristics of normally distributed data sets. The normal distribution was discovered by the German mathematician Carl Gauss (1777–1855), after whom it is sometimes named – the *Gaussian distribution*. Gauss was able to express the regularity of the distribution in mathematical terms, and from that definition has sprung a huge area of statistical theory that we can use to advantage.

5.7 The mathematical definition of the normal distribution

The pattern of probability changes through the normal distribution is typically bell-shaped, with its peak at the mean. It can be applied only to interval and ratio scale data. In theory therefore it should be described by a curve and not by the series of discrete classes that constitute a histogram.

One means by which such a curve could be approximated would be to gather large amounts of data, thereby allowing us to classify them into ever smaller classes as the data set grew (Figure 5.4). But to do so would require often impossibly large data sets. Fortunately we need not resort to this method of determining the precise character of the normal distribution, and the mathematical equation that describes the bell-shaped curve can come to our assistance. This numerical expression is given in Equation 5.2 in which it should be noted that it relies only on quantities already introduced in previous chapters:

$$Y = \frac{1}{\sigma\sqrt{2\pi}} e^{-0.5(X-\mu)^2/\sigma^2}$$

(5.2)

Equation 5.2

Y = height of the curve at point X

e = the constant 2·7183 . . .

π = constant 3·1416 . . .

μ = the mean of all observed Xs

σ = the standard deviation of X

X = individual values of X

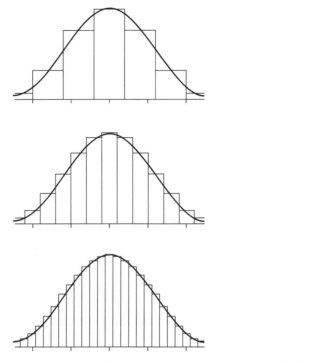

FIGURE 5.4 The effect of decreasing class intervals on an idealised histogram form showing improved approximation to the normal curve with increasing sample size and class numbers

We need know only the mean (μ) and the standard deviation (σ) to be able to calculate the height of the curve (Y) at any point (X) along its range. While the equation is less than inviting, the principles of its application are the same as for the simpler expressions introduced in section 2.5. An unknown quantity (Y) is estimated from known terms, which are X (any chosen point on the measurement scale), the mean and the standard deviation of a sample of observations of X, and the two constants e and π. The mean and standard deviation will, of course, vary from sample to sample, but e and π are fixed for all instances. Repetitive substitution of X will provide enough points on the curve for it to be plotted, should we wish to do so.

Before progressing further we should note an important distinction between any such derived continuous curve and the probability histogram. In the latter the heights of each column are directly proportional to the probability of a randomly chosen event falling within that class. This is not the case for the normal curve, where its height above the base line is not a similarly direct measure of probability, and represents instead a quantity known as the *probability density function* (PDF). A full discussion of the PDF would take us far beyond the scope of this book, but some of its features can be understood if it is recalled that the measurement scale consists of an infinite number of points, and not a finite number of classes. Such points have no width or area, and probability statements can be applied only to ranges along such a continuum and not to individual locations. For example, we can correctly ask what the probability is of annual rainfall being between 500 and 600 mm, but it would not make mathematical sense to ask what the probability is of getting an annual total of exactly 790·5 mm for example (see Figure 5.5).

We can now turn to consider these points, but before doing so we should review the methods by which the form of the normal curve can be estimated without recourse to the challenging mathematics and repetitive substitutions expected for Equation 5.2. The MINITAB system provides a means of fitting a 'perfect' normal distribution to any given sample of data. The sample mean and the standard deviation can be used to describe the theoretical perfectly normal distribution of the background 'population' from which the sample was drawn. In this case the mean annual rainfall is 643·3 mm and the standard deviation is 101·5 mm. The command sequence **Calc > Probability Distributions > Normal** will bring up the dialogue box in Figure 5.6, into which must be entered the mean and standard deviation of the sample of data, together with the column (C1) in which the various values of X have previously been entered. In this case we have chosen 50 mm intervals between 200 and 1,250 (these were held in a file RAINPDF.MTW), but they need not be regular nor restricted in number and can, if preferred, be typed in at the keyboard. The space for **Probability density** should be checked. The PDF value for each of these is then entered by MINITAB into the specified column (C2) on the same row of the worksheet as the respective values of X.

The total area beneath the normal curve has a notional value of 1·0, which equates to a probability of 1·0 as all possible events must fall somewhere along the measurement spectrum. It is, however, important to notice that unlike the probability histogram with its definite upper and lower class limits, the normal curve can theoretically extend to

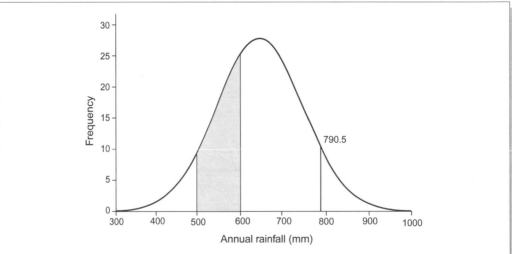

FIGURE 5.5   The normal curve showing (shaded) the area covered between two points on the horizontal scale. No corresponding area defines a single point

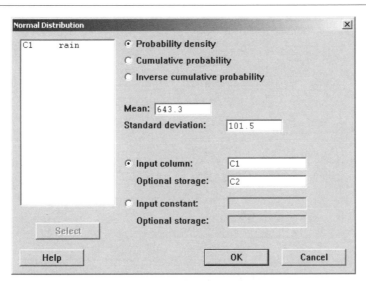

FIGURE 5.6 **Normal Distribution** dialogue box in MINITAB showing the requirements for deriving the PDF values for a normal distribution with mean of 643·3 and a standard deviation of 101·5. The values of *X* are held in column 1 (C1), and the results in column 2 (C2)

infinity in either direction, and is not constrained within the range of observed values only. We could, for example, have estimated a PDF value at $X = 1,500$ mm. The resulting PDF would be very small, but it would not be zero.

5.8 The standardised normal curve

The precise form of the normal curve will vary from case to case as the means and the standard deviations change. For example, in Figure 5.7a we can see that three samples have the same standard deviation or 'spread', but are distinguished by three different means. In Figure 5.7b, the means of three samples are the same, but the standard deviations differ. To realise the full potential of our knowledge of the normal distribution such differences must be removed by *standardisation* of the data. This is achieved by reference to the standard deviation of the sample in question. Individual observations can be converted to the equivalent *z-scores* by expressing their departure from the mean as a proportion of that standard deviation. For example, an observation that is exactly one and a half standard deviations above the mean will have a z-score of 1·5; an observation that is two standard deviations below the mean will have a z-score of –2·0. This standardisation process is expressed algebraically by Equation 5.3. When all the observations have been so converted, the new data set will have a mean of zero and a standard deviation of 1·0 irrespective of the raw values.

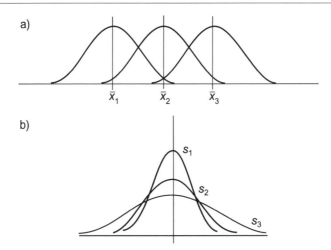

FIGURE 5.7   Generalised normal distributions showing (a) different means but similar standard deviations, and (b) similar means but different standard deviations

$$z = \frac{X - \mu}{\sigma}$$
(5.3)

Equation 5.3

z = required standardised value

μ = mean of variable X

σ = standard deviation of variable X

X = raw value of X

A few examples will illustrate this point, and we can see how the rainfall data used in Figure 5.3 can be converted to z-scores. Remembering that the mean and standard deviation are 643·3 and 101·5 mm respectively, the following conversions are easily performed.

Example 1: the z-score for a rainfall of 800 mm.

$$z = \frac{800 - 643·3}{101·5} = \frac{156·7}{101·5} = 1·54$$

Example 2: the z-score for a rainfall of 500 mm

$$z = \frac{500 - 643·3}{101·5} = \frac{-143·34}{101·5} = -1·41$$

Example 3: the z-score for a rainfall of 1,050 mm

$$z = \frac{1050 - 643 \cdot 3}{101 \cdot 5} = \frac{406 \cdot 7}{101 \cdot 5} = 4 \cdot 01$$

The effect of these conversions is to express all observations in terms of standard deviations about the mean. Thus both positive and negative z-scores are possible depending upon whether the selected value is greater or less than the mean. In example 1, 800 mm is 1·54 standard deviations above the mean, but in example 2, 500 mm is 1·41 standard deviations below the mean and, hence, negative. We need not, however, resort to hand calculations to standardise a data set; MINITAB can do so automatically by following the command route **Calc > Standardize**. The required column of data (we have again used the data in file SUNDRAIN.MTW) is then specified in the **Standardize** window (Figure 5.8), together with the column into which the standardised data should be entered (C2), click on **OK**, and the process is completed, and the standardised values can be saved in the work file.

This standardisation process can also be applied to the equation for the normal distribution (5·2) rendering it more simple. The terms σ and μ can be replaced by 1·0 and zero respectively, while the expression $(X - \mu)/\sigma$ can be simplified to z, giving the following expression:

$$Y = \frac{1}{\sqrt{2\pi}} e^{-0 \cdot 5z^2} \tag{5.4}$$

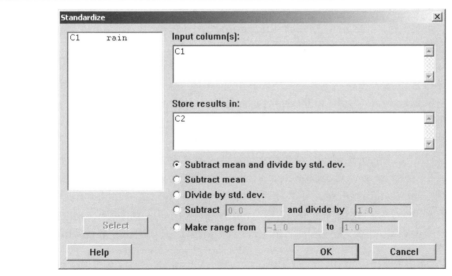

FIGURE 5.8 MINITAB **Standardize** dialogue box with specification for a data column and a storage column for the standardised observations

Equation 5.4

z = standardised variable (see Equation 5.3)

e = the constant 2·7183 . . .

π = the constant 3·1416 . . .

Y = the height of the curve at point z

By this procedure the expression retains its characteristic form, but the individual effects of differing means and standard deviations have been eliminated to produce curves that are mathematically identical with zero mean and unit (1·0) standard deviation.

5.9 The normal curve and probability

In general terms the character of the normal distribution is one in which events close to the mean are the most likely, becoming more improbable as one moves away from the central point (the mean). Exceedingly large or extremely small values are possible, but increasingly improbable. However, the nature of much geographical data imposes limitations on the realisation of such ideal properties. All ratio scale data (see section 4.1) such as crop yields, monetary income and rainfall have a zero point below which the distribution cannot extend.

Accepting these qualifications, we can nevertheless make confident statements about the probabilities of events falling within specified ranges of a normally distributed variable, but this can be most conveniently undertaken by using the standardised data. We have already stated that the area beneath the standardised normal curve has a notional value of 1·0, and must include all possible events. We know also that the distribution is perfectly symmetrical and that half the area must, therefore, lie above the mean and the other half below. Hence there is a 0·5 probability that any observation will be greater than the mean and a 0·5 probability that it will be less. Usefully, our understanding of the normal distribution goes far beyond this simple conclusion and, using the mathematics of calculus, we can estimate the relative areas beneath the curve between any two selected points that we might choose. These relative areas are also, importantly, the probabilities of events falling within those same ranges. So often are these quantities required that we need not venture into the calculation of them, and can instead refer to published tables. Appendix I contains such a table from which the area (probability) between the mean and any z-score can be read off directly. A few examples will serve to clarify the table's great usefulness.

Example 1: What is the probability of an observation (event) occurring within the range $z = 0·0$ and $z = +0·75$?

We need to know the relative area below the curve between these two points (Figure 5.9). Appendix I is arranged to provide such probabilities (relative areas) between 0·0

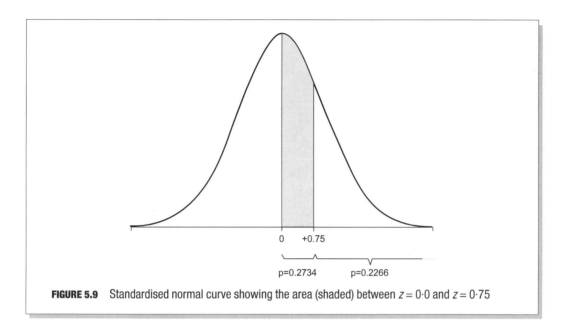

FIGURE 5.9 Standardised normal curve showing the area (shaded) between $z = 0.0$ and $z = 0.75$

and any specified value of z. The required probability, accurate to four places, may be read off directly from the table. In this example the resulting figure is 0.2734, i.e. the probability of an event falling within the range zero to $z = 0.75$ is 0.2734 or 27.34 per cent. Because the distribution is symmetrical about the mean, the probability of an event between zero and $z = -0.75$ would also be 0.2734.

Example 2: What is the probability of an observation (event) occurring with a z-value of 0.75 or greater?

The required probability is now between 0.75 and infinity. But, as the probability for an event between zero and $z = 0.75$ is 0.2734, and we know that the probability for any event greater than $z = 0.0$ is 0.5, it follows that:

$$p(z > 0.75) = 0.5 - 0.2734 = 0.2266$$

Example 3: What is the probability of an event falling within the range $z = 1.5$ and $z = -0.8$?

The same principles apply but the question must be answered in two parts, one dealing with the probability for the range $z = 0.0$ to 1.5, and the other for $z = 0.0$ to -0.8 (Figure 5.10). From Appendix I we see that:

$$p(z > -0.8) = 0.2882 \text{ and } p(z < 1.5) = 0.4332$$

thus

$$p(1.5 > z > -0.8) = 0.4332 + 0.2882 = 0.7214$$

and there is a 0.7214 (72.14%) probability that the event will fall within the range $z = -0.8$ to $z = 1.5$.

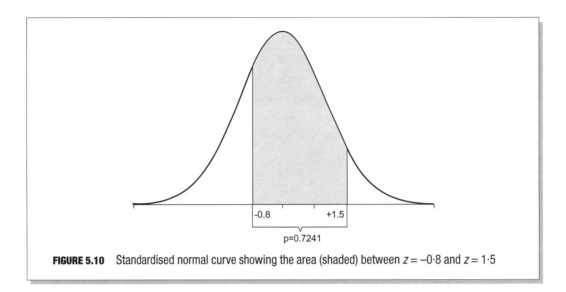

FIGURE 5.10 Standardised normal curve showing the area (shaded) between $z = -0.8$ and $z = 1.5$

Example 4: From the earlier rainfall example, we can determine the probability of a single year's total being between, for example, 600 and 700 mm. We must first convert these quantities to their z-score equivalents. The mean in 643·3 mm and the standard deviation 101·5 mm, thus:

$$z_{600} = \frac{600 - 643 \cdot 3}{101 \cdot 5} = -0 \cdot 43$$

and

$$z_{700} = \frac{700 - 643 \cdot 3}{101 \cdot 5} = 0 \cdot 56$$

Because the range covers both sides of the mean ($z = 0.0$) we must read off the two probabilities and then add them. Thus $p(z < 0.56) = 0.2123$ and $p(z > -0.43) = 0.1664$ and the probability of an annual rainfall at this site of between 600 and 700 mm is $0.2123 + 0.1664 = 0.3787$ (or 37·87%).

5.10 Further applications of the normal distribution

Any normally distributed variable has, as we have seen, predetermined probabilities of events falling within any specified range. We have also seen that these ranges are most conveniently described in terms of z-values. The table in Appendix I indicate that there is, for example, a 0·3413 probability that an observation will lie between the mean and +1·0 standard deviations ($z = +1.0$), from which we calculate that there is 0·6826 (0.3413×2) probability that the observation will be within one standard deviation either side of the mean ($z = \pm 1.0$). On the same basis there is a 0·9545 probability that an observation lies within two standard deviations ($z = \pm 2.0$), and a 0·9973 probability that it lies within three standard deviations ($z = \pm 3.0$) – see Figure 5.11. Most importantly

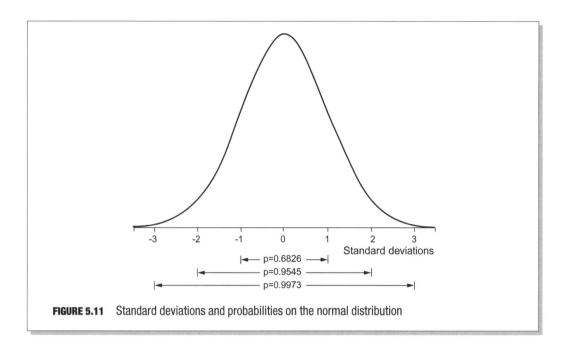

FIGURE 5.11 Standard deviations and probabilities on the normal distribution

these probabilities apply over all normally distributed variables be they hydrologic, climatic, economic etc., without exception.

It is, however, more convenient to express such probabilities of ranges about the mean in a different way. Thus, the 0·95 (or 95 per cent) probability limits are often quoted, giving the range within which an observation will lie with 0·95 (95 per cent) probability. This does not correspond exactly with the two standard deviation ranges, but it is not difficult to establish the z-value to which it relates, and the published tables can again be used. Appendix I present only half of the symmetrically distributed z-values. We must work 'backwards' therefore and find the z-value that corresponds to the probability 0·95/2, or 0·475. This is in fact 1·96. Expressed another way, there is a 0·95 (or 95 per cent) probability that an event will fall within 1·96 standard deviations either side of the mean. Correspondingly, events so extreme as to fall beyond those same limits, will do so with a probability of only $1 - 0.95 = 0.05$ (or 5 per cent). Figure 5.12 summarises this important concept that will reappear under many guises in the following chapters.

For any normally distributed variable these z-values of ±1·96 are readily converted back into 'raw' data. Consider the rainfall example again. From Equation 5.3 we know that, for the upper 0·95 probability limit (X), we have:

$$1.96 = \frac{X - 643.3}{101.5}$$

therefore, by transposition:

$$X = 643.3 + 1.96 \times 101.5 = 842.2 \text{ mm}$$

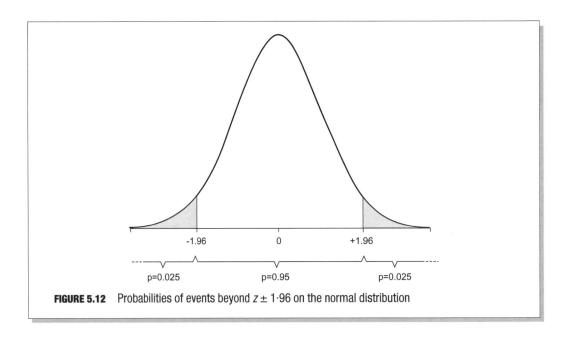

FIGURE 5.12 Probabilities of events beyond $z \pm 1.96$ on the normal distribution

and, by the same process, the lower limit is:

$$X = 643.3 - 1.96 \times 101.5 = 444.4 \text{ mm}$$

From which we conclude that there is a 0·95 probability that annual rainfall at this site will be between 444·4 and 842·2 mm, and only a 0·05 probability that it will exceed either of those two limits.

More generally, the required limits for any probability range can be expressed as:

$$X = \mu \pm z_c \sigma \tag{5.5}$$

Equation 5.5

μ = mean of variable X

z_c = critical z-value for selected limits

σ = standard deviation of variable X

X = required raw observation

Table 5.2 lists the most popularly used probability ranges for events around the mean of a normal distribution (0·90, 0·95, 0·99 and 0·999 – or respectively, 90, 95, 99 and 99·9 per cent limits). The table also gives the complementary probabilities for events outside of those ranges, and the more everyday expressions of the latter. For example, the 0·05

TABLE 5.2 Extreme probabilities and associated critical z-values

Probabilities of events about the mean		Critical z-value
Within the range	Beyond the range	
0·90	0·10 or 1 in 10	± 1·647
0·95	0·05 or 1 in 20	± 1·960
0·99	0·01 or 1 in 100	± 2·575
0·999	0·001 or 1 in 1000	± 3·290

(5 per cent) probability of an event falling outside of the 0·95 (95 per cent) limits can be expressed as 1 in 20 chance.

5.11 The binomial distribution

Thus far only the normal distribution has been examined, but other probability distributions exist to which geographical data conform. Two of the more important are the binomial and the Poisson distributions. Both apply to a range of natural events, but the manner of their application, and their data requirements are quite different from those of the normal case. Nevertheless, there are links between all three, and their importance lies in the possibility of using them to extend our ability to analyse geographical data. In common with the normal distribution, both the binomial and the Poisson distribution can be defined in rigorous mathematical terms. They can also be summarised through their respective measures of central tendency, dispersion and skewness.

The properties of the binomial distribution were first defined by James Bernoulli in the late seventeenth century, and it is sometimes referred to as the *Bernoulli distribution*. It describes the probability distribution of events for which there can be one of only two possible outcomes: for example, the flip of a coin, which can result in either a head or a tail. But, unlike the normal distribution, it has no single characteristic form, and its shape will vary according to the sequence length or number of trials and the probabilities of the two outcomes. Of the two possible outcomes, we must distinguish one (it doesn't matter which) as a 'success', and the other as a 'failure'. The binomial distribution is primarily concerned with the probabilities of the different numbers of successes over a number of trials. If, as in the case of coin flipping, the probabilities for a success and a failure are the same (0·5), the distribution for the two over any trial length must be identical. This equality exists only when p(success) = p(failure) = 0·5; as soon as one of them changes, so must the other and the two distributions will differ accordingly.

The binomial distribution is concerned, not with measurements along a continuum, but with countable events, e.g. the number of heads in coin flipping trials. As result it is discrete and not continuous in form. Fractional values are not possible, and the flips of a coin can, for example, yield only 0, 1, 2, 3 etc. successes. The equation that describes the binomial distribution produces not a curve, but a histogram, each bar of which represents the probability of 0, 1, 2 . . . N successes, where N is the trial length. If the probability of X successes in a sequence of trial length N is denoted by $p(X)$, then

$$p(X) = \binom{N}{X}(j^X)(1-j)^{N-X}$$

(5.6)

Equation 5.6

$\binom{N}{X}$ = the combinational expression

j = probability of a success

X = specified number of successes

N = sequence length (number of trials)

To understand how this definition operates, we must proceed by steps. Of the quantities indicated in Equation 5.6 only the *combinatorial expression* requires any elaboration. The binomial distribution uses factorials (see section 2.6) to determine the number of permutations of X items that can be abstracted from a total of N items. It is not the result of dividing N by X but is expressed as:

$$\binom{N}{X} = \frac{N!}{X!(N-X)!}$$

(5.7)

If we need to know how many different permutations there are of three successes in five trials, we would proceed as follows: on this case $X = 3$ and $N = 5$, so that

$$\binom{5}{3} = \frac{5!}{3!(5-3)!} = \frac{120}{6(2)} = 10$$

from which we get the result that there are ten possible permutations of three successes in five trials. In the context of coin flipping this means that there are ten ways in which the five trials could fall in such a way that three of them include a head.

These principles may now be included in a simple example. What is the probability of obtaining four heads ($p(4)$) from a sequence of six flips of a coin? By substitution in Equation 5.6 we get:

$$p(4) = \binom{6}{4}(0.5^4)(1-0.5)^{6-4}$$

$$= \frac{720}{24(2)}(0.5)^4(0.5)^2 = 15 \times 0.0625 \times 0.25$$

$$= 0.2344$$

Thus we find that there is a probability of 0·2344 that in any sequence of six flips of a coin, four will be heads. Because in this case the probability of a success (head) is the same as that of a failure (tail), the same result applies to four tails in six flips. This is, however, only part of the picture. To complete the distribution, we need also to know the probability of 0, 1, 2, 3, 5 and 6 successes in six trials. This requires that Equation 5.6 is applied to each of these situations in turn. The results are tabulated in Table 5.3 and depicted in Figure 5.13.

From Table 5.3 we see that the chances of getting six heads ($X = 0$) or six tails ($X = 6$) is very remote ($p = 0.0156$), and the most probable outcome is that we will get three heads ($p = 0.3125$). In addition notice there are 20 ways in which a trial of six can produce three successes, but only one in which it can produce six successes.

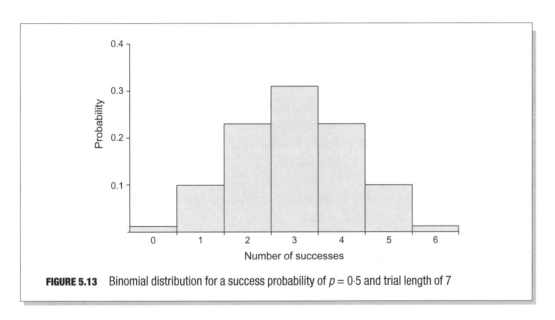

FIGURE 5.13   Binomial distribution for a success probability of $p = 0.5$ and trial length of 7

TABLE 5.3   Derivation of elements of the binomial distribution for $N = 6$ and p (success) $= 0.5$

X	$\binom{N}{X}$	j^X	$(1 - j)^{N-X}$	$p(X)$
0	1	1	0·0156	0·0156
1	6	0·5	0·0313	0·0939
2	15	0·25	0·0625	0·2344
3	20	0·125	0·125	0·3125
4	15	0·0625	0·25	0·2344
5	6	0·0313	0·5	0·0939
6	1	0·0156	1	0·0156

Note: 0! and anything raised to the power of 0 are all, by convention, 1·0.

5.12 Moments of the binomial distribution

Provided that the probability of a success remains 0·5, then the binomial distribution will be symmetrical regardless of the sequence length. Differences between the probabilities of a success (j) and a failure ($1 - j$) will manifest themselves as distributional skewness. An example is provided by the probability of a rainfall day in Durham (see section 5.3). If a dry, rainless day is defined as a success, then $j = 0.37$. The probability of a failure is 0·63. Let us consider a trial length of five days. In that period six outcomes are possible, either 0, 1, 2, 3, 4, or 5 dry days. Table 5.4 summarises the distribution of probabilities using Equation 5.6, and Figure 5.14 plots the results in graphical form showing the degree of skewness now introduced into the distribution.

Just as the normal distribution can be summarised by reference to its central tendency, dispersion and skewness, so too can the binomial. The meaning and interpretation of

TABLE 5.4 Derivation of probabilities on the binomial distribution for dry days in Durham, where p(success) $= 0.37$

X	$\binom{N}{X}$	j^X	$(1-j)^{N-X}$	$p(X)$
0	1	1	0·0992	0·0992
1	5	0·37	0·1575	0·2914
2	10	0·1369	0·2500	0·3423
3	10	0·0507	0·3969	0·2012
4	5	0·01874	0·63	0·0590
5	1	0·00693	1	0·00693

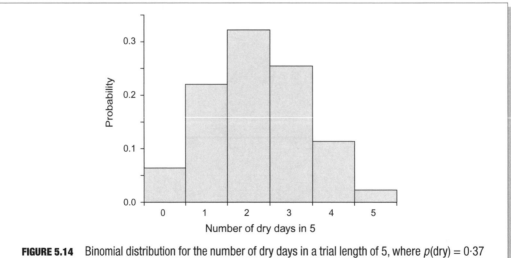

FIGURE 5.14 Binomial distribution for the number of dry days in a trial length of 5, where p(dry) $= 0.37$

these *moments* are much the same as in the normal case, but their derivation differs owing to the very different characters of the two distributions.

The mean of the binomial distribution is best described as the long-term average number of successes in repeated sequences of trial length N. This is analogous to the situation for the normal distribution in which the most probable events cluster about the mean. The binomial mean (μ) is found from:

$$\mu = Nj \tag{5.8}$$

where N is the sequence length and j the probability of a success. A sequence of six flips of a coin (in which $N = 6$ and $j = 0\cdot5$) has a mean, and most probable outcome, of three. The situation is not, however, always so straightforward. Using the Durham rain days example, we find that the mean for a six trial sequence with a rain day deemed as a success is:

$$\mu = 6 \times 0\cdot63 = 3\cdot78$$

How can we reconcile a fractional mean with a distribution of discrete events measured using whole numbers only? To do so, it must be recalled that the mean is the theoretical average number of rain days for all six-day sequences. As such it need not be a realisable integer quantity, but should reflect the underlying tendency to centrality.

The variance, standard deviation and skewness of a binomial distribution are obtained with correspondingly undemanding equations. Again, however, fractional outcomes are possible. Thus:

$$\text{variance} = \sigma^2 = Nj(1 - j) \tag{5.9}$$

$$\text{standard deviation} = \sigma = \sqrt{[Nj(1 - j)]} \tag{5.10}$$

$$\text{skewness} = \alpha_3 = \frac{j - (1 - j)}{Nj(1 - j)} \tag{5.11}$$

The characteristics implicit in these measures of the binomial distribution are similar to their normal distribution counterparts. It would not, for example, be expected that every N-trial sequence would provide exactly the same, or necessarily the most proba-ble, outcome. Some degree of variation from one sequence to another is all but certain. More specifically, any six flips of a coin will not necessarily yield three successes. On different occasions 2, 4, 1, 5, or even 0 or 6 successes might occur. The variance and standard deviation measure this variation about the mean tendency, while skewness measures the degree of distributional asymmetry.

5.13 Using MINITAB to estimate binomial distributions

Table 5.4 and Equation 5.6 suggest that calculating a binomial distribution can be a lengthy process. Fortunately MINITAB can undertake the task for us, needing the user only to specify the probability of a success and the trial length. For example, if we

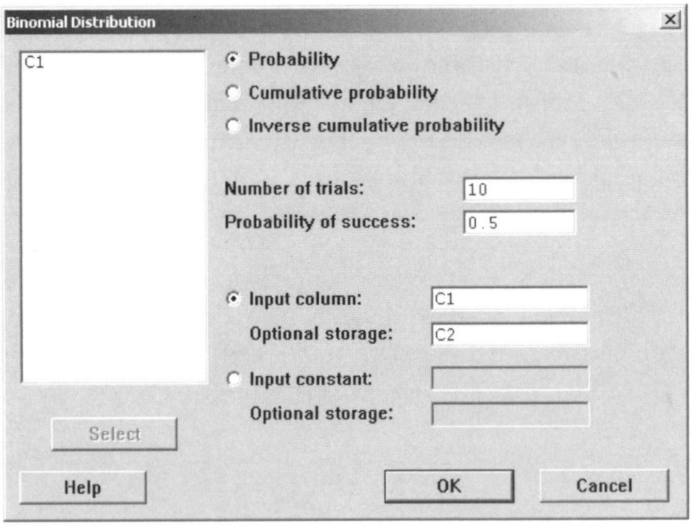

FIGURE 5.15 MINITAB **Binomial Distribution** dialogue box requesting the probability distribution with a success probability of $p = 0 \cdot 5$ over a trial length of 10

wanted the distribution for ten flips of a coin we would follow the command sequence **Calc > Probability Distributions > Binomial**. This would bring up the dialogue box in Figure 5.15 in which we need to indicate that the **Probability** option is required. We must supply also the **Number of trials** and the **Probability of success** in their respective spaces. The **Input column** (C1 in this case) is the column in which each required element of the distribution is entered. In this case we want the probabilities for 0, 1, 2. . .10 successes, and these numbers are entered in C1 beforehand. If we want the resulting probabilities to appear in the worksheet window we must specify a column number in the **Optional storage** space. In this example we have specified C2. If this is left blank, the results are displayed in the Session window (provided that the **Editor > enable commands** box has been checked). This option does not provide any of the moments of the distribution, and these would need to be calculated using Equations 5.9 to 5.11.

5.14 The binomial distribution and continuous scale data

The binomial distribution is applicable only to *dichotomous* variables; those with only two possible outcomes. But dichotomous variables may also be derived from the two-fold subdivision of variables measured on the continuous scale. This is particularly useful where such variables have a critical threshold value. Human behaviour, for example, may change abruptly at 65 with retirement and social geographers might regard age in this context as a dichotomous variable, with age being not a specific number but categorised as either above or below retirement age. But firmer links exist between the binomial and the normal distribution. Consider the case for increasing values of N: as the trial length becomes longer, the number of combinations of outcomes grows proportionally and the columnar histogram of the distribution begins to resemble that for a continuous distribution (see Figure 5.4 for an example of this effect). Provided that p(success) is close to 0·5 the histogram will tend towards a normal distribution curve with surprising rapidity. As a working rule, if both Nj and $N(1 - j)$ are greater than 5·0, then approximation to the normal distribution can be assumed. Hence, if $j = 0·5$ for all sequences of length greater than 10 the distribution can be regarded as approximately normal in character. For $j = 0·3$ the sequence must be 16 or longer for this assumption to be valid. Under these circumstances it is possible to express outcomes on the binomial distribution in terms of z-values, using the moments of the latter and equating them with those of the normal distribution. Thus, because a z-value is derived from:

$$\frac{\textit{difference between the individual and the mean}}{\textit{standard deviation}}$$

It follows that, using Equations 5.8 and 5.10:

$$z = \frac{X - \mu}{\sigma} = \frac{X - Nj}{\sqrt{[Nj(1 - j)]}} \tag{5.12}$$

Equation 5.12

μ and σ = normal mean and standard deviation

Nj = binomial mean

$\sqrt{[Nj(1 - j)]}$ = binomial standard deviation

X = individual observation/outcome

This useful convention allows us to express deviations from the binomial mean as a z-value with, importantly, all the attendant probabilistic properties outlined earlier in this chapter.

5.15 The Poisson distribution and its estimation using MINITAB

This distribution is named after its French discoverer, and it has proved to be a fruitful area for the study of geographical and spatially-organised data. It has, however, much in common with the binomial and the normal distribution, not least our ability to describe it mathematically and to estimate its moments. While the binomial distribution can be used when probabilities of a success and of a failure are not vastly dissimilar, problems arise when the two become enormously different. It is under these circumstances that the Poisson distribution might be considered. This is clearly the case when dealing with 'point' events in space or in time; when events can be counted and located, but non-events cannot. For example, a shop location is a point in geographical space, but it is not sensible to consider the number of non-shop points, of which there is an infinity. This eliminates any possibility of attaching empirical and binomial probabilities to the presence (success) of absence (failure) of a shop. Stream junctions, factory locations, crime locations and many other geographical phenomena fall into this same category.

As an example we can study the location of grocers' shops on Sunderland, England. The first task is the critical one of delimiting the study region, which in this case was the built-up area of the city. The issue is not, however, always resolved so easily, and it is important to recall that the final outcome can be influenced by the geographic limits set to the study area (see also Chapter 13). Figure 5.16 shows the present study area, here composed on 200 metre grid squares. From the original map, the number of grocers in each square was counted to give the average density of points per square. This quantity is denoted by λ (lambda) and is vital in the description of the Poisson distribution, for which Equation 5.13 is the formal expression. Each shop has now become an 'event' and this equation allows us to estimate the elements of the distribution, i.e. the probabilities ($p(X)$) that any square will contain 0, 1, 2, 3, 4 etc. events.

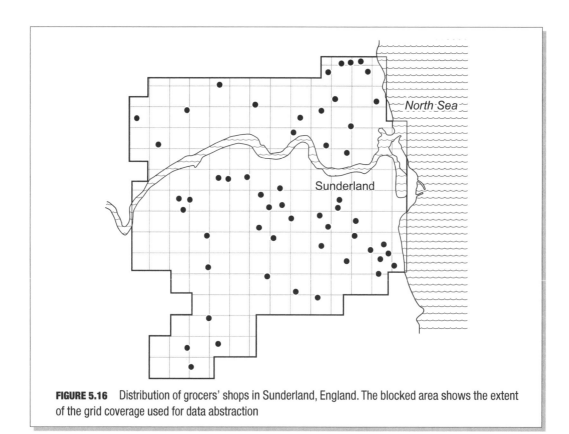

FIGURE 5.16   Distribution of grocers' shops in Sunderland, England. The blocked area shows the extent of the grid coverage used for data abstraction

$$p(X) = \frac{\lambda^X}{X!} e^{-x}$$ (5.13)

Equation 5.13

λ = average density of events

e = the constant 2·7183 . . .

$X!$ = factorial of number of events per unit

The number of events per grid square may vary between zero and a theoretical limit of infinity. In practice the distribution need be evaluated only within realistic limits determined by the researcher. In this case six would be such a limit, not because higher numbers are impossible, but because they would be extremely unlikely. As only whole numbers of events can be predicted, the distribution is discrete, and should be plotted as a histogram, and the probabilities of 0, 1, 2, 3, etc. events in any one square need to be estimated separately using Equation 5.13. These probabilities would then apply equally to all squares in the study area. The importance of the original definition of λ is now evident, as the derived probabilities depend largely upon its value, and this can change with the extent of the study area and the size of grid square used to define the original counting procedures – both of which are at the discretion of the researcher.

In the current example there are 55 shops scattered unevenly over 135 grid squares. Giving a value of $\lambda = 0.407$. With only this information we can calculate the probability distribution. For example, the probability of a square having two shops is found from:

$$p(2) = \frac{0.407^2}{2!} \times 2.7183^{-0.407}$$
$$= \frac{0.166}{2} \times 0.6656 = 0.0552$$

We need, however, the probabilities for the other values of X up to six. Fortunately we need not resort to individual calculation of these as MINITAB can again be used to provide the answers. The command route to use is **Calc > Probability Distributions > Poisson**. This will bring up the dialogue box in Figure 5.17. We need first of all to have entered into the worksheet the number of events per square for which we require a probability; in this case 0, 1, 2, 3, 4, 5 and 6 etc. These were entered in C1, and this column needs to be specified in the **Input column** space. If the output is to be placed in the worksheet, that column too must be specified in the **Optional storage** space. The default will list the results in the Session window. We need also to specify that the **Probability** is required by highlighting that option, and type in the value for the **Mean** of the observed data, then click on **OK**. The results are shown in Figure 5.18 and have been used to produce the distribution histogram in Figure 5.19.

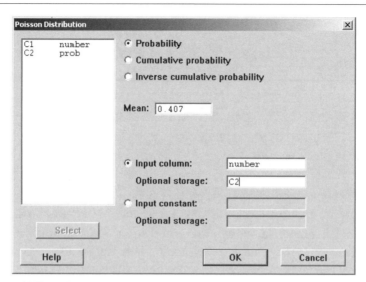

FIGURE 5.17 MINITAB **Poisson Distribution** dialogue box requesting the probability distribution for a mean of 0·407. The input column has been labelled as 'number' and the results have been sent to C2 ('prob') (see Figure 5.18)

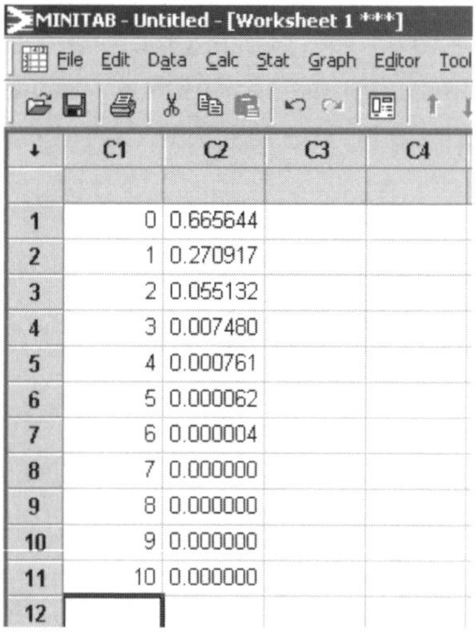

FIGURE 5.18 Section of the MINITAB worksheet window showing the results of the Poisson distribution task described in Figure 5.17

The very low probability than any one square will have six grocers' shops, with the yet smaller probabilities for seven or more demonstrates why the distribution need not be calculated over a wide range of X. However, only the full range of $X = 0$ to X of

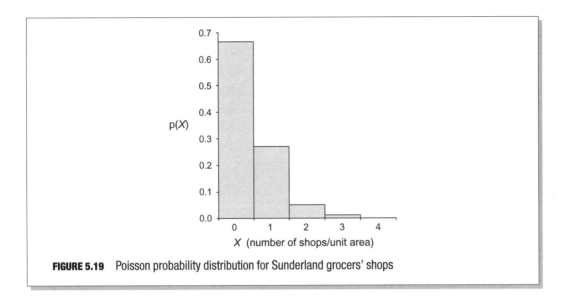

FIGURE 5.19 Poisson probability distribution for Sunderland grocers' shops

infinity embraces the whole of the theoretical distribution, therefore only $p(0) + p(1) + p(2)...p(\infty) = 1.0$. As the sum of the probabilities to $X = 6$ is 0·99928, we can deduce that the probability of seven or more shops in a square is only 0·00072.

5.16 Moments of the Poisson distribution

The Poisson distribution has its own measures of central tendency, dispersion and skewness. Their calculation is simple, and is based on the observed density of events (λ). One of the most characteristic qualities of the Poisson distribution is the equality of the variance and the mean, and the remaining moments are transformations of this quantity, and are defined as follows:

$$\text{Mean} = \mu = \lambda \tag{5.14}$$

$$\text{Variance} = \sigma^2 = \lambda \tag{5.15}$$

$$\text{Standard deviation} = \sigma = \sqrt{\lambda} \tag{5.16}$$

$$\text{Skewness} = \alpha_3 = \frac{1}{\sqrt{\lambda}} \tag{5.17}$$

The current example uses points per unit area, but other events may be studied as points in time, e.g. events per hour, per day or per year. The mean can, therefore represent events or points per unit area, or per unit time. The mean may also, as is the case with the binomial distribution, be a fractional quantity. The average density of Sunderland grocers' shops was, for example, 0·407 per 200 m square. Clearly no square can contain only 0·407 of a point, and it represents a tendency rather than an achievable quantity. On the other hand, different squares contain different numbers of events;

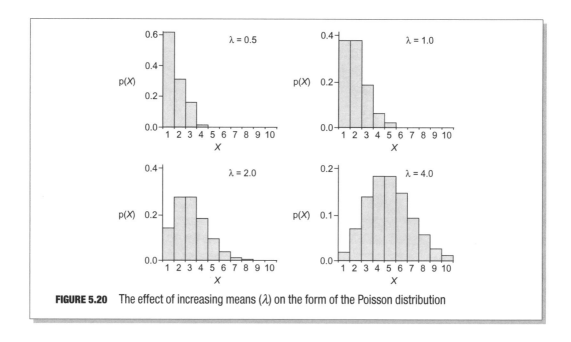

FIGURE 5.20 The effect of increasing means (λ) on the form of the Poisson distribution

some have zero shops, others one, others two etc. The data are, in this sense, scattered about the mean, and the variance measures the degree of this statistical spread of the data.

The inherent properties of the Poisson distribution dictate that measurable skewness is a common characteristic. Negative frequencies are, of course, impossible, while probabilities tend to tail away towards the higher values of X. These two features often combine to produce the degree of skewness evident in Figure 5.20. There are, nonetheless, links with the normal distribution. As the density of points (λ) increases, the Poisson distribution tends to greater symmetry and to the normal form. This transformation is illustrated in Figure 5.20, in which λ increases from 0·5 to 4·0.

These changes can be accommodated in a simple transformation of the equation for z:

$$z = \frac{X - \mu}{\sigma} = \frac{X - \lambda}{\sqrt{\lambda}} \tag{5.18}$$

by which individual observations can be expressed as standardised departures from the mean using Equations 5.14 and 5.15.

5.17 Probability and expectation

The three distributions introduced in this chapter are all definable in quantitative terms. They are, therefore, quite different from the arbitrary probability distributions inferred from nominal data introduced in section 5.5. But they share the capacity to predict the probability that any one event or individual will fall within a predetermined range or class. In the case of Sunderland shops for example, we can estimate probability of any one square having zero, one, two, etc. shops within it. These probabilities values can be easily converted into expected frequencies (under a perfect Poisson distribution) by multiplying $p(X)$ by the number of squares (135 in this case). The *expectation* (E) of an event is therefore found from:

$$E(X) = N \times p(X) \tag{5.19}$$

Thus the expected number of squares with zero grocers' shops is given by:

$$E(0) = 135 \times 0.6654 = 89.826$$

In this example, the observed number of squares with no shops differs little from the expected number (96 as opposed to 89.826).

But why might observed frequencies not follow the predicted patterns? To answer this question, we need to emphasise a point hitherto overlooked. The normal, binomial and Poisson distributions apply to variables consisting of independent events scattered, literally, randomly about their respective means. No external, non-random, forces are acting to predetermine that events fall into one or another range or class. Not only is this *independence* an important requirement in many forms of data analysis, but the randomness associated with it requires that variation about the expected pattern is to be anticipated. We might, for example, find that the locations of the residences of those contracting a particular disease are clustered together in a seemingly non-random manner. This suggests that independence of events has been lost, and that contagion is controlling the outbreaks. Similarly, some retail functions tend to cluster for purposes of economic advantage. The question is, at what point do the departures indicate that non-random, controlled and process-driven events are taking place? This distinction between random and non-random occurrences, associations and geographical behaviour generally, is at the very core of many of the chapters that follow.

Samples and populations

6.1 Introduction

THE READER SHOULD NOW be aware of the important distinctions between statistical populations and the samples drawn from them. Chapter 3 introduced the theory of sampling and how samples can be designed to accommodate the needs of the geographer. Chapter 5 has also drawn attention to the fact that samples can be used to interpret the properties of the original populations. Samples and sampling are an important part of geographical research, and much has been written about them, and now we need to consider some of these issues in more detail.

We must begin with conventions. A wide variety of symbols have been adopted for use in statistics, and a distinction is made between those used to describe the properties of a sample, and those for the population. When describing the parameters of a population it is common practice to use Greek symbols. Thus the mean is denoted by μ, and the standard deviation by σ. Latin symbols are preferred for sample parameters, where the mean is denoted by $\bar{X}$ and the standard deviation by s. Table 6.1 summarises the most commonly used symbols. It should be noted that the size of a finite population is often referred to by N but sample sizes by n, though this is the least consistently observed element of the algebraic conventions.

6.2 Estimates of reliability: standard errors

Samples do not necessarily reflect the precise characteristics of the populations from which they are drawn. Even the most well-designed sampling scheme cannot guarantee to do so, and any sample is capable of misrepresenting its population. Although our knowledge of a population may be vague and limited by the necessity of examining it only through the medium of a sample, we need not be equally uncertain about the reliability of the sample estimates of such parameters as the mean and the standard deviation, and methods exist with which to determine the limits of their accuracy; these will now be reviewed.

Our initial interest is with samples containing 60 or more observations per variable. These are described as *large samples*, although some statisticians take the limit as being

TABLE 6.1   Symbols used for describing the characteristics of samples and populations

Parameter	Population symbol	Sample symbol
Mean	μ	$\bar{X}$
Standard deviation	σ	s
Variance	σ^2	s^2
Skewness	α_3	α_3
Number of observations	N	n

less, even as few as 30. The virtue of large samples is that the so-called *central limit theorem* can be applied to them. The principle of this theorem is best explained as follows: if a very large number of samples of size n were drawn from a population, the distribution of the derived sample means – one coming from each sample – would be normal. It is these sample means that provide what is termed the *sampling distribution*. By far the most useful aspect of such sampling distributions is that they are normal irrespective of the distribution of the background population. Thus even a skewd population would yield a normally distributed set of sample means! In all cases the mean of the sampling distribution ($\mu_{\bar{x}}$) is the same as the mean of the background population μ, which is expressed algebraically as:

$$\mu = \mu_{\bar{X}} \tag{6.1}$$

For infinite populations, we could never know either of these quantities with absolute accuracy, but larger samples would bring us closer to the true figure.

These principles can be applied if we consider the example of daily discharge data for the River Clyde. These data are stored in the files CLYDE_Q.MTW and CLYDE_Q.SAV and were downloaded from the UK National River Flow Archive (see section 3.6). They were used to prepare the generalised distribution in Figure 6.1 in which a high degree of skewness can be seen. This same figure also shows the sampling distribution of means based on a sample size of 60 drawn randomly from the data file. It is important to note that this sampling distribution has the familiar normal or Gaussian shape and represents a graphical expression of the central limit theorem.

Under all but the most exceptional of circumstances we would take only one such sample from a population. We might, therefore, imagine ourselves to be in a poor position to have any knowledge of the distribution of the sample means. Fortunately this is not the case, and with just one sample and its attendant standard deviation the sampling distribution's properties can be calculated. In particular, the standard deviation of the sample means about the unknown population mean (a quantity more correctly termed the *standard error of the sample means*) can be estimated. Only two quantities are

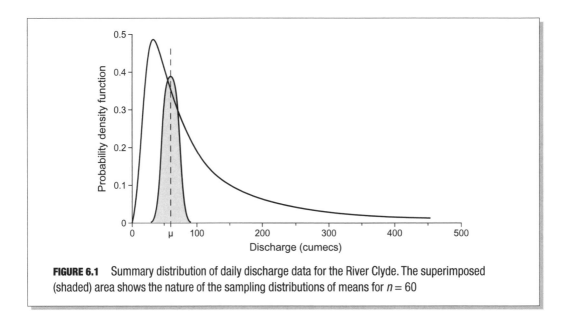

FIGURE 6.1 Summary distribution of daily discharge data for the River Clyde. The superimposed (shaded) area shows the nature of the sampling distributions of means for $n = 60$

required for this: the sample's standard deviation and size. These combine to provide the standard error of the sample mean ($\sigma_{\bar{X}}$) from:

$$\sigma_{\bar{X}} \frac{s}{\sqrt{n}}$$

(6.2)

Equation 6.2

$\sigma_{\bar{X}}$ = standard error of sample means

s = standard deviation of the sample

n = sample size

Clearly such standard errors will vary from case to case. Equally clearly, because $\sigma_{\bar{X}}$ decreases as n increases, larger samples provide means that are more likely to be close approximations to that of the population than will small samples. In this way Equation 6.2 gives substance to the intuitive notion that the bigger samples are more reliable. More importantly, however, such sampling distributions share all those probabilistic properties already described in Chapter 5 for the normal distribution.

6.3 Confidence limits and standard errors

It follows from what we know of the normal distribution, and the fact that it applies equally to sampling distributions of large samples, that we can determine the probability of the sample mean lying within any specified limits about the population mean; the latter of which lies at the centre of the sampling distribution. There is, however, a problem in that we do not know the population mean. We can, however, adjust our thinking on this matter by transposing the roles of population and sample means. Thus, while we start by stating that there is, for example, a 0·683 probability of the sample mean lying within one standard error (standard deviation) either side of the population mean, we can legitimately argue that there is also a 0·683 probability that the unknown population mean will be within one standard error of the known sample mean, a 0·954 probability that it will be within two standard errors (Figure 6.2), and a 0·997 probability that it will be within three standard errors, and so on through the range of probabilities on the normal distribution.

The discharge data for the River Clyde show how these principles might be applied. A random sample of 60 observations gave a mean of 57·83 cumecs (cubic metres per second), and a standard deviation of 44·82 cumecs. How reliable is this estimate of the unknown population mean? To answer this question we must first evaluate Equation 6.2 to find the standard error of the sampling distribution of means:

$$\sigma_{\bar{x}} = \frac{44\cdot82}{\sqrt{60}} = 5\cdot79 \text{ cumecs}$$

From which we conclude that there is 0·683 probability that the population mean lies within 5·79 cumecs either side of the sample mean of 57·83 cumecs. In numerical terms these limits equate to:

57·83 ± 5·79 = 63·62 and 52·04 cumecs

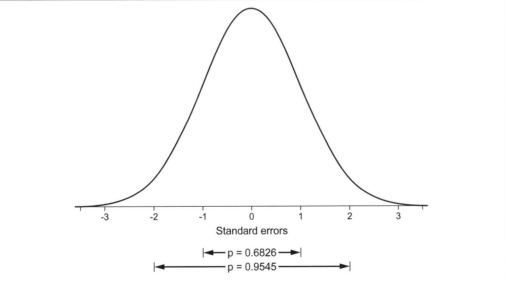

FIGURE 6.2 Normal distribution with probabilities of the population mean lying within one and two standard errors either side of the sample mean

Such values are known as *confidence limits* and they enclose a range of probabilities known as the *confidence interval*. Traditionally, these limits are described in percentage terms, and we might refer to the above as the 68·3 per cent limits. But the properties of the normal curve are well understood and, as noted in section 5.10 it is often easier to use more convenient limits such as the 95 or the 99 per cent, although we are free to choose any limits that we wish. The critical values that enclose the 95 and the 99 per cent confidence limits are ±1·96 and ±2·58 standard errors respectively. The general algebraic expression for these limits is given by:

$$\overline{X} \pm z_c \times \sigma_{\overline{X}}$$

(6.3)

Equation 6.3

$\overline{X}$ = sample mean of variable X

z_c = critical z-value for selected confidence level

$\sigma_{\overline{X}}$ = standard error of sample means

The 95 per cent limits would, on this basis, be given by:

$$57\cdot83 \pm 1\cdot96 \times 5\cdot79 = 69\cdot18 \text{ and } 46\cdot48 \text{ cumecs}$$

and the 99 per cent limits from:

$$57\cdot83 \pm 2\cdot58 \times 5\cdot79 = 72\cdot77 \text{ and } 42\cdot89 \text{ cumecs}$$

From these results we note that greater confidence that the population mean lies within a specified range can be gained only at the expense of widening the confidence intervals; the range for 95 per cent confidence is 22·7 cumecs, but rises to 29·88 cumecs if we want to be 99 per cent certain. In theory we can never be 100 per cent certain. The only means by which the confidence can be narrowed without prejudice to the reliability of the results is by increasing the sample size (n).

6.4 Samples and standard deviations

The mean is commonly the first point of departure in statistical descriptions of samples, but it is rarely the only one. The standard deviation is also important in providing a clear expression of the behaviour of a geographical variable. Fortunately, assessments can also be made of the degree of uncertainty attached to sample estimates of the population's standard deviation, and the central limit theorem applies equally in respect of this parameter. Hence, if all possible samples of size n were drawn from a population, the distribution of the sample standard deviations would again be normal irrespective of the distribution of the background population. The standard error of sample standard deviations is given by:

$$\sigma_s = \frac{s}{\sqrt{(2n)}} \qquad (6.4)$$

Equation 6.4

s = sample standard deviation

n = sample size

σ_s = standard error of the sample standard deviations

As the sampling distribution of standard deviations is also normal, the confidence limits may again be estimated. The strategy is identical to that used for sample means, and can be generalised as:

$$s \pm z_c \times \sigma_s \qquad (6.5)$$

in which z_c is the critical z-value for the chosen confidence level, e.g. 1·96 for the 95 per cent level etc.

As an example, we can continue to use the daily discharge data for the River Clyde. The random sample of 60 observations gave a standard deviation of 44·82 cumecs. But how reliable is this as an estimate of the population standard deviation? To answer this question we must first calculate the standard error of the sampling distribution using Equation 6.4, from which we get:

$$\sigma_s = \frac{44·82}{\sqrt{(2 \times 60)}} = 4·09 \text{ cumecs}$$

This standard error can now be used to estimate the 95 per cent confidence limits as follows:

$$44·82 \pm 1·96 \times 4·09 = 36·80 \text{ to } 52·84 \text{ cumecs}$$

Hence we can be 95 per cent certain that the population standard deviation lies between these two limits. Other limits can be estimated by substituting the appropriate quantities, e.g. 2·58 for the 99 per cent limits instead of 1·96.

6.5 Samples and non-parametric data

Thus far we have concerned ourselves only with samples measured on the interval and ratio scales. There are, however, many occasions when geographers will work with nominal data; here again, the central limit theorem can come to our assistance.

Proportions and non-parametric data generally are often derived from questionnaire surveys. The UK Government's 10 per cent Census report offers a good example, and we can review the employment statistics, which allocates each individual to an employment category. We might therefore have the number of unemployed people expressed as a proportion of the total population. But, given that the figure is an estimate based on only 10 per cent of the population, how reliable is it? If we took a very large number of 10 per cent samples each would differ and we could gain an idea of the sampling distribution of the proportion. We would, however, again find that they are normally distributed. More usefully, we can take just one 10 per cent sample, and use Equation 6.6 to estimate the standard error of the distribution of proportions (σ_p). If p is the sample proportion and n the sample size:

$$\sigma_p = \sqrt{\left[\frac{p(1-p)}{n}\right]} \tag{6.6}$$

This standard error again possesses all those properties now familiar from the normal distribution, and they can be used to determine the confidence limits. In a similar fashion to Equations 6.3 and 6.5, these limits can be written as:

$$p \pm z_c \times \sigma_p \tag{6.7}$$

As an example, the UK 10 per cent sample Census of 1981 (Office of Population Censuses and Surveys 1984) indicated that of the 136,771 people of working age in Wales, 15,596 were classified as unemployed, giving a proportion of 15,596/136,771 = 0·114. Our problem is to determine the reliability of such an estimate. The standard error of this proportion is given by:

$$\sigma_p = \sqrt{\left[\frac{0{\cdot}114 \times (1-0{\cdot}114)}{136771}\right]} = 0{\cdot}00086$$

from which we can estimate the 95 per cent confidence limits. Remembering that the critical values of z for these limits are ±1·96, we use Equation 6.7 as follows:

$$0{\cdot}114 \pm 1{\cdot}96 \times 0{\cdot}00086 = 0{\cdot}114 \pm 0{\cdot}0017$$

In other words, we can be 95 per cent certain that the true population proportion of unemployed people in Wales was between 0·1123 and 0·1157. These relatively narrow confidence limits are the usual result of the very large sample size.

6.6 Small samples

We have seen how large samples will reduce error margins in estimating population parameters. But caution is always required when sample size falls below the critical limit of 60. Such *small samples* can be examined using procedures that take account of their peculiarities. Large samples provide sampling distributions that are normal irrespective of the background population. In small samples, however, the sampling distributions are no longer perfectly normal and tend to follow the so-called Student's *t*-distribution, even

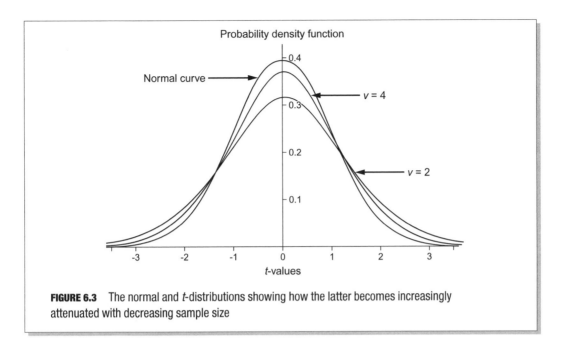

FIGURE 6.3 The normal and *t*-distributions showing how the latter becomes increasingly attenuated with decreasing sample size

when the background population is normal. Where background populations are known to be non-normal it is recommended that small samples should be avoided as even greater uncertainties attach to the sampling distributions.

The *t*-distribution is not unlike the normal. It is continuous and, in theory, extends from plus to minus infinity. Although also 'bell-shaped' its precise form varies with sample size, and in this important sense it differs from the normal distribution, which is independent of sample size. For very small sample sizes the curve is attenuated relative to the normal form but, as n increases it approximates ever more closely to the normal form. Coincidence is generally assumed for $n = 60$ (Figure 6.3).

The distribution was discovered in the 1930s by an industrial statistician, William Gosset, who published his findings under the pseudonym 'Student'. The variability of this distribution presents us with few difficulties because its form is mathematically definable and *t*-tables, not unlike the *z*-table (Appendix I) in their layout, have been prepared to indicate the probability of events falling within specified ranges of *t*. In the case of the normal distribution there is, as we know, a 0·95 probability of an event falling within the range $z = -1·96$ to $z = +1·96$. To find the corresponding limits on the *t*-distribution we use the tables in Appendix II. But attention must also be given to the sample size, which is expressed through the *degrees of freedom* – a quantity that is, in most cases, one less than the sample size $(n - 1)$. The critical *t*-values are arranged in rows according the degrees of freedom (denoted by v). The columns are arranged according to the various probabilities, usually the most commonly used such as 0·999, 0·99, 0·95 and 0·90. If our interest is with the 0·95 limits we focus on that column. The required critical value is found then by reference to the appropriate row number determined by the degrees of freedom. The distribution is perfectly symmetrical over all values of v, and the negative values need not, therefore, be listed. The table columns are, however, arranged according to the *tailedness* of the task in hand. The distinction between *one-tailed* and *two-tailed* situations is discussed fully in section 7.5, and need not be introduced in this context. For the moment we can justifiably assume that we are dealing only with two-tailed situations, in which confidence limits on both sides of the estimate are required.

Returning to the river discharge example, a second sample of only 20 observations provided a mean of 46·67 cumecs and a standard deviation 33·469. The standard error of the sampling distribution of this mean is again calculated using Equation 6.2, so that

$$\sigma_{\bar{x}} = \frac{33 \cdot 469}{\sqrt{20}} = 7 \cdot 48$$

We can now determine the limits within which the population mean lies with, say, 95 per cent confidence. The sample size is 20, which gives degrees of freedom (v) of 19. From Appendix II the critical t-values for 0·95 is found to be ±2·09. This converts to limits of:

$$46 \cdot 67 \pm 2 \cdot 09 \times 7 \cdot 48 = 31 \cdot 04 \text{ and } 62 \cdot 30 \text{ cumecs}$$

Expressed in everyday terms, there is a 0·95 probability that the population mean discharge lies between 31·04 and 62·30 cumecs. These limits are wider than in the sample of 60 observations, and reflect the small sample size and consequently larger standard error. Had we wished to be 99 per cent certain of our limits, they would have been yet wider. The corresponding critical value is 2·86, giving

$$46 \cdot 67 \pm 2 \cdot 86 \times 7 \cdot 48 = 25 \cdot 28 \text{ to } 68 \cdot 06 \text{ cumecs}$$

It is worth noting from Appendix II that the t-values (for 19 degrees of freedom) are greater than those on the normal distribution, which are 1·96 and 2·58, and that they become even larger as v decreases. This has the effect of widening the confidence interval with respect to those that prevail for the normal distribution. This is as we expect, because we are dealing with less reliable estimates from small samples. Thus, sample size is now of greater importance because it not only controls the standard error of the sampling distribution, but it also now contributes to the critical t-values.

A concluding comment of the question of degrees of freedom is required. The principles of this concept are demonstrated if we consider a sample of ten numbers that add, say, to 17·5. We can regard this quantity as fixed for our sample of data. But of the ten constituent elements nine can be regarded as being free to assume any value whatsoever. This requires, however, that these nine must predetermine the tenth in order for the total to remain at 17·5, and it has no freedom to vary. We say that one degree of freedom has been lost. There are many examples in the following chapters where reference is made not to sample size but to such degrees of freedom. Furthermore there are instances where more than one degree of freedom can be lost from a sample, but these will be considered as they arise. More generally, degrees of freedom are preferred to sample size as they reduce unwanted bias in sample estimates. Small sample variances, for example, are often under-estimates of the population figure. Variance (Equation 4.4) for a large sample is found by dividing the sum of squared deviations about the mean of the sample by the sample size, but it is preferable to divide not by n but by the degrees of freedom $(n - 1)$ in such cases. Thus we can write:

$$variance = \frac{sum\ of\ squares}{degrees\ of\ freedom}$$

or, more algebraically,

$$\hat{\sigma}^2 = \frac{\Sigma\left(X - \overline{X}\right)^2}{n - 1} \tag{6.8}$$

Equation 6.8

X = individual observation on variable X

$\overline{X}$ = sample mean of variable X

n = sample size

$\hat{\sigma}^2$ = 'best estimate' of population variance

Readers should note the use of the $\wedge$ symbol, which indicates that the parameter is a *best estimate*, and may not be absolutely correct. It is a symbol that we will come across later.

6.7 Samples and standard errors in MINITAB

The standard error of the mean for any sample of data can be easily derived in MINITAB using the command sequence **Stat > Basic Statistics > Display Descriptive Statistics**. This brings up the **Display Descriptive Statistics** window (Figure 6.4) in which the column containing the sample data is entered in the **Variables** space. The **Statistics** button is then clicked to bring up the **Descriptive Statistics** window. As many items as necessary can be 'checked', but in this case only those for the Mean, SE of mean, Standard deviation, Maximum, Minimum and Skewness have been requested. After clicking **OK** on both windows, the results appear in the Session screen, listing those parameters that were checked. The results using the complete River Clyde discharge data (CLYDE_Q.MTW) of 365 observations are shown in Figure 6.5, from which the standard error of the mean, based on this one year's sample of daily discharges is seen to be 1·90 cumecs (for the earlier sample of only 60 observations it was much larger at

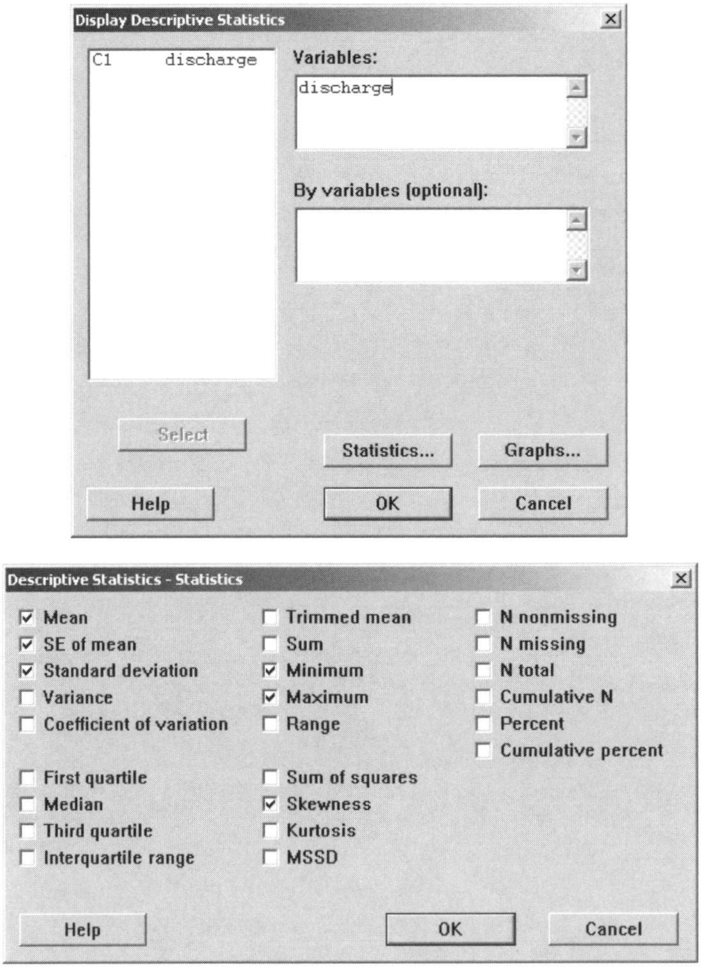

FIGURE 6.4 Dialogue box sequence in MINITAB for determining the standard error of estimate for the mean (and other measures) of a sample of data stored in column C1. Clicking on the **Statistics** button in the upper window provides the lower in which various statistics can be requested

Results for: Clyde_Q.MTW

Descriptive Statistics: discharge

Variable	Mean	SE Mean	StDev	Minimum	Maximum	Skewness
discharge	45.89	1.90	36.28	14.48	247.10	2.25

FIGURE 6.5 **Session** window in MINITAB showing results for the **Basic Statistics** command with statistics requested in Figure 6.4

5·79 cumecs). However, even this much larger sample of 365 observations remains just that – a sample – and such results can then be converted to the appropriate confidence limits by reference to the equations cited above.

6.8 Testing sample data for normality

Much has been written in the preceding pages about normality in the statistical distribution of data. Data that are normally distributed present the researcher with many opportunities for detailed investigation of the variable being measured, and some of the properties of the normal distribution have already been put to valuable use in this chapter. Moreover, data normality is a prerequisite for most statistical tests introduced later that use interval or ratio scale (parametric) data. Before considering such tests it is important therefore to review the means by which data sets can be assessed for their degree of normality.

We have already seen that simple histograms of the data (Figure 6.1) can identify cases of extreme skewness, and a numerical measure of this characteristic can be requested in MINITAB (Figures 6.4 and 6.5, see also section 4.9). Where skewness is present there is a tendency for the two principle measures of central tendency, the mean and the median, to differ. As we saw in section 4.6, a few extreme values at one or the other end of the range of observations will displace the mean in that same direction, but the effect on the median is less marked, with the result that in positively-skewed data the mean tends to be greater than the median, while in the negatively-skewed case it will be less (see Figure 4.11). There are, however, situations in which a more objective method is required to determine the normality or otherwise of a data set. One possibility is to convert the skewness of the data into an equivalent z-value. If the latter exceeds some predetermined critical value, usually ±1·96 or 2·58, we might conclude the data to be significantly skewed and, therefore, non-normal, but to do so we need to establish the *standard error of the skewness* ($\sigma_{\alpha3}$). We can use SPSS to provide the information required to undertake this simple task, and our need is only for the skewness value itself and its standard error. The skewness of perfectly normal data is 0·0, and to convert any individual estimate to its z-value we need to determine its standardised departure from the normal zero state using Equation 6.9.

$$z_{\alpha3} = \frac{\alpha_3 - 0.0}{\sigma_{\alpha3}}$$

(6.9)

Equation 6.9

$z_{\alpha3}$ = skewness z-value

α_3 = skewness

$\sigma_{\alpha3}$ = standard error of skewness

Continuing with the example of the discharge data from the River Clyde, in SPSS we follow the command sequence **Analyze > Descriptive Statistics > Descriptives**. This brings up the **Descriptives** window in Figure 6.6 in which we click on the **Options** button to bring up the second window, in which we check those parameters that we require. In this case we have chosen the Mean, Std. deviation, Variance, Skewness and S.E. mean (the standard error of skewness appears automatically with skewness). We conclude the process by clicking the **Continue** and **OK** buttons. The results are shown in Figure 6.7.

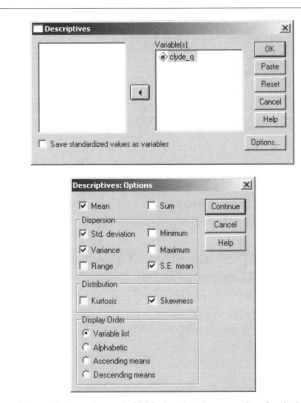

FIGURE 6.6 **Descriptives** dialogue boxes in SPSS showing the procedure for deriving the standard error of skewness of the River Clyde discharge data

Descriptive Statistics

	N	Mean		Std.	Variance	Skewness	
	Statistic	Statistic	Std. Error	Statistic	Statistic	Statistic	Std. Error
CLYDE_Q	365	46.8939	1.8991	36.28280	1316.442	2.245	.128
Valid N (listwise)	365						

FIGURE 6.7 **Descriptives** output from SPSS based on the options in Figure 6.6. The standard error of skewness does not need a specific instruction, and appears automatically when the skewness measure is requested

We can now use Equation 6.9 to provide the skewness z-value, which is

$$z_{\alpha3} = \frac{2 \cdot 245 - 0 \cdot 0}{0 \cdot 128} = 17 \cdot 54$$

Such extreme z-values fall far beyond even the 0·01 (1 per cent) limits of $z = \pm2·58$, from which we conclude that the data are significantly skewed.

There are, usefully, other means by which the normality of a data set can be established. A useful graphical approach is that of producing a *probability plot*. If the data are normally distributed, the probability plot of the sample's points will produce a straight line on the graph, otherwise a curved plot will result. MINITAB will perform this task using the command sequence **Stat > Basic Statistics > Normality test**. This will bring up the window in Figure 6.8 in which we enter the data column in the appropriate space, but of the three statistics options we need only 'check' the Anderson-Darling statistic. After clicking the **OK** button, the probability plot in Figure 6.9 will appear. Notice the highly curved nature of the plot, and the manner in which it departs from the straight, diagonal line that normally distributed data would follow – a sure indication of skewness. More usefully, the display also gives the Anderson-Darling (AD) statistic of 27·22, and its associated probability – in this case <0·005. This statistic is a measure of the overall departure of the points from the straight line (normal) case. The probability value attached to the AD statistic is, in effect, the probability that the population could be normally distributed but in the case of this sample an unrepresentative degree of skewness has been captured in the sampling process. The usual probability limits beyond which such departures would be regarded as showing significant and non-random skewness are usually either

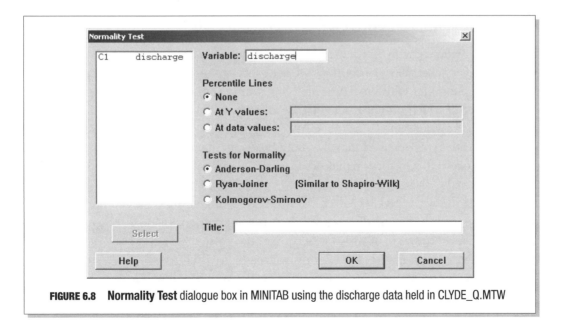

FIGURE 6.8 **Normality Test** dialogue box in MINITAB using the discharge data held in CLYDE_Q.MTW

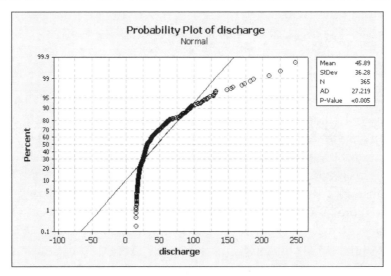

FIGURE 6.9 Probability plot from MINITAB for River Clyde daily discharge observations showing the deviation from the straight line that indicates marked non-normality in the data

0·05 or 0·01. In this example, such a small probability (less than 0·005) is much lower than either conventional limit, and it is highly unlikely therefore that the sample skewness arises from a non-representative sample of a normal population, and we must conclude therefore that the data are genuinely skewed.

6.9 Transforming non-normal data

Despite the frequency with which the normal distribution is encountered there remain many instances when the distributions of data sets are manifestly not normal, and we need to be familiar with procedures by which this problem may be overcome; the most common of which is some form of transformation of the data to render them more normal in their distribution.

We have already established that the daily discharge data for the River Clyde are significantly skewed. A histogram of the data was prepared in MINITAB (see section 4.4) to give Figure 6.10.

Fortunately many positively skewed distributions can have a measure of normality imposed on them by data transformations. Such transformations can assume a number of forms, the most common of which is to convert the positively skewed raw data into their respective logarithms. This can performed easily in MINITAB with the command sequence **Calc > Calculator**. This brings up the Calculator window (Figure 6.11). The pull down menu of transformations (**Functions**) allows the appropriate changes to be made. In this case we double click **Log 10**, this will be placed in the **Expression** window

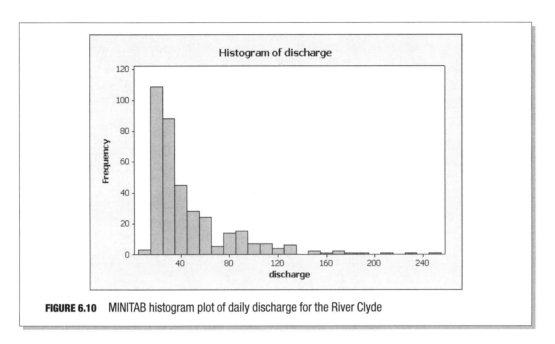

FIGURE 6.10 MINITAB histogram plot of daily discharge for the River Clyde

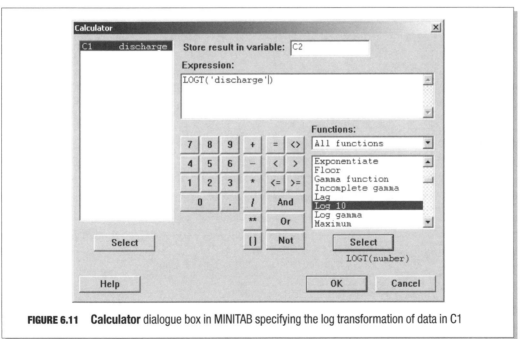

FIGURE 6.11 **Calculator** dialogue box in MINITAB specifying the log transformation of data in C1

(as LOGT note), we then add the variable name (which, in common with MINITAB practice, needs to be in single quotes) or the column of data (in the form Cx) to be transformed. Using the **Store result in variable** space we indicate the column into which the new data will go, and click on **OK**. The log-transformed variable is now stored in that column and can be treated as any other variable. The histogram of those logarithms yields a different picture (Figure 6.12) that, while not providing for perfect normality in the data, offers some improvement. Table 6.2 shows also that the mean and median of these logged data are closer, and the skewness values also indicate the change in the character of the distribution.

Such logarithmic transformations 'work' because smaller numbers less than 1·0, as they approach zero, become ever larger negative quantities when logged (see section 2.3), thereby 'spreading' the lower magnitude tail outwards. Conversely, the long tail at the upper end of the distribution is compressed in its logarithmic form as, for example, 10 becomes 1, 100 becomes 2 while 1,000 becomes only 3. Logarithmic transformations are often useful for ratio scale data where zero is the lower range cut-off point. Users need, however, to be alert to the fact that while negative values in ratio scale raw data are impossible, they will occur in the log-transformed data when raw values are less than 1·0. Users must remember also that some degrees and forms of skewness cannot be corrected using logarithms, and that logarithms cannot be formed from negative numbers.

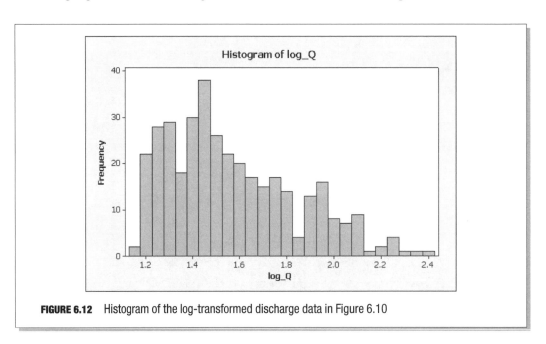

FIGURE 6.12   Histogram of the log-transformed discharge data in Figure 6.10

TABLE 6.2   Comparison of means and standard deviations for raw and for log-transformed data of daily discharge for the River Clyde at Daldowie

	n	Mean	Median	Skewness	Standard deviation
Raw data	365	45·89	31·08	2·25	36·28
Log-transformed data	365	1·566	1·493	0·70	0·273

Units: cubic metres per second (cumecs).

Negative skewness occurs much less commonly in geographical data. Where it does the problem may be resolved by taking the squares, even in extreme cases, the higher powers of the raw data. This would have the effect of extending or 'stretching' the upper end of the distribution. The MINITAB **Calc > Calculator** option used to log transform the data can be used to produce squares, but this is not available from the pull down menu in the window and the keypad must be used to enter the transformation 'by hand' in the **Expression** space in Figure 6.11. If the raw data are held in C1 the instruction to square these values would be **C1**2**. This would have to be typed in the space. To cube the data, the instruction would read **C1**3**. Such transformations can also be undertaken in SPSS. The procedure is broadly similar and requires the commands **Transform > Compute** to bring up the window in which the procedures can be defined (see details on the CD files SPSS4 and SPSS5 for examples).

Such processes of normalisation are now easy to undertake using statistical software, but a note of caution needs to be sounded: the temptation to juggle with data, sometimes without complete success, in an attempt to impose high degrees of normality should be resisted. Geographers should, rightly, be concerned to use appropriate data but, equally, they need to be able to interpret the results of the various statistical analyses that they may carry out. Where data have undergone elaborate forms of transformation, such interpretations may be difficult.

7

Testing hypotheses using parametric and non-parametric data

7.1 Introduction

ALL GEOGRAPHERS FORM GENERAL impressions in the course of their work that are the beginnings of ideas and hypotheses. We might observe that some forms of retail function cluster more readily than others, or that steep slopes are associated with particular types of rock. But whatever the nature of such speculations and hypotheses, we would always want to know if they are correct. We can do this by objectively assessing them against reality, often using statistical methods.

The first step in assessing the validity of any hypothesis is that of measurement, and here we might encounter the first of our problems. While some phenomena can be measured on one or more scales (nominal, ordinal, interval or ratio), others have no agreed form of quantification. Slopes may be measured by degrees of inclination (ratio scale), rock hardness on the Moh's scale (ordinal scale), and rock type can be allocated to a lithological type (nominal scale). But how might we measure some aspects of human behaviour such as attitudes to the environment or to crime? There are, unfortunately, some cases where it may not be possible to measure exactly the phenomena in question. Consequently we have to draw a distinction between theoretical and operational definitions or concepts. For example, a geomorphologist might be interested in hillside morphology, hence the theoretical concept is that of hillside shape. In operational terms, however, a more precise and pragmatic definition is required. What, exactly, is meant by hillside morphology? Is it overall slope, the slope of the steepest section, the variability of slope or its degree of curvature? Indeed, how are we to define and demarcate the length and section of hillside to be studied? Such problems of definition are so commonplace that we often overlook them.

The substitution of operational for theoretical concepts is similar to translating from one language to another, and care must be taken not to change inadvertently the sense of the concepts in question. Once armed with a reliable operational concept, however, we can proceed to the stage of testing its validity. The term 'testing' is here used in the specific context of *statistical tests*, the study of which will occupy the remainder of this chapter.

7.2 The null hypothesis

Statistical tests require numerical data collected within a rigorous sampling framework, and drawn from a specified population as explained in Chapter 4. During the process of gathering data the researcher must take every precaution to ensure that the samples are unbiased and representative of the populations from which they are drawn. No matter how sophisticated a statistical test might be, it cannot produce reliable results from unreliable data.

In this chapter attention will be confined to *univariate* methods – those that analyse the data for one variable only. There may, however, be more than one sample of such data and, for example, we might examine the differences between two (or more) samples of data measuring the same phenomenon. Later chapters will review how we might examine the behaviour of two or more variables, the so-called *bivariate* and *multivariate* cases. Though the different tests, of which there are many, vary in their precise procedures, they share the important function of testing the hypotheses formulated by the researcher. Remarkably, however, the hypotheses that they test are not general, geographical statements, but the so-called *null hypothesis* (designated by H_0). Indeed, the null hypothesis is indispensable in statistical methods, and is expressed as one of 'no difference'. For example, that there is 'no difference between the average slopes on two different lithological rock types', or that there is 'no difference between the degree of clustering of two different retail functions'. In other cases the observed data might be compared with some hypothetical state. For example, we might hypothesise that there is no difference between an observed scatter of retail functions and some specified, perhaps random or even regular spatial pattern or distribution. Such statements of no difference may well run counter to our expectations or understanding of the problem, but it is important that it is always presented, and tested, in this fashion. We must, therefore, see the null hypothesis as different from our general or working hypothesis on which it is based. The statistical test leads to a decision to accept or reject the null hypothesis. If it is rejected then we must accept the alternative hypothesis (H_1). This alternative hypothesis is the logical counterpoint to H_0, and states that there *is* a difference between the two data sets, and that those differences are too great to be attributed to random variation. Hence we may distinguish three forms of hypothesis:

- the research or working hypothesis – this is a general, perhaps lengthy, statement of the factors governing the behaviour of the variable in question
- the null hypothesis (H_0) of no difference
- the alternative hypothesis (H_1) of differences that are too great to be attributable to random variation.

The latter two are statistical statements only and the null hypothesis is the testable expression of the working hypothesis. Whether we believe it to be true or not is immaterial. Statistical tests allow us to reach decisions on H_0. They clarify our understanding of the problem, but the decision to accept or to reject the H_0 is not an end in itself, merely a step along the path of investigation. It is clear that all three forms of hypothesis are linked, but only after the acceptance, or rejection, of H_0 should we return to review the original working hypothesis. This might be a cherished collection of thoughts and speculations that fails to withstand the rigorous scrutiny of a statistical test. On the other hand seemingly weak arguments might be supported following closer analytical examination. The real challenge in research is to explain and account for the factors that underlie these, occasionally surprising, conclusions.

7.3 An introduction to hypothesis testing: the one-sample *t*-test for parametric data

We have already come very close to classical hypothesis testing when, in Chapter 6, we introduced the concept of the sampling distribution of means and proportions. In these cases we had a sample mean (or proportion) and we wanted to know if they could be regarded as representative of the populations from which they were drawn. The null hypothesis in such instances would be to the effect 'that there is no difference between the sample and population mean', or 'that there is no difference between the sample and population proportion'. In order to decide whether to accept or to reject the null hypothesis we need to produce a *test statistic*. Sometimes, as in this case, the test statistic will be a *z*-value (a *t*-value if the sample size is small – see section 6.6). But other tests will produce different forms of test statistic, some of which we will examine in later sections. The key point is that we know the statistical distribution of all these statistics, and can therefore assess the random probability of any one of them being equalled or exceeded in much the same way as we did with the normal distribution. This is usually accomplished by reference to published tables or, more helpfully, the random probability of the test statistic in question is listed in the SPSS or MINITAB output. As we have seen with *z*- and *t*-statistics, bigger values lie at the extreme ends of the distribution, and are less likely to occur by chance. Small values are more likely to have arisen by chance. In general, whenever a test statistic is found to have a low probability of having arisen by chance we tend to reject H_0 (and accept H_1), and when there is a high probability of it having arisen by chance we accept H_0 (and reject H_1). Much, therefore, depends on the limit beyond which the probability of the test statistic is regarded as so remote that H_0 is rejected. This critical probability has to be determined by the investigator before the test begins, and it is used to define the *rejection region of* H_0 on the probability distribution in question.

Let us suppose that we are undertaking a study of death rates in the UK. The overall mean death rate was found to be 11·59 per 1,000 population. But, when examining these raw data we see that the data for the ten Scottish regions (with a mean of 13·04 deaths per 1,000 population, and a sample standard deviation of 1·179) are different from those for the UK as a whole. This contrast is the basis of our working hypothesis, and from it might stem a number of public health and other issues. However, to test this hypothesis it needs to be recast as a null hypothesis – that there is *no difference* between the mean death rates in Scottish regions compared with the UK as a whole. The alternative hypothesis is that the death rates differ by a degree that cannot be accounted for by random variation within a *common population*. We are, in effect, testing for differences between a sample mean (death rates in the Scottish regions) and a known population (death rates for the whole of the UK).

The null hypothesis can be tested using an adaptation of the sampling distribution of means introduced in the previous chapter. Equation 7.1 will provide the test statistic. Notice that we are taking the difference between the population and sample mean $(\overline{X} - \mu)$ and dividing this difference by the standard error of the sample means (see also Equation 6.2). In this case, and because the sample size is small (10), the result is a test statistic that conforms to the *t*-distribution. Had the sample size been over 60 the result could have been regarded as a *z*-statistic on the normal distribution.

$$t = \frac{\overline{X} - \mu}{s / \sqrt{n}} \tag{7.1}$$

Equation 7.1

$\overline{X}$ = sample mean

μ = population mean

s = sample standard deviation

n = sample size

Before calculating t we must decide on the *significance level*, i.e. the probability beyond which we will conclude the test statistic to be so unlikely as not to be attributable to random variation and must, therefore, be the result of some influential factor(s) that contribute to death rates in Scotland. Conventionally the choice is between the probabilities of 0·05 (5 per cent) or 0·01 (1 per cent), though in theory we can select any significance level that we consider suitable. We will adopt the 0·05 significance level. As our test statistic follows the *t*-distribution, and we know the sample size, we can use Appendix II to estimate the *critical t-statistic* that delimits the rejection region. In this case the degrees of freedom are 10 – 1, or 9. The test is two tailed because we are not specifying in our working hypothesis that the sample mean is either greater or less than the population mean, merely that it is different. This gives critical *t*-statistics of ±2·26. Thus if test statistic t is greater than 2·26 *or* less than –2·26, it falls within the rejection

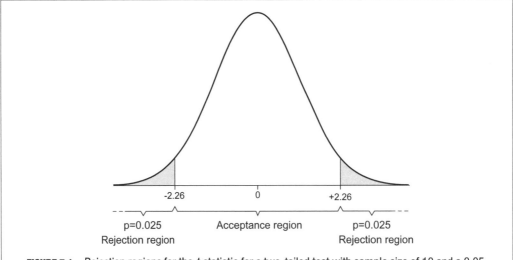

FIGURE 7.1 Rejection regions for the *t*-statistic for a two-tailed test with sample size of 10 and a 0·05 significance level

region for H_0. This idea is presented in graphical form in Figure 7.1. In this example we derive the test statistic from,

$$t = \frac{13 \cdot 04 - 11 \cdot 59}{1 \cdot 179 / \sqrt{10}} = \frac{1 \cdot 45}{0 \cdot 373} = 3 \cdot 887$$

Because the test statistic is more than the critical 2·26 in a two-tailed test, we must reject H_0, and conclude that there are genuine differences between Scottish regional death rates and those of the UK as a whole. Had it been less than −2·26 we would also have rejected H_0 as the rejection region is distributed equally over both extreme ends of the distribution.

Although the arithmetic is straightforward, such *one-sample t*-tests can be carried out using SPSS. The command sequence is **Analyze > Compare Means > One-Sample T Test**. The **One-Sample T Test** window then allows you to specify the column that contains the sample of data (we have used the data in the small file SCOTMORT.SAV). The test has a default population mean (**Test Value** in the window) of 0·0, but you can enter any value here; using the same data as above this value is 11·59 (Figure 7.2). The results are straightforward, and are shown in Figure 7.3. The table includes the *t*-statistic, the degrees of freedom (df) and the (two-tailed) probability of the former being equalled or exceeded by chance alone (Sig.). This form of output does not give the critical *t*-value that must be exceeded for H_0 to be rejected and Sig. is therefore of great importance in this and other tests in the output of which it is commonly listed. It allows us to dispense with tables of critical values and, if this probability value is equal to or less than the selected significance level, which in this example is 0·05, H_0 must be rejected. Because

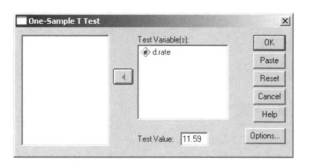

FIGURE 7.2 **One-Sample T Test** dialogue box in SPSS. Note the specification of 11.59 as the **Test Value** (population mean). The **Options** button allows confidence bands other than the default 95 per cent to be specified

One-Sample Test

			Test Value = 11.59			
	t	df	Sig. (2-tailed)	Mean Difference	95% Confidence Interval of the Difference	
					Lower	Upper
D.RATE	3.887	9	.004	1.4500	.6061	2.2939

FIGURE 7.3 Output display for **One-Sample T Test** in SPSS

here Sig. is 0·004, we must reject the null hypothesis. This information is followed by the difference between the sample and specified population means and, finally, we have the upper and lower limits of the 95 per cent confidence interval. These are the limits within which lies, with 95 per cent confidence, the difference between the population mean and the 'true' (and theoretically unknown) mean for Scottish regions. In this latter respect it must not be forgotten that the test is based on a sample, and another sample will yield a different mean death rate. This final item in the output listing informs us that in 95 per cent of such samples, the difference between sample (Scottish) and population (UK) means will be between 0·6061 and 2·2939.

In conclusion, we have identified in this section a strategy common to all statistical tests:

- the creation of a working hypothesis
- the statement of the null hypothesis
- the selection of the significance level
- the statistical test of the data and calculation of the test statistic
- the decision to accept or reject the null hypothesis.

7.4 Errors in statistical testing

The statistical test is a useful device, but it does not guarantee an accurate result, and there is always a possibility, however remote, of the null hypothesis being rejected when it is in fact correct. Conversely, there is also a chance of it being accepted when it is false. In this example we decided that H_0 would be rejected if the random probability of the test statistic being equalled or exceeded was 0·05 or less. Such remote random probabilities suggest that the differences result not from chance, but from some underlying causal factor or factors. This significance level, usually denoted by α (alpha), is, however, also the probability of incorrectly rejecting H_0, being simultaneously the probability that such test statistics might indeed be the result of chance alone with no intervening causal factors being at work. Expressed otherwise, it is the very nature of the statistical distribution in question that at the 0·05 (0·01) significance level there is a 5 per cent (1 per cent) chance of such extreme statistics being equalled or exceeded as a result of random, non-causal, variation.

To wrongly reject H_0 is to commit a *type I error*. The risk of making type I errors is reduced by decreasing the value of α to 0·01 or less. But in doing so we increase the chance of accepting H_0 when it is incorrect. This is known as a *type II error*. The probability of the latter is denoted by β (beta), and the *power* of a test is measured as shown in Equation 7.2:

$$\text{power} = 1 - \beta \tag{7.2}$$

In general terms, the risk of a type II error is reduced by raising α above 0·05, to 0·1 or more. The weakness of adhering rigidly to a policy of either 0·05 or 0·01 significance levels should now be clear. The appropriate significance level (α) should be determined by close attention to the practical consequences of committing type I or type II errors. For most teaching purposes this problem does not arise and either α of 0·05 or 0·01 is sufficient. But in the worlds of industry and commerce these errors may have grave financial costs or dangers, and steps must be taken to minimise the risk of incurring the more costly of the two types of errors.

7.5 One- and two-tailed tests

The one-sample *t*-test has thus far been described as a two-tailed test because no specification was made of the direction of departure of the sample from the population mean, i.e. not that one was greater or less than the other, merely that there was a difference. As a result the rejection region was divided evenly between the two extreme ends of the *t*-distribution (Figure 7.1).

There is often a need, however, to indicate in the alternative hypothesis not only that a difference exists, but that the difference is in a specified direction. In the death rate example it would have been sensible to stipulate not only that the sample mean was different from the population mean, but also that it was greater. In other words we would specify that death rates in the Scottish regions were higher than those for the UK as a whole. The test would, therefore, assume a *one-tailed* character. In such cases care must be taken to allocate the rejection region to the correct end of the distribution in question. Equation 7.1 shows that for the sample mean ($\bar{X}$) to be greater than the population mean (μ) the *t*-statistic would have to be positive, and the rejection region concentrated at the upper end of the distribution (Figure 7.4).

This reorganisation also changes the critical value that defines the rejection region as it is now concentrated at one end of the distribution. Table 7.1 lists the critical *z*-values on the normal distribution for both one- and two-tailed cases and for $\alpha = 0.05$ and 0.01. Those for the two-tailed case will be familiar from earlier sections, but notice how they differ from the one-tailed critical values. In marginal cases the decision to accept or to reject H_0 might depend therefore upon the tailedness of the test, which should therefore be decided with care.

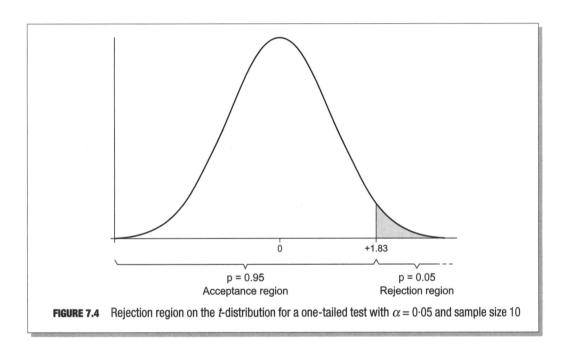

FIGURE 7.4 Rejection region on the *t*-distribution for a one-tailed test with $\alpha = 0.05$ and sample size 10

TABLE 7.1 Critical *z*-values for the 0·05 and 0·01 confidence limits using one- and two-tailed tests

Tailedness	Critical z-values	
	0·05 level	0·01 level
One-tailed test	−1·645 **or** +1·645	−2·33 **or** +2·33
Two-tailed test	−1·96 **and** +1·96	−2·58 **and** +2·58

Let us reconsider the earlier example in which we made no suggestion regarding the direction of difference between sample and population means. The null hypothesis (of no difference) remains unchanged, but our working hypothesis now states that death rates in Scotland are higher than those of the UK as a whole. The alternative hypothesis would express this view by stating not only that there was a difference between the means, but that the sample mean would be greater than the population mean by a degree that could not be accounted for by random variation within a common population. In this case any negative test statistic would automatically lead to H_0 being accepted as it would result from the population mean being greater than the sample mean. But what is the new critical limit for the one-tailed rejection region? To determine this we can again consult Appendix II. The significance level remains at 0·05, and the degrees of freedom are again 9, but the column for a one-tailed significance value of 0·05 must now be consulted. This gives a critical value of 1·83. Notice that because the 0·05 area of the rejection region is now at one end of the distribution, the defining critical value is less than for its two-tailed counterpart. Any t-statistic equal to or greater than +1·83 falls within the rejection region, and as the test statistic was +3·887 this is clearly the case.

A one-tailed one-sample t-test can be carried out in MINITAB using the command sequence **Stat > Basic Statistics > 1-sample t . . ..** In Figure 7.5 the data (from the file SCOTMORT.MTW) are held in **C1**, and the **Test mean** of 11·59 needs to be added as indicated. The **Options** box then allows the one-tailed option to be specified in the **Alternative** box where the choices are 'less than', 'not equal' and 'greater than'. The first and last options are those for the one-tailed test, and the 'not equal' indicates a two-tailed test. In the current example we need to specify 'greater than' the convention being (see Equation 7.1) that the population mean is subtracted from the sample mean and that our interest is with a sample mean that is greater than the population mean. The results are shown in Figure 7.6 in which we have:

- the sample size (N), mean (Mean) and standard deviation (StDev)

- the smallest value of the sample mean that would allow us to reject H_0 with 95 per cent confidence (95% Lower Bound); in effect the lower limit of the rejection region.

- the t-statistic (T) and associated random probability (P) for the population-sample mean difference.

It is clear that the observed mean exceeds the 'lower bound' and H_0 is rejected.

Had the sample size been greater than 60, the test statistic would have been normally distributed and the corresponding z-test could have been run with the instructions **Stat > Basic Statistics > 1-sample z . . ..** The procedures are all but identical to those of the t-test.

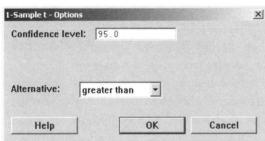

FIGURE 7.5   **One-sample t-test** and **Options** dialogue boxes in MINITAB. The latter specifies that the sample mean should exceed the population mean. The 95.0 confidence level equates to a 0.05 (5.0%) significance level.

FIGURE 7.6   MINITAB **Session window** output for one-tailed one-sample t-test with $\alpha = 0.05$ for the death rate data in file SCOTMORT.MTW and a population mean of 11·59

7.6 Choosing a statistical test

The one-sample t- (or z-) test is only a single example of the many that are at the disposal of the researcher. Others exist, not all of which can be introduced here. All differ from each other in their arithmetic procedures, but all are the same in testing a null hypothesis on the basis of a test statistic with a known distribution.

The choice of test is often dictated by the data to hand and a range of *parametric tests* exist that use data measured at the interval and ratio scales. These are more powerful than the *non-parametric tests* that use nominal or ordinal scale data, but require that the raw data are normally distributed (or can be transformed to normality). The non-parametric tests are less powerful, but enjoy the advantage of being *distribution free*, the data not having to meet the same stringent requirements as those for parametric procedures. In addition, the data might be structured in terms of the number of samples. Tests can, as above, be *one-sample* in character in which a single set of data is compared with a measured or hypothesised population. On the other hand two samples might be compared and we could, for example, compare death rates between southern and northern England. There are also k-sample cases in which three or more samples might need to be compared. In all such cases only one variable is used such as death rates, average income etc. but the division into the k samples will be made on the basis of another variable that might be region (differences between different places), income (differences between different socio-economic groups) etc.

Table 7.2 summarises the tests to be introduced in this chapter. We have chosen examples of statistical tests categorised by the number of samples (one, two and k) and by the data requirements (parametric and non-parametric). Some of the tests are known by the names of the mathematicians who originally developed them and studied the distribution of the respective test statistics. The list is by no means exhaustive, but will meet most needs. It should also be remembered that the distinctions between them may be blurred by the nature of the data. The normality requirement for parametric tests

TABLE 7.2 Examples of statistical tests categorised by number of samples (one, two and k) and by data requirements (parametric or non-parametric)

	Non-parametric		Parametric
Sample	**Nominal**	**Ordinal**	**Interval/ratio**
1	χ^2 *one-sample test (section 7.13)	Kolmogorov-Smirnov test (section 7.9)	One-sample t- or z-test (section 7.3)
2	χ^2 two-sample test (section 7.15)	Mann-Whitney test (section 7.10)	t-test for difference between two means (section 7.7)
k	χ^2 k-sample test (section 7.15)	Kruskal-Wallis test (section 7.11)	Analysis of variance (section 7.8)

* known as a chi-square test.

may limit their applicability but, fortunately, if serious doubts exist about a sample of interval or ratio scale data they can always be reduced to ordinal scale by ranking them, or even to nominal scale by putting the observations into groups or classes. The data are thereby rendered non-parametric, and the distribution-free qualities of the non-parametric tests can be used to advantage. In any case where parametric tests are to be used it is good practice to test for normality using the methods described in section 6.8. Having already introduced the one-sample parametric case, we will continue with the two- and k-sample counterparts.

7.7 Parametric tests: *t*-test of difference between two sample means

Whereas the one-sample t-test compares a single mean with some population figure, this form of t-test compares two sample means, with a view to determining if they could have been drawn from the same background population. Data need to be measured on the interval or ratio scales, and although the test is tolerant of modest degrees of skewness they should be checked beforehand. This test exists in two forms; the simpler from the mathematical point of view requires also that the variances of the two samples are not grossly dissimilar. If such differences are encountered a variant form can be used which is thought by some to be more reliable in both cases. This latter form treats the two variances as separate entities. If the differences between the variances is not great, the form of test can be used in which the variances are 'pooled' to a common quantity.

Nevertheless the two forms are identical in principle and derive their test statistics from the division of the difference between the sample means by the *standard error of the difference of sample means*. Thus:

$$t = \frac{difference\ between\ means}{standard\ error\ of\ the\ difference} = \frac{\overline{X} - \overline{Y}}{\sigma_{\bar{x}-\bar{y}}} \qquad (7.3)$$

Equation 7.3

$\overline{X}$ = mean of sample X

$\overline{Y}$ = mean of sample Y

$\sigma_{\bar{x}-\bar{y}}$ = standard error of the difference between the means

The reader will already be aware from Chapter 6 of the concept of the standard error in sampling distributions of means, standard deviations and proportions. In the same manner we can imagine the distribution of differences between pairs of sample means drawn from a common population. Replicate two-sample data abstractions will each provide a difference between the derived pairs of means. These differences are distributed as t for

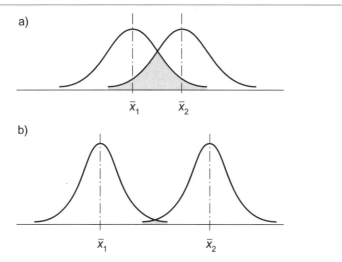

FIGURE 7.7 Generalised sample normal distributions showing (a) overlap and no significant difference the means, and (b) minimal overlap and significant difference between the means

small samples, and as z for large samples. Fortunately we can, again, determine the nature of the distribution from just one pair of samples. Where differences between means are large, but the variance is relatively small, large test statistics will result, and the H_0 of no difference between the sample means can usually be rejected. Figure 7.7 depicts the principles of the two-sample t-test in which the significance of the difference depends upon the spread and overlap of the two sample distributions.

As an example we will take annual runoff from two geologically and climatologically distinct areas: South East England and the Southern Uplands of Scotland (data source: *Hydrological Data UK 1990 Yearbook*, Institute of Hydrology 1991). The latter is an area of impermeable Palaeozoic sediments and high rainfall, the former of permeable Cainozoic sediments and lower rainfall. The original data are in files RUNOFF_T_TEST.MTW and RUNOFF_T_TEST.SAV on the CD. We suspect that geology and climate combine to create important contrasts in the hydrological setting as expressed in runoff figures (measured here in directly comparable units of millimetres depth of water), with significantly more runoff from the Scottish sites – but we need to test this supposition. The null hypothesis is one of no difference between the mean runoff from the two areas, i.e. that they are drawn from the same population of data, and any differences are attributable to chance alone. The alternative hypothesis states that the difference between the sample means is too great to be attributed to chance and reflects a real difference between the hydrological settings of the two regions. Because we are specifying also that the Scottish sample mean ($\bar{X}$) is greater than that for South East England ($\bar{Y}$), the test is one-tailed.

Having confirmed the normality of the two samples, the next step is to compare their variances. We can use either MINITAB or SPSS (see Chapter 4) to do this, and we find that the two differ: 66,752 for southern Scotland, and 9,164 for South East England. We must now test their equality by taking the ratio of the larger to the smaller estimate. This simple process yields what is termed an F-variance ratio statistic. Importantly, the distribution of F is known and the tables of critical values appear in Appendix VI. Because the distribution depends on the degrees of freedom of the two estimates a separate table is required for each significance level, and we have included those for the most commonly used: 0.01, 0.05 and 0.10. The degrees of freedom of the greater (v_1) and the lesser (v_2) variances are found from $n - 1$, where n is the respective sample size (they do not need to be the same). If the observed F-statistic (variance ratio) is greater than that tabled for given α and degrees of freedom then the H_0 of no difference between the two variances is rejected. In that sense, it is a test within a test, but follows the same strategy.

In this example:

$$F = 66,752/9,164 = 7.284$$

The two degrees of freedom are $v_1 = 20$ and $v_2 = 20$. Interpolating the 0.05 significance level table (Appendix VI) the critical F-statistic is found to be 2.16. We must, therefore, reject H_0 as the test F-statistic is greater than this critical value. In doing so we then have to adopt the form of t-test in which the two variances are treated separately and not 'pooled' to provide a single figure.

Our next task is to define the rejection region for H_0 of no difference between the two sample means. The sample sizes are small and the test statistic is distributed as t, and we have already decided that the test is one-tailed as the mean for the Scottish data should be greater than that for South East England. We will adopt the 0.05 significance level, leaving us with only the degrees of freedom (v) to be determined. This, however, is not straightforward in this case, and has to be calculated using Equation 7.4 that takes into account the two sample sizes and their respective variances.

$$v = \frac{\left[\left(s_x^2/n_x\right) + \left(s_y^2/n_y\right)\right]^2}{\left[\dfrac{\left(s_x^2/n_x\right)^2}{\left(n_x - 1\right)}\right] + \left[\dfrac{\left(s_y^2/n_y\right)^2}{\left(n_y - 1\right)}\right]} \tag{7.4}$$

This calculation gives 24.12 degrees of freedom, for which the one-tailed critical t-statistic (Appendix II) is $+1.71$. This defines the lower limit of the rejection region and any test statistic (t) that is greater than this places H_0 within it.

The formula for the test statistic, expressed generally in Equation 7.3, can now be written in full:

$$t = \frac{\overline{X} - \overline{Y}}{\sqrt{\left(\dfrac{s_x^2}{n_x - 1} + \dfrac{s_y^2}{n_y - 1}\right)}} \tag{7.5}$$

Equations 7.4 and 7.5

$\bar{X}$ = sample mean of variable X

$\bar{Y}$ = sample mean of variable Y

s_x^2 = sample variance of X

s_y^2 = sample variance of Y

n_x = sample size of variable X

n_y = sample size of variable Y

Neither Equation 7.4 nor 7.5 are as difficult to evaluate as they appear. We may already have the two variance estimates from the preliminary F-test of variance equality. Both these and the samples means can be derived from SPSS or MINITAB should they be needed. However, these systems will provide complete results for the t-test, and this would be the preferred option if large data sets are being used.

In SPSS the data should be entered in two columns, one of which contains the sample data, in this case of mean annual runoff in millimetres per year for both regions. The other column lists the group to which each observation belongs. This is coded using numbers. In this example (see below and Figure 7.8) code **1** identifies the southern Scottish data and **2** those for South East England. In this example the **Value labels** (see section 2.9) option has been used to attach a name to each of the code numbers, and 1 has been set to 'S Scotland' and 2 to 'SE England'. The sample data files also include the names of the drainage basins for each observation.

The required command sequence is **Analyze > Compare Means > Independent-Samples T Test**. This brings up the **Independent-Samples T Test** dialogue box

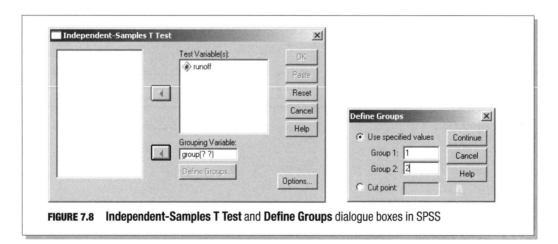

FIGURE 7.8   **Independent-Samples T Test** and **Define Groups** dialogue boxes in SPSS

Independent Samples Test

		Levene's Test for Equality of Variances		t-test for Equality of Means						
									95% Confidence Interval of the Difference	
		F	Sig.	t	df	Sig. (2-tailed)	Mean Difference	Std. Error Difference	Lower	Upper
RUNOFF	Equal variances assumed	11.604	.002	10.652	38	.000	656.2500	61.61031	31.52646	80.97354
	Equal variances not assumed			10.652	24.120	.000	656.2500	61.61031	29.12612	83.37388

FIGURE 7.9 Results table using the two-sample *t*-test in SPSS using data in file RUNOFF_T_TEST.SAV

(Figure 7.8), in which the data column identifier is entered in the **Test Variable(s)** space, and the column for the group allocations is entered in the **Grouping Variable** space. The **Define Groups** button must now be clicked to bring up the dialogue box in which the two group identifying codes are entered. We have used 1 and 2, but any two numbers could have been adopted. The **Continue** and the **OK** buttons then bring up the results screen (Figure 7.9). Notice that two sets of results are given, one of which is appropriate for the unequal sample variance case, the other when the variances are similar and can be pooled. The output table also provides the following results:

- the preliminary *F*-test, known here as 'Levene's Test for the Equality of Variances'. This is based on slightly different propositions than the simple variance ratio test outlined above, and is useful where data show tendencies to non-normality.
- the *t*-statistic with the degrees of freedom and its random probability (denoted by 'Sig. (2-tailed)'). This allows us to accept or to reject H_0 where the test is two-tailed. If 'Sig.' is less than α, H_0 is rejected.
- the difference between the two sample means and the standard error of that difference.
- the '95% Confidence Interval of the Difference' are the limits within which the difference of the two (unknown) population means will lie with that probability (other limits can be specified in **Options** window).

In the case of one-tailed tests the table requires reinterpretation, and the rejection region can only be determined by consulting the appropriate column of critical statistics in Appendix II (see above). It is important to note that SPSS always establishes the difference between the means on the basis of the group with the higher code number (2 (SE England) in this case) being subtracted from that with the lower code number, which in this case was 1 (S Scotland). Where two-tailed tests are used this point is of no importance, but this convention must be recalled whenever one-tailed tests are being used as the two groups need to be 'ordered' to take into account the wording of H_1.

In the present example the *F*-test of variance equality confirms that the two samples cannot be pooled (F = 11·604, Sig. = 0·002). The difference between the sample means is 656·25, with a standard error of 61·61. The former divided by the latter (see Equation 7.5) provides the test statistic t of 10·652, which is far greater than the critical tabled (one-tailed) value of 1·71, and H_0 is, consequently, rejected.

Had the sample variances not been significantly different, the upper row of results could have been consulted. The standard error of the difference between the means would, in this case, be given by:

$$\sigma_{\bar{x}-\bar{y}} = \sqrt{\left(\frac{n_x s_x^2 + n_y s_y^2}{n_x + n_y - 2}\right)\left(\frac{n_x + n_y}{n_x n_y}\right)} \qquad (7.6)$$

In which the terms are the same as in Equations 7.4 and 7.5. The degrees of freedom are more readily calculated, and now depend only upon each sample size minus 1:

$$v = (n_x - 1) + (n_y - 1) \qquad (7.7)$$

This gives the larger v of 38. While in this case the two approaches do not result in differences regarding H_0's rejection or acceptance, this is not always the case and care should be taken to use the appropriate procedure.

7.8 Parametric tests: one-way analysis of variance for k samples

The one-way analysis of variance derives its name from the fact that it discriminates between sample means on the basis of one variable only. It is similar to the two-sample t-test, but is used when three or more samples have been drawn.

The samples of data need to be normally distributed and, again, the sample variances should not be grossly dissimilar. The test, nevertheless, is tolerant on both counts. Analysis of variance assesses the probability of k samples having been drawn from the same population. It does so by decomposing the variance of the whole data set into the *within-groups* and the *between-groups* components. The former represents the variation of the individual observations about their respective sample means, the latter is the variation of the k sample means about the mean for whole data set. The ratio of these two variances yields an F-statistic, the random probability of which can be determined from the tables in Appendix VI in the manner outlined in the previous section. In this case the between-groups is always divided by the within-groups variances. The degrees of freedom remain v_1 for the greater of the two, and v_2 for the lesser. They depend, respectively, upon the total number of observations across all samples, and on the number of samples (k). If the test F-statistic exceeds the critical value at the selected significance level, the H_0 of no difference between sample means is rejected. Naturally for any k samples drawn from a common population some random variation about the sample means will exist, as will sample mean variation about the overall mean and some overlap between the sample distributions will occur. The F-test helps us to decide whether the observed differences between sample means and degrees of overlap could have arisen by chance – the samples having been drawn from such a common population – or

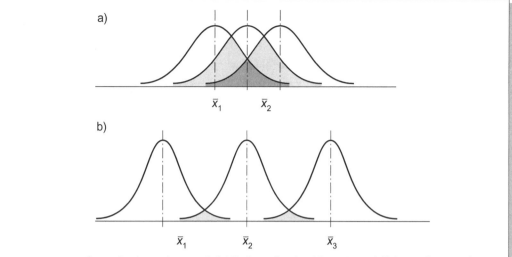

FIGURE 7.10   Generalised sample normal distributions showing (a) greater and (b) lesser degrees of inter-group overlap

if they are so great as to be explicable only by having been drawn from different populations. Figure 7.10 shows the idealised differences between these two conditions.

Interest focuses on the within- and between-groups variances. If the between-groups component far exceeds the within-groups, then high F-ratios will result. If the inter-group contrasts are less well marked, the F-statistic will be smaller with a greater degree of overlap between the groups. It is important to note that because three or more samples are used (in contrast to the t-test's two) there is no question of 'tailedness' in analysis of variance tests. In the following example we want to extend our study of regional runoff to include data for the North of England. Do these observations constitute yet another distinct hydro-climatological group that differs from the other two? Our null hypothesis would be one of no difference between the three sample means. While our alternative hypothesis would state that the differences between the means were greater than could be expected from random variation within a common population. We will use the 0·01 significance level for this exercise.

Having formulated the various hypotheses and defined the significance level, we can now consider the execution of the test. The within-groups variance (s_w^2) is found by dividing the sum of squared deviations of all observations about their respective sample means by the appropriate degrees of freedom, which is the total number of observations (n) minus the number of samples (k). Thus:

$$s_w{}^2 = \frac{\text{within-groups sum of squares}}{\text{within-groups degrees of freedom}} = \frac{\sum\limits_{j=1}^{k}\sum\limits_{i=1}^{j}\left(X_{ij} - \overline{X}_j\right)^2}{n-k} \tag{7.8}$$

where $\bar{X}_j$ are the k group means and X_{ij} are the individual observations within each group.

The between-groups variance (s_b^2) is based on the squared deviations of each sample mean $(\bar{X}_j)$ about the mean of the whole data set $(\bar{X}_t)$. These squares are, however, weighted to take account of the number of observations in each sample (n_j), which do not need to be the same:

$$s_b^2 = \frac{between\text{-}groups\ sum\ of\ squares}{between\text{-}groups\ degrees\ of\ freedom} = \frac{\sum_{j=1}^{k} n_j \left(\bar{X}_j - \bar{X}_t\right)^2}{k-1} \tag{7.9}$$

The between-groups degrees of freedom are given by the numbers of samples (k) less one. The required F-statistic is given by:

$$F = s_w^2 / s_b^2 \tag{7.10}$$

These calculations can be tedious to perform manually, but both MINITAB and SPSS can produce the results using simple instruction sequences. The data are set out in the same fashion for both systems, with the runoff data in one column and the group identifier in another (see section 7.7 and CD files RUNOFF_ANOVA.MTW and RUNOFF_ANOVA.SAV). The command sequence in SPSS is **Analyze > Compare Means > One-Way ANOVA**. This brings up the window in Figure 7.11 in which the variable under study (**runoff**) is entered in the **Dependent List**, and the column with the group identifiers (**group**) in the **Factor** space. In the current example the data have been entered in group-based blocks: all of group 1, then all of group 2 and so on. But this need not be the case and both SPSS and MINITAB will identify the data by group in whatever order they are entered. Neither is it vital that all groups have the same number of observations. The North of England sample, for example, has only 17 data

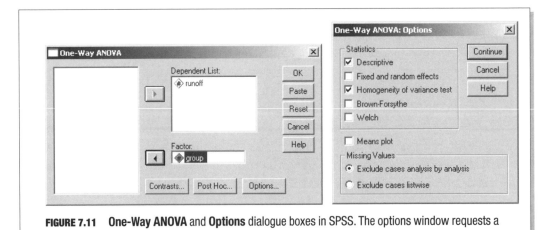

FIGURE 7.11 **One-Way ANOVA** and **Options** dialogue boxes in SPSS. The options window requests a summary of output statistics (Descriptives) and the execution of the Homogeneity of variance test

points as opposed to the 20 of the other two. It is, however, advisable not to allow great disparities between sample sizes as this can create problems for variance homogeneity.

SPSS offers several possibilities for more advanced forms of analysis, but we will keep matters simple at this stage. The **Options** button is useful (Figure 7.11), and we should tick the **Descriptive** and the **Homogeneity of variance test** boxes. The latter is similar to that used in the *t*-test. It is often overlooked, but is important if the results are to be reliable. Clicking the **Continue** and **OK** buttons will then bring up the results in the output window (Figure 7.12). The Descriptive table (not shown) provides basic, but often useful, information on the character of the samples (means, standard deviations and standard errors of means, for example). This is followed by the test for variance homogeneity. In this case Sig. (the random probability of *F*) is 0·004, and the variances are concluded not to be homogenous. The researcher can, and many do, continue with the test, but it is important to indicate in any written report that the results may not be wholly reliable. The three sample means are 879·6 mm for southern Scotland, 479·8 mm for northern England, and 223·4 mm for South East England. These differences are quite large, but are they significant?

The ANOVA (*analysis of va*riance) table in Figure 7.12 offers the answer. Here are to be found the between-groups and the within-groups sums of squares, degrees of freedom and mean square (the variance). From the latter two the *F*-statistic is derived and its random probability (Sig.) is given, avoiding the need to consult the tables of critical values. In this example the *F*-statistic is 60·458 and Sig. is less than 0·001 (reported as 0·000), allowing us to reject H_0 of no difference between the means, and to conclude more generally that the southern Scottish, northern England and South East England regions are significantly different in their hydrological characteristics.

We have thus examined methods by which one-, two- and *k*-sample parametric data can be examined for differences. Each test carries important assumptions regarding normality of the data, homogeneity of the sample variances and the nature of the data

Test of Homogeneity of Variances

RUNOFF

Levene Statistic	df1	df2	Sig.
6.043	2	52	.004

ANOVA

RUNOFF

	Sum of Squares	df	Mean Square	F	Sig.
Between Groups	4362762	2	2181381.089	60.458	.000
Within Groups	1876222	52	36081.188		
Total	6238984	54			

FIGURE 7.12   Output in SPSS for the analysis of variance test using data in file RUNOFF3.SAV

(interval or ratio scale measurements). But suppose that our data are measured on the ordinal or the nominal scales, or that problems of normality or homogeneity cannot be resolved. What can we do? Fortunately, there is a range of statistical tests that use non-parametric data. They are therefore *distribution free*. They are also useful where only small samples of data are available. If we recall that questionable parametric data can be re-expressed in ordinal form (by ranking) or in nominal form (by grouping frequencies of occurrence within classes), this large group of tests can be seen to be very useful, and we will now turn to consider some of them.

7.9 Non-parametric tests using one-sample ordinal data: the Kolmogorov-Smirnov test

The Kolmogorov-Smirnov test (hereafter the K-S test) is particularly suitable when comparing one sample with some theoretical or hypothesised set of data. It uses ordinal data and concentrates on cumulative frequencies in those ordered series. In the case of both the sample and the hypothetical data sets, the cumulative frequencies are measured as proportions in the range zero (0) to one (1). The two cumulative distributions are then compared between corresponding points. The largest such difference (irrespective of sign) provides the test statistic, here known as D. The distribution of D when subject only to random variation is known and summarised in Appendix IV. The null hypothesis, here of no difference between the two cumulative distributions, is rejected when D exceeds the tabled critical value for the chosen significance level and sample size.

A popular application of this test is in the comparison of observed data with those representing a known statistical distribution. Reverting to the example of the spatial scatter of grocers' shops (section 5.16) we can compare the observed scatter with that hypothesised to result from purely random processes. If the latter were the case, the statistical distribution of points would conform to a Poisson (by definition, random) distribution. The two data sets consist of the observed and expected frequencies of squares containing 0, 1, 2, 3 etc. shops. Table 7.3 lists the observed data set giving

TABLE 7.3 Observed and hypothesised frequencies of grocers' shops for the Kolmogorov-Smirnov test (the derived test statistic D is in bold)

Shops per square	Observed frequency	Expected frequency	Cumulative observed frequency ($S_n X$)	Cumulative expected frequency ($F_o X$)	Difference
0	96	89·826	0·7111	0·6654	**0·0457**
1	27	36·595	0·9111	0·9365	0·0254
2	9	7·4544	0·9777	0·9917	0·0140
3	2	1·0124	0·9926	0·9992	0·0066
4	1	0·1031	1·000	0·9999	0·0001

the number of occasions when grid squares contained 0, 1, 2, 3 and 4 shops (none were observed with 5 or more). The table also gives the corresponding numbers for shops had they been scattered at random across the area and, therefore, conforming to a Poisson distribution. These latter data were estimated by the method of expectations detailed in section 5·17. The two ordered lists of frequencies are then cumulated and converted into proportions of the total (135). The differences between the two sets of proportions are then calculated, the test statistic D being the largest of them. Thus:

$$D = \text{maximum } |S_n X - F_o X| \tag{7.11}$$

Where $S_n X$ refers to the observed distribution, and $F_o X$ to the hypothesised or expected distribution. Notice the use of 'modulus' brackets to indicate that the sign of the difference is ignored. This has the effect of ensuring that the test is two-tailed.

In the current example we will adopt the 0·05 significance level. The critical value for D is easily determined by reference to Appendix IV, which is arranged in columns according to α, or by simple calculation. The rows are arranged by sample size (n), which in this case is the number of grid squares used in deriving the shop frequency counts. It is not the number of shops. No correction need be made for degrees of freedom, but when n exceeds 35 the tabled data are replaced by critical values obtained by use of the equation appropriate to each significance level (see Appendix IV). Hence the critical D-statistic for $\alpha = 0·05$ is given by:

$$D = 1·36/\sqrt{n} \tag{7.12}$$

In this case:

$$D = 1·36/\sqrt{135} = 0·117$$

Those test statistics that are greater than the critical value will lie within the rejection region for H_0. In our example the test statistic is 0·0457 and, as this is less than the critical value, we accept H_0 and conclude the two distributions are not significantly different. This being the case we conclude, more generally, that the spatial scatter of shops conforms to the Poisson distribution and is random with no tendency to clustering, or to regularity in pattern.

The K-S test can be carried out using SPSS (but not MINITAB) with the command sequence **Analyze > Nonparametric Tests > One-Sample K-S Test**, which brings up the window shown in Figure 7.13. The column with the data (typed in or from a data file) is transferred to the **Test Variable List** space, and the appropriate **Test Distribution** box is ticked (in this case **Poisson**, but note that others are possible). We do not need any of the options for this task, and clicking the **OK** button will yield the results in Figure 7.14.

Data entry can be tedious because SPSS expects the shop (or other variable) count for each individual square (or other unit of division of space or time). The data for this

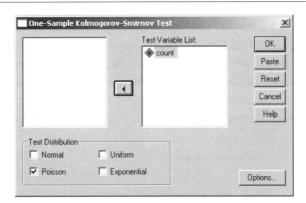

FIGURE 7.13 SPSS dialogue box the **One-Sample Kolmogorov-Smirnov Test**. This example requires a test to be conducted using a Poisson distribution

One-Sample Kolmogorov-Smirnov Test

		COUNT
N		135
Poisson Parameter[a,b]	Mean	.41
Most Extreme Differences	Absolute	.046
	Positive	.046
	Negative	-.025
Kolmogorov-Smirnov Z		.531
Asymp. Sig. (2-tailed)		.940

a. Test distribution is Poisson.

b. Calculated from data.

FIGURE 7.14 Output listing for the one-sample Kolmogorov-Smirnov test using SPSS. These results are based on the data in file SLAND_SHOPS.SAV

exercise are held in the file SLAND_SHOPS.SAV where the layout can be viewed. The column headed 'Count' has 96 cells with zero, 27 with one, nine with two etc. The results (Figure 7.14) are, allowing for rounding, the same as those for the manual method cited above. The count of shops (N) is given, followed by the mean of the Poisson distribution and the maximum positive and negative differences between the two cumulative distributions (the lesser of the two is not needed). The test statistic is not, however, given as D but as its equivalent z-score that is derived from:

$$z = \sqrt{n} \times D \tag{7.13}$$

The following two-tailed significance value is the random probability of z being equalled or exceeded. This would need to be less than α for us to reject H_0; clearly it is not ($z = 0.531$) and, as with the earlier method, we accept it and conclude that the distribution is not significantly non-random and is, therefore, Poisson in character.

7.10 Non-parametric tests using two-sample ordinal data: the Mann-Whitney test

The K-S test has a two-sample counterpart, but another procedure is often preferred, namely the Mann-Whitney test (henceforth the M-W test). One of the advantages of this test is its suitability for very small samples of as few as three observations, although it remains equally suitable for larger sets of ordinal scale data.

The following example analyses regional variations in agricultural activity in England. It is commonly thought that climate and terrain of northern and western England favour pastoral farming, whereas southern and eastern districts are more suited to arable farming. Using data for the proportions of land under pasture, eight English regions can be ranked from the least to the most pastoral. This is an example of how parametric data (the proportions of area devoted to pastoral farming) are reduced to ordinal scale data by the process of ranking. In doing so, the problem of determining the distribution of such a small data set disappears, and it becomes distribution free. For the purposes of the M-W test each of the regions must be allocated to one of the two samples, in this example either the north/west (NW) or the south/east (SE) sample. This process is summarised in Table 7.4. The observations are ranked from the smallest (1) to the largest (n). Where the original parametric data tie for a rank, the two are given the average of the two ranks that they would have occupied had they been different. For example if two observations are tied on the third rank, both are ranked at 3·5, but with no fourth ranked observation, the next being fifth. It is advisable not to have many ties.

The null hypothesis is one of no difference between the mean ranks of the two samples. The alternative hypothesis states that the differences are too great to be attributed to random sampling from a common population, and one sample ranks higher than the other. To test H_0 we must define the *object group*, which in this case consists of the south/east (SE) group of, supposedly, less pastoral regions. The object group is that which ranks higher (closer to 1) than the other. If the two samples' ranks are indeed different, we would expect to see some degree of segregation in the ranked listing. The test statistic (U), which measures the degree of segregation, has a distribution that is known, enabling us to define the rejection region for H_0.

TABLE 7.4 Data for the Mann-Whitney test of proportions of pastoral agriculture in north/west (NW) and south/east (SE) groups of regions in England (*Source*: Central Statistical Office 1981)

Region	East Anglia	East Midlands	Yorkshire	Home Counties	North	West Midlands	North West	South West
Proportion of pasturage	0·132	0·330	0·366	0·368	0·507	0·579	0·654	0·662
Rank	1	2	3	4	5	6	7	8
Sample group	SE	SE	NW	SE	NW	NW	NW	NW

For such a small sample the U-statistic is obtained by a simple counting procedure. Each member of the object group (and here we see the importance of its definition) is taken in turn, and the number of members of the other group that precede them are counted. The test statistic is the sum of these counts. In the present example we therefore consider each of the SE group in turn. The first two members of this group rank 1 and 2 in the list, and are therefore not preceded by any members of the other NW group, and both count as zero in their contributions to the test statistic. Only one of the object group, the Home Counties, is preceded by any member of the NW group, this being Yorkshire. Hence the U-statistic is compiled as follows:

$$U = 0 + 0 + 1 = 1$$

It is obvious that the greater the segregation of the ranks, the smaller will be U. This renders the M-W test unusual in requiring a small test statistic in order for H_0 to be rejected. The tables in section (a) of Appendix V provide, for small samples, the probabilities of different values of U. Another point may be noted; the distribution is unlike those we have used thus far in that it is discrete and only integer quantities are possible. If the tabled probability of U is less than the significance level chosen for the test, H_0 is rejected. This probability is found by reference to the table in Appendix V(a) that is specific for n_2 (the larger of the two groups – in this case 5), within which the value of n_1 (the size of the smaller group) and of U directs us to the appropriate cell of the matrix of probabilities. For $n_1 = 3$ and $U = 1$, the tabled probability is 0·036 that the test statistic will be equalled or exceeded. With a 0·05 significance level we would reject H_0 of no difference (although had we used $\alpha = 0·01$ we would have accepted it). When used in this manner the test has an inevitable one-tailed character as the object group determines the arithmetic of the test statistic's derivation. If we had been using the test in a two-tailed fashion, not being concerned which group preceded the other in the rankings, this tabled probability would be doubled to give 0·072. This has the important consequence of requiring us to accept H_0 of no difference.

Where sample size of one group exceeds eight, Equation 7.14 might be preferred to counting, where:

$$U = n_1 n_2 + \frac{n_1(n_1+1)}{2} - R_1 \tag{7.14}$$

Equation 7.14

n_1 = size of smaller group

n_2 = size of larger group

R_1 = sum of ranks of group 1

The tables of critical values for such larger samples are given in (d) to (f) of Appendix V. The layout is slightly different from those of (a) to (c), and the tables are ordered by significance level, with the critical values of U forming the body of the matrix, with n_1 and n_2 providing the column and row definitions. The key point with these tables is to recall that H_0 is rejected only if the test statistic is *less than* the critical value. A further note of caution to be sounded is that Equation 7.14 can yield two values for U if, for example, the larger or object group has been wrongly identified. The tables are prepared for the smaller of the two estimates of U. If the alternative (incorrect) value is denoted by U_1, it is possible to confirm which of the two quantities has been produced by using Equation 7.15:

$$U_1 = n_1 n_2 - U \tag{7.15}$$

Yet further changes take place when sample sizes exceed 20 as the distribution of U then approximates to the normal with a mean of μ_u and a standard deviation σ_u, so that:

$$\mu_u = \frac{n_1 n_2}{2} \tag{7.16}$$

and

$$\sigma_u = \sqrt{\left[\frac{n_1 n_2 (n_1 + n_2 + 1)}{12}\right]} \tag{7.17}$$

The test statistic is derived from Equation 7.15, but is then converted to its equivalent z-score. In general terms:

$$z = \frac{\textit{difference from the mean}}{\textit{standard deviation}}$$

hence in this case

$$z = \frac{U - \mu_u}{\sigma_u} \tag{7.18}$$

The critical z-values are then established by reference to the tables of normal probabilities (Appendix I), having decided α and the tailedness of the test (i.e. is one particular group specified to have higher (or lower) ranks than the other, thereby determining the sign of the z-statistic required for rejection of H_0, or is a difference between them – irrespective of sign – all that is needed for rejection?).

Both SPSS and MINITAB will carry out the M-W test. In this example we will use SPSS with the same data as above. The appropriate data files are held as PASTORAL.SAV and, for use with MINITAB, PASTORAL.MTW. The command sequence is **Analyze > Nonparametric Tests > Two Independent Samples**. Having done this the window in Figure 7.15 will appear in which we must specify the column with the data and, as with the t-test (section 7.7), this is followed by the **Define Groups** option in which we allocate numbers to identify the two groups (again, 1 and 2 will suffice). The data are stored with

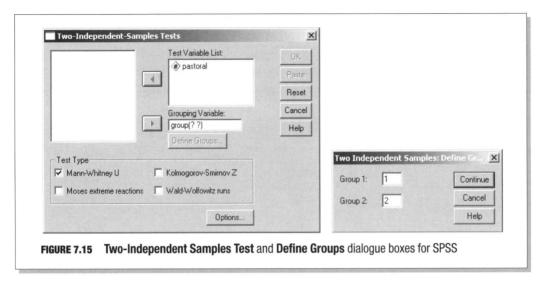

FIGURE 7.15 **Two-Independent Samples Test** and **Define Groups** dialogue boxes for SPSS

Ranks

	GROUP	N	Mean Rank	Sum of Ranks
PASTORAL	NW	5	5.80	29.00
	SE	3	2.33	7.00
	Total	8		

Test Statistics[b]

	PASTORAL
Mann-Whitney U	1.000
Wilcoxon W	7.000
Z	-1.938
Asymp. Sig. (2-tailed)	.053
Exact Sig. [2*(1-tailed Sig.)]	.071 [a]

a. Not corrected for ties.

b. Grouping Variable: GROUP

FIGURE 7.16 Results table for the Mann-Whitney test in SPSS using file PASTORAL.SAV

the observations in one column, and the group identifier in another. We must also check the box in **Test Type** for the Mann-Whitney U test. The default significance level is 0·05. Clicking the **Continue** and the **OK** buttons will then bring up the results (Figure 7.16). The 'Ranks' table lists the mean rank of the two groups and the sums of the ranks with each group. More useful is 'Test Statistics' table, which provides a number of results, the most important of which is the Mann-Whitney U statistic (1, as in the worked example above). It also gives two probabilities for U; the 'asymptotic' significance should be used only for large samples. Where sample size is small the 'exact significance' is preferred. To derive the one-tailed figure the exact significance figure should be divided by 2. This gives 0·036 and (allowing for rounding errors) agrees with the worked example above.

You will also have noticed an additional quantity, the Wilcoxon W statistic, together with its equivalent z-value, 7·0 and −1·938 respectively. This is similar to U and is the sum of ranks for the lower ranked group $(1 + 2 + 4 = 7$, see Table 7.4). As a z-value it can be treated as any other. In this case, for the one-tailed test, the critical tabled z-value for

$\alpha = 0.05$ is -1.645 (see Table 7.1). Thus H_0 is again rejected, although it would be accepted at the 0.01 level for which the critical z-value is -2.33.

The M-W test can be run on MINITAB, but the data need to be ordered in columns for which each contains the data for one of the groups (see file PASTORAL.MTW and CD file MINITAB3). The output focuses only on the W statistic, and U is not included.

7.11 Non-parametric tests using k-sample data: the Kruskal-Wallis test

The Kruskal-Wallis test is the non-parametric counterpart to the analysis of variance test. It allows us to compare three or more samples of the same variable. It requires only ordinal scale data, but is commonly used for small samples of parametric data where assumptions of normality cannot be confidently made.

The data are ranked by reference to the measurement variable over all observations, irrespective of their group membership. The smallest observation is ranked 1 and so on. Ties are again dealt with (as in the M-W test) by averaging over the two ranks that the two observations would have taken had they been different. The test then proceeds by summing the ranks within each of the k samples (groups). This gives a rank sum (R_j) for each group. These values are then included in Equation 7.19 to give the test statistic H.

$$H = \frac{12}{n_s(n_s - 1)} \sum_{j=1}^{k} \frac{R_j^2}{n_i} - 3(n_s + 1) \qquad (7.19)$$

Equation 7.19

n_i = number of observations in group j

n_s = total number of observations

R_j = sum of ranks for group j

For groups of sample sizes less than five, the tables of H-statistics in Appendix VII should be used in which the critical values are found by reference to the different combinations of group sizes at the selected significance level. The degrees of freedom are given by $k - 1$, where k is the number of groups under test.

In principle, greater inter-group differences in ranks provide larger H-statistics which, if greater than the critical value, cause H_0 of no difference between the mean ranks of the samples to be rejected. The test is most often used for small groups, but is equally applicable to larger samples if its distribution-free qualities are required. The following example is for a small sample, and uses the incidence of deserted villages (measured as desertions per 100 sq. km) in three English regions: the South East, the Midlands and the North. Only fragmentary historical data are available, but we suspect

TABLE 7.5 Density of deserted medieval villages in three English regions prepared for use in the Kruskal-Wallis test (*Source*: Beresford and Hurst 1971)

South East			Midlands			North		
County	**Density[1]**	**Rank**	**County**	**Density**	**Rank**	**County**	**Density**	**Rank**
Kent	1·85	3	Northamptonshire	1·46	2	Northumberland	3·16	9
Surrey	1·07	1	Nottinghamshire	3·03	7	W Yorkshire	2·08	5
Hampshire	3·00	6	Oxfordshire	3·94	10	E Yorkshire	6·20	12
			Leicestershire	3·10	8	N Yorkshire	2·06	4
			Warwickshire	5·08	11			
Rank sum		10			38			30

[1] deserted villages per 100 sq. km.

important inter-regional contrasts to be at work and this test might indicate if the observed differences are genuine, or the result only of random variation.

The data are first ranked across the whole data set irrespective of groups, only then are they set out in the groups as shown in Table 7.5.

The H_0 under test is of no difference between the mean ranks of the three samples. The alternative hypothesis is that such differences are greater than can be expected from random variation within a common population. All such k-sample tests are, by their nature, non-directional and the tailedness of the test is not a factor. We will use $\alpha = 0.05$, and the arithmetic procedures based on the data and sub-totals in Table 7.5 are given by:

$$H = \left[\frac{12}{12\,(12+1)} \right] \left[\frac{10^2}{3} + \frac{38^2}{5} + \frac{30^2}{4} \right] - 3\,(12+1) = 3.08 \qquad (7.20)$$

Appendix VII shows that the critical H value for $\alpha = 0.05$ and sample sizes 3, 4 and 5 is 5·631. Thus H_0 is accepted as the test statistic does not exceed this value, and our original hypothesis of inter-regional differences in village desertions is thrown into doubt.

The question of tied observations has already been mentioned in connection with the M-W and the K-S tests. Where there are ties in the K-W test they are dealt with in the same way, but should they occur in large numbers a correction (C) must be applied to H such that:

$$C = 1 - \frac{\left(T^3 - T \right)}{\left(n_s^3 - n_s \right)} \qquad (7.21)$$

Where T is the number of ties and n_s the total number of observations. In most cases C is close to 1·0, but becomes smaller as T increases and should always be used if more than 25 per cent of the observations are tied. Corrected H is found from $H \times C$.

MINITAB can be used to perform the Kruskal-Wallis test, and the required sequence of commands is: **Stat > Nonparametrics > Kruskal-Wallis . . ..** This brings up the window in Figure 7.17. The data file (DES_VILLAGES.MTW), usefully, has the same layout as that for SPSS, and lists the individual observations (deserted village rates: des-rate) in one column with the group allocation (by numbers: 1, 2 and 3 in this example) in another. The data column is entered in the **Response** box, and the group column in the **Factor** box. The results table is relatively straightforward (Figure 7.18), and provides, by groups, the sample size (N), median of the raw data, the average of the ranks, and the z-score or standardised measure of the departure of that particular group from the overall mean. Most importantly, the final line lists the test statistic H, the degrees of freedom (DF) and the random probability of H. The former is 3·09 but, with a probability of 0·214, the H_0 of no difference between the groups has to be accepted as it exceeds the significance level of 0·05.

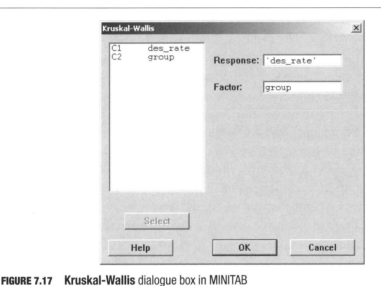

FIGURE 7.17   **Kruskal-Wallis** dialogue box in MINITAB

Kruskal-Wallis Test: des_rate versus group

```
Kruskal-Wallis Test on des_rate

                        Ave
group     N   Median   Rank        Z
1         3    1.850    3.3    -1.76
2         5    3.100    7.6     0.89
3         4    2.620    7.5     0.68
Overall  12             6.5

H = 3.09  DF = 2   P = 0.214

* NOTE * One or more small samples
```

FIGURE 7.18   Results table in MINITAB for the Kruskal-Wallis test from file DES_VILLAGES.MTW

The data file DES_VILLAGES.SAV can be used to run the K-W test in SPSS. The results are set out in much the same fashion, and can be obtained using the commands **Analyze > Nonparametric Tests > K Independent Samples**. The instructions follow the same sequence as used in the M-W test (see CD file SPSS10).

Where there are more than five observations in each group, the tables cannot be used and the test statistic can be assumed to be distributed as what is known as a χ^2 (chi-square) statistic with $k - 1$ degrees of freedom, where k is the number of samples. The χ^2 distribution will be dealt with in detail in the next three sections.

7.12 Non-parametric tests for nominal data: the χ^2 (chi-square) test

On many occasions geographers collect nominal (categorical) data that cannot be analysed by techniques such as the Mann-Whitney (U) test or Kruskal-Wallis (H) test, both of which require the data to be in at least ordinal categories. You will recall that the parametric t-test (section 7.7) uses the mean as its criterion for differentiating between samples, and that the U and H tests both use medians to assess statistical differences between samples. Accordingly, if we wish to examine nominal scale data we must employ a different range of methods employing data that do not utilise measures of central tendency such as the mean or median. When using nominal data we are restricted to comparing frequencies in the categories with which the data are described. One of the most useful methods for making such comparisons is the χ^2 (chi-square) test. Although not as powerful as either the parametric tests or some of the non-parametric procedures, it enjoys the advantage of simple data requirements and is widely used. It can be employed in the one-sample form when an observed set of frequencies is compared with some hypothesised series or population, in which case it is used as a *goodness-of-fit* test. It can also be used in the two- and k-sample cases where independent samples are compared.

7.13 The χ^2 one-sample test

Suppose that we wanted to assess whether the voting habits of Exeter residents differed significantly from those of the UK as a whole. Table 7.6 lists the numbers of votes cast in Exeter for the different parties (notice that the various minor parties have been grouped together as 'Other'). These constitute a set of 'observed' frequencies. The χ^2 test, is, however, based on the differences between such observed frequencies and those expected under a null hypothesis of no difference, which in this case is one of no difference between the local (Exeter) and UK national patterns of voting. We need, therefore, to estimate how many people would have voted in each category had the distribution exactly followed the national trend; these constitute the 'expected' frequencies under H_0. To determine these expected frequencies we need to know how the national vote was distributed. This distribution is given, as proportions, in Table 7.6 from which the required expected frequencies can be calculated. For example, the total number of votes cast in Exeter was 52,616. Nationally the proportion of the votes cast for the Labour party was 0·407. If the same had been true in Exeter there would have been 52,616 × 0·407, or 21,414·7 votes cast for Labour, although in this case the numbers can be rounded without prejudice to the final result. The same procedure can be applied to the other three categories to complete Table 7.6 that now provides all the data that are required in order to estimate the χ^2 test statistic, which is given by:

$$\chi^2 = \sum_{i=1}^{n} \left[\frac{(O_i - E_i)^2}{E_i} \right]$$

(7.22)

Equation 7.22

O_i = observed frequencies

E_i = expected frequencies under H_0 of no difference

From Table 7.6 we see that the χ^2 test statistic is the sum of the various $O - E$ components, and:

$$\chi^2 = 1,066·5 + 301·9 + 1,009·0 + 69·2 = 2,446·6$$

Clearly the magnitude of the test statistic increases as differences grow between the observed and expected frequencies. However, as with other statistical tests, the issue of whether a difference is statistically significant rests on the probability that the test statistic could have occurred due to chance. This is decided by the degrees of freedom and the choice of significance level. The distribution of the χ^2 is known, and the critical statistics that define the rejection region are presented in Appendix III. The degrees of

TABLE 7.6 Observed and expected frequencies for Exeter compared with UK national voting habits. Also shown are the proportions on which the expected values have been calculated and the sub-totals that provide the final test statistic of 2,446·6 (*Source*: BBC Vote 2001)

	Labour	Conservative	Liberal Democrat	Other	*Total*
Observed frequency (*O*)	26,194	14,435	6,512	5,475	*52,616*
UK proportion of the vote	0·407	0·317	0·183	0·093	*1·00*
Expected frequency (*E*)	21,415	16,679	9,629	4,893	*52,616*
$(O - E)^2/E$	1,066·5	3,01·9	1,009·0	69·2	***2,446·6***

freedom are given by $n - 1$ (where n refers to the number of categories in the table and *not* to the number of observations). In this case we will use the 0·01 significance level and the degrees of freedom are $4 - 1 = 3$, although the nature of the χ^2 test dictates that it can never be one tailed. From Appendix III we see that the critical χ^2 statistic that defines the rejection region for H_0 is 11·34. The test statistic, however, is 2,446 and is far greater than the critical value. As a result, we reject H_0 and conclude that the voting patterns in Exeter differ significantly from the overall UK national pattern and cannot be attributed to random variation.

One of the most useful elements of the χ^2 test is that understanding of the data can be gained through examining the table of observed and expected frequencies. In this case it is evident that the difference is caused by a relatively weak Conservative and Liberal Democrat vote (the observed frequencies are lower than the expected), while the Labour and the Others performed better than was anticipated.

Finally, it was noted that the date requirements for the χ^2 test were relatively limited, but they are not altogether absent, and the following should be noted:

- The χ^2 test can only be carried out using absolute frequencies and not percentages or proportions.

- The null hypothesis should not yield any expected frequencies of zero.

- No more than 20 per cent of the categories should have fewer than five as their expected frequency.

7.14 The χ^2 one-sample test in SPSS

The computation of the χ^2 test statistic need not be, as we have seen, a laborious process if the number of categories is small. Nevertheless SPSS can be usefully employed to speed up the procedures.

In SPSS, we need to enter two columns of data in the Data View window, one a string variable referring to party (Labour, Liberal, etc.) and another with the observed number of votes for each, as shown in Figure 7.19. We have, however, entered the total number of people voting for each party, and SPSS will count each cell as an individual observation if we do not indicate that they are each to be 'weighted' so that the quantities will be recognised as the total number of voters allocated to each category. This must be done before we embark on the χ^2 test. To weight the data in this fashion, we use the instruction **Data > Weight Cases**, upon which the dialogue box in Figure 7.20 will appear.

As the names of the political parties have been entered as a string variable, only the name of the variable that lists the number of votes (**votes** in this example) will appear as an option in the dialogue box. Select this variable and place it in the **Frequency Variable** box, clicking also the **Weight Cases by** button. Click **OK**. Each cell will now be treated as a category frequency count.

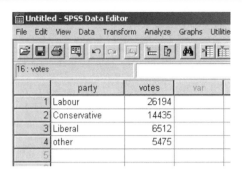

FIGURE 7.19 Data View window in SPSS showing the layout of the spreadsheet data layout for the χ^2 voting test

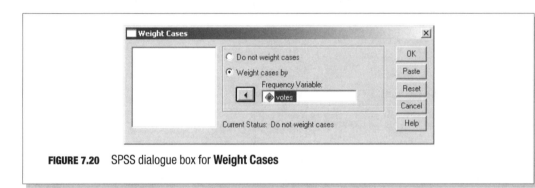

FIGURE 7.20 SPSS dialogue box for **Weight Cases**

To perform the χ^2 one-sample test itself, we use the instructions **Analyze > Nonparametrics > Chi-Square**. In the dialogue box (Figure 7.21), place the variable that contains the weighted numbers (**votes** in this example) in the **Test Variable List** space, and ensure that under the **Expected Values** heading, the button **Values** is ticked.

You will now be able to enter in sequence all of your expected values by typing the expected count into the box adjacent to the **Values** button and then clicking **Add** after each entry. You must do this in the *reverse* order that you have entered the data in the **Data View**, which in this case means putting the expected counts for Others first, then Liberal Democrat and so on backwards through the list. Note that if we had a null hypothesis that required no difference between any of the observed frequencies (in other words that all categories should have the same number of voters) we would have checked the **All categories equal** button, there would be no need to enter any expected frequencies and the system would apply the same number automatically in each cell of expected values. This figure would be derived from the total count over all categories divided by the number of categories, i.e. 52,616/4 = 13,154. In this case such a null hypothesis would make little sense, but there are many situations in which the null hypothesis would require equal numbers of expected frequencies in all categories.

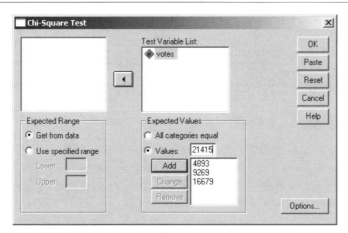

FIGURE 7.21   Dialogue window in SPSS for the χ^2 test. At this point the final expected frequency is about to be included by clicking the **Add** button

Numbers voting

	Observed N	Expected N	Residual
5475.0	5475	4893.0	582.0
6512.0	6512	9629.0	-3117.0
14435.0	14435	16679.0	-2244.0
26194.0	26194	21415.0	4779.0
Total	52616		

Test Statistics

	Numbers voting
Chi-Square[a]	2446.626
df	3
Asymp. Sig.	.000

a. 0 cells (.0%) have expected frequencies less than 5. The minimum expected cell frequency is 4893.0.

FIGURE 7.22   SPSS output for the one-sample χ^2 test of voting patterns

Returning to the example, the commands listed above generated the output in Figure 7.22. The observed and expected counts appear in the first output table, the 'Residual' referring to the differences between them. The χ^2 statistic of 2,446·6 is provided in the second output table. There are three degrees of freedom (df), while Asymp. Sig. of <0·000 indicates the probability that the test statistic could have arisen by chance. Because the latter is less than the selected significance level (0·01), we can reject the null hypothesis of no difference between national and Exeter voting habits without need to make recourse to the table of critical values.

7.15 The two- and *k*-sample χ^2 test

If we want to compare two or more samples measured on nominal scales we need to take a slightly different approach. Suppose for example that we had data relating to modes of travel to work and we wanted to know whether there was a statistically significant difference in the preferences of male and female commuters. In this example

TABLE 7.7 Observed (and expected) frequencies for a small travel to work survey showing the preferences for modes of travel by male and female respondents

	Bus	Car	Train	Total
Female	4 (6·2)	13 (8·6)	6 (8·1)	23
Male	9 (6·8)	5 (9·4)	11 (8·9)	25
Total	13	18	17	48

a survey provided 48 respondents whose modes of travel to work were either bus, train or car. The observed frequencies for two- and k-sample tests are set out with a row for each sample, and column for each of the categories into which the samples are divided. In this case we have only two samples (male and female) and three categories for each sample (the three modes of transport), but the same principle applies for larger numbers of samples and of categories. The null hypothesis is one of no difference between males and females in respect of mode of travel to work. From Table 7.7 we can see that there are differences, although the picture is not clear. But we can treat males as one sample and females as another and use the χ^2 k-sample test to determine the significance of the differences between them.

In such two- and k-sample cases the test statistic is again distributed as χ^2 but, compared with the one-sample case, differences exist in the manner in which the expected frequencies are estimated and in the derivation of the test statistic itself. The test requirements noted above still apply, and we also require an expected frequency under H_0 for each category, which are now provided by

$$E_{ij} = \frac{row\ total \times column\ total}{overall\ total} \tag{7.23}$$

For example, the expected number of males who travel to work by car (E_{12}) is found from the marginal totals in Table 7.7, so that

$$E_{12} = \frac{23 \times 18}{48} = 8 \cdot 6$$

The process is repeated for all cells (see Table 7.7), at the conclusion of which we can use Equation 7.24 to provide a test statistic based on observed and expected counts over all categories and samples. This requirement is indicated by the double summation sign, which indicates that all r rows and k columns have to be included in the calculations.

$$\chi^2 = \sum_{i=1}^{r} \sum_{j=1}^{k} \left[\frac{\left(O_{ij} - E_{ij}\right)^2}{E_{ij}} \right] \tag{7.24}$$

The degrees of freedom (v) are provided by the number of rows minus one, multiplied by the number of columns minus one, thus:

$$v = (r-1) \times (k-1) \tag{7.25}$$

The significance level is chosen (0·05 in this example) and the test statistic is compared with the tabled value in Appendix III. In this case we have two rows and three columns so that $v = 2$. The derived χ^2 statistics is based on the six $O - E$ differences, one for each cell, and has a value of 6·9. From Appendix III the critical value is found to be 5·99. As the test statistic exceeds this value, it falls within the rejection region and the null hypothesis of no difference between male and female modes of transport is rejected. Inspection of the matrix of observed and expected frequencies indicates that differences arise largely from the higher than expected number of males and fewer than expected number of females who travel to work by car.

Let us suppose, however, that we have the same two-sample gender-based set of data, but categorised only by private (car) and public (bus and train) means of transport. This represents a special case, and is termed a *2 × 2 contingency table* in which the frequencies are set out as in Table 7.8. The χ^2 test statistic must now be estimated from Equation 7.26, which includes a correction that takes into account some problems presented by such data matrices. The equation uses only the observed frequencies, keyed in by the alphabetic cell identifiers in Table 7.8.

$$\chi^2 = \frac{n \left(\left| AD - BC \right| - n/2 \right)^2}{(A+B)(C+D)(A+C)(B+D)} \tag{7.26}$$

In all such cases the degrees of freedom is 1. But this can be a very awkward equation to evaluate by hand when the frequencies are large, and the benefits of either SPSS and MINITAB, both of which use this equation for all 2×2 cases, are readily apparent. In this example the test statistic is 5·30. From Appendix III the critical value at the 0·05 level is found to be 3·84. As the test statistic exceeds this, H_0 is again rejected, and we confirm that there are significant gender preferences with respect to public and private means of transport. This test statistic includes the continuity correction, but had we used Equation 7.25 (which does not) and estimated expected values from Equation 7.23 we would have derived an over-estimated test statistic of 6·89. In this case the contrast has no influence on our decision to accept or reject the null hypothesis, but this will not always be the case.

Although this method does not rely on estimated frequencies, Table 7.8 indicates that the significance of this test is a consequence of a female preference for private transport, but a male preference for public means for travel to work. Both of these cells have relatively high frequencies, and the other two (males using private transport and females using public transport) record far fewer responses.

7.16 The χ^2 two- and *k*-sample test in SPSS

The computation of the two-sample (and any *k*-sample) case in SPSS requires a number of steps. Using our travel to work data, we have two samples based on gender, each

TABLE 7.8 Observed frequencies for gender preferences for journey to work categorised by public or private means

	Private	Public
Female	13 (*A*)[1]	10 (*B*)
Male	5 (*C*)	20 (*D*)

[1] The cell alphabetic indicators are those used in Equation 7·26.

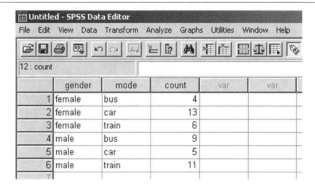

FIGURE 7.23 Example of data layout for the two-sample chi-square test in SPSS. Note how the sample categories are specified by the combinations of gender and mode of transport

with categories for mode of transport (bus, car or train). Both 'gender' and 'mode' are entered in SPSS as string variables that define the categories, but do not give quantities. We must also provide SPSS with the counts under each of the six possible categories. These are entered in the Data View window and set up as in Figure 7.23. Where there are more than two samples or more than three categories, the data input sequence is extended by introducing the additional sample-category combinations.

Once again, as with the one-sample case, we need first of all to use the **Weight Cases** option for the variable that contains the frequencies. This having been done we next need to *cross-tabulate* the data and then specify that we wish to perform a Chi-Square analysis. This is done by following the command sequence **Analyze > Descriptive Statistics > Crosstabs** to obtain the dialogue box in Figure 7.24 in which we transfer the row and column categories into their respective spaces.

This last instruction sets up the matrix of raw data, but we must click on both the **Statistics** and **Cells** buttons to complete the set-up. The **Statistics** box provides the options in Figure 7.25 and allows us to specify a **Chi-square** test. The other options relate to more complex analyses of nominal and ordinal data that need not concern us here. The **Cells** button brings up the other dialogue box in Figure 7.25 in which we request the output to include both the observed and the expected frequencies. These

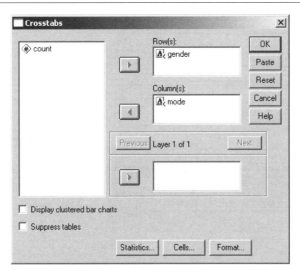

FIGURE 7.24 **Crosstabs** dialogue window in SPSS with the two sample designators having been transferred into the **Row(s)** and **Column(s)** boxes

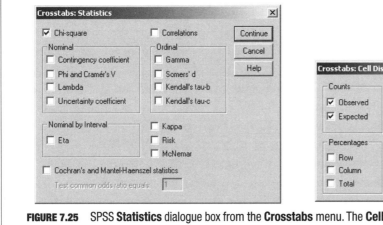

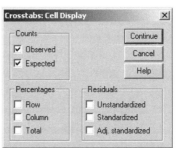

FIGURE 7.25 SPSS **Statistics** dialogue box from the **Crosstabs** menu. The **Cell Display** box is also shown, indicating a request for observed and expected frequencies to be listed in the output

are useful for the later analysis of the results. Although not requested here, you can obtain percentages for the row and column totals, and there is also the option of examining the residuals (the difference between the observed and expected values) in raw form and also in a standardised format. Click **Continue** on **Cells** and **Statistics** boxes, which returns you to the **Crosstabs** dialogue box. Click on **OK** and the output tables in Figure 7.26 are then generated.

GENDER * MODE Crosstabulation

			MODE			
			bus	car	train	Total
GENDER	female	Count	4	13	6	23
		Expected Count	6.2	8.6	8.1	23.0
	male	Count	9	5	11	25
		Expected Count	6.8	9.4	8.9	25.0
Total		Count	13	18	17	48
		Expected Count	13.0	18.0	17.0	48.0

Chi-Square Tests

	Value	df	Asymp. Sig. (2-sided)
Pearson Chi-Square	6.878ª	2	.032
Likelihood Ratio	7.066	2	.029
N of Valid Cases	48		

a. 0 cells (.0%) have expected count less than 5. The minimum expected count is 6.23.

FIGURE 7.26   Output tables for the SPSS two-sample χ^2 test of gender vs mode of travel to work

The first table provides the cross-tabulation with observed and expected frequencies, and the various marginal totals. The second section provides the results as follows:

- Pearson Chi-Square statistic. In common with the other test statistics, the associated degrees of freedom and the random probability (Asymp.Sig.) are also provided. This test statistic is preferred in most k-sample cases.

- Likelihood ratio: a variation of the chi-square method that will be similar to Pearson Chi-Square statistic where frequency counts are high.

- The number of *cases*, but not to be confused with the degrees of freedom (df = 2 in this example).

In this example, the differences between observed and expected frequencies are relatively large resulting in a correspondingly large test statistic (χ^2 = 6.88). The SPSS output dispenses with the need for tables of critical values, and we can use the random probability of the test statistic (Asymp.Sig.) to arrive at a decision on H_0. In this example it is 0.032, which, being less than the significance level of 0.05, allows us to reject H_0 of no difference in terms of gender and preferred mode of transport to work. Note, however, that we would have accepted H_0 if we had adopted the 0.01 significance level.

The example of gender preferences for public or private transport can also be tested in SPSS using the same procedures as outlined above. The data are entered in the same way, with columns for 'gender' and for 'means', the frequencies then being entered in the 'count' column. The output (Figure 7.27) is, however, slightly different as SPSS identifies this as a 2×2 contingency table.

The first table, as before, lists the observed and expected frequencies; the latter calculated from Equation 7.23. The second table, however, has two additional items:

GENDER * MEANS Crosstabulation

| | | | MEANS | | |
			private	public	Total
GENDER	female	Count	13	10	23
		Expected Count	8.6	14.4	23.0
	male	Count	5	20	25
		Expected Count	9.4	15.6	25.0
Total		Count	18	30	48
		Expected Count	18.0	30.0	48.0

Chi-Square Tests

	Value	df	Asymp. Sig. (2-sided)	Exact Sig. (2-sided)	Exact Sig. (1-sided)
Pearson Chi-Square	6.817[b]	1	.009		
Continuity Correction[a]	5.348	1	.021		
Likelihood Ratio	6.998	1	.008		
Fisher's Exact Test				.016	.010
N of Valid Cases	48				

a. Computed only for a 2x2 table

b. 0 cells (.0%) have expected count less than 5. The minimum expected count is 8.63.

FIGURE 7.27 Output from SPSS for the chi-square test of public/private mode of travel vs gender

- Continuity correction – this is the corrected version of the χ^2 statistic, sometimes referred to as Yates' correction, which is applied whenever the data are in the form of a 2×2 table. It is to be preferred to the Pearson Chi-Square statistic for all such cases.

- Fisher's Exact test – this is mainly used when the sample data are small. Unusually for nominal data, this has a one- and two-tailed form.

The continuity correction (which gives a test statistic of 5·35) stands in contrast to the uncorrected Pearson statistic of 6·82. The random probability (Asymp. Sig.) of the former is 0·021 and, as this is less than the significance level of 0·05, the null hypothesis can be rejected. The output also alerts us to the requirement that no more than 20 per cent of the cells should have fewer than 5 as their expected frequency. When this limitation is violated, SPSS usefully indicates that the test is invalid. Should this be the case the best course of action is to obtain more data and increase the observed counts in all cells. But where there are several categories it may be possible to merge them, thereby providing higher frequencies in the aggregated groups and raising also the values of the expected frequencies. In effect, this was done in this example in which the public transport category consists of bus and train counts. It was also used in the earlier Exeter voting example where a large number of small parties were grouped together as 'Other'. There will be some loss of statistical detail by this process, but usually this is compensated by the test being rendered valid.

In the above examples it was assumed that the frequencies to be entered into the various cells of the χ^2 were known. In many situations this may not be the case and the researcher will have only a matrix of original observations of the character exemplified in TRAVEL_DATA.SAV. Here can be found questionnaire data listing case by

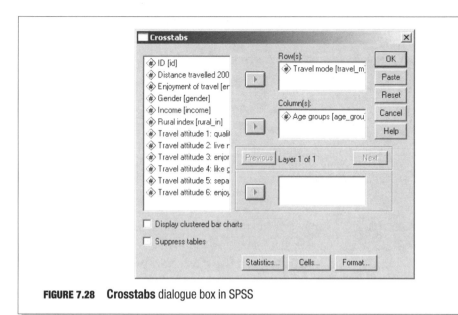

FIGURE 7.28 **Crosstabs** dialogue box in SPSS

Travel mode * Age groups Crosstabulation

Count

		Age groups					Total
		18-30	31-45	46-60	61-75	Over 75	
Travel mode	Car	2	1		4	1	8
	Bus	1		2	3		6
	Train	3	8	3		1	15
Total		6	9	5	7	2	29

FIGURE 7.29 Simple cross-tabulation matrix of nominal data in SPSS

case such categorical attributes as gender, mode of transport and attitudinal responses to questions on work and quality of life. This is a small sample but the problem of counting the cross-tabulated frequencies by hand remains problematic and subject to error, the more so with larger data sets. Fortunately SPSS (and MINITAB, see CD file MINITAB6) can conduct the process more efficiently. Suppose that we wanted to cross-tabulate 'age groups' (1 = 18 to 30, 2 = 31 to 45 and so on to 5 = 75 or more) with travel mode (1 = bus, 2 = car and 3 = train) to examine if travel habits differed by age of respondent. The instructions **Analyze > Descriptive Statistics > Crosstabs** would call up the dialogue box in Figure 7.28 into which 'age groups' are designated to form the rows and 'travel mode' the columns. SPSS will produce the required table. The χ^2 test on the resulting 3×5 matrix of frequencies can be carried out clicking the **Statistics** button that produces a simple option dialogue box (not shown). In this procedure we do not need to 'weight cases' as was done previously, and the system recognizes the character of the data. The cross-tabulated output are presented in the Output viewer

(Figure 7.29) and can be used for simple inspection, although in this example the low frequencies in some cells will infringe the test requirements noted above. In MINITAB the process is similar andrequires the instructions **Stat > Tables > Cross Tabulation and Chi_Square . . .** toinitiate the process.

7.17 Conclusions

Earlier chapters have discussed the preliminary treatment of statistical information. Useful though such methods are in the summarising of data, it is only within the setting of hypothesis testing that geographical theory can be developed. Here we have reviewed a wide range of parametric and non-parametric tests. The latter are useful because of their distribution-free qualities, making them useful not only for non-parametric data but also for interval/ratio scale data where samples are small or seriously skewed. Parametric tests, while more powerful, are more demanding of data, and require acceptable degrees of normality and relatively large sample sizes. Such differences notwithstanding, all such procedures can be seen to have the same overall strategy:

- the formulation of a research hypothesis
- the choice of a test appropriate to the data and aims of the study
- formulation of the null and alternative hypothesis
- selection of the significance level and definition of the rejection region for H_0
- calculation of the test statistic
- acceptance or rejection of H_0.

CHAPTER

8

Methods of correlation analysis

8.1 Introduction

A GREAT DEAL OF geographical analysis involves studying the relationships between two or more variables. This chapter focuses on those statistical techniques that enable us to measure and determine the strength of a statistical relationship between two variables. A number of different methods of correlation analysis are available to us, and Table 8.1 indicates those that are most commonly used. The decision as to which particular measure to employ will depend on the type of data we have (degree of skewness, sample size etc.) and their scale of measurement (see Chapter 4). The power of the different types of correlation analysis varies, and it is generally recognised that the product-moment or Pearson's correlation coefficient (r), which uses interval/ratio scale data, is the best in that respect. For example, it has been calculated that Spearman's rank correlation coefficient, which uses ordinal data, is only 91 per cent as efficient as Pearson's. This means that if in a sample of 100 cases from a bivariate normal population, the product-moment coefficient is significant, it will require a sample of 110 cases of the same population to achieve the similar reliability using the Spearman coefficient.

Regardless of the form of correlation analysis we select, the outcome is always expressed as a numerical coefficient that describes the direction and character of the relationship between two variables. The values of such coefficients can vary only between –1 and +1. These extremes represent, respectively, the perfect negative and positive relationship between variables. In the former case, the value of one variable increases as the other decreases, and in the latter the two increase (or decrease) together. A value of 0·0 indicates the absence of any correlation-based relationship. Correlations can often be qualitatively assessed using *scatter diagrams* on which the two variables are plotted. How perfect positive ($r = 1·0$) and negative ($r = –1·0$) correlations appear are shown in Figure 8.1a and c, respectively, while Figure 8.1b indicates the scatter of points that might arise when there is no correlation ($r = 0·0$). Between these extremes there exists a range of less distinct cases and although we might make a visual assessment of the degree of association the following sections explain how coefficients can be used to measure correlation in a more objective fashion.

TABLE 8.1 Types of correlation coefficients and their data requirements

Type of correlation	Measurement scale	Data characteristics
Pearson's (r)	Interval or ratio	Both variables must be in parametric form
Spearman's rank (r_s) and Kendall's tau (τ)	Ordinal	Both variables must be in ranked form
Biserial (r_b)	Nominal	Requires one variable to be dichotomous, the other can have more categories
Phi coefficient (ϕ)	Nominal	Both variables must be dichotomous

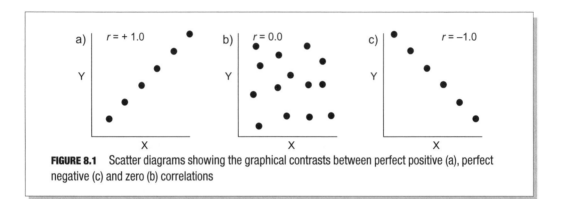

FIGURE 8.1   Scatter diagrams showing the graphical contrasts between perfect positive (a), perfect negative (c) and zero (b) correlations

8.2 The product-moment correlation coefficient

As with all parametric tests (see Chapter 7) the product-moment correlation coefficient makes assumptions about the data being tested, namely:

- data need to be measured on the interval/ratio scales
- the two variables should each approximate to a normal distribution.

Small samples bring their own problems and need to be treated more cautiously, especially regarding the assumption of data normality.

The Pearson product-moment correlation coefficient is based on the concept of *covariance*, which is related to data variance. While variance is used to measure the variability of a sample of data about its mean, covariance develops this idea but measures the correspondence or covariation of the two variables together. As discussed in section 4.7, the variance is estimated on the basis of the sum of squared deviations of individual observations about their mean. Covariance, on the other hand, depends on the sum of the products of the deviation of each pair of observations about their respective means. In algebraic terms this is expressed as:

arisen by chance, without reflecting any real association between the populations of the variables in question. Interest here focuses on the null hypothesis (H_0), which is usually one of no difference between the observed (r) correlation and a zero correlation. We might paraphrase this as an H_0 of no correlation. There are various methods by which this null hypothesis can be tested, but the easiest method is by consulting tables of critical correlations in Appendix VIII.

To establish the significance of any observed correlation coefficient, we need to take account of the sample size (n) and the significance level that we have adopted. It should be remembered that when sampling from bivariate populations the sample size is the number of pairs of observations and not the total number of individual observations. We must also decide on the tailedness of the test; are we specifying merely that the correlation differs from zero and make no suggestion as to whether it is positive or negative, or that it differs in one specified direction and that the coefficient is either positive or negative? The former represents the two-tailed case, and the latter the one-tailed.

Using the earlier rainfall example, let us adopt the 0·05 significance level and stipulate in the alternative hypothesis (H_1) that we expect observed r to be greater than zero, i.e. the test is one-tailed and the correlation coefficient is positive, with annual rainfall and altitude increasing together. The table is arranged by reference to sample size (n), which determines the row, and by significance level and tailedness, which determine the column. The conditions for the current example direct us to the first column in Appendix VIII (one-tailed 0·05 significance), from which we obtain a critical correlation coefficient of +0·306. Our observed r must exceed this value in order for us to reject H_0 of no correlation. As the coefficient from section 8.2 is +0·645, it exceeds the critical value and we conclude that the two variables are significantly and positively correlated to a degree that cannot be accounted for by random variation.

8.4 Spearman's rank correlation for ordinal scale data

In certain circumstances, we may wish to assess the relationship between variables measured at the ordinal scale. Alternatively, we may have a small sample or entertain doubts about the normality of our data distribution such that we could not apply the product-moment correlation test. We could transform the data to impose some degree of normality upon it (section 6.9), but in the context of correlation analysis other, easier, alternatives are available to us. Most importantly, there are methods of correlation that employ ranked (ordinal) data, in which form they are distribution free. These data may consist of interval and ratio scale observations that have been converted to ranks. Two types of ordinal-based correlation coefficient are available: Kendall's tau and Spearman's rank (Table 8.1). Both are equally powerful, although Spearman's rank correlation coefficient (r_s) is the easier to compute, available in both MINITAB and SPSS (section 8.7) and more widely used.

Spearman's rank correlation requires only that data be on the ordinal scale and consist of at least five pairs of observations. It is therefore of particular use when small samples only are available and no reliable information is available regarding the distribution of the data. Each pair of observations consists of two ranks. If the correlation is perfectly positive, the sequence of the two paired ranks will be identical. Usually, however, there are differences between the rankings and the correlation coefficient (r_s) is derived from these differences. Such numerical differences (D) are squared and then summed for inclusion in Equation 8.3:

$$r_s = 1 - \frac{6\Sigma D^2}{n(n^2 - 1)} \qquad (8.3)$$

Equation 8.3

D = difference between ranks of corresponding values of X and Y

n = number of pairs of X and Y values

Where data are converted from the interval/ratio scales, ties may occur but, in most cases, these can be dealt with using the methods described in section 7.10.

In geographical analysis, Spearman's rank correlation is used fairly frequently and is commonly utilised with interval/ratio data when conditions of normality are not met. Rank correlation also becomes particularly important when geographers are researching cognitive perception in behavioural studies and where ordinal data is a common form of measurement.

This can be demonstrated by the example in Table 8.3, which compares the environmental dislikes of a sample of residents from the London Borough of Stockwell with those of residents in the rest of Greater London. The various dislikes are ranked within each sample and Spearman's rank correlation can be used to measure whether there is any relationship or degree of similarity between the perceptions of residents of the two areas. Taking the sub-totals from Table 8.3, we can substitute them into Equation 8.3 to give

$$r_s = 1 - \frac{6 \times 88}{11(11^2 - 1)} = +0.60$$

In terms of these 'dislikes', a value of −1·0 would have indicated that the two areas had completely different perceptions of environmental issues, whereas a coefficient of +1·0 would indicate perfect comparability. A correlation of 0·60 lies towards the upper end of the scale, and suggests that there are degrees of similarity between the perceptions of the two groups. As our data are based on a sample, we must proceed to test the significance of the coefficient. Might it have arisen by chance? The null hypothesis to be tested is that of no difference between the observed correlation and one of zero.

TABLE 8.3 Comparisons, by rank, of environmental dislikes in Stockwell and Greater London (*Source*: Madge and Willmott 1981)

Dislikes	Stockwell ranks	Greater London ranks	Difference between ranks (D)	Difference squared (D^2)
Immigrants	1	2	−1	1
Dirt, litter etc.	2	7	−5	25
Lack of facilities	5	4	1	1
Crime, vandalism	3	5	−2	4
Lack of open space	8	10	−2	4
Children, young people	4	6	−2	4
Council services	6	3	3	9
Traffic problems	7	1	6	36
Schools	10	8	2	4
Noise	9	9	0	0
Shopping facilities	11	11	0	0
			Total	88

When we are testing the significance of Spearman's rank correlation, we can use one of two methods, depending upon sample size:

For smaller samples – it is better to use prepared tables of the type presented in Appendix IX. These tables are used in the same way as those for the product-moment coefficient. Taking the results from Table 8.3, we can assess the significance of the observed coefficient for which we will adopt the 0·05 significance level. Our alternative hypothesis asserts that the correlation should be positive, and the test is therefore one-tailed. With a sample size $n = 11$, we obtain from the table a critical correlation coefficient of +0·536. As our observed coefficient is larger than this (+0·60), we can reject the null hypothesis of zero correlation and conclude that the perceptions of residents of the two areas are, indeed, statistically similar.

For larger samples – it is sometimes preferable to convert the rank correlation coefficient into an equivalent *t*-value, where:

$$t = r_s \sqrt{\left(\frac{n-2}{1-r_s^2} \right)} \tag{8.4}$$

The derived t-statistic can then be treated in the same manner as those in Chapter 7. The tailedness of the test must be established, as must the significance level, but in the case of rank correlation methods the significance testing procedures operate with $n - 2$ degrees of freedom. Comparisons with the table of critical values will allow the null hypothesis to be accepted or rejected. In this example we derive from Equation 8.4 a t-statistic of $+2 \cdot 85$ and, as Appendix II indicates a critical t-statistic of $+1 \cdot 83$ (for 9 degrees of freedom, a significance level of $0 \cdot 05$ and a one-tailed test), we can again reject H_0 of no correlation.

8.5 Measures of correlation for nominal scale data

If we want to examine the relationship between two variables measured on the nominal scale, we need to consider other types of correlation statistics (Table 8.1). The most useful measures are the *point biserial coefficient* and the *phi coefficient*, each of which deals with different forms of data.

Suppose we want to examine the relationship between two variables, one measured on a continuous scale, while the other is a dichotomous variable that can only take the values of, say, 1 or 0. In our example, variable Y represents population totals in a sample of ten villages in South West England, and variable X indicates the presence or absence of a village post office (Table 8.4). The continuous variable (Y) can therefore be divided into two sub-groups depending on the value of X, i.e. villages with a post office ($X = 1$) and those without ($X = 0$). We can term these sub-groups Y_0 and Y_1. The point biserial coefficient (r_b) is then given by Equation 8.5, in which the means of the sub-groups (Y_0 and Y_1) need to be calculated, together with the standard deviation (s_y) of the complete set of data for variable Y:

TABLE 8.4 Raw data for point biserial coefficient between village population and existence of a post office in Wiltshire (*Source*: Wiltshire County Council 1979)

Village	Population (Y)	Post office (X)
Bowden Hill	200	1
Corsley	200	1
Bishops Cannings	250	0
Poulshot	250	0
Compton Bassett	250	1
Seend Cleeve	300	0
Hilmarton	300	1
Hormingsham	320	1
Worton	310	1
Broughton Gifford	750	0

$$r_b = \frac{\overline{Y_1} - \overline{Y_0}}{s_y} \sqrt{\left(\frac{n_1 n_0}{n(n-1)} \right)} \tag{8.5}$$

From the procedures outlined and the data workings from Table 8.5, we have all the information to allow us to use Equation 8.5. Hence:

$$r_b = \frac{263 \cdot 3 - 387 \cdot 5}{159 \cdot 4} \sqrt{\left(\frac{6 \times 4}{90} \right)}$$

$$= -0 \cdot 40$$

Equation 8.5

n = total number of observations

n_0 = number of observations with $X = 0$

n_1 = number of observations with $X = 1$

and $\quad \overline{Y_0} = \dfrac{\Sigma Y_0}{n_0} \qquad \overline{Y_1} = \dfrac{\Sigma Y_1}{n_1}$

$$S_y = \sqrt{\left(\frac{n \Sigma Y^2 - (\Sigma Y)^2}{n(n-1)} \right)}$$

As with other correlation measures, the point biserial can vary between +1 and –1. We can assess the significance of our results by employing a t-test. The null hypothesis in this case is that of no correlation, i.e. the presence of a post office is not determined by village size. In common with all such tests, we must select a significance level, say 0·05, and decide on the tailedness of the test. As the variable used to discriminate the groups is at the nominal scale and has no natural order, the test is used in its two-tailed form. The degrees of freedom are given by $n - 2$, giving us 8 in this example. From Appendix II we obtain a critical t-statistic of ±2·31, while the coefficient's t-statistic can be found from Equation 8.6.

$$t = r_b \sqrt{\left(\frac{n-2}{1-r_b^2} \right)} \tag{8.6}$$

Using the data from Table 8.4, we get a t-statistic of –1·23. As this does not exceed the critical value of 2·31, it therefore fails to fall within the rejection region on the t-distribution, and we must accept H_0 of zero correlation and conclude that the presence or absence of a post office does not, in this case, depend on population.

TABLE 8.5 Calculation of $\bar{Y}_0$ and $\bar{Y}_1$ for the point biserial correlation data in Table 8.4 (sub-totals are in bold)

Y_0	Y_0^2	Y_1	Y_1^2
250	62,500	200	40,000
250	62,500	200	40,000
300	90,000	250	62,500
750	562,500	300	90,000
. . . .	. . . .	320	102,400
. . . .	. . . .	310	96,100
1,550	**777,500**	**1,580**	**431,000**

$\bar{Y}_0 = 1{,}550/4 = 387{\cdot}5$ $\qquad\qquad\qquad$ $\bar{Y}_1 = 1{,}580/6 = 263{\cdot}3$

The nature of the point biserial correlation requires that certain assumptions underlie its application. Thus, the value of the continuous variable should be normally distributed. Furthermore, the two sub-samples of the dichotomous variable should not be vastly different in terms of the number of observations. Tests have shown that the more equal these sub-groups are, the more accurate the test becomes.

The point biserial coefficient is only applicable if one variable is measured on the interval or ratio scale. When we want to use correlation between two dichotomous variables, other statistics need to be considered. Under these conditions we can use the *phi coefficient*, which represents an extension of the χ^2 test but uses only 2×2 contingency tables (see sections 7.13–15). However, unlike χ^2 values, the phi coefficient can only vary between $-1{\cdot}0$ and $+1{\cdot}0$. The two tests also differ in another fundamental way in that the phi coefficient, like other correlation statistics, tells us about the strength and direction of a relationship between two variables, whereas χ^2 is more concerned with assessing the distinctiveness of the two samples.

There are two methods of calculating phi (ϕ) according to whether the χ^2 value has already been derived. If it has not, we need to apply Equation 8.7

$$\phi = \frac{AD - BC}{\sqrt{[(A+B)(C+D)(A+C)(B+D)]}} \tag{8.7}$$

Table 8.6 gives the definitions of the terms used in the equation in which the letters refer to the arrangement of cells in the contingency table. In this example we want to determine whether there is any correlation between the location of retail centres (local or city centre) used for food shopping by car and by non-car owning households. The null hypothesis is that there is zero correlation between the two variables of car ownership and shop location. From Equation 8.7 we get:

TABLE 8.6 Calculation of the ϕ coefficient between car ownership and shopping behaviour.

	City shops	Local shops	Total
Households with a car	295 (A)[1]	95 (B)	390
Households without a car	27 (C)	83 (D)	110
Total	322	178	

[1] The cell alphabetic indicators indicate their roles in Equation 8.7.

$$\phi = \frac{(295 \times 83) - (95 \times 27)}{(390 \times 110 \times 322 \times 178)}$$

$$\phi = +0.44$$

This phi coefficient indicates that some degree of association exists between the variables, though, as will be shown, it is not easy to determine the significance of this figure.

If we had already established the χ^2 statistic for this data set, we could have determined the phi coefficient from Equation 8.8 in which the χ^2 statistic is divided by the total frequency count (n), which is 500 in this example.

$$\phi = \sqrt{\left(\frac{\chi^2}{n}\right)} \tag{8.8}$$

Unfortunately, there is no method of finding confidence limits for ϕ, and in order to test its significance, it must be treated as a χ^2 statistic. We may already have that figure, if not but we do have ϕ, we need only transpose Equation 8.8 to give:

$$\chi^2 = \phi^2 \times n \tag{8.9}$$

If we do this, we obtain in this example a χ^2 statistic of 97. This exceeds the critical value of 6.64 derived from Appendix III (with $\alpha = 0.01$, and remembering that there is only ever 1 degree of freedom in such cases). We must therefore reject H_0 of no correlation between the two variables, and conclude that in our study area, shopping patterns are determined, at least partly by car ownership.

8.6 Correlation analysis in MINITAB

Table 8.2 has shown that the preparation of a product-moment correlation coefficient is a simple, but highly repetitive process in which computers can offer great assistance. Both SPSS and MINITAB have options for calculating correlation coefficients. In neither system are we restricted to producing just one correlation at a time, and it is possible to enter several variables for correlation analysis, the results of which will be presented in the form of a *correlation matrix* in which a coefficient is calculated between each possible pairing of the selected list of variables.

To examine how correlations can be produced using these systems we will use a set of socio-economic data for 46 English counties. The full data set is available on the CD in the files COUNTY.MTW (for use in MINITAB) and COUNTY.SAV (for use in SPSS). Our interest will lie, however, with only four of the variables; death rate in deaths per 1,000 population ('death'), percentage unemployment rates ('unemploy'), gross weekly earnings in £s ('gwe') and crime rate measured in reported crimes per 100,000 population ('crime'). A correlation matrix can be produced in MINITAB by requesting the instructions **Stat > Basic Statistics > Correlation**. In the resulting dialogue box (Figure 8.2), the required variables are selected from the list and transferred to the **Variables** box. We will leave the **Display p-values** option checked, and by clicking on **OK** will produce the correlation matrix in the Session window (Figure 8.3).

The matrix lists all possible correlations between the variables. These range between 0·064 for the crime and weekly earnings pairing, to –0·522 for that between death rates and weekly earnings. In the latter case there is a strong suggestion that death rates rise with falling levels of income. The figures beneath each correlation coefficient (the P-Value) are their associated random probabilities, i.e. the probabilities that the correlation coefficients are due to chance alone, and there is no underlying association between the two variables. With these values we can dispense with the need for tables of critical values as outlined in section 8.3 and, if we are working to the 0·05 significance level, all correlations with probabilities of less than 0·05 would be significant. In this example only the death rate/earnings, death rate/unemployment and crime rate/unemployment

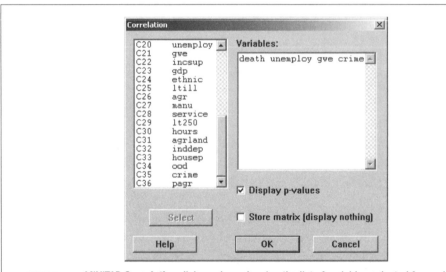

FIGURE 8.2 MINITAB **Correlation** dialogue box, showing the list of variables selected for analysis

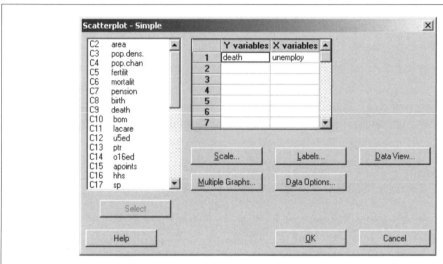

Correlations: death, unemploy, gwe, crime

```
              death    unemploy      gwe
unemploy     0.341
             0.020

gwe         -0.522      -0.251
             0.000       0.092

crime       -0.168       0.332     0.064
             0.265       0.024     0.671


Cell Contents: Pearson correlation
               P-Value
```

FIGURE 8.3 MINITAB correlation coefficient matrix showing the coefficient (above) and its associated random probability (below) analysis

FIGURE 8.4 Dialogue box in MINITAB for the preparation of a scatter diagram

correlations are significant at this level (and only death rate/earnings at the 0·01 level). In the other cases the *p*-value exceeds 0·05 and the correlations are deemed not significant.

It is often useful to have a scatter diagram of bivariate relationships of this nature. These can also be produced in MINITAB by the commands **Graph > Scatterplot**. The immediate MINITAB response is to present some options for the graph, of which the default of the **Simple** graph is generally preferred. The dialogue box (Figure 8.4) then appears and allows us to specify the two variables to be plotted; one for the **Y variable** and one for the **X variable**. These can be allocated by double clicking from the variable list. Notice that we can, if we wish to do so, produce more than one graph by adding further variables to the list. The result for death rates against unemployment is shown in Figure 8.5. It should be pointed out that while there is significant correlation between

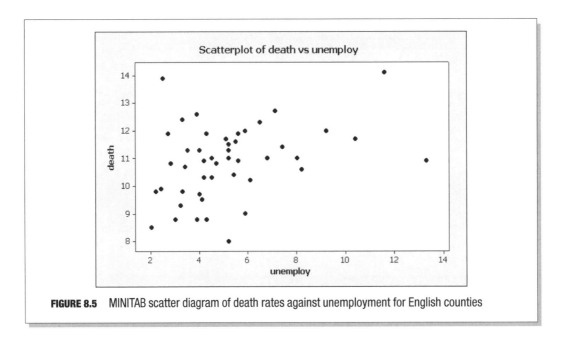

FIGURE 8.5   MINITAB scatter diagram of death rates against unemployment for English counties

these two variables, the graph shows a high degree of scatter of the data points and warns against relying on subjective estimates of correlation based on scatter diagrams alone.

8.7 Spearman's rank correlation analysis using SPSS

The procedures by which we estimate correlation coefficients using SPSS are the same for the product-moment and the rank correlations, and the appropriate coefficient is selected in the dialogue box. If the Spearman's rank correlation is selected, SPSS will automatically convert the observations into ranks (if they are not already in that form), but MINITAB requires that we undertake this operation as a separate exercise. MINITAB only allows one variable at a time to be ranked, and does so with the commands **Data > Rank**. The dialogue box (Figure 8.6) allows us to specify the variable to be ranked, but requires also that we allocate a column where the ranks are to be held. In this case we will use the next free column, C38. We have chosen the variable for unemployment in this example, but the process would have to be repeated for each variable to be included in any matrix of Spearman's rank correlations. This matrix would then be estimated using the same series of instructions as indicated in the preceding section (**Stat > Basic Statistics > Correlation**), but the variables selected to be processed would now be the ranked data, and the output in the form of Spearman coefficients.

In SPSS the process is more straightforward and the instructions **Analyze > Correlate > Bivariate** will bring up the dialogue box in Figure 8.7. We will transfer the same four variables for processing but untick the **Pearson** box and tick that for **Spearman**.

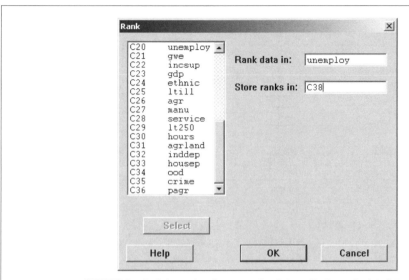

FIGURE 8.6   MINITAB **Rank** dialogue box for converting interval/ratio scale data into rank-ordered form

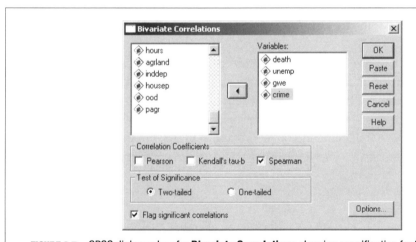

FIGURE 8.7   SPSS dialogue box for **Bivariate Correlations** showing specification for the Spearman coefficient

Notice that we can also elect to use a one- or two-tailed form of the analysis. The results are presented in Figure 8.8. Each cell of the matrix indicates the Spearman correlation coefficient, its random probability, the sample size and an indication is also given of those coefficients that are significant at the 0·05 or 0·01 levels. In this example we should note that the general level of correlation is higher than for the product-moment case. This is particularly so for correlations involving unemployment, for which the

Correlations

			DEATH	UNEMP	GWE	CRIME
Spearman's rho	DEATH	Correlation Coefficient	1.000	.339*	-.544**	-.167
		Sig. (2-tailed)	.	.021	.000	.268
		N	46	46	46	46
	UNEMP	Correlation Coefficient	.339*	1.000	-.311*	.380**
		Sig. (2-tailed)	.021	.	.035	.009
		N	46	46	46	46
	GWE	Correlation Coefficient	-.544**	-.311*	1.000	-.029
		Sig. (2-tailed)	.000	.035	.	.846
		N	46	46	46	46
	CRIME	Correlation Coefficient	-.167	.380**	-.029	1.000
		Sig. (2-tailed)	.268	.009	.846	.
		N	46	46	46	46

*. Correlation is significant at the .05 level (2-tailed).

**. Correlation is significant at the .01 level (2-tailed).

FIGURE 8.8 Correlation matrix output in SPSS format

correlation with earnings and crime rates have gone up from −0·251 and 0·322 to −0·311 and 0·380, respectively. In part this reflects the degree of skewness in the unemployment data (α_3 = +1·46), but the conversion of the raw data to ranks has eliminated this problem by rendering the data 'distribution free'. In such cases the Spearman correlation is the more reliable of the two, although it may not necessarily improve the degree of correlation.

It is clear therefore that the choice of correlation coefficient is determined largely by the character of the available data. In particular, care needs to taken with interval and ratio scale data to ensure that they conform to the requirements of normality implicit in the product-moment correlation coefficient. Where doubts exist, it is better to use the less powerful, but more reliable method of Spearman's rank correlation.

Simple linear and non-linear regression

9.1 Introduction

IN CHAPTER 8 WE examined methods of assessing the statistical relationship between two variables. The correlation coefficient is one such measure of association but, useful as this measure might be, it does not allow us to predict the numerical value of one variable based on the other. Neither does correlation make any assumptions on causation, for example that it is one of the variables that controls the behaviour of the other. The importance of regression analysis is that it goes much further than correlation, and it enables us to make a numerical prediction of one variable by reference to another. In order, however, to embark on this procedure we must decide on the *direction of causation*, and which is the *dependent variable* and which is the *independent*, i.e. which variable controls the other. Statistical convention dictates that the dependent variable is termed Y, and the independent variable X. For example, mean annual UK rainfall is known to increase with altitude. In this situation rainfall (Y) could be argued to depend on altitude (X). The reverse would not make scientific sense, although in some situations the dependency relationships are far less easy to distinguish, especially in areas of human geography.

We will deal firstly with linear regression in which incremental changes in X produce a consistent response in Y across the range of observed Xs, i.e. the two variables are linearly related. We will also only consider the case of a single predictor (Chapter 10 deals with multiple predictors). Simple linear regression is a valuable predictive and modelling tool, allowing geographers to recreate, in numerical terms, the way in which one variable controls another. It is, however, a parametric test and requires data at the interval or ratio scale. It requires also that these data are not significantly skewed in their distributions. Although pairs of variables may be found to be linearly related, there is no implication of perfection in the relationship and, as exemplified in Figure 8.5, some degree of departure from a perfect relationship must always be expected.

In essence, simple linear regression methods 'fit' a straight line through scatters of points. In section 2.5 we saw that straight lines can be described in algebraic terms that allow them to be plotted on sheets of graph paper. It was also shown that the Y term (in the context of regression methods this is the dependent variable) is related to the term X (the independent variable) through two constants, a and b. If we know the values of the two constants we can plot the line and predict Y for any value of X (see, for example, Table 2.7). The problem is, how to determine these two values? Many different results will be obtained if we rely on a visual judgement to determine the *best-fit line*. Clearly, we require an objective method, based on a consistent criterion. Statisticians, for very important reasons that we cannot discuss here, adopt the criterion of *least squares*, whereby the best-fit line passes through the scatter of plotted points in such a way that the sum of the squared departures of each point from the line (always measured in terms of Y) is at a minimum. For each set of two variables there is only one such solution.

Figure 9.1 is a simplified expression of the above principles, in which we have indicated the difference (V) between each observation of Y and the best-fit line. We should also notice that the constant b is, in the current context, described as the *regression coefficient*, but that it also describes the slope of the line. The constant a is known as the *intercept term*, and is the point on the Y axis through which the line passes. In algebraic terms it is the value of Y when $X = 0.0$.

9.2 Estimating the linear regression model

Equation 9.1 is the full expression of the simple linear regression model. It differs from the straight line equation only by the inclusion of the error term e that recognises the degree of scatter of points (observations) about the line:

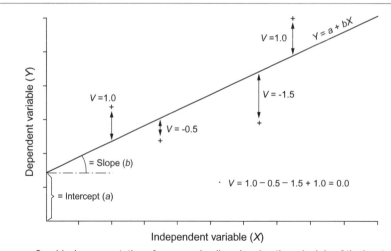

FIGURE 9.1 Graphical representation of a regression line showing the principle of the least-squares criterion, and the graphical interpretation of the intercept term (*a*) and the regression coefficient (slope of the line, *b*). The regression line is fitted by reference to the differences (*V*) between the line and the individual data points

$$Y = a + bX + e \qquad\qquad (9.1)$$

In the following example we will use two variables (death rate and gross weekly earnings) from the data files COUNTY.MTW or COUNTY.SAV that we have already employed in correlation studies in Chapter 8. It might be expected that death rates (measured in deaths per 1,000 of the population) are related to, and might depend upon, gross weekly income (in £s), hence the former will be taken as the dependent variable, and the latter as the independent. The correlation between the two is significant at the 0·01 level and $r = -0.522$. Low incomes, therefore, are generally associated with high death rates and vice versa. The scatter diagram of the relationship is shown in Figure 9.2.

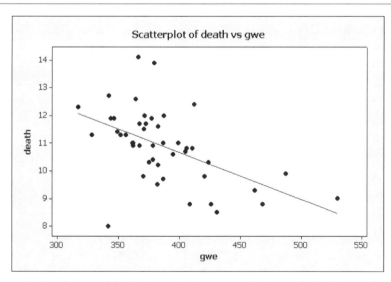

FIGURE 9.2 Scatter diagram of death rates against gross weekly income for English counties. The best-fit regression line has also been included. This graph was prepared in MINITAB using the command sequence **Graph > Scatterplot > With Regression**

The principal task in regression analysis is to establish the values of the intercept term (a) and the regression coefficient (b) for the least-squares line that summarises this relationship. There is no requirement at this stage to determine the error term, and this is dealt with in section 9.5 where the question of *residual* values is examined. The value of b can be determined from Equation 9.2:

$$b = \frac{\sum x_i y_i}{\sum x_i^2} \qquad (9.2)$$

Equation 9.2

$$x_i = (X_i - \bar{X})$$

$$y_i = (Y_i - \bar{Y})$$

Thus each individual observation of X and of Y has their respective mean subtracted from them. In one case these pairs of differences are multiplied (xy), and in the other, those for X alone, are squared, as illustrated in Table 9.1. Both sets of products are summed and the division of the sum for xy by that for x^2 provides the least-squares estimate of b.

The least-squares criterion also has the important consequence that the line must pass through the *data centroid* – the point where the $\bar{X}$ and the $\bar{Y}$ co-ordinates intersect. It follows therefore from Equation 9.1 and by transposition that:

TABLE 9.1 Abridged work sheet and sub-totals for estimating coefficients in the simple regression model for death rate and gross weekly income

Observation (*i*)	Weekly earnings (*X*)	Death rate (*Y*)	$(X_i - \bar{X})$ (*x*)	$(Y_i - \bar{Y})$ (*y*)	x^2	*xy*
1	378·0	10·9	−8·67	0·03	75·16	−0·26
2	348·7	11·4	−37·97	0·53	1,441·72	−20·12
3	343·7	11·9	−42·97	1·03	1,846·42	−44·26
4	372·3	11·7	−14·37	0·83	206·49	−11·93
....	....	....	....	....	....	....
45	366·9	11·7	−19·77	0·83	390·85	−16·41
46	370·3	9·8	−16·37	−1·07	267·98	17·52
Means	386·665	10·874		Totals	76,002·56	−1,286·67

regression coefficient (b) = −1,286·67/76,002·56 = −0·01693.
intercept term (a) = 10·874 − (−0·01693 × 386·665) = 17·42.

$$a = \bar{Y} - b\,\bar{X} \tag{9.3}$$

Table 9.1 shows how the data might be treated manually to provide the sub-totals required for Equations 9.2 and 9.3.

In this example, the least-squares regression line described by the equation is estimated to be

$$Y = 17{\cdot}42 - 0{\cdot}01693X \tag{9.4}$$

The regression coefficient, in common with the correlation coefficient for these two variables, is negative. Thus, as gross weekly earnings increase, the death rate falls. The regression coefficient also tells us that for each unit change (£1) on the earnings scale, the death rate changes by 0·01693 deaths per 1,000 of population. This response rate is constant throughout the range of X, and we can use Equation 9.4 to predict death rates for any given gross weekly earnings. This predictive capacity distinguishes correlation from regression, but there are other contrasts. Most importantly, the correlation and regression coefficients are quite different. The former can vary only between +1 and –1 (see Chapter 8), and the correlation coefficient's value remains the same even if the units by which a variable is measured are changed. For example, if we changed the units of measurement of gross weekly earnings from £s to euros, and the death rate units of deaths per thousand to deaths per hundred of the population, the value of the correlation coefficient will not change. Matters are quite different with regression coefficients. These are *scale-dependent*, and if the units are changed so does the value of the coefficient. Moreover, regression coefficients are not constrained within the limits +1 to –1, and can assume any value depending on the units used in the two variables. Regression and correlation coefficients for any two variables will share signs, but nothing more.

Let us now consider the matter in more detail. Figure 9.2 shows the way in which the least-squares line describes and summarises the relationship between gross weekly earnings and death rate. Notice, however, that even with the high degree of correlation ($r = -0{\cdot}522$), the points do not fall exactly on the line, and are scattered either side of it. On the other hand, all values of Y that are predicted using the Equation 9.4 must, by mathematical definition fall on, and be part of, that line. These predictions can be termed *best estimates* of Y, and are conventionally denoted by $\hat{Y}$, so that

$$\hat{Y} = a + bX \tag{9.5}$$

This leads us to consider the purpose of regression models. With them, we seek to explain the changes (variance) of the dependent variable that results from changes (variance) of the independent variable. For each observation X in our data set there is a corresponding dependent observation (Y) and, importantly, a best-estimate value ($\hat{Y}$) that results from substituting X into the least-squares equation. For example the observed death rate for Merseyside is 12·0 deaths per 1,000 population. Given the

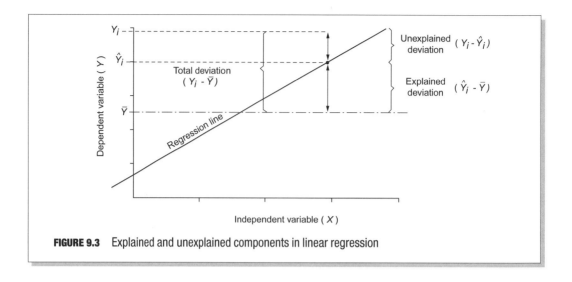

FIGURE 9.3   Explained and unexplained components in linear regression

area's average gross weekly income of £387·4, the best-estimate death rate is given by:

$$\hat{Y} = 17 \cdot 42 - 0 \cdot 01693 \times 387 \cdot 4 = 10 \cdot 9 \text{ deaths per } 1,000 \text{ population}$$

In this example, the observed death rate is much higher than that which might be expected given the gross weekly income. The differences between the pairs of Y and $\hat{Y}$ values are known as *residuals*, but not all are by any means as great as in this example, but these collective differences reflect the degree to which the model cannot explain all of the variance in Y. If we can measure the variance of all observed Ys about the least-squares line we will have a measure of *unexplained* (or *residual*) variance. On the other hand the degree to which the corresponding $\hat{Y}$ values (essentially the best-fit line) vary about the mean of Y is a measure of the *explained* variance. Figure 9.3 expresses this concept in graphical form.

The use of explained and unexplained variance as a means of significance testing has already been introduced in our study of one-way analysis of variance (section 7.8). We can now develop these ideas in the setting of regression analysis.

9.3 Significance testing in simple regression

Regression procedures will fit lines through any scatter of points, regardless of the existence or otherwise of any causal relationship between the variables. We need, therefore, to determine the significance of any equation that is produced, and this can be done by reference to the explained and unexplained variances noted above. In all such situations (see also Equation 7.8)

$$variance = \frac{sum\ of\ squares}{degrees\ of\ freedom} \tag{9.6}$$

and we can again use the variance ratio (F) to determine the significance of the findings. In section 7.8 our interest was in the between- and within-groups variances. Here it is between the explained and unexplained variances that result from the regression equation's attempt to explain the variation in Y by means of a summary linear equation. The explained variance is, as noted above, the variance of the best-fit line about $\bar{Y}$, while the unexplained component is the variability of observed values of Y about the line. The former's degrees of freedom depend upon the number of predictor terms (k) used in the equation to account for Y. This is always 1 in simple regression. The degrees of freedom for the unexplained variance depends upon the number of observations (n), each of which will contribute to the unexplained variance by virtue of its residual value. If we denote the explained (sometime known as the regression) variance by s_y^2, and the unexplained (residual or error) variance by s_e^2, then:

$$s_y^2 = \frac{\sum(\hat{Y}-\bar{Y})^2}{k} \tag{9.7}$$

and

$$s_e^2 = \frac{\sum(Y-\hat{Y})^2}{n-k-1} \tag{9.8}$$

Equations 9.7 and 9.8

$\hat{Y}$ = best-estimate of Y

$\bar{Y}$ = mean of Y

Y = individual observations of Y

n = number of pairs of observations

k = number of predictors

The variance ratio F is found from the ratio of the explained to the unexplained variance:

$$F = s_y^2/s_e^2 \tag{9.9}$$

As usual in such situations, we must set up a null hypothesis, which here is one of 'no explanation of Y in terms of X'.

Table 9.2 shows how the F-statistic can be derived for the death rate-gross weekly earnings example. For each observation, the best estimate of Y ($\hat{Y}$) must be calculated using Equation 9.4. The individual differences of $\hat{Y}$ from the observed values, and from

TABLE 9.2 Abridged work sheet and analysis of variance table of data required to determine the *F*-ratio of the regression model for death rate predicted by gross weekly earnings

Observation (*i*)	Index of deprivation (*X_i*)	Mortality (*Y_i*)	Predicted *Y* (*Ŷ_i*)	Residual (*Y_i−Ŷ_i*)	(*Y_i−Ŷ_i*)²	(*Ŷ_i−Ȳ*)	(*Ŷ_i−Ȳ*)²
1	378·0	10·9	11·020	−0·120	0·0144	0·146	0·0213
2	348·7	11·4	11·517	−0·117	0·0137	0·643	0·4134
3	343·7	11·9	11·601	0·299	0·0894	0·727	0·5285
4	372·3	11·7	11·117	0·583	0·3399	0·243	0·0590
....	....	....	....	....	....	....	....
45	366·9	11·7	11·208	0·492	0·2421	0·334	0·1116
46	370·3	9·8	11·151	−1·351	1·8252	0·277	0·0767
Means	386·665	10·874		Totals	58·0862		21·7842

Analysis of variance table

Source of variance	Sum of squares	Degrees of freedom	Variance	*F*-ratio
Explained	21·7842	1	21·7842	16·5
Unexplained	58·0862	46 − 1 − 1	1·320	
Total	79·8704	46 − 1		

the $\bar{Y}$ can then be listed and the respective squares can be calculated. The sums of the columns give the required sums of squares. The degrees of freedom can be easily derived (see Equations 9.7 and 9.8). We will use the 0·05 significance level, and from Appendix VIb we can see that the critical *F*-ratio for 1 and 44 degrees of freedom is 4·07 (by interpolation). The test statistic ($F = 16·5$) far exceeds this, and H_0 of no explanation can be rejected, and the model concluded to provide a significant degree of explanation of death rates in terms of income.

A useful additional feature of this 'manual' method is that the correlation coefficient and the coefficient of explanation (see Chapter 8) can be estimated from the ANOVA table. The coefficient of explanation (r^2) is given by the ratio of explained (or regression) to total sums of squares of Y, the correlation coefficient being the square root of that estimate. Thus:

$$r = \sqrt{\left(\frac{regression\ sum\ of\ squares\ of\ Y}{total\ sum\ of\ squares\ of\ Y}\right)} = \sqrt{\left[\frac{\sum\left(\hat{Y}-\bar{Y}\right)^2}{\sum\left(Y-\bar{Y}\right)^2}\right]}$$ (9.10)

In the current example (see Table 9.2) we obtain:

$$r = \sqrt{(21{\cdot}7842/79{\cdot}8704)} = 0{\cdot}522$$

You will have noted, however, that square roots can be positive or negative, and the correlation coefficient therefore either + or $-0{\cdot}522$. The correct sign can be determined by consulting the scatter diagram or the derived regression coefficient. In this case it is negative.

9.4 Confidence limits in simple linear regression

One of the most important features that governs the reliability of any estimate of Y that we make, is the scatter of points about the best-fit line. If the scatter is wide, the predictions will have more uncertainty than when the scatter is narrow. We estimate this degree of scatter by a quantity known as the *standard error of the residuals*. In Table 9.2 we determined the unexplained or error variance (s_e^2) to be $1{\cdot}320$. The standard error of the residuals (s_e) is the square root of this:

$$s_e = \sqrt{1{\cdot}320} = 1{\cdot}149$$

Recalling from section 6.3 that standard errors correspond to standard deviations, this means that 68 per cent of the residuals should lie within a band $1{\cdot}149$ units (deaths per 1,000 of population) wide each side of the regression line.

This is, however, only one source of uncertainty. There is another. Regression equations are usually estimated on the basis of sampled data from unknown populations. As such they are subject to sampling variations, and estimates of a and b must be regarded as indicators of the unknown population parameters α and β, respectively. Figure 9.4 is a graphical expression of the consequences of these sampling variations. The intercept term (a) governs vertical location of the line, the variation of which will result in a possible error range indicated in Figure 9.4a. The regression coefficient (b), on the other hand, controls the slope of the line, and pivots through the data centroid. Variations in b result in the error range shown in Figure 9.4b. The combined effect of these two sources of error are summarised in Figure 9.4c in which the error range is defined by two curves either side of the regression line. In detail, these curves are hyperbolic in form, but their important characteristic is that they define error bands that become greater as they depart either side of the mean. We can, thus, distinguish, on the one hand, *confidence intervals* for the line itself and, on the other, *prediction intervals* that describe the degree to which estimates of Y vary about the line. The latter are wider and reflect the collective uncertainties due to the scatter of points about the line and to the estimates of the coefficients a and b. Because our interest usually lies with the best estimates of the dependent variable $(\hat{Y})$, it is the prediction intervals (PI) that are of most concern. The standard error of PI $(SE_{\hat{Y}i})$ depends, in part, upon the standard error of the residuals (s_e) and is given by:

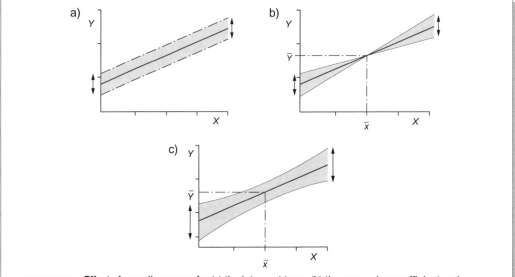

FIGURE 9.4 Effect of sampling errors for (a) the intercept term, (b) the regression coefficient and (c) the combined effect of both

$$\text{SE}_{\hat{Y}i} = s_e \sqrt{\left[1 + \frac{1}{n} + \frac{\left(X_k - \overline{X}\right)^2}{\sum_{i=1}^{n}\left(X_i - \overline{X}\right)^2} \right]}$$

(9.11)

Equation 9.11

n = sample size

X_k = the value of X for which the PI of Y is required

X_i = all observations i of X

$\overline{X}$ = mean of Xs and s_e = standard error of the residuals

We will now consider two values for X_k, one of which is close to the mean (£380), the other of which is more extreme (£520) and determine the prediction intervals for the two estimates of death rate that are produced using Equation 9.4. These are respectively, 8·62 and 10·99 deaths per 1,000 population. Taking the estimate of 10·99 deaths per 1,000 population first; by reference to sub-totals already available from Table 9.1 and substitution into Equation 9.11 we get:

$$\text{SE}_{\hat{Y}i} = 1 \cdot 149 \sqrt{\left[1 + \frac{1}{46} + \frac{(380 - 386 \cdot 665)^2}{76,002 \cdot 56} \right]} = 1 \cdot 162$$

The same process for $X_k = 520$ gives an answer of 1·288. But these are the standard errors for PI; if we want to determine the corresponding 95 per cent limits we must multiply these by the appropriate factor. If the sample size were larger than 60 we could take the values for the normal distribution of ±1·96, but because the sample size is only 46 we should refer to the t-distributions in Appendix II to derive these figures. By interpolation the t-statistics that embrace two-tailed 95 per cent of the distribution are ±2·01. Thus we can be 95 per cent certain that the 'real' death rate for average weekly income of £380 will be between the limits:

$$10·99 ± 2·01 × 1·162 = 8·65 \text{ and } 13·33 \text{ deaths per 1,000 population,}$$

and range of 4·68 deaths.

For an average weekly income of £520 we have limits of:

$$8·62 ± 2·01 × 1·288 = 6·03 \text{ and } 11·21 \text{ deaths per 1,000 population,}$$

and a range of 5·18 deaths.

We should notice first, how much wider the PI band is at the extreme end of the range of observed values compared to the narrower limits close to the mean. Secondly, the wide intervals are themselves a salutary warning that, even with relatively strong correlations and with powerful analytical tools at our disposal, any predictions that we might make can often be hedged about by notable uncertainty.

9.5 Analysis of residuals

Reference has already been made to residuals – the departure of the observed from the estimated values of the dependent variable. Residuals are an important part of regression analysis. Not only do their magnitudes contribute to the prediction limits, but their general character has also implications for the regression model.

It is often useful to express residuals not as absolute values but in a standardised form in which each of them is measured in terms of the number of standard errors by which it departs from the regression line. We have seen already in section 5.8 how data sets can be expressed in this *standardised* form. This is another expression of that transformation, in which the difference between observed and estimated values (Y_i and $\hat{Y}$) is expressed as a proportion of the standard error of the residual (s_e):

$$\text{standardised residual} = \frac{Y_i - \hat{Y}}{s_e} \tag{9.12}$$

Such transformation helps to identify the truly unusual residuals; those that depart significantly from the line and indicate individuals (counties in the current example) that do not conform to the general trend and, perhaps, warrant closer attention. The mapping of residual analysis of spatially-based observations, of which counties are a good example,

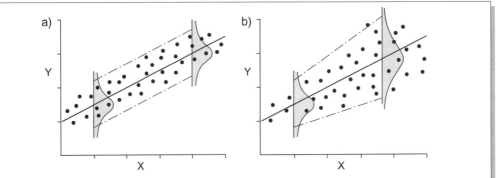

FIGURE 9.5 Representations of conditions of (a) homoscedasticity (equal spread of residuals along the regression line) and (b) heteroscedasticity (varying scatter of residuals about the line)

can also help to identify clusters or regions of positive or negative residuals. Again, this often helps to direct further studies by demonstrating important spatial patterns not readily apparent in the raw data.

There are, however, other aspects of residual analysis that are more fundamental to regression analysis. For the model to be wholly reliable, the residuals should be distributed normally about the line (Figure 9.5). In this way the standardised residuals have, importantly, zero mean and unit variance. In addition, the degree of scatter should not vary greatly along the range of X. This is a requirement of *homoscedasticity*. If it is not fulfilled the data are said to be *heteroscedastic*, and the regression equation may be unreliable for some purposes. A further requirement is that there should independence between the residuals and, consequently, that there be no *autocorrelation* among them. Autocorrelation is indicated by either long runs of positive or negative residuals along the regression line or, on the other hand, by rapid and regular fluctuations of residuals. These two conditions are shown in Figure 9.6.

If the conditions for zero autocorrelation and for heteroscedasticity are met, our predictions of Y will not be subject to undue error. We might be satisfied with a visual check of the plots of our data to confirm this, but if we are in any doubt, it is better to use an objective method. One of the most widely used measures of autocorrelation is the Durbin-Watson d-statistic, the derivation of which is relatively simple and based on the sequence of residuals so that:

$$d = \frac{sum\ of\ successive\ squared\ differences}{sum\ of\ squared\ residuals}$$

in algebraic form, this is represented by:

$$d = \frac{\sum (e_i - e_{i-1})^2}{\sum e_i^2} \tag{9.13}$$

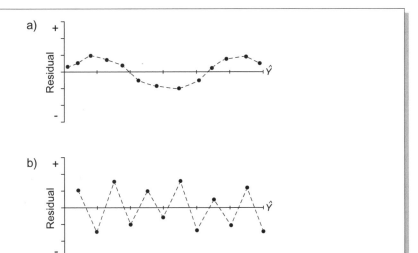

FIGURE 9.6 Representation of (a) positive, and (b) negative autocorrelation in regression residuals. The horizontal axis represents $\hat{Y}$ (predicted Y), and is an expression of the regression line and the manner in which the residuals are scattered about it

In the case of positive autocorrelation (Figure 9.6a) differences between adjacent residuals are not great and d tends towards zero. If, on the other hand, adjacent differences are large, d tends towards its maximum value of 4·0. When there is little autocorrelation, d-statistics tend towards 2·0.

The decision to accept or reject the null hypothesis of zero autocorrelation is not easily arrived at. Appendix X lists the bounds for the rejection regions on the d-distribution. The limits are obtained by reference to the sample size n (the number of residuals in the series), the number of independent terms k (always 1 in the case of simple regression) and the chosen significance level. Upper (d_u) and lower (d_l) values are given in the tables, and are used to define the two rejection regions for H_0. One is the rejection region for positive autocorrelation, the other for negative autocorrelation. In addition, a zone of acceptance of H_0 can be delimited about $d = 2·0$, leaving two areas along the distribution where the test is indeterminate. Figure 9.7 offers a graphical description of this partitioning of the statistical distribution.

We can now test the death rate/earnings model for autocorrelation. Either absolute or standardised residuals can be used; we will use the former. A sample of the working is shown in Table 9.3. It is important to note that the residuals must be ordered in terms of the predicted values of Y.

From the sub-totals in Table 9.3 the Durbin-Watson d-statistic is given by:

$$d = 126·96 / 58·086 = 2·186$$

If we adopt the 0·05 significance level we should turn to Appendix Xa to find the lower (d_l) and upper (d_u) bounds with which to define the rejection regions of d. As $k = 1$ and

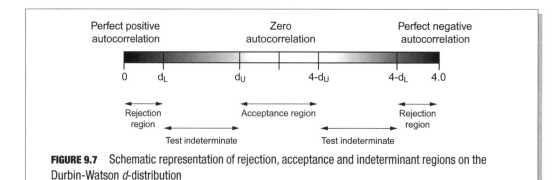

FIGURE 9.7 Schematic representation of rejection, acceptance and indeterminant regions on the Durbin-Watson d-distribution

TABLE 9.3 Derivation of the Durbin-Watson d-statistic. Only some of the data are shown, but note that $\hat{Y}_i$ must be ranked in ascending order

Predicted Y ($\hat{Y}_i$)	Observed Y (Y_i)	Residual $e = (Y_i - \hat{Y}_i)$	Squared residual (e^2)	Successive difference ($e_i - e_{i-1}$)	Squared difference ($e_i - e_{i-1})^2$
8·451	9·0	0·549	0·3014		
9·175	9·9	0·725	0·5256	0·176	0·0310
9·493	8·8	−0·693	0·4802	−1·418	2·0110
. . . .	. . . .	. . . .	. . . .	. . . .	. . . .
11·630	12·7	1·070	1·1449	0·771	0·5944
11·642	8·0	−3·642	13·2642	−4·712	22·2029
11·867	11·3	−0·567	0·3215	3·075	9·4556
12·050	12·3	0·250	0·0625	0·817	0·6675
Sums			58·086		126·960

$n = 46$, we find these figures to be, respectively, 1·475 and 1·566. Using now the method outlined in Figure 9.7, the results are listed in Table 9.4 from which we can conclude that the H_0 of no autocorrelation can be accepted. The areas where the test is uncertain are relatively narrow on this case, but they become larger with smaller samples.

9.6 Simple linear regression in MINITAB

It will be clear from the above account, that the calculation of regression equations and the treatment of residuals is relatively simple from the mathematical point of view, but repetitious, and demanding in terms of time. Both SPSS and MINITAB can be

TABLE 9.4 Acceptance, rejection and indeterminate region on the Durbin-Watson d-distribution for $k = 1$ and $n = 46$ for $\alpha = 0.05$

Range of d	Definition
0–1·475	Reject H_0 (significant positive autocorrelation)
1·475–1·566	Test indeterminate
1·566–2·434	Accept H_0
2·434–2·525	Test indeterminate
2·525–4·0	Reject H_0 (significant negative autocorrelation)

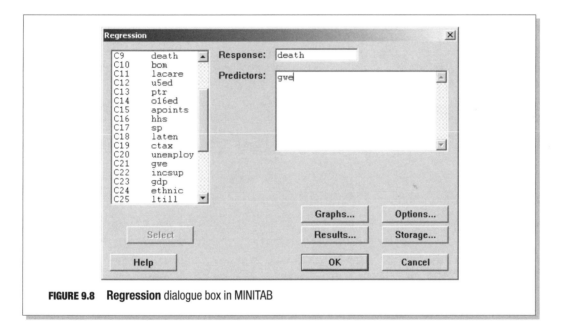

FIGURE 9.8 **Regression** dialogue box in MINITAB

particularly helpful in arriving quickly at reliable results. Let us run MINITAB using the two variables, average gross weekly earnings (gwe) and average death rate (death) for English counties. These data can be found in a MINITAB work file COUNTY.MTW on the CD, and can be loaded directly into the package. The command sequence **Stat > Regression > Regression** will bring up the window in Figure 9.8 in which 'death' is entered as the **Response:** and 'gwe' as the **Predictor:**. The **Options** button will allow us to check the box (not shown) to request the Durbin-Watson statistic if it is required.

The results are presented in tabular form (Figure 9.9), in which the following information is presented:

```
Regression Analysis: death versus gwe

The regression equation is
death = 17.4 - 0.0169 gwe


Predictor        Coef    SE Coef       T      P
Constant       17.420      1.620   10.75  0.000
gwe         -0.016929   0.004168   -4.06  0.000


S = 1.14897   R-Sq = 27.3%   R-Sq(adj) = 25.6%


Analysis of Variance

Source          DF       SS       MS       F      P
Regression       1   21.782   21.782   16.50  0.000
Residual Error  44   58.086    1.320
Total           45   79.869


Unusual Observations

Obs  gwe    death     Fit   SE Fit  Residual  St Resid
 14  341    8.000  11.642    0.254    -3.642    -3.25R
 32  530    9.000   8.451    0.620     0.549     0.57 X
 34  379   13.900  10.999    0.172     2.901     2.55R
 36  366   14.100  11.229    0.191     2.871     2.53R
 39  487    9.900   9.175    0.451     0.725     0.69 X

R denotes an observation with a large standardized residual.
X denotes an observation whose X value gives it large influence.
```

FIGURE 9.9 Standard linear regression output from MINITAB. This example uses data from the file COUNTY.MTW

- the regression equation

- a table that provides the standard error (SE Coef) of each coefficient, a *t*-statistic (T) and probability value for *t* (P). The standard errors for the coefficients reflect, as noted above, the fact that each is based on a sample, and is subject to a degree of imprecision. The associated *t*-statistic is derived from:

$$t = c / (\text{standard error of } c) \tag{9.14}$$

where *c* is the coefficient estimate.

- the next row lists the standard error of the residuals (S), the coefficient of explanation (R-Sq) and the so-called adjusted (adj) coefficient. The latter attempts to describe more accurately the explanation offered by the model, although the differences with the unadjusted coefficient are usually slight.

- the analysis of variance table includes the information displayed in the worked example (Table 9.2). Note that MS is 'mean square' or variance.

- the 'Unusual Observations' is a list of observations that are unusual either because they have large residual values, or because the original observations exercise a large influence of the model. It should, in this context, be noted how the standard error of the estimate (SE Fit) varies, being smallest close to the mean but much larger for

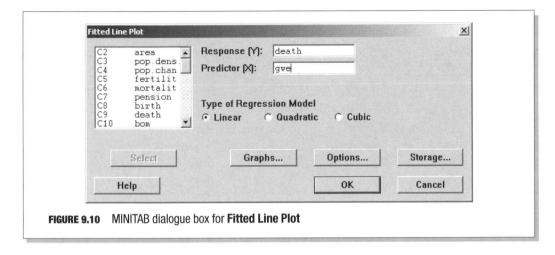

FIGURE 9.10   MINITAB dialogue box for **Fitted Line Plot**

the extreme values of X (the principles of this aspect of regression modelling were introduced in section 9.4).

We can also request a scatter diagram of the data that will, helpfully, include the least-squares line and the confidence (CI) and prediction intervals (PI) for the specified significance level. The commands **Stat > Regression > Fitted Line Plot** will present the window in Figure 9.10. The variables are allocated conventionally with 'death', the dependent variable, entered as **Y** and 'gwe' as **X**. Use the options button to bring up the **Options** window (not shown, but see later Figure 9.16) in which you need only check the **Display confidence interval** and **Display prediction interval** boxes to have them included in the output. All other boxes can be left at default; that for the confidence and prediction limits is 95 per cent. Clicking the **OK** buttons will, as usual, produce the result.

The output graph (Figure 9.11) includes a useful summary of the regression analysis, as well as providing a view of the behaviour of the data points. Notice how the large negative residual, identified in Figure 9.9 as number 14 (county of Rutland) in which the observed death rate is much lower (–3·642 standard errors) than is predicted, stands out. The two large positive residuals, where death rates are higher than predicted, are also clearly anomalous. These are numbers 34 (East Sussex) and 36 (Isle of Wight). Although regression analysis is a method for summarising overall trends, such individual cases can often be usefully examined in more detail and suggest the influence of other variables: an issue pursued in the following chapter on multiple regression.

Attention has already been drawn to the varying width of the prediction and confidence intervals. If precise numbers need to be attached to those intervals, they can be calculated using the MINITAB commands **Stat > Regression > Options**. This brings up the dialogue box in Figure 9.12 in which we enter the value of X for which the prediction and confidence intervals are required. In this example we will use, as we did earlier £380. This figure is entered in the box **Prediction intervals for new observations**. The

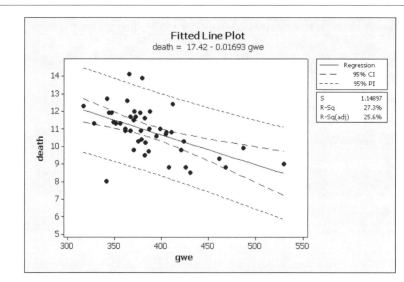

FIGURE 9.11   Output graph from **Fitted Line Plot** option in MINITAB. Notice the inclusion (see text) of the 95 per cent confidence and prediction intervals

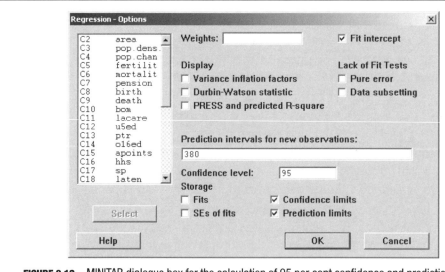

FIGURE 9.12   MINITAB dialogue box for the calculation of 95 per cent confidence and prediction intervals in regression analysis

default confidence level is 95 per cent. Although not elected here, this option can also be used to request a Durbin-Watson statistic. The results (not shown) provide the regression output in Figure 9.9, but appends to it the required confidence and prediction interval limits. This operation has, however, to be repeated for each 'new observation' but is often useful where predicted values are the focus of attention.

9.7 Non-linear regression

Many bivariate relationships in geography are linear in character, but there are a number in which incremental changes in the predictor variable (X) are not accompanied by correspondingly uniform changes in the dependent variable (Y). Such relationships are said to be *non-linear* and are summarised by curves, and not by straight lines. This is not, however, to suggest that a best-fit curve, as opposed to a best-fit straight line, cannot be produced. The difficulty often lies in the fact that there are many possible forms of non-linear relationships. The general character of the equations of curves has been introduced in section 2.5 to which reference can usefully be made.

The following sections deal with only one example of non-linear relationships, but the methods with which it can be explored by SPSS and MINITAB apply to a much wider range, some of which will be briefly mentioned. The easiest way to determine if a relationship is obviously non-linear is to construct a scatter plot using either SPSS or MINITAB.

Figure 9.13 summarises the relationship between population density and distance from the centre of a city, in this case for Kingston-upon-Hull (East Yorkshire). The raw data are available in files HULL.MTW and HULL.SAV on the CD. It is clear that density

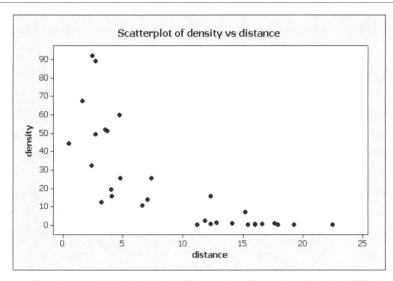

FIGURE 9.13   Changing population density with distance from the centre of the city of Kingston-upon-Hull (*Source*: Office of Population Censuses and Surveys 1973). This graph was plotted using MINITAB **Graph > Scatterplot** commands

does not 'decay' linearly with distance, but falls away quickly close to the centre, but at a slower rate as distance increases. It is equally clear that it would be inappropriate to estimate a linear regression equation to describe this relationship. So what can be done? The first task in any such exercise is to select from the many different forms of non-linear equation that might summarise the relationship. Although there are, in theory, many hundreds of such equations, in reality the choice is often reduced to one of a number of 'families' of curves. The most common of those useful to geographers are:

the simple power curve	$Y = aX^b$	(9.15)
the simple exponential curve	$Y = ae^{bX}$	(9.16)
the simple logarithmic curve	$Y = a + b \log X$	(9.17)
the quadratic curve	$Y = a + bX + cX^2$	(9.18)
the cubic curve	$Y = a + bX + cX^2 + dX^3$	(9.19)

Equations 9.15 and 9.17 have been discussed and illustrated in section 2.5, but none of them is notably different from the now familiar linear equation $Y = a + bX$. All have one dependent term (Y) and one predictor term (X). They also have constants a, b and, in some cases, c and d, all of which require estimation before the curve can be plotted or used for predictive purposes. Differences lie in the inclusion in Equation 9.16 of the universal constant e (which is equivalent to $2\cdot7183\ldots$ as explained in section 2.3), and in the arithmetic roles of the constants a and b. The latter acts either as a multiplication factor (as it does in the linear model), or as a power. The constant a can be either additive (Equations 9.17, 9.18 and 9.19) or multiplicative (Equations 9.15 and 9.16). In the case of curve selection to describe the example of population decline with distance from city centre, we are fortunate and can be guided by the fact that it is often suggested that such a relationship is *exponential* in form, and the change in the value of the dependent term is fixed by proportion, i.e. the population density might fall by 10 per cent over the first kilometre from the centre, then by 10 per cent of that new value over the next kilometre, and so on. The *negative exponential* form of the curve has other characteristics that make it suitable in situations such as these. First, it is *asymptotic* with respect to the X axis, i.e. it can approach ever more closely to the axis, but not cross it. Thus, negative values of Y are impossible; a reasonable restriction when summarising population densities. Secondly, the curve originates on the Y axis at a point equivalent to the value for a – as it does in the linear case – from where Y decreases with increasing X. The model assumes, therefore, that the population density is greatest at the city centre and decreases outwards from that focus. In many situations, however, there will be no such a priori reasoning, and a certain amount of 'trial and error' might be required to determine which family of curves provides the optimum description of the relationship and, help-fully, both SPSS and MINITAB allow different models to be easily tested on the same data set. In general, Equations 9.18 and 9.19 offer greater flexibility, but at the cost of lengthier expressions.

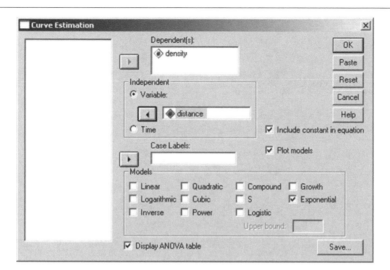

FIGURE 9.14 The SPSS **Curve Estimation** dialogue box specifying an exponential model with a full ANOVA report table

9.8 Estimating non-linear parameters using SPSS

Using the example of the population density for 31 civil parishes and electoral wards around the city of Kingston-upon-Hull, we have hypothesised that the relationship between the two variables (density and distance from the city centre) might be exponential in character. The data are available on the CD in the file HULL.SAV. The SPSS command sequence to examine these data and the exponential hypothesis is **Analyze > Regression > Curve Estimation**. This will bring up the window in Figure 9.14, in which we can specify the Dependent (density) and the Independent (distance) terms in the now familiar fashion. We can also specify the form of non-linear function with which to describe the relationship between the two. Several are available, but we should check the boxes for **Exponential**, and, to ensure a full report, for **Display ANOVA table**. We should 'untick' the default **Linear** box, which would otherwise give us results for the linear as well as the exponential model.

The results of this exercise (Figure 9.15) show firstly that the two variables are highly correlated ($r = -0.897$) although, rather confusingly, described as 'multiple R'. The output is otherwise broadly similar to that in Figure 9.9 with estimates of R^2, adjusted R^2 and the standard error (of the residuals). The ANOVA table reveals also that the model is significant at the 0.01 level (the significance of F is 0.000 and less than this critical value), with an F-ratio of 118.97. The best-fit parameters of the model are provided in a form similar to that for the linear output (Figure 9.9). The coefficient a ('constant') has a value of 91.454, while b is -0.2984. The associated t-statistics and significance values for

```
Dependent variable.. DENSITY          Method.. EXPONENT

Listwise Deletion of Missing Data

Multiple R           .89667
R Square             .80401
Adjusted R Square    .79725
Standard Error       .95786

                Analysis of Variance:

              DF    Sum of Squares      Mean Square

Regression     1         109.15057         109.15057
Residuals     29          26.60727           .91749

F =     118.96624     Signif F =   .0000

------------------- Variables in the Equation -------------------

Variable                 B      SE B       Beta       T   Sig T

DISTANCE          -.298380   .027356   -.896666  -10.907   .0000
(Constant)        91.454450 28.331356             3.228   .0031
```

FIGURE 9.15 SPSS ANOVA report table for the exponential model of population density change with distance from the centre of Kingston-upon-Hull

both constants are also given. Both constants are highly significant and when placed into Equation 9.16, the equation that expresses this 'best fit' expression becomes:

$$Y = 91·454e^{-0·2984X} \tag{9.20}$$

in which the best estimate of the city centre population density (where $X = 0·0$) is 91·454 people/sq. km, with density declining as distance increases. Although the details are not shown (the readers are invited to undertake the task for themselves), the results of fitting other functions to the data using the same procedures all produce lower F-ratios of explained to unexplained variance: 66·6 for the power function, 41·64 for the logarithmic, 26·6 for the quadratic and only 17·34 for the cubic. On this evidence, our initial hypothesis regarding the exponential character of this relationship is justified.

9.9 Estimating non-linear parameters in MINITAB

Non-linear regression can also be conducted in MINITAB. The command sequence **Stat > Regression > Fitted Line Plot** will bring up the window already shown in Figure 9.10 in which the variables can be allocated to the **Y** and **X** categories as necessary. However, at this stage, only the **Quadratic** and **Cubic** non-linear functions are available. Should we wish to test either the power, exponential or logarithmic form we need to log-transform one or both of the variables. Logarithmic transformations have the important effect of linearising these non-linear relationships, and in this transformed state the **Linear** option will provide the required equation parameters although, as shown below, some further

TABLE 9.5   Summary of transformations required to linearise different families of curves

Expression	X term	Y term
$Y = a + b \log X$	Convert to logs	No transformation needed
$Y = ae^{bX}$	No transformation needed	Convert to logs
$Y = aX^b$	Convert to logs	Convert to logs

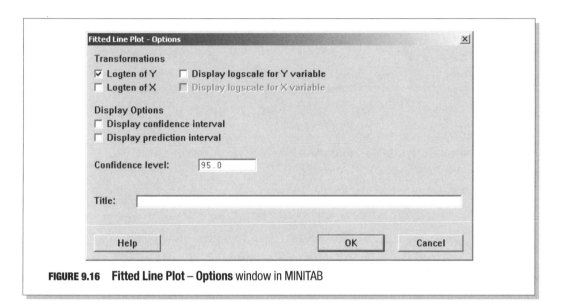

FIGURE 9.16   **Fitted Line Plot – Options** window in MINITAB

manipulation of the results is required. Table 9.5 summarises the different logarithmic transformations that are required to linearise the exponential, power and logarithmic functions. In order to fit the exponential function to the data we need log-transform only the Y (density) variable. This is done by clicking the **Options** button to bring up the window in Figure 9.16. The box **Logten of Y** is ticked (although not requested in this example, you can also reset the confidence level and request that confidence and prediction intervals are plotted).

Clicking on the **OK** buttons will bring up the results. The tabulated output is not shown, but is set out in a similar fashion to that in Figure 9.15 listing the equation, its coefficients, R^2 values and various standard errors. Helpfully, a graph of the fitted curve is automatically produced (Figure 9.17), which shows the degree to which the exponential curve summarises the scatter of points. It will, however, be readily noticed that the 'best-fit' equation at the head of the plot differs from that given in SPSS, and is in the form:

logten(density) = 1·961 – 0·1296(distance)

In common with the other two functions (the logarithmic and the power), the equation is expressed using the log-transformed elements; in this case **logten(density)** instead of

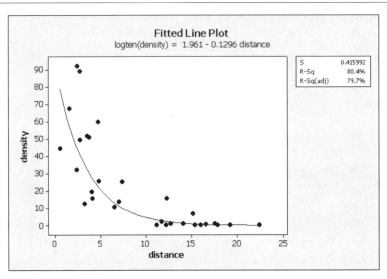

FIGURE 9.17 Graph output in MINITAB showing the result of fitting an exponential curve to the population density/distance data for Kingston-upon-Hull

density. To express the model in its untransformed and curvilinear state, those items have to be antilogged (see section 2.3 for guidance on this procedure). The coefficient *a* (with a value of 1·961) is always expressed in terms of the *Y* variable and is therefore in logarithmic form and requires antilogging, which gives 91·41. Coefficient *b* is more complicated, and in the exponential model is contained within the expression *b*log*e*, and can be unravelled only with some arithmetic manipulation. The output gives a value of –0·1296, and recalling that *e* = 2·7183, we have

$$-0\cdot1296 = b \times \log e = b \times \log(2\cdot7183) = b \times 0\cdot4343$$

from which it follows that

$$b = -0\cdot1296 / 0\cdot4343 = -0\cdot2984$$

and therefore, as before

$$Y = 91\cdot41 e^{-0\cdot2984X} \tag{9.21}$$

Rounding errors, always a problem in these situations, account for the slight differences between these results and those in Equation 9.20. Readers are encouraged to use the data sets on the CD (HULL.MTW) to rerun these data using the power functions (log transform *X* and *Y*) and the logarithmic function (log transform only *X*). Conversion of the results of these operations is simpler. In the case of the power function the equation is given in the form:

$$\text{logten}(Y) = a_1 + b_1 (\text{logten}(X)) \tag{9.22}$$

where both estimated $a_1 + b_1$ can be antilogged without, as in the exponential case, further adjustment, to provide the a and b terms in Equation 9.15. However, no such antilogging of the coefficients is necessary in the logarithmic form

$$Y = a + b (\text{logten}(X))$$

and the equation is evaluated simply by taking logarithmic values of X.

In all non-linear cases, the SPSS and MINITAB output provides not only the coefficient values (or equivalent terms that can be re-expressed after conversion), but sufficient information to test any null hypothesis of no explanation of the Y in terms of X, and to compare the efficiency of one family of non-linear models with any other, thereby identifying the most appropriate of them.

10

Multiple regression and correlation

10.1 Measuring multivariate relationships

MANY OF THE PROBLEMS studied by geographers are of a complex nature, involving a number of interacting variables. In such circumstances bivariate statistical methods are inadequate tools, and attention needs to turn to multivariate methods. Here, again, the procedures depend upon the nature of the data and the objectives of the research. Multiple regression is a direct development of the 'simple' methods introduced in Chapter 9. It allows hypotheses of no explanation of the dependent variable to be tested, and the nature of variable interactions to be explored by objective methods. The importance of all forms of multivariate methods cannot be overstated. We have seen in Chapter 9 that we would be fortunate if the behaviour of any one geographical variable could be satisfactorily accounted for by only one other, and it is often the case that high degrees of 'explanation' can be achieved only by using multiple regression in which two or more predictor variables are adopted.

As Figure 10.1 shows, there exists a wide range of multivariate methods. We can distinguish those concerned with the analysis of dependence, in which one variable is identified for study and is then examined in terms of its dependence on others. For example, in multiple regression we attempt to account for variation in the dependent variable through variation in a number of predictor variables. Similarly, *canonical correlation* techniques extend this analysis to examine the interdependence between groups of variables – the so-called *predictor* and the *criterion* groups. As such it provides a link to the second group of techniques that are concerned more specifically with the interdependence that might exist between all variables with no reference to any particular one of them as being 'dependent'. This interaction may range from complete mutual independence to close interdependence where each variable is a function of the others. In these cases we can use *principal component analysis* or *factor analysis* to transform the original data into a smaller number of new, usually uncorrelated, 'synthetic' variables, each of which represents the collective behaviour of groups of the original variables. There exist also methods by which multivariate approaches can be used to place individuals into groups or categories. These are useful in situations where

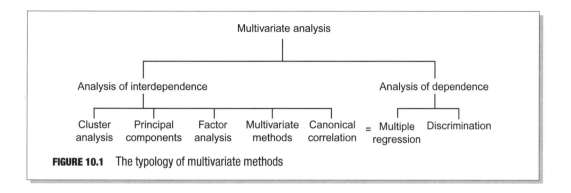

FIGURE 10.1 The typology of multivariate methods

we want to identify similarities between individuals or groups. *Cluster analysis* and *discriminant analysis* fall into this category. Principal components, factor, cluster and discriminant analyses are all reviewed in the following chapters, meanwhile we will concentrate on multiple regression and correlation as direct developments from their 'simple' counterparts in Chapter 9.

10.2 Multiple linear regression

Multiple regression attempts to predict the variation in a single dependent variable (Y) on the basis of two or more predictor terms. The multiple regression equation takes the form:

$$Y = a + b_1X_1 + b_2X_2 + \ldots b_nX_n \pm e \qquad (10.1)$$

Equation 10.1

a = intercept term

b_1 to b_n = partial regression coefficients

e = random error term

The principal purpose in undertaking multiple regression is to improve the degree of explanation of the dependent variable. So let us see how we can take the simple model used in Chapter 9 and, by the inclusion of an additional variable increase its predictive capacity. You will find a copy of the complete data file (COUNTY.SAV and COUNTY.MTW) in the CD that comes with this book. The model, as we left it in Chapter 9, predicted English death rates on the basis of gross weekly earnings, but our data set includes other variables among which is household size. The latter has a strong correlation with death rates ($r = -0.827$) and we might suppose that this variable may

TABLE 10.1 Change in regression model parameters from including a new variable (household size) in the existing simple model that relies only on gross weekly earnings to predict death rates

Predictor(s) of death rate	Coefficient of explanation (R^2)	Standard error of estimate	Regression (explained) sum of squares	F-value
Gross weekly earnings	0·273	1·149	21·782	16·50
Gross weekly earnings and household size	0·764	0·662	61·023	69·62
Change	+0·491	−0·487	+39·241	+53·12

also be an important controlling factor. This new, least-squares multiple regression equation is given by:

$$Y = 56·506 - 17·685X_1 - 0·00963X_2$$

Where X_1 is household size and X_2 is gross weekly earnings. Notice how the value of the regression coefficient for earnings has changed from the 0·01693 of the simple case (see section 9.2) and, more importantly, the effect that the inclusion has on such important parameters as the coefficient of explanation, the standard error of estimate and the model's F-value (Table 10.1). The means by which this new, multivariate, model can be estimated will be reviewed later, meanwhile we should observe that in every respect the improvement in the regression model is notable, and suggests that the new variable makes an important contribution to predicting death rates. Not all variables in the data set could be expected, however, to provide such marked levels of improved explanation, and the methods by which we select the most appropriate of them will occupy much of this chapter.

In the case of simple (bivariate) regression or correlation, the scatter of points can be represented in graphical form. This cannot be done in the multivariate case in which each variable (dependent and independent) requires an axis for its representation. Thus one dependent and three predictor variables takes us into the unimaginable realm of four-dimensional space. Such geometrical oddities notwithstanding, the principle of adopting the least-squares criterion remains important, and is adopted to define the 'best-fit surfaces' through n-dimensional space. This concept can be illustrated by the case of two predictors and one dependent variable – a three-dimensional example – and is demonstrated in Figure 10.2 where a 'best-fit plane' can be seen to pass through a scatter of points, each of which is located in three-dimensional space by reference to the three axes or dimensions, namely the Y, X_1 and X_2 observations for each data point. The error term in the simple case is represented graphically by the 'distance' above or below the best-fit line and the observed values of Y, in this case these 'distances' are those of individual observations above or below the best-fit, two-dimensional plane.

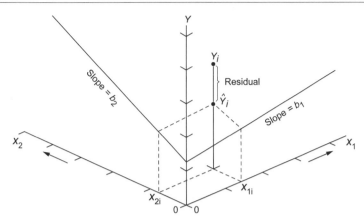

FIGURE 10.2 Representation of a regression plane in three-dimensional space. Any point can be uniquely located by reference to its value on the three axes (dimensions). The residual or error term is the difference between the observed value of Y and its predicted counterpart ($\hat{Y}$)

In most cases the assistance of SPSS or MINITAB is needed to calculate the least-squares parameters for Equation 10.1. The derived coefficients are correctly termed the *partial regression coefficients*, and they measure the effect that the predictor term in question has on the dependent term when the other predictors are present but, importantly, held constant. In this sense the multiple regression model is more correctly expressed as follows:

$$Y = a + b_{01 \cdot 2}X_1 + b_{02 \cdot 1}X_2 \ldots \pm e \qquad (10.2)$$

In which subscript 0 represents the dependent term (Y), and $b_{01 \cdot 2}$ is the partial regression coefficient representing X_1's influence on Y with variable X_2 held constant *but not excluded*. Similarly, the coefficient $b_{02 \cdot 1}$ represents X_2's influence on Y when X_1 is held constant. In geometrical terms (Figure 10.2) the two partial coefficients of a two-predictor model are the slopes of the regression plane where they intersect the vertical planes of their respective axes.

It should, however, be remembered that the partial regression coefficients, in common with their simple counterparts, are *scale dependent* and have magnitudes that are partly determined by the units in which X_i and Y are measured. If, for example, we have a model that predicts rainfall from a number of independent terms, and the data are converted from inches to millimetres, the magnitude of the partial regression coefficients will change, even though the underlying relationship does not. This raises a potential problem in multiple regression because we should not be tempted into assessing the importance of the each predictor by reference to its partial regression coefficient, and large values do not imply greater importance. Such comparisons are best made through the medium of *beta weights*. These can be determined using Equation 10.3 that has the effect of standardising the coefficients and allowing the responses of the dependent variable to each of the independent terms to be assessed more directly.

$$B_i = b_i(s_x/s_y) \tag{10.3}$$

Equation 10.3

B_i = beta coefficient for variable X_i

b_i = partial regression coefficient for variable X_i

s_x = standard deviation of variable X_i

s_y = standard deviation of dependent variable Y

The use of beta coefficients is illustrated in the earlier example in which death rates (Y) for English counties is predicted on the basis of household size (X_1) and mean gross weekly earnings (X_2). The multiple regression equation was shown to be:

$$Y = 56 \cdot 506 - 17 \cdot 685X_1 - 0 \cdot 00963X_2$$

The coefficient for X_1 shows the change of death rate with respect to household size, but holding constant the gross weekly earnings. The coefficient for X_2 shows the rate of change of death rate with gross weekly earnings, but now holding constant the household size. Both partial regression coefficients are negative, indicating that death rates decrease as each of the predictors increase. But these are unstandardised coefficients from which it would be wrong to conclude that household size has a much greater influence on death rates than do gross weekly earnings. The corresponding beta coefficients were found to be $-0\cdot736$ (for X_1) and $-0\cdot297$ (for X_2). We may now conclude, with greater certainty, that the household size has a more marked influence than gross weekly income, but the distinction is much less than might have been inferred from the original regression coefficients.

10.3 Multiple and partial correlation

In the previous section attention was focused on the character of the multiple regression equation, and the nature of its components, but in many instances our initial interest may lie with the explanatory capability of the model as a whole. This can be found from the *multiple coefficient of explanation* (R^2), which is linked to the *multiple correlation coefficient* (R). The latter is a direct counterpart to the simple correlation coefficient (r in section 8.2), but measures the association between the dependent variable and, in effect, a group of two or more predictor variables. It can be found by the decomposition of the total sum of squares of the dependent variable about its mean (ss_y). In common with simple regression, this can be expressed in two components; that which is explained by the regression model (ss_r), and that which cannot, the so-called residual or error sum of squares (ss_e). In all cases $ss_r + ss_e = ss_y$. The multiple correlation coefficient is derived from:

$$R^2 = ss_r / ss_y = \frac{\Sigma(\hat{Y} - \bar{Y})^2}{\Sigma(Y_i - \bar{Y})^2}$$

(10.4)

Equation 10.4

$\hat{Y}$ = predicted value of Y

Y_i = observed value of Y

$\bar{Y}$ = mean of Y

Equation 10.4 expresses the proportion of the variation in the dependent variable that is accounted for by the collective variation of the predictors, and its square root gives the multiple correlation coefficient. It does not, by itself, confirm the significance of the regression model (that will be tested later), but it often acts as a useful initial indicator of its general utility.

In the earlier example (Table 10.1) the R^2 value was 0·764, indicating that 76·4 per cent of the variation of county-based death rates could be accounted for by variation in the two predictor variables. In section 9.3 the F-ratio was determined by reference to the explained (regression) and unexplained (residual) variances, each of which were obtained by dividing their corresponding sums of squares by their respective degrees of freedom. In multiple regression we employ the same principle, with the difference that the regression and residual degrees of freedom have to take account of the number of predictors (k), which will now be greater than 1. The equations and quantities needed to evaluate the sums of squares and variances are summarised in Table 10.2. In later sections we will see how these quantities are presented in the computer package outputs.

TABLE 10.2 Summary of quantities needed to test the statistical significance of a multiple regression model, where k = number of predictors and n = sample size. The variances are found by dividing the sum of squares by the corresponding degrees of freedom

Source of variation	Sum of squares	Degrees of freedom
Regression	$\Sigma(\hat{Y} - \bar{Y})^2$	k
Residual	$\Sigma(Y - \hat{Y})^2$	$n - k - 1$
Total	$\Sigma(Y - \bar{Y})^2$	$n - 1$

In the same way as we examined partial regression coefficients, so too can we study *partial correlation coefficients*. These measure the correlation between the dependent variable and each of the individual predictors but, again, holding constant all other predictors in the model. They share with simple correlation coefficients the characteristic of varying only between +1 and −1 and are not, therefore, scale dependent. The partial correlation coefficient between one variable and, say, two others would be written as $r_{01 \cdot 2}$ where 0 and 1 represent the two variables to be correlated, and 2 the third, included but constant, item. Similarly $r_{02 \cdot 1}$ represents the partial correlation between variables 0 and 2, but with 1 now being held constant. This convention can be extended to include as many variables as necessary. Correlations are estimated for only two variables at a time, all others being held constant. Thus, with four variables we might have $r_{01 \cdot 23}$. They are, therefore, quite different from the multiple correlations described above, and should not be confused with them. Partial correlations are extremely useful when we want to examine the intrinsic association between two variables in complex multivariate situations.

The number of 'controlled' variables determines the order of the correlation. Simple correlations are *zero-order*. First-order partial correlations have only one controlled variable, but can be derived from the various zero-order correlations (r_{01}, r_{02} and r_{12}) between each of the variables in the data set. Thus:

$$r_{01 \cdot 2} = \frac{r_{01} - (r_{02})\,(r_{12})}{\sqrt{(1 - r_{02}^2)}\,\sqrt{(1 - r_{12}^2)}} \qquad (10.5)$$

The equation can be easily adapted to provide any one of the three partial correlations possible with the data set ($r_{02 \cdot 1}$ and $r_{2 \cdot 01}$). For higher order partial correlation we must rely on computer packages such as SPSS and MINITAB.

Because correlation coefficients (partial and zero-order) are scale-independent they provide another easy means of checking the associations between variables in multivariate data sets. In this sense they are similar to, but not identical with, beta weights. The latter indicate the numerical response of the dependent variable to changes in the independent variable; as such, they are a measure of 'numerical sensitivity'. In contrast, the partial correlations provide a measure of how much of the total variability in the dependent variable can be accounted for by variability in the predictor(s).

The relationships between zero-order and partial correlation coefficients are not always obvious or predictable. In many cases the move from zero-order to partial correlations will not only lead to a change in the absolute correlation between the two principal variables in question, it might even lead to a change in sign. This point can be illustrated by considering again the example of death rates. Table 10.3 provides the matrix of zero-order and first-order partial correlations between the three variables. The two first-order partial correlations reveal a slightly different picture and, in both cases (death rate with gross weekly earnings, $r_{01 \cdot 2}$ and death rate with household size, $r_{02 \cdot 1}$) the

TABLE 10.3 Zero-order and first-order partial correlations for English county-based statistics of death rate, income and household size

	Y	X_1	X_2
Death rates (Y)	1·000		
Gross weekly earnings (X_1) (partial coefficient – X_2 constant)	−0·522 (−0·503)	1·00	
Household size (X_2) (partial coefficient – X_1 constant)	−0·827 (−0·822)	0·306	1·00

correlations remain negative but are slightly weaker than their zero-order counterparts. In some measure this is because the household size and gross weekly earnings variables are themselves positively correlated, and this slightly obscures, and inflates in this case, the relationship when viewed through the medium of zero-order correlations. Partial correlations help to remove this distorting effect by controlling the third (or further) variables in the data set. Because of this potential to obscure the true character of statistical association between variables, researchers are often advised that the various predictors in their models should not be correlated between themselves. This is, however, a largely unrealisable ambition, and raises thereby the thorny issue of *multicollinearity*.

10.4 Data requirements and multicollinearity

Multiple regression models impose the same demands on the data as do the simple models (see Chapter 9). Each variable must be examined to check if the distributions are acceptably close to the normal case. In some instances, data transformations may be needed, in other cases they may not. Where mixed transformed and untransformed variables are included, the multiple regression model may assume some peculiar forms that need to be recalled to mind when the results are being interpreted, or predictions of the dependent variable are being made. Such transformations are legitimate, but may obscure the outcomes.

These cautionary observations notwithstanding, it is multicollinearity that most often creates problems. The term refers to the situation where correlation exists between several predictor variables. When two predictors are strongly correlated their respective zero-order correlations with the dependent variable may often suggest similarly strong degrees of association to exist. The difficulty of multicollinearity results from the fact that in multiple regression we might be tempted to employ two such variables, both of which appear to have a strong correlation with the dependent item, only to find that one of them emerges as having a very weak partial influence, and its seemingly strong zero-order association results only from its correlation with the other. To a limited extent, this was the case in the current example. We should be alerted to such a possibility by the zero-order correlation matrix, in which such multicollinearity can be quickly identified. Equally, if only a slight increase in the multiple correlation coefficient over the zero-order correlation is found after inclusion of a seemingly well correlated second predictor, we can reasonably conclude multicollinearity to exist. Where, on the other hand, the addition of further variables to the multiple correlation model yields significant increases to the coefficient we can be confident that the new variable is making an independent contribution to our attempts to 'explain' variation of the dependent term.

Where many variables are involved the situation may be difficult to interpret. Generally, the more widespread is the multicollinearity within the set of predictors, the more ambiguous and less reliable are the results of multiple regression. Only by careful inspection of the computer output can the worst pitfalls be avoided, and the temptation to include, with little preliminary thought, as many variables as possible because of the ease with which the software can handle large data sets must be resisted.

Depending on the degree of multicollinearity, two possible methods are available to solve the problem. One is to use an objective 'filtering' method such as *stepwise regression*, in which variables are added or subtracted successively from the data set until an optimum resolution with respect to the number of variables and the degree of explanation has been achieved. Alternatively, if all variables are included we might then adopt factor analysis or principal components analysis (see Chapter 11) to simplify the data set and to produce a series of orthogonal (uncorrelated) synthetic variables each of which represents the combined effects of different combinations of the original, much larger, set. Multiple regression might then proceed using these new 'variables'. But these methods are complex and computationally demanding. In addition they might, again, create problems at the important stage of interpretation of the results.

10.5 Using SPSS to determine partial correlation coefficients

Partial regression coefficients of any order can easily be determined using SPSS. To obtain the results given in Table 10.3 above, the following sequence of commands were used: **Analyze > Correlate > Partial**. This produced the dialogue box in Figure 10.3. The two principal variables to be correlated are transferred to the **Variables** box, and the one (or more) variables that are to be held constant are transferred to the **Controlling for** box. In this example we are partially correlating death rates with gross weekly earnings, but holding household size constant. The two-tailed statistics are produced by default, but can be changed if necessary to one-tailed. Clicking the **OK** button produces the matrix of results (Figure 10.4) in which the partial correlation ($r_{01 \cdot 2} = -0.5034$ in this case) is given together with its random probability (p) and the degrees of freedom (notice that one degree is lost for each variable in the correlation set). In common with other such measures, the partial correlation coefficient can be regarded as significant and the H_0 of

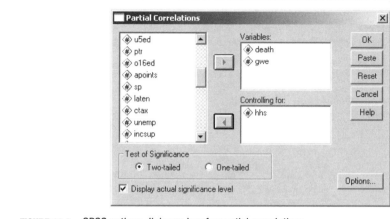

FIGURE 10.3   SPSS options dialogue box for partial correlations

```
     -  P A R T I A L    C O R R E L A T I O N    C O E F F I C I E N T S  -

    Controlling for..    HHS

                    DEATH        GWE

    DEATH          1.0000      -.5034
                  (     0)     (    43)
                   P=  .        P=  .000

    GWE            -.5034      1.0000
                  (    43)     (     0)
                   P=  .000     P=  .

    (Coefficient  /  (D.F.)  /  2-tailed Significance)

    "  .  " is printed if a coefficient cannot be computed
```

FIGURE 10.4   Screen output in SPSS for partial correlation analysis

no explanation rejected only if p is less than the selected significance level (usually 0·05 or 0·01). MINITAB can also be used to produce partial correlation coefficients, but the procedure is complex and is not described here (see CD file MINITAB7).

10.6 Multiple regression modelling with SPSS

Turning now to multiple regression models, these can be easily produced using SPSS or MINITAB. The command sequence is all but identical to that used in simple regression: **Analyze > Regression > Linear**. The difference lies in the selection of variables, and in this case two or more predictors can be transferred into the **Independent(s)** box (Figure 10.5).

The manner in which the results are displayed (Figure 10.6) is broadly the same as in the simple case and has three important elements.

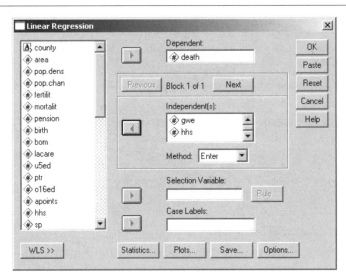

FIGURE 10.5 **Linear Regression** dialogue box in SPSS set up for a multiple regression model in which gross weekly earnings (gwe) and household size (hhs) are predictors and death rate (death) the dependent variable

Model Summary

Model	R	R Square	Adjusted R Square	Std. Error of the Estimate
1	.874[a]	.764	.753	.6620

a. Predictors: (Constant), HHS, GWE

ANOVA[b]

Model		Sum of Squares	df	Mean Square	F	Sig.
1	Regression	61.023	2	30.511	69.617	.000[a]
	Residual	18.846	43	.438		
	Total	79.869	45			

a. Predictors: (Constant), HHS, GWE

b. Dependent Variable: DEATH

Coefficients[a]

Model		Unstandardized Coefficients		Standardized Coefficients	t	Sig.
		B	Std. Error	Beta		
1	(Constant)	56.506	4.235		13.343	.000
	GWE	-9.63E-03	.003	-.297	-3.820	.000
	HHS	-17.685	1.869	-.736	-9.462	.000

a. Dependent Variable: DEATH

FIGURE 10.6 SPSS results for a multiple regression model predicting death rate (DEATH) from household size (HHS) and gross weekly earnings (GWE)

- The Model Summary gives the multiple correlation coefficient ($R = 0.874$) and the multiple coefficient of explanation ($R^2 = 0.764$) and the standard error of estimate.

- The ANOVA table shows the partition of variance (mean square) between the explained (regression) and unexplained (residual) components, giving an F-value in this example of 69·617. The associated Sig. Value is the random probability of F. Where Sig. is less than the significance level, the H_0 of no explanation by the regression model can be rejected.

- The statistics for the individual elements of the model are given in the Coefficients table. 'Constant' refers to the intercept term, while the partial regression coefficients are indicated by the codes given to each predictor (GWE and HHS). Notice, however, the use of *floating point* format for the GWE coefficient in which –9·63E–03 indicates that the term is –0·00963. Also given are the beta weights (standardised coefficients). Each term has an associated standard error, t-value and significance that reflects the fact that the results are based on what is, in effect, a sample. These statistics reflect sampling variability (see section 9.4) and the associated measure of uncertainty in the derived model parameters.

The regression equation could be written as:

$$\text{death} = 56.506 - 17.685 \,(\text{hhs}) - 0.00963 \,(\text{gwe})$$

It is shown to be significant at the 0·01 level as Sig. = 0·000, and both predictor coefficients appear to be important, having high t-statistics.

10.7 Stepwise regression using MINITAB

Stepwise regression is an objective procedure that helps the researcher to rationalise a data set with a large number of variables. MINITAB conducts this complex process in such a way that the results are easily understood, and will be exemplified below. The SPSS procedures are similar and activated by selecting **Stepwise** in the **Method** box options in Figure 10.5. In both systems, the researcher includes as many predictors as he or she wishes, and the system sorts the various combinations to find the optimum that balances the number of predictors against the degree of explained variance. This objective method is always to be preferred to the inclusion of a large number of variables into some fixed model determined by the researcher in the hope that something suitable will emerge.

In the following example we will use a number of variables in the data file COUNTY.MTW. We will again specify death rate as the dependent term, but now ask MINITAB to examine eight additional variables (household size, percentage single parent families, average council tax, percentage unemployment, gross weekly earnings, percentage of population on income support, proportion ethnic population and crime rate) as possible predictors. Some of these we might expect to have a greater influence than others, but it will be interesting to see what optimum model MINITAB produces.

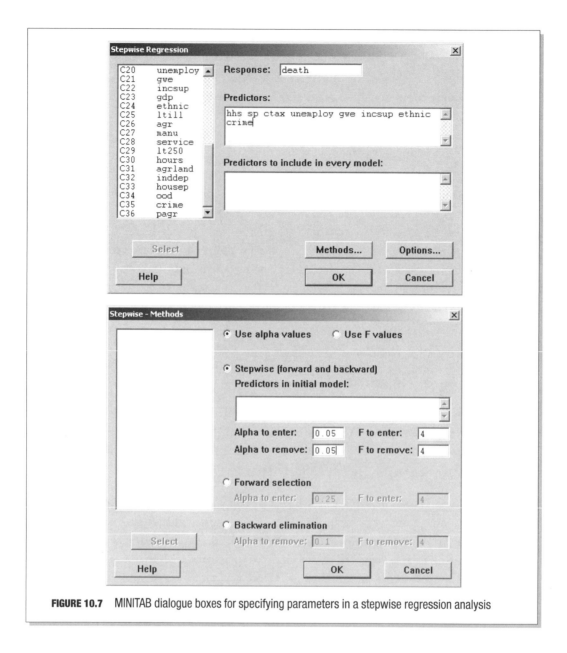

FIGURE 10.7 MINITAB dialogue boxes for specifying parameters in a stepwise regression analysis

The command sequence **Stat > Regression > Stepwise** will produce the dialogue boxes in Figure 10.7. In the first window we specify the dependent variable (**Response**) and the various predictors. We must also remember to click the **Methods** button, as we need to indicate which stepwise method to use, and how the system should determine whether or not a variable should be accepted into the regression set. Three methods are available to us: *stepwise* in which variables can be added or removed to yield the optimum solution; *forward selection* in which variables are added but once added cannot

```
Results for: COUNTY.MTW

Stepwise Regression: death versus birth, sp, ...

   Alpha-to-Enter: 0.05  Alpha-to-Remove: 0.05

Response is death on 8 predictors, with N = 46

Step              1        2        3
Constant      57.95    56.51    57.21

hhs           -19.9    -17.7    -18.4
T-Value       -9.76    -9.46   -10.06
P-Value       0.000    0.000    0.000

gwe                   -0.0096  -0.0093
T-Value                 -3.82    -3.82
P-Value                 0.000    0.000

sp                               0.156
T-Value                           2.12
P-Value                          0.040

S             0.757    0.662    0.637
R-Sq          68.40    76.40    78.68
R-Sq(adj)     67.68    75.31    77.15
Mallows C-p    17.9      4.7      2.4
```

FIGURE 10.8 MINITAB results for stepwise regression using socio-economic variables thought to control death rate

be removed; and *backwards elimination*, which begins with all variables and successively removes them, after which they cannot be re-entered. In most situations the more flexible **Stepwise** method is preferred, and that is the case here. The system needs also to know, by either the statistical significance of the variable, or the change that it makes to the model's *F*-value, whether it is to be included or removed. In this example we will specify choice by significance (**Alpha to enter** and **Alpha to remove**). To do this click on the **Use alpha values** button and enter the chosen significance level (0·05) in the two boxes. Notice that we can specify, should we wish to do so, particular variables that have to be included in every model, or a variable that has to be included in the initial step. These options are not taken here, but can be useful if the researcher has particular insight into the problem and knows certain variables to be important irrespective of the statistical parameters that have been set.

The results (Figure 10.8) show, step by step, how the model has evolved and the order in which variables were added (using the selection criteria noted above). The output identifies three predictors as the optimum model, these being household size, gross weekly income and percentage on income support (incsup). Each variable's partial regression coefficient at each stage is listed (but note that they change as the model develops), together with the associated T-statistics and P-values. At the foot of each column can be found the standard error of estimate (S), the R^2 value and Mallows C-p statistic. As the model improves, the standard error of estimate decreases, while R^2 increases. The Mallows C-p statistic is specific to stepwise regression and measures the efficiency of the model based on its standard error, the number of terms (including the intercept), and standard error of the model that includes all variables in the data set. An efficient model is one in which the C-p statistic is close to the number of terms. In the current example, the final C-p statistic is 2·6 and not greatly different to the number of terms in the model. The final model is such that further additions to the regression set will not significantly increase the 'explained' sum of squares, while removal of any one of the variables would lead to a significant decrease.

This form of output is, however, limited, and should the researcher want to know more about the final stepwise model, a multiple regression exercise using the selected variables should be run in which, for example, the ANOVA table, beta weights etc. can be examined. It is worth examining the degree to which the selected optimum model improves upon the two-predictor version summarised in Table 10.1. The MINITAB results using the three predictors can be found using the command sequence **Stat > Regression**, which brings up the same window as shown in Figure 10.7. The variables are entered as usual, and produce a multiple regression equation with the form:

$$\text{death} = 52{\cdot}87 - 16{\cdot}8 \text{ (hhs)} - 0{\cdot}0080 \text{ (gwe)} + 0{\cdot}113 \text{ (incsup)}$$

The other derived statistics for this equation are given in Table 10.4, which also includes the summary of results from the original two-variable model in Table 10.1. MINITAB has identified only one additional variable as making a statistically significant contribution at the selected 0·05 level. It is, therefore, the optimum model from that objective point of view, but the researcher should always be alive to the possibility of making decisions to exclude, or even include, other variables if justified on scientific grounds.

10.8 Residuals in multiple regression

Chapter 9 discussed the conditions of variable and residual behaviour that had to be complied with before any regression model can be regarded as reliable. All of those conditions apply with equal force to multiple regression models. Once again, a careful study of the residuals will do much to direct subsequent research. This is particularly

TABLE 10.4 Regression model parameters based on a two-predictor and three-predictor model for death rates

Predictors of death rate[1]	Coefficient of explanation (R^2)	Standard error of estimate	Regression (explained) sum of squares	F-value
hhs and gwe	0·764	0·662	61·02	69·62
hhs, gwe and incsup	0·817	0·590	65·24	62·42
Change	+0·053	−0·072	+4·22	−7·20

[1] Where hhs = household size, gwe = gross weekly earnings and incsup = percentage on income support.

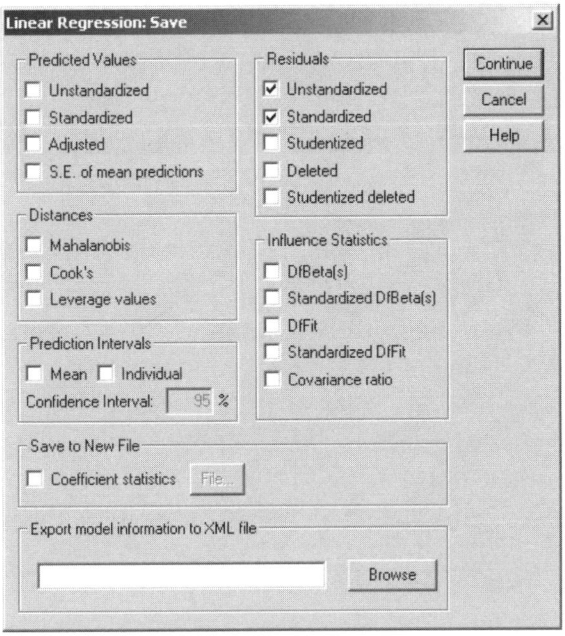

FIGURE 10.9 **Save** options window in SPSS regression procedures. This set up requests only standardised and unstandarised residual listings to be saved

the case in multiple regression, where variables for inclusion need to be selected with care. For example, the presence of a high degree of autocorrelation in the residuals may suggest a problem with the data but, more probably indicates the action of another variable, which, if included, would eliminate this problem and improve the model's predictive capacity thereby lowering the standard error of estimate.

Residual analysis is of great importance. Fortunately we can request a listing of all the residuals from the regression model by clicking the **Save** button in the SPSS procedures (see Figure 10.5), which will bring up the option window in Figure 10.9. Our immediate interest, using the stepwise model above, is only with the absolute residuals and their standardised equivalent values. We need to tick the boxes for these two items, which are then entered automatically in the **Data view** window, being placed in the next immediately free columns and headed **res_1** and **zre_1** respectively as in Figure 10.10 in which form the data file can be saved for later reference.

It is often helpful to examine these residuals to identify anomalous cases that might be genuinely unusual or could be the result of an error somewhere in the data entry or recording. Using the three-predictor model identified above, the largest standardised residuals are for the counties of Tyne and Wear (–1·931) and Bedfordshire (–2·550), where the observed death rates are lower than predicted, and the Isle of Wight (1·673),

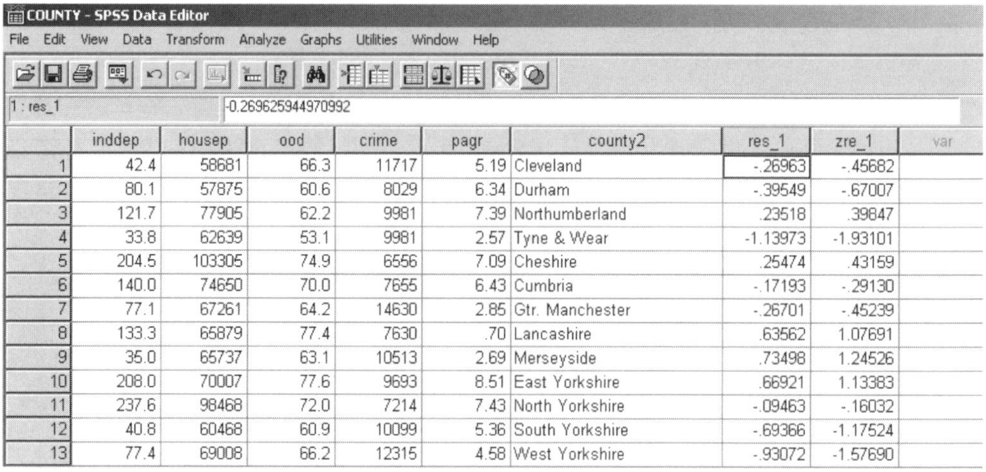

	inddep	housep	ood	crime	pagr	county2	res_1	zre_1	var
1	42.4	58681	66.3	11717	5.19	Cleveland	-.26963	-.45682	
2	80.1	57875	60.6	8029	6.34	Durham	-.39549	-.67007	
3	121.7	77905	62.2	9981	7.39	Northumberland	.23518	.39847	
4	33.8	62639	53.1	9981	2.57	Tyne & Wear	-1.13973	-1.93101	
5	204.5	103305	74.9	6556	7.09	Cheshire	.25474	.43159	
6	140.0	74650	70.0	7655	6.43	Cumbria	-.17193	-.29130	
7	77.1	67261	64.2	14630	2.85	Gtr. Manchester	-.26701	-.45239	
8	133.3	65879	77.4	7630	.70	Lancashire	.63562	1.07691	
9	35.0	65737	63.1	10513	2.69	Merseyside	.73498	1.24526	
10	208.0	70007	77.6	9693	8.51	East Yorkshire	.66921	1.13383	
11	237.6	98468	72.0	7214	7.43	North Yorkshire	-.09463	-.16032	
12	40.8	60468	60.9	10099	5.36	South Yorkshire	-.69366	-1.17524	
13	77.4	69008	66.2	12315	4.58	West Yorkshire	-.93072	-1.57690	

FIGURE 10.10 SPSS Data view listing showing the inclusion of absolute (res_1) and standardised (zre_1) residuals using the Save option in Figure 10.9

where the observed death rate is much higher than is predicted. All three might warrant closer attention.

MINITAB automatically identifies and lists the most anomalous individuals in the regression data set under a heading of **Unusual Observations**, in which all residuals of more than two standard errors are itemised together with other individuals that while not necessarily being significant in their residual, exercise a notable influence on the model. For example, item 30 in the data set (West Sussex) has an exceptionally high death rate, indeed the highest in the country, and is identified by this criterion.

In Chapter 9 attention was given to the means by which confidence and prediction intervals could be calculated for individual cases. It will be clear that for multiple models the arithmetic is very demanding but, fortunately, we can use the same MINITAB option as described in section 9.6. But the **Prediction intervals for new observations** box must now have 'new observations' for all predictors, entered in the order in which they appear in the regression model. These intervals can be thought of as extending through n-dimensional space, where n is the number of terms in the model. Nevertheless, the concept of interval bands of reliability remains valid, and useful.

Finally, we can use the **Plot** option in SPSS regression procedures to produce a scatter diagram, the inspection of which allows us to draw some general conclusions regarding the overall character of the residual set. To employ this option click on the **Plots** button in the first option window (Figure 10.5). This will bring up the dialogue box in Figure 10.11, in which we need only transfer the specified items into the appropriate **Y** and **X** spaces to allow us to produce a graph. In this example we will plot the standardised residuals (ZRESID) against the standardised predicted values (ZPRED). If, as is required by

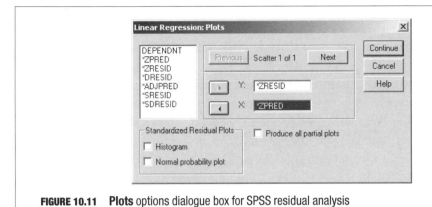

FIGURE 10.11 **Plots** options dialogue box for SPSS residual analysis

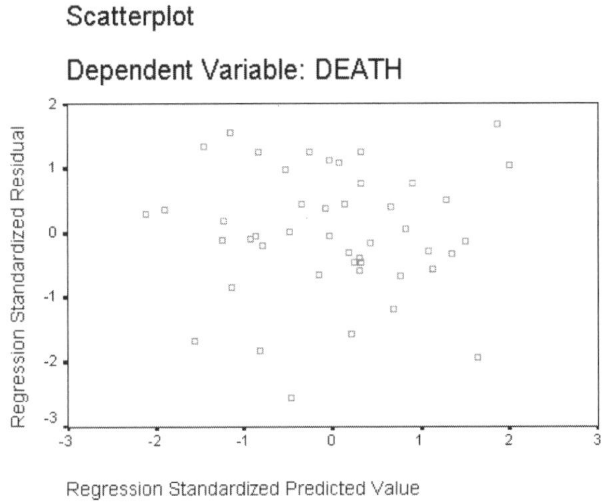

Scatterplot

Dependent Variable: DEATH

FIGURE 10.12 Plot of residuals against predicted values of the dependent variable *Y* based on the regression model predicting death rates on the basis of gross weekly earnings, household size and percentage of population on income support

regression theory, the residuals have no trend and are homoscedastic (see section 9.5), the plot of these two measures should have no pattern. Any trends would indicate that these important assumptions are not being fully met. The results, using the three-predictor model of death rates based on household size, weekly earnings and percentage of population on income support are shown in Figure 10.12 in which the random scatter of points suggests that the assumptions of residual behaviour have been met. Although this is a purely visual, slightly subjective, exercise, it is a useful and important one in regression analysis.

10.9 Problems and assumptions

Geographers are now more aware than ever of the difficulties inherent in the indiscriminate and poorly directed use of powerful statistics packages. Two areas present particular difficulties. The first of these relates to important assumptions regarding the nature, especially the normality, of the data used for regression and other analytical methods. The second area encompasses the tendency for an unquestioning dependence on the results of statistics packages, which is ill advised when insufficient attention has been given to the suitability of the data for the test and to the sampling frame in which the data are gathered.

On the other hand, it is has been observed that the often-quoted need for data normality is subordinate, particularly in regression analysis, to more pressing requirements. As noted above, the urge to transform data and to impose high degrees of normality upon them can lead to problems at the important stage of interpretation of the results. The reliability of the individual regression coefficients is responsive to other preconditions than normality. At the most fundamental, but often overlooked, level, data accuracy is critical. Regression equations acknowledge errors in Y, but assume that X is measured to a much higher degree of reliability. Rarely is this the case. Furthermore, even in situations of great reliability and accuracy, there is always the issue how closely the data represent the phenomena that they are held to represent. For instance, in the earlier examples we might legitimately enquire how closely gross weekly income represents 'wealth'. Might not net income, or disposable income after unavoidable expenditures act as better measures? An earlier example also included household size as a seemingly useful predictor of death rates, but we need also to question exactly what this parameter is indicating and how much it reflects other correlated variables. Notice that it was not selected by the stepwise procedures, despite its strong zero-order correlation with death rates. But even if we harbour such doubts, there remains the issue of data availability, and the most desirable measures may, quite simply, not be available. This goes back to the opening sections of Chapter 7 in which we considered some fundamental aspects of measurement.

Lastly, it is important that observations used in regression analysis should be randomly selected and independent of each other. For geographers, this latter requirement can present some difficulties. Much of our data are spatially organised; contiguous spatial units such as counties, regions and nations contribute an underlying tendency to spatial autocorrelation. Much has been written on this theme, but many of the problems have yet to be fully resolved. Fortunately, it is within the compass of most geographers to, at the very least, check the reliability and character of their data, and to take some steps to counter such non-compliances. Even when this cannot be done, a recognition of the problem, and due caution in the interpretation of the results is wise counsel.

11

Factor analysis and related techniques

11.1 Introduction

THE AIM OF THIS chapter is to introduce the practical aspects associated with factor analytical methods. A full consideration of the theory of factor analysis would take us far beyond the scope of this book and, therefore, our attention will be confined largely to the way in which the MINITAB and SPSS systems deal with the practicalities of using these techniques, and how geographers can understand and interpret the results. We shall start by examining the possible uses of factor analysis, before discussing the variety of techniques that are available to the researcher.

Factor analytical methods can take several variables and identify possibly useful combinations, more properly termed *factors* or *components*, of those variables thereby reducing a large volume of data to a smaller and more manageable set of information. This reduction process may be necessary for a number of reasons, although two main ones can be identified. First we may wish to produce combinations of the original data that can be used as new variables in some further analysis. For example, we may use factor analysis to combine independent variables in multiple regression and thereby reduce the effect of multicollinearity (section 10.4). By this means a poorly understood but large body of data covering a range of variables may be rendered more comprehensible and manageable, with a few factors replacing a much larger number of original variables. Second, we may use it for exploratory purposes, in an attempt to detect and identify groups of functionally related variables. We may be guided in this approach by an established degree of understanding of the variables' interrelationships, or the strategy may be one of exploratory investigation and of testing an hypothesis which predicts a number of factors or components. As we shall see the two approaches require rather different methods of factor analysis. It is within the area of exploratory analysis that many geographical uses of factor techniques are to be found, although as such work advances the studies tend to become less investigative and more analytical. The factors (in effect, groups of variables) that are identified by these methods, though of a purely statistical character in terms of their derivation, are far more than mere numerical devices when set within the wider interpretational framework and they may indicate much of the functionality of the data set. This important point is well illustrated in the origins of factor analysis. Factoring methods spring from psychological researches undertaken in the 1930s in which well-understood concepts, such as intelligence, could be measured only on the basis of several parameters and no single practical measure could be relied upon. Factoring methods, however, allowed several parameters to be combined to form a single 'intelligence factor'. In the same way, geographers may wish to measure attributes of selected areas, such as urban decay, social status or social well-being, all of which are combined effects of several measurable variables but none of which individually and adequately encompasses our meaning of the terms. Before proceeding further, it should be stressed that the term factor analysis does not refer to a single technique, but covers a variety of approaches, though they all share important characteristics. Initially, we can recognise three main stages in their application, each of which may offer the researcher a choice of methods (Table 11.1).

In the first stage most factor analyses require a matrix of product-moment correlation coefficients as the basic data input. At this point the alternatives are between those matrices based on correlations between different variables for a group of observations, or of taking a matrix of correlation coefficients measuring the degree of similarity between a set of individuals based on a number of variables or attributes. In the first instance we may examine the behaviour of a set of variables sampled across different areas, such as counties, cities or some other set of spatial units. As a result we produce a correlation matrix of the selected variables as in Chapter 8 – this is called *R-mode factoring*. We might note that the focus of attention is on the variables, while the geographical or spatial dimension, if present at all, appears only as part of the sampling strategy. But, as geographers, we might be more concerned to look at the degrees of similarity between the areas and to distinguish spatially-based, rather than variable-based, arrangements and groupings. We might therefore produce a correlation matrix not of the variables but of the areas. In effect the roles of variables and cases are exchanged. Pairs of areas, which

TABLE 11.1 A simplified view of options in factoring methods

Stage	Option types	Terminology
Correlation	Between variables	R-mode factoring
	Between individuals	Q-mode factoring
Extraction of initial orthogonal factors	Variance assumed to be common	Principal components analysis
	Variance apportioned to common and unique categories	Factor analysis
Rotation to final factors	Uncorrelated	Orthogonal
	Correlated	Oblique

have similar attributes, will display a strong positive correlation (though we might prefer to call it now a similarity index), and those pairs with contrasting values across the variables will have a strong negative correlation. This approach is referred to as *Q-mode factoring*. Though Q-mode factoring is often valuable to geographers it requires a large number of variables with which to measure each case – ideally, at least as many variables as cases are required for successful Q-mode factoring.

The second stage, often known as *factor extraction*, is to explore the possibilities of data reduction by constructing a new, and smaller, set of variables based on the interrelationships in the correlation matrix. There are two approaches to this second stage – principal components analysis and factor analysis. In both of these strategies, new variables (components or factors) are defined as mathematical transformations and combinations of the original data. In the factor analysis model the assumption is made that the correlations are largely the result of some underlying regularity in the basic data. Specifically, it assumes that the behaviour of each original variable is partly, indeed it would be hoped largely, influenced by the various factors that are common to all the variables. The degree to which this is the case is expressed through what is termed the *common variance*. A further element is known as the *unique variance* and is an expression of the variance that is specific to the variable itself and to errors in its measurement. The latter effect clearly influences the usefulness of the derived factors. In contrast, principal components analysis makes no such assumptions about the structure of the original variables. It does not presuppose any element of unique variance to exist within each variable, and the variances are assumed to be entirely common in character. This important concept is expressed graphically in Figure 11.1. We should use

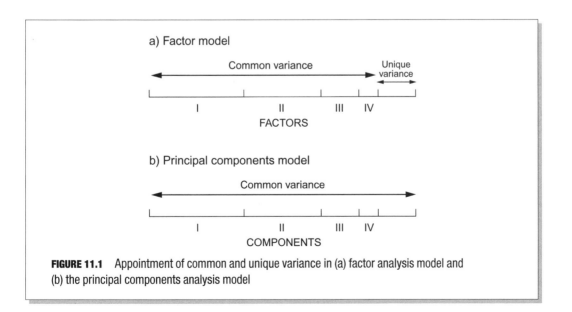

FIGURE 11.1 Appointment of common and unique variance in (a) factor analysis model and (b) the principal components analysis model

principal components analysis as a purely exploratory tool when we have little understanding or knowledge of the data with which we might be working. Factor analysis, on the other hand, presupposes that we have sufficient understanding to know how many significant factors are to be expected and the degree of common variance for which they account. These differences have practical implications and will be examined in more detail in section 11.3.

The final stage in which variations in the method are possible is in the search for interpretable factors. This is the point at which we analyse the character of the factors and qualities that they represent. To help us in this process we might choose to refine or clarify the factor model. To achieve this a number of options are available, one of which is known as *factor rotation*. Up to this point the various factors can be thought of as being geometrically orthogonal, i.e. at right angles to each other in *n*-dimensional space, in the same way that the two axes on a graph are orthogonal in two-dimensions. In the statistical sense this ensures that they are uncorrelated with one another. We may, however, rotate these axes as a fixed set through *n*-dimensional space in order to account for a greater degree of the variance of the original data. In this case the factors remain *orthogonal* and, by definition, uncorrelated. But we may also rotate the axes independently so that they become *oblique* to one another. This may further increase the utility of the factoring model, but a degree of correlation will now exist between the different, now non-orthogonal, factor axes. These points are discussed more fully and are exemplified in section 11.6.

11.2 Theoretical considerations and terminology

Before we examine the operational aspects of the group of techniques known as factor analysis we must consider a little of its theoretical background. There are two approaches, one based on algebraic solutions and the second on geometric interpretations. It is the latter upon which we shall focus. Let us start by considering the case of simple correlations. In Figures 8.1, 8.5 and 9.2 we saw how the relationship between two variables can be expressed by means of a scatter diagram with X and Y axes defining the two variables in question. Had the points fallen perfectly along a straight line the correlation would have been +1·0. On the other hand, had there been no correlation between the two variables the points would have formed a vaguely circular scatter on the graph with no apparent trend. From the point of view of the geometry of such graphs, these two extremes – the perfect (ignoring for the moment the question of the sign) and the zero correlation – represent the two limiting conditions between which all other states will plot on a graph in the form of ellipsoidal scatters of points with varying degrees of eccentricity or elongation. This characteristic is illustrated in Figure 11.2, which shows two extreme cases together with an intermediate condition. The latter in particular draws attention to the important point that all such ellipses can be described by reference to a major and minor axis. The former runs the length of the ellipse, the minor axis lying at right angles to it.

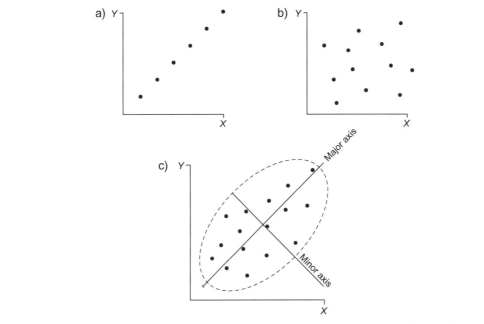

FIGURE 11.2 Graphical representation of the relationship between pairs of variables. Diagram (a) shows perfect correlation, (b) zero-correlated variables and (c) the intermediate state in which the principal components can be viewed as orthogonal axes

The major axis can be viewed as representing the common variance between the two variables and is in some ways comparable to a regression line. The minor axis is more akin to the residual variance, i.e. that which is not accounted for by the major axis. Thus, when we have a perfect relationship the major axis is at its greatest length and the minor axis disappears. As the scatter of points spreads and departs from a perfect relationship, the major axis shortens and the minor axis lengthens until there is zero correlation and the two are of the same length. These two axes represent the only two possible components of a two-variable factor model. Where correlations are strong the two variables can be reduced to the one dominant component (major axis) of the plot and the minor axis, being relatively trivial, can be overlooked. Notice that at most we can only have as many components as we have variables.

Thus far we have done little more than consider the simple two-variable case. The great virtue of factor analytical methods is that they can perform this task of estimating components on data sets containing many variables or cases (depending upon whether we use an R- or Q-mode approach). The problem is that such n-variable models require a similar number of geometric dimensions and cannot be represented in graphical form. Hence the principal axis of the hyperellipsoid (an ellipse in n-dimensional space) may represent the combined effects of not two, but several, inter-correlated variables. At the same time we are no longer restricted to just two components or axes and can have as many as we have variables. The second (orthogonal) component might no longer, as above, represent the residual element, but might indicate the combined effects of another group of variables. This axis will be 'shorter' than the principal axis but may nevertheless account for a significant proportion of the variability of the data set not accounted for by the latter. A third axis or component may take up a little more of the remaining variability and represent the effect of a third group of variables and so on until all the variability is accounted for. As with the addition of terms in multiple regression, there will come a time when the inclusion of further components fails to help significantly in our attempts to explain the data set's variability. The 'lengths' of the derived axes, or components, are therefore important. They can be easily determined by computer programs in which the axes or factors, more properly termed *eigenvectors*, are estimated and their statistical length measured by what are termed their *eigenvalue*.

We can develop these principles with a simple example. Let us consider the relationships between three variables given by the hypothetical product-moment correlations in Table 11.2. From these data it is possible to calculate each variable's importance (each will be different) on the first component or factor. This quantity is more correctly termed the *loading* of the variable on the factor, and is a function of the square root of the sum of all the possible correlation entries in the appropriate column of the correlation matrix. This sum includes the diagonal elements, which, as the measure of the variables association with itself, is 1·0, and the duplicate correlation entries either side of this principal diagonal. The column sums are given in Table 11.2. They add to 7·2, the square root of which is 2·68. The correlation between any variable X_i, and the first factor is found by dividing the appropriate column sum of correlations by the square root of the sum of all the correlations in the matrix. Thus, for example, the loading of variable X_1 on this first factor is given by 2·3/2·68 = 0·86. Furthermore, as these loadings are a measure of the collective correlation between the variables and the first factor, their respective squares represent the proportions of the variance of that particular variable accounted for by the factor (see the discussion of coefficients of explanation in section 8.2). When the squares

TABLE 11.2 Hypothetical correlation matrix for factor loading calculations

	X_1	X_2	X_3	
X_1	1·0	0·6	0·7	
X_2	0·6	1·0	0·8	
X_3	0·7	0·8	1·0	
Sum of correlations	2·3	2·4	2·5	Overall sum = 7·2
Factor loading[1]	0·86	0·89	0·93	

[1] Factor loading = column sum/√(total sum of correlations).

TABLE 11.3 Factor loadings and eigenvalues for a hypothetical example

Variable	Loading	Squared loading
X_1	0·86	0·74
X_2	0·89	0·79
X_3	0·93	0·86
		Eigenvalue = sum = 2·39

of the loadings of all the variables on the one factor are summed they provide therefore a measure of the variance of the whole data accounted for by that factor. This important quantity is the eigenvalue of the factor. Table 11.3 shows how the eigenvalue of factor 1 is derived from our simple example. To establish the importance of the first component we can relate it to the total variance of the original data by dividing it by the number of variables (n) in the data set (Equation 11.1). The answer is usually expressed as a percentage.

$$\text{Percentage of variance} = (\lambda_1 / n) \times 100\% \tag{11.1}$$

Equation 11.1

λ_1 = eigenvalue for factor 1

n = number of original factors

In this case the eigenvalue of 2·39 is divided by 3; giving 0·797 and indicating that 79·7 per cent of the total variance is accounted for by this first component. The next step would normally be to estimate the eigenvalue for the second component. This would be extracted from what is termed the *residual correlation matrix*. The maximum percentage of explanation possible by this second factor is limited to that not accounted for by the first, in the example, 100 – 79·7 or 20·3 per cent. In statistical terms this second component will be wholly uncorrelated with the first and, in geometrical terms, the two will be orthogonal to each other in n-dimensional space. In principal components analysis the process could continue until we had as many factors as variables, by which stage all the correlations would have been accounted for and, theoretically, the sum of the eigenvalues should equal to n and, therefore provide 100 per cent explanation. In factor analysis we would, however, normally confine ourselves only to those factors with an eigenvalue of 1·0 or more. On purely qualitative grounds these might be regarded as 'significant' components.

Factor analysis differs from principal components analysis in one further important regard. This concerns the concept of *communality*, which is the proportion of variance of each variable accounted for by the common factors, i.e. the common variance identified in section 11.1 and Figure 11.1. It is important to recognise that the communality of each variable is the quantity that appears in the principal diagonal of the correlation matrix used to initiate all factoring procedures. In principal components analysis the behaviour of each variable is assumed to be wholly explained by the factors or components that are common to all the variables. By inference, therefore, there is no variation that is unique to each variable and not accounted for by the cumulative effect of all possible factors or components, and each variable correlates perfectly (1·0) with itself. On the other hand, the technique known specifically as factor analysis makes no such assumptions. The correlation matrix in the case of factor analysis will have principal diagonal elements (communalities) that are less than 1·0. The degree to which each variable's communality differs from 1·0 is a measure of its unique variance that, in turn, cannot be accounted for by the common factors. The difficulty in this approach is that we do not know the communalities to be entered in the principal diagonal. This problem is resolved in some computer packages by the use of iterative techniques in which initial estimates are made, sometimes from a preliminary principal components analysis, and the program then runs to give revised communalities. Further adjustments are then made, the program reruns and so on until the results converge upon consistent figures. This final estimate is guided by the multiple coefficient of explanation (R^2) between the variable in question and all others in the data set. Higher R^2 values will indicate smaller degrees of unique variance and vice versa.

Each variable will, as we saw in Table 11.3, have a different loading on each of the derived components or factors. A generally reliable estimate of communality of any one variable is provided by the squares of its loadings summed across all the 'significant' components, i.e. commonly those with eigenvalues greater than 1·0. This total represents the collective percentage variance of the variable accounted for by the components. These quantities, one for each variable in the data set, must be less than 1·0, though their magnitudes are determined by the efficacy of the 'significant' components. If the latter account for the large proportion of the total variance, then the derived communality estimates will be close to 1·0, otherwise they will be much smaller. In MINITAB and SPSS iterative procedures may throw up communality estimates greater than 1·0, causing the procedures to prematurely conclude.

11.3 Factor analysis and principal components analysis: further comparisons

As we explained in section 11.1, principal components and factor analysis represent the two different forms of factoring methods. Geographers have used both. From our point of view, the main points of interest are, first, in the distinctions between them and, secondly, how to decide on which is the more appropriate in any given case.

Examining first the differences between the techniques, we have already drawn attention to some of the main contrasts. The principal components models assume a closed system in which all statistical variation is accounted for by the variables themselves. Hence the communality values are set to 1·0 and, ultimately, we would expect to account for the whole variance of the data set. As a minimum requirement we would want very high correlations between the variables, thereby minimising the unique variance. This approach is often favoured because of its simplicity and its solution to the problem of estimating communalities.

Factor analysis, on the other hand, might be regarded as a more realistic approach to research problems as it does not presuppose a closed system in which the variables wholly explain each other's behaviour. Thus, in most studies we would acknowledge that we have not collected data on all possible variables and that error variation would be attached to each of them. This allows for this uncertainty by allocating a residual and unexplained variance element unique to each variable.

Given these differences we can go on to consider the criteria for selecting one model in preference to the other. Under certain conditions both models will give similar results, for example, when all the variables are highly inter-correlated. If, however, some of the correlations are low the use of 1·0 as communality entries will be an over-estimate through which the principal components and the factor analysis methods will produce divergent results. In general, the factor analysis approach is the more realistic. It acknowledges that errors in measurement will occur, but it also requires a general knowledge of the underlying factorial structure of the data. In contrast, principal components models deal with more limiting cases; no underlying structure is assumed and the search is one based largely on the data reduction. The general characteristics of the two methods are listed in Table 11.4.

Clearly from what we have said, factor analysis provides a more comprehensive model for most geographers and, for this reason, most of what follows is aimed more specifically at this approach.

11.4 Factor analysis: data input

The preparation of any factor analysis model can be broken down into the procedures summarised in Table 11.1. These start with the data matrix, from which a correlation

TABLE 11.4 Essential characteristics of principal components and factor analysis

	Principal components analysis	**Factor analysis**
Assumptions	A closed system with no assumptions about the underlying variable structure; identifies only common variance	Realistic assumptions concerning errors in measurement; identifies common and unique variance
Best conditions	High correlations between a large number of variables and the need for simple data reduction	As for principal components, but it will also deal with a small correlation matrix and permits a wider range of analysis and interpretation

matrix can be derived. The next steps would normally consist of deriving the initial orthogonal factors, then rotating them to achieve a better degree of explanation of the original data's variance, the listing of the loading of each variable on each factor and, finally, although optional and dependent on the researcher's needs, the listing of the so-called factor scores for each case, rather than each variable, on each of the factors (this option is reviewed in section 11.7 below). For the moment we will concentrate on the first stages, those where the raw data and their correlation matrix are the focus of interest. The correlation matrix, however, may not be the only form of data input and the covariance matrix or the raw statistics could also be used. Nevertheless the correlation matrix might be preferred if only because it allows for the easier identification of possible groupings of variables upon which the later factors may converge.

One of the main decisions to be taken with regard to the raw data surrounds the question of transformations. In common with other parametric methods, it is assumed that the data are not significantly non-normal in their distribution and, because the procedures rely so heavily upon correlation coefficients, that the relationships are linear. Distributional transformations may be necessary if these conditions are not met. But, as in so often the case, the final interpretation may be hampered through transforming the data and the user should weigh carefully the requirements of the procedures against the problems of interpretation at a later stage.

The problems posed by the units used to measure the raw data are more easily solved. In any study the different variables will have not only a number of scales upon which they can each be measured (temperatures in degrees Fahrenheit or Celsius, income in sterling or dollars, etc.) but the magnitudes will also differ between the variables (income per week might measure in hundreds, but household sizes only in twos, threes or fours in most cases). All variables could be given equal statistical weight by expressing them in standardised form. Fortunately this is rarely necessary as correlation coefficients are scale-independent.

Of greater importance is the selection of variables to be used in factoring methods. The selection will, in part, depend upon data availability. Nevertheless the derived structure of the factors will be determined by the choice of variables. For example, in urban or social studies, if the original variables included many that measure demographic characteristics, clearly this would be reflected in the composition and character of the factors. It is often advisable therefore to achieve some kind of balance across the selected variables with regard to what they measure. The decision as to which variables to include is obviously difficult and no clear guidelines exist; although when using factor analysis, rather than principal components analysis, the prerequisite of a working hypothesis may well help.

Finally there is the question of the number of variables. The effect of including a large number of variables that measure similar characteristics and are highly correlated is merely to increase the importance of the factor through which they are represented, without necessarily changing the overall factor structure. Again, some balance should be achieved between the variables. The overriding consideration, in R-mode analysis, is that there should be many more cases than variables. In Q-mode analysis the reverse requirement prevails and there should be many more variables than cases.

11.5 Factor analysis using SPSS

SPSS and MINITAB permit the use of all of the types of factor analysis that we have outlined in the previous sections. To demonstrate the power and utility of the computer packages and the technique, we will use a subset of the data already referred to in Chapters 9 and 10, relating to various demographic and social variables in the English counties (this can be found on the CD in the file COUNTY.SAV). Those variables chosen for this exercise and their key names are listed in Table 11.5. They are deliberately diverse in character, ranging from death and birth rates to education and income statistics. The question we might pose is whether there is an empirical basis for grouping these nine variables into a smaller number of factors. It should be evident at this stage that these questions necessarily pose exploratory rather than confirmatory questions. In other words, we need to examine if there are significant relationships among the variables and how these relationships can be expressed in the grouping of variables into a smaller number of factors. If new factors from these variables could be created, we might more easily be able to interpret the data and generalise their behaviour.

We will examine these questions in SPSS. The appropriate instructions for MINITAB are provided on the CD. We initiate the analysis with the command sequence **Analyze > Data Reduction > Factor**. The resulting dialogue box is shown in Figure 11.3.

The variables which are to be included in the analysis should be placed into the **Variables** box on the right by selecting each one in turn and transferring it using the

TABLE 11.5   Data variables from the file COUNTY.SAV used in the factor analysis examples

SPSS name	Description of variable
birth	Live births/1,000 population
death	Death rate/1,000 population
sp	Single parents as percentage of all households
hhs	Household size
ctax	Average council tax
o16ed	Percentage school children staying for post-16 education
u5ed	Percentage under 5s in education
unemp	Percentage of workers unemployed
gwe	Gross weekly earnings

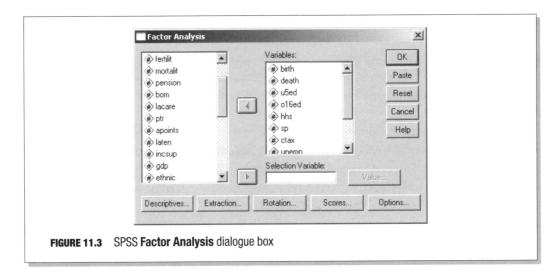

FIGURE 11.3 SPSS **Factor Analysis** dialogue box

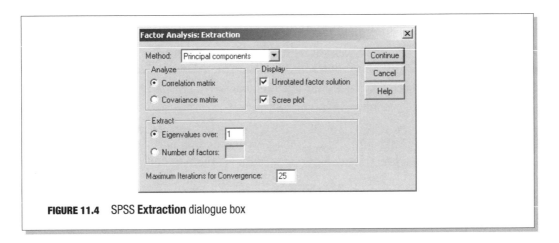

FIGURE 11.4 SPSS **Extraction** dialogue box

input arrow. The first consideration after adding the variables concerns the method of factor analysis to be used. SPSS provides a range of methods in the **Extraction** dialogue box, opened by clicking on the **Extraction . . .** button at the bottom of the main dialogue box. This brings up the dialogue box in Figure 11.4.

The method to be used can be selected by clicking the arrow on the pull down menu. The two that are most likely to be of use are those methods that we have covered in this chapter – **Principal components** (the default setting) and **Principal axis factoring** (more commonly termed factor analysis). As this is an initial, more exploratory, form of analysis we will select the Principal components option. By default (see the **Display** options in Figure 11.4) such results are unrotated. Under the **Display** section, you should also check that you have selected a **Scree plot**. This is a useful diagrammatic tool for examining the decrease in eigenvalues (levels of explained variance) as more factors are extracted. The **Extract** section should have the **Eigenvalues over** button checked, with the number 1 (normally the default) typed in the box, but we should make no specification on the number of factors yet. This is because in the first instance, we need to establish the strength of the significant eigenvalues, i.e. those with values greater than 1·0, before deciding how many will be retained for later analysis and rotation.

Returning to the main dialogue box, we click **OK** (the other optional dialogue boxes are considered below in due course). The major elements of the output are shown in Figure 11.5. The tables provide a review of the level of variance explained by the

Communalities

	Initial	Extraction
BIRTH	1.000	.732
DEATH	1.000	.880
U5ED	1.000	.601
O16ED	1.000	.736
HHS	1.000	.784
SP	1.000	.825
CTAX	1.000	.683
UNEMP	1.000	.666
GWE	1.000	.569

Extraction Method: Principal Component Analysis

Total Variance Explained

Component	Initial Eigenvalues			Extraction Sums of Squared Loadings		
	Total	% of Variance	Cumulative %	Total	% of Variance	Cumulative %
1	3.039	33.764	33.764	3.039	33.764	33.764
2	2.337	25.972	59.737	2.337	25.972	59.737
3	1.101	12.229	71.965	1.101	12.229	71.965
4	.860	9.553	81.518			
5	.559	6.217	87.734			
6	.471	5.232	92.967			
7	.262	2.909	95.876			
8	.255	2.832	98.708			
9	.116	1.292	100.000			

Extraction Method: Principal Component Analysis.

Component Matrix[a]

	Component		
	1	2	3
BIRTH	-.618	.521	-.281
DEATH	.872	-.200	-.284
U5ED	.448	-.300	.557
O16ED	-.401	-.531	.541
HHS	-.701	.367	.398
SP	.228	.867	.148
CTAX	.379	.639	.363
UNEMP	.560	.586	9.294E-02
GWE	-.732	.127	-.132

Extraction Method: Principal Component Analysis
a. 3 components extracted.

FIGURE 11.5 SPSS output using principal components analysis procedures

different factors generated by the analysis as well as much other useful information and can be interpreted in the following way:

- **Communalities** – as described above, principal components analysis assumes this to be 1·0 in the first instance. The column headed 'Extraction' indicates the degree of common variance attributed to each variable after the analysis is complete and the data better understood. In the case of death rates this is as high as 88 per cent, but for gross weekly income it falls to 56·9 per cent.

- **Initial eigenvalues** – these appear in the table for Total Variance Explained. For each factor, the eigenvalues are provided, with an estimate of the percentage variance and cumulative percentage variance of the total that the component explains. Accordingly, for factor 1, the eigenvalue is 3·039, and it explains 33·764 per cent of the total variance.

- **Extraction sums** – at this stage, this section of the table is somewhat obsolete. Because we asked SPSS to extract all factors with eigenvalues over 1, it re-states the data from the left-hand side of the table. Nonetheless, it is clear that the first three factors (eigenvalues > 1·0) collectively account for nearly 72 per cent of the total variance.

- **Component matrix** – although we may not have an immediate use for this information, the output also includes the loadings of each variable on the three components with eigenvalues greater than 1·0.

The number of factors we should retain for further analysis is always a difficult decision. One viewpoint is that factors should only be retained where eigenvalues are over 1·0, since if an eigenvalue is less than this the factor explains less than the variance of one variable. Indeed, Figure 11.5 demonstrates that nearly three quarters of the total variance is accounted for by these three factors; a good figure for social science data. However, the pattern of eigenvalue decline has also to be considered and it has been argued that where there is a significant change in eigenvalue levels, there should be a decision only to extract those factors above this point. The standard way of assessing this has been to use what is termed a *scree plot*. SPSS will provide scree plots (see Figure 11.4), an example of which is shown in Figure 11.6.

The scree plot shows that three factors do indeed have eigenvalues over 1·0. After factor 2, however, there is a suggestion of a marked decrease in the decline of eigenvalues (equivalent to the increase in explained variance). As a result we may decide to retain only the two most important factors for further analysis on the basis that the third is barely above 1·0. Furthermore, factor 3 only accounts for 12·2 per cent of the variance, and is not much more important than factor 4 which accounts for a further 9·6 per cent, and it might be reasonable to exclude both. But these decisions tend to be matters of judgement rather than of objective exercise.

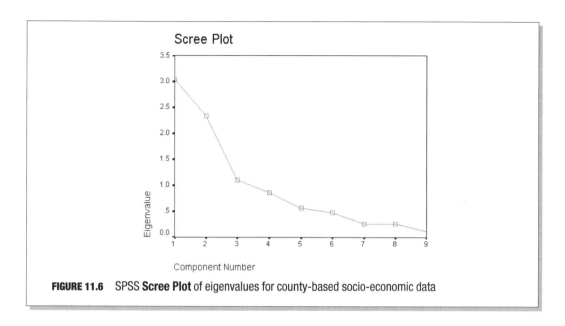

FIGURE 11.6 SPSS **Scree Plot** of eigenvalues for county-based socio-economic data

Having decided to extract two factors, we need to provide SPSS with the necessary commands to analyse these two factors in isolation. To do this, we repeat the command **Analyze > Data Reduction > Factor** and in the main dialogue box, again we click on **Extraction . . ..** In this case, we check the button **Number of factors** and type in the number we wish to analyse (in our case 2). We can also now request the option for factor analysis (**Principal axis factoring**) and can consider the possibility of factor rotation, to which attention can now be given before completing the sequence of options and commands.

11.6 Methods of factor rotation

To a large extent the aim of factor analysis is to define new variables or factors that adequately and clearly describe the original variables. The ideal situation would, therefore, be where each variable loads heavily onto one factor and has little or no relation to the remaining factors. However, this solution is rarely the case, with loadings on different factors being often quite similar (Figure 11.5). Where this occurs, there is an indication that the initially defined factors are not adequately explaining the variance in the data set or providing an unambiguous structure to the variables. Notice, for example in Figure 11.5 how O16ED (over 16s in education) loads similarly across all three factors. To overcome this difficultly, we can use a technique called *rotational factor analysis*, which attempts to simplify the factor structure and identify more clearly the groupings of variables. In each case, the relationship of one axis to each other are fixed. They remain orthogonal, but can be rotated collectively in directions that might account for more of the variance among the original variables. Within the general orthogonal

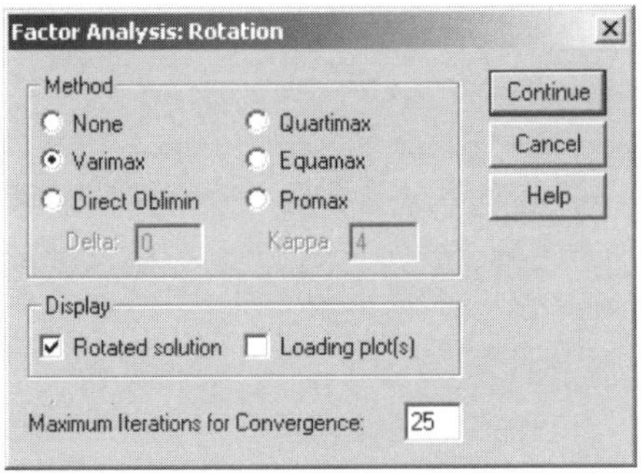

FIGURE 11.7 SPSS **Rotation** dialogue box

model used thus far in this chapter there are three rotational methods offered by SPSS: *quartimax*, *equimax* and *varimax*. The latter is the most widely used, depending as it does on a simplification of the columns of the factor matrix, thereby maximising the sum of the variances of the squared loadings in each column; hence the term varimax. The mathematical origins of these three methods need not concern us here, but rather we must now focus on how a varimax solution assists us in providing for a clearer understanding of the data.

To undertake a varimax rotation in SPSS, we go back to the dialogue box generated by the command **Analyze > Data Reduction > Factor**, but now click on the **Rotation . . .** button. This will bring up the box shown in Figure 11.7. Of the various extraction methods available, we select **Varimax**, and then click on **Continue** and **OK**.

The partial output from these commands is provided in Figure 11.8, and it can be usefully compared with that from the initial exercise in Figure 11.5. The elements of the output are listed thus:

- **Communalities** (not shown) – because we are using factor analysis, the initial communalities are not zero, and the final values are lower than those in principal components, indicating lower common variance.

- **Total variance explained** – this lists the eigenvalues of all factors, but provides details, in initial and rotated form, for the two factors that were requested. Notice how the rotational process changes the distribution of explanation between these two.

- **Factor matrices** – these are given for the original (not shown here) and the rotated factors. The degree to which the unrotated and rotated loadings of the variables differ should be noted. The problem of matching loadings of O16ED noted previously, is completely removed by rotation: it now loads far more favourably on factor 2.

- **Factor transformation matrix** (not shown here) – this is difficult for beginners to interpret, but when the matrix cell elements differ, it suggests that oblique rotation might be usefully explored.

Total Variance Explained

Factor	Initial Eigenvalues			Extraction Sums of Squared Loadings			Rotation Sums of Squared Loadings		
	Total	% of Variance	Cumulative %	Total	% of Variance	Cumulative %	Total	% of Variance	Cumulative %
1	3.039	33.764	33.764	2.608	28.982	28.982	2.458	27.307	27.307
2	2.337	25.972	59.737	1.952	21.689	50.671	2.103	23.364	50.671
3	1.101	12.229	71.965						
4	.860	9.553	81.518						
5	.559	6.217	87.734						
6	.471	5.232	92.967						
7	.262	2.909	95.876						
8	.255	2.832	98.708						
9	.116	1.292	100.000						

Extraction Method: Principal Axis Factoring.

Rotated Factor Matrix

	Factor	
	1	2
DEATH	-.896	.249
HHS	.733	-2.18E-02
BIRTH	.693	.121
GWE	.606	-.208
U5ED	-.405	-5.68E-03
SP	.233	.922
UNEMP	-.198	.705
CTAX	-2.78E-02	.619
O16ED	.109	-.503

Extraction Method: Principal Axis Factoring.
Rotation Method: Varimax with Kaiser Normalization
a. Rotation converged in 3 iterations.

FIGURE 11.8 Output listing of factor loadings for the Varimax rotation method in factor analysis

Such tables are of unquestionable value, but the next, and important, part of the analysis can only be undertaken by the researcher. This requires that some interpretation is made of the 'character' of the two factors, taking into account the variables that load strongly on each of them. This is obviously made simpler when loadings for any one variable differ between the factors. Emphasis is given to variables that load heavily on a factor, whether in a positive or a negative sense. In this case we might offer the following interpretations.

Factor 1 – this is highly associated with the variables relating to demographic factors such as death rate (–0·896), birth rate (0·693) and household size (0·733). The difference in signs suggest that in general high death rates are associated with low birth rates and low household sizes and vice versa. Gross weekly earnings (0·606) also loads heavily, but is less easy to interpret in the 'demographic' context of this factor. The latter's score on factor 1 is strong, but there is also a lower, but not unimportant, score on factor 2. We might decide, after consideration of this ambiguity, to overlook, perhaps even exclude this variable on the basis that its scores make it difficult to attach it to either of the two factors.

Factor 2 – this is associated with various social variables, of which the proportion of single parents (0·922), unemployment (0·705), council tax levels (0·619) and proportion of over 16s in education (–0·503) all load heavily. The table also shows how those variables that loaded heavily on factor 1, are now far less important – a good sign that the factoring exercise is yielding largely unambiguous results. The balance of loadings suggests here that where unemployment levels and single parent numbers are high, the numbers progressing to post-16 education are lower, and vice versa.

In summary, therefore, factor 1 could be said to relate to demographic factors, while factor 2 has a more socio-economic and educational character. These labels will evidently always be in some dispute as they are assigned by the researcher, but in this case, there does appear to be a relatively clear division between essential demographic and social factors. The value of these findings is that we are now able to compare counties according to composite variables, as well as resolving some of the complexities of the data set.

Section 11.1 has already indicated that solutions can be sought by rotating the axis as a single orthogonal set. A further option that is available is to select an oblique solution. In such cases the factors are rotated independently of one another. In doing so they lose their mutually orthogonal relationship and, depending on the angle between the factors (or axes, if we retain a more geometrical terminology), will become correlated between themselves. The closer to $90°$, the more orthogonal is the relationship, but as the angle decreases the correlation rises. This may not be an entirely unrealistic representation of the data as groups of variables, while possessing distinctive characteristics, may also be linked and are not necessarily orthogonal (and uncorrelated). From the results of our example thus far we might anticipate that the 'demographic' and the 'social' factors may not themselves be wholly uncorrelated or causally independent. On the other hand we must be careful when rotating factors not to merely reproduce our original data set! A further difficulty with oblique rotations is that there are no unique solutions and many decisions, especially those connected with the freedom to rotate the factors, are in the hands of the researcher and consequently subjective in character.

The oblique rotation approach also alters a fundamental assumption in orthogonal factoring, which is that any variable will, ideally, load as $+1\cdot0$ on one axis only, and as zero on all others. This is no longer true and the consequences of this change further complicate matters by producing two sets of loadings. The first, the so-called *structure loadings* are analogous to the loadings of variables on orthogonal models and represent, in geometrical terms, the independent projections of each variable onto each factor. Such perpendicular projections, or loadings, overlook any non-orthogonal relationship between the factors. The second set, the *pattern loadings*, again represent the loadings of each variable of each factor, but now that loading takes into account the fact that orthogonality no longer exists. In simple geometrical terms these are not the perpendicular projections of a variable onto any one factor but a projection whose line is parallel to the other factor. The degree to which that projection departs from the perpendicular depends upon the angle between the two factors. The contrasts between the two interpretations are summarised graphically in Figure 11.9. The whole issue of course

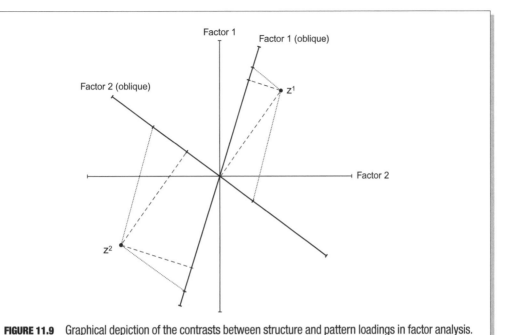

FIGURE 11.9 Graphical depiction of the contrasts between structure and pattern loadings in factor analysis. The geometry of the structure loadings is shown by chain lines, and that for pattern loadings by dotted lines

becomes more complicated when three or more axes are involved, but the same basic geometric principles apply no matter how many factors are extracted.

To examine the differences with the orthogonal solution discussed above, we will undertake an oblique rotation using SPSS by again using the **Analyze > Data Reduction > Factor** command and then by clicking on the **Rotation** button in the dialogue box (not shown) and selecting **Direct Oblimin** (the oblique rotation option, rather than **Varimax**, but see also Figure 11.7). To provide for appropriate comparison of the results, we will again choose to extract two factors. In this case, the output in Figure 11.10 is generated and can be compared to that in Figure 11.8. The output is set out in a similar fashion to those for orthogonal rotations, but includes different tables for pattern and structure loadings on the two selected factors. The two factors account for just over 50 per cent of the variance, and while there are small differences between the loadings provided in the two tables for factors 1 and 2, the general pattern of results is unchanged, suggesting that our choice of an orthogonal varimax rotation was a good one in the first instance and that oblique rotation has not added significantly to the explanation of the data.

11.7 The use of factor scores

One significant output from factor analysis is the relationship that each case (county in this example) has with each factor. The representations of these relationships are known

Pattern Matrix[a]

	Factor	
	1	2
DEATH	.887	.194
HHS	-.736	2.416E-02
BIRTH	-.704	.165
GWE	-.597	-.171
U5ED	.407	-3.11E-02
SP	-.287	.941
UNEMP	.159	.696
CTAX	-7.53E-03	.620
O16ED	-8.12E-02	-.499

Extraction Method: Principal Axis Factoring.
Rotation Method: Oblimin with Kaiser Normalization
a. Rotation converged in 4 iterations.

Structure Matrix

	Factor	
	1	2
DEATH	.910	.299
HHS	-.733	-.063
BIRTH	-.684	.081
GWE	-.618	-.242
U5ED	.403	.017
SP	-.175	.907
UNEMP	.242	.715
CTAX	.066	.619
O16ED	-.141	-.509

Extraction Method: Principal Axis Factoring.
Rotation Method: Oblimin with Kaiser Normalization

FIGURE 11.10 SPSS Oblique rotation results showing pattern and structure loadings

as *factor scores*. Geographers can use such scores to examine the values of each case and their relationship to each extracted factor, thus providing the possibility of examining spatial relationships and case-wise degrees of similarity (or dissimilarity). Because each factor takes all the variables into account we can estimate their net effect for each case (or county in the current example) on each factor. It is these quantities that constitute the factor score. Remember, however, that each variable will load on each factor to different degrees, and each factor will yield scores that emphasise the character of that factor, whether it be social, demographic or some other collection of attributes.

Usefully, factor scores can provide the means by which geographers may make spatial generalisations based on specific factors and the manner in which cases score on those factors. To take our example of county data, we defined two factors, one relating to demographic and the other to social data. We might be interested in examining whether, for example, there are spatial patterns for social variables (which we would expect). We could of course map each variable separately and make a visual comparison of any spatial patterns that appear. But the great virtue of factor analysis is that we need only plot a single map based on the factor scores from the second, more social, factor. These are expressions of all the variables' influences but give special importance

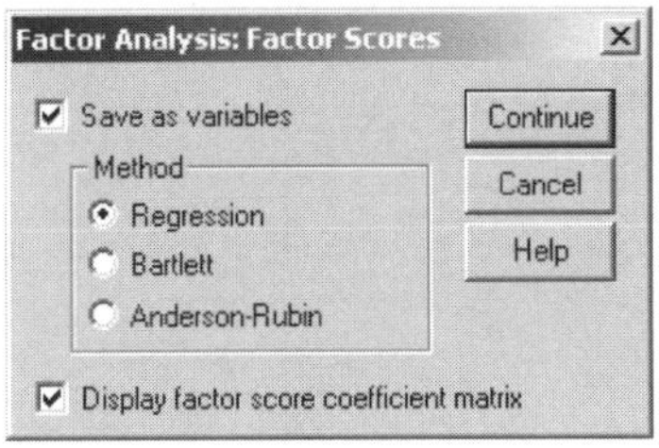

FIGURE 11.11 SPSS **Factor Scores** dialogue box

(see Figure 11.8) to those social variables that load heavily on that factor: the proportion of people unemployed, the percentage of single parents and the levels of council tax. SPSS will calculate factor scores on the basis of the strength of the variables on each factor, with those given the highest loadings providing the greatest contribution to the scores. The factor score for any one case is based on the *factor score coefficients*, which can be regarded as similar to regression coefficients.

SPSS can be instructed to provide the factor score coefficients, and to execute the calculations that give the factor scores. These are replicated over each abstracted factor and stored in columns in the **Data View** window. To accomplish this task we would go to the original factor analysis dialogue box (**Analyze > Data Reduction > Factor**) and click on the **Scores . . .** button to bring up the dialogue box in Figure 11.11. The next step is to check the **Save as Variables** box and select the **Regression** button (this indicates the method used to calculate the factor scores). To display the factor score coefficients we need also to tick the box for **Display factor score coefficient matrix**. Then click on **Continue** and **OK** to obtain the results. The matrix of coefficients is presented in the Output Viewer, but the case-by-case factor scores for each factor are stored in columns in the Data View window with column headings of the form **fac1_1, fac2_1** etc.

Figure 11.12 shows the factor score coefficient matrix for the current data set. These factor score coefficients are not, however, comparable with factor loadings and they reflect quite different aspects of the relationship between the variables in the data set. The factor scores for each case are calculated on the basis of these coefficients but, importantly, using the standardised observations and not the untransformed raw data. Thus, for factor one, the factor score (*FC1*) for any case is given by:

$$FC1 = 0.185 \text{ (birth)} - 0.880 \text{ (death)} - 0.034 \text{ (u5ed)} - 0.046 \text{ (o16ed)} - 0.149 \text{ (hhs)} +$$
$$0.304 \text{ (sp)} - 0.071 \text{ (ctax)} - 0.072 \text{ (unemp)} + 0.051 \text{ (gwe)}$$

and for factor two (*FC2*) by:

$$FC2 = 0.035 \text{ (birth)} + 0.120 \text{ (death)} - 0.023(\text{u5ed}) - 0.063 \text{ (o16ed)} - 0.013 \text{ (hhs)} +$$
$$0.788 \text{ (sp)} + 0.039 \text{ (ctax)} + 0.119 \text{ (unemp)} - 0.105 \text{ (gwe)}$$

Factor Score Coefficient Matrix

	Factor	
	1	2
BIRTH	.185	.035
DEATH	-.880	.120
U5ED	-.034	-.023
O16ED	-.046	-.063
HHS	-.149	-.013
SP	.304	.788
CTAX	-.071	.039
UNEMP	-.072	.119
GWE	.051	-.105

Extraction Method: Principal Axis Factoring.
Rotation Method: Varimax with Kaiser Normalization
Factor Scores Method: Regression.

FIGURE 11.12 SPSS factor scores coefficient matrix

Notice how similar the above expressions are to the multiple regression models used in Chapter 10. But instead of a dependent variable, the equation yields a single factor score for each county based on its various attributes. The manner in which these factor scores are presented in the Data view window is shown in Figure 11.13.

Interpretation of each score for each case can be undertaken by reference to a simple set of principles. For a case to achieve a high score on any factor, it must have a high value for variables with positive loadings and a low value for variables with negative loadings. Conversely, for a case to have a low factor score, it must have low value on variables with positive loadings and a high value on variables with negative loadings. To understand this more fully we can examine the factor solution provided in Figure 11.8. For factor 1, which relates mainly to demographic variables, we can see that death rate has a negative loading, while birth rate, household size and gross weekly earnings all have positive loadings. Accordingly, our computed factor scores in the new column **fac1_1** will reflect those relationships, with those cases having higher scores relating to counties that have higher birth rates, incomes and household sizes and low death rates. Thus Outer London (where birth rates are high but death rates low) has a high factor score of 2·17, while the Isle of Wight (where birth rates are low but death rates high) scores lowest with –2·63. Clearly, scores will represent a spectrum of values, but with the general rule being that the higher the score, the more likely the county is to have higher birth rates and lower death rates. Nevertheless, we must be careful when interpreting such data that we do not equate very high factor scores with only high birth rates and low death rates and so on, and we should recall that we are dealing with 'composite' variables, and that gross weekly income and household size are also important variables on factor 1.

To indicate the great value of factor scores to geographers in drawing several variables together into a single measure, Figure 11.14 plots the results for factor 2 (the 'social' factor). It needs to be recalled (see Figure 11.8) that the strongly loaded positive factors are such variables as death rate, percentage single parent families and

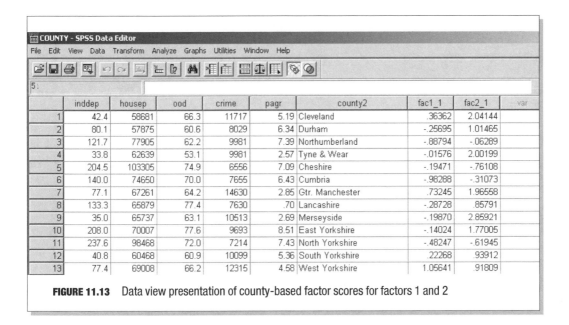

FIGURE 11.13 Data view presentation of county-based factor scores for factors 1 and 2

unemployment. The major negatively loaded variable is the proportion of pupils engaged in post-16 education. As a result, all counties with high factor 2 scores will have high measures on these positive variables, but have fewer than average pupils staying on for post-16 education. It is immediately noticeable that such counties tend to concentrate in the north of England, with an outlier in the West Midlands. On the other hand, the low scoring counties (with low unemployment, low death rates etc. but high levels of post-16 education) are concentrated in the south-east of the country.

11.8 Problems in the application of factor analysis

In common with most other multivariate statistical techniques applied to geographical problems, factor analysis has attracted a degree of criticism. Among statisticians there are those who dismiss the method as an elaborate way of doing something that can only ever be crude, namely the picking out of clusters of interrelated variables. In these debates such people favour the mathematical clarity of principal components analysis. However, countering such criticism is the work of the pro-factor analysts, whose studies are mainly rooted within the social sciences. To these people the advantages of factor analysis are the objectivity of the method and its more realistic assumptions of the data structures.

These debates have encouraged geographers to question the methods and two main issues have emerged. The first concerns how factor analysis should be used by geographers, a problem that to a large extent is created by the very flexibility of the method. Without perhaps fully appreciating it to be the case, geographers have used factoring methods in one of three ways:

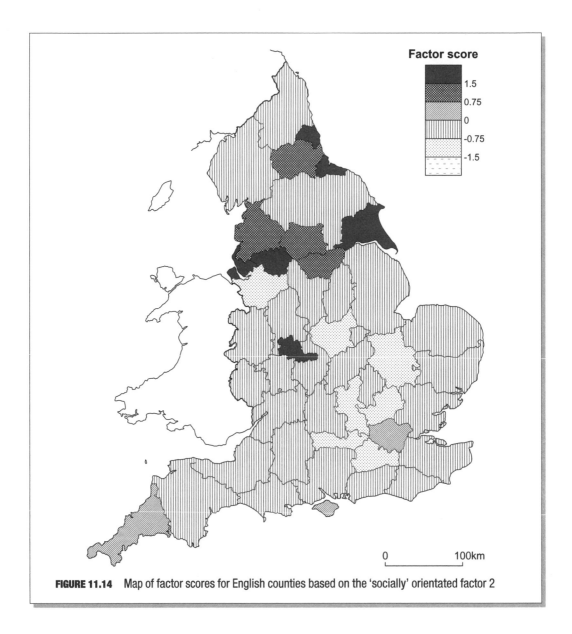

Factor score

■	1.5
▦	0.75
▨	0
▥	-0.75
⠂	-1.5

0   100km

FIGURE 11.14   Map of factor scores for English counties based on the 'socially' orientated factor 2

1   to attempt to create some order in a large body of poorly understood data;

2   to explore working hypotheses and to measure the related dimensions of sets of variables; and

3   to analyse patterns of factor loadings.

These uses may be complicated by the variety of methods that exist to solve each problem and the question is quickly raised of which is the best method. The problem becomes yet more vexing when different programs, using different methods, produce different results from the same data. Such problems cannot be fully resolved unless geographers explore the advantage and limitations of different factor models in the light of their own clearly defined needs.

The second problem is that of interpretation. One way in which this problem arises is through the study of factor loadings of the variables. These represent the square roots of the proportions of standardised variation of each variable on each factor (see section 11.2). Thus these factors are not as substantive as their numerical size might indicate. We might, in this sense, overestimate the importance of groups of variables and we might lay too great a stress on pairs of variables that are poorly correlated.

Variable selection is also a perennial problem. Some workers have gone so far as to suggest the selective removal of variables that score low on all derived factors, thereby simplifying the data structure. But the necessities of subjective assessment would normally make this inadvisable. Other problems result from the mismatch between census enumeration districts (the usual unit in British studies) and social groups. For example, large counties will inevitably contain a wide diversity of social groups and attributes. This may introduce spurious internal heterogeneity into each spatial unit making it thereby more difficult to abstract useful factors. In general, however, factor analysis, when used with suitable caution and awareness of its advantages and disadvantages, provides a notable addition to the geographer's range of analytical techniques.

Cluster analysis

12.1 Classification and segmentation

IN CHAPTER 11 WE examined the idea of data reduction; that is of minimising the number of variables with which we have to work, with a view to refining our data set for further analyses. Such reductions help when examining the links between many variables or when drawing conclusions about their general characteristics. In this chapter we will continue this theme of data reduction, but for a rather different purpose. It is often said that there are specific groups in society that can be related by attitudes or perceptions; for example the 'types' of people who are most likely to buy a particular sort of car, hold particular political views or conduct themselves in particular ways. But such categorisation is by no means restricted to human beings. In a similar fashion, regions and spatial units such as counties, states or cities can be grouped and classified, while other popular subjects for grouping are biological features such as plant and animal communities. Furthermore, for many scientists classification is an important first step in investigation and research. In the following examples we will concentrate on the grouping of individuals according to their behaviour and attitudes, but the potential for applying these methods widely across others areas in geography must not be overlooked.

Classifying individuals has great utility as a research tool, enabling the investigator to examine the types of individuals (animate and inanimate) through their collective measured attributes. However, the problem is how, exactly, should such individuals be classified? Should this be done arbitrarily or randomly? In the first instance, we might choose to assign individual cases to a particular group on the basis of assumptions that we already have about the data. By this means we might decide to allocate seemingly similar individuals into a particular category. For example, we might have conducted a questionnaire survey and measured four attitudes on Likert agreement scales. We could then assess the degree of agreement across these four attitudes for each individual. The higher total scores would indicate generally higher degrees of agreement. We might then choose to select groupings on the basis of these raw scores (i.e. those scoring above 25, above 20 and so on). However, the problem with this approach is that it assumes that general agreement with one concept or attitude is reflected in all others and hides any variability in agreement between specific attitudes. It does not, for example, take into account the difference between one individual who scores highly on the first three of the hypothetical questions and low on the fourth and another who scores high on the final three but low on the first. They will have similar scores, but for different reasons.

Cluster analysis techniques are more sophisticated and introduce greater, but not necessarily complete, objectivity. They allow the researcher to examine how cases in a dataset are related to each other across a range of variables. We have already argued that the arbitrary approach of grouping individuals simply according to their total score on a combined measurement scale would disguise variations in questionnaire response profiles. Cluster analysis, however, overcomes this problem by comparing how statistically similar to each other the scores of individuals are over a range of different measurement scales. In contrast to the above, one-dimensional measure of 'similarity' in which all measures are accumulated into one index, it does so by measuring the statistical distance between individuals in n-dimensional space, where n is the number of measured attributes. These distances are measures of similarity. By this means, it is easier to identify groups that would not readily emerge if we used only total scores across all scales.

12.2 Cluster analysis: theory and application

Cluster analysis is based on the concept of similarity (the numerical aspects of similarity are examined below). In cluster analysis groups are formed by the pairing of individual cases within a dataset according to how similar they are on either a series of two or more scales or measures. This *similarity* is measured in a number of different ways, according to what types of groups need to be identified. More importantly it is also based on the measurement of the statistical distance between any two individual observations or groups of observations. In cluster analysis, observations are related and paired to each other on the basis of these distances, which are defined by the differences between the scores of one observation on the relevant variables and the corresponding scores of another observation. Distance (D) is based on the notion of $n \times v$ dimensional space, where

$$D = (n, v) \tag{12.1}$$

Equation 12.1

D = dimensional space

n = number of observations

v = number of variables

This *n*-dimensional distance itself can be measured in a number of ways, the main ones being:

- *Euclidean distance* is a standard measure of distance using the square root of the sum of squared differences between each score for two observations.

- *Pearson distance* is the square root of the sum of squared differences between observations divided by their variances. This method is used to standardise distance where measures operate over different magnitude ranges (see below for more information on standardising variables).

- *Manhattan distance* is the sum of absolute differences between scores in observations. This method reduces the influence of outliers in the calculation of distance between groups of more than one individual.

Having identified how distance is measured between the individual observations or groups (also known as clusters), it is important to examine how clusters are formed and then amalgamated into larger clusters. We have already noted that clusters were joined on the basis of their 'similarity'. This can be assessed using a range of different *linkage* methods for pairing observations or clusters together. This is an important point, since we have assumed up until now that there is only one method of joining observations and clusters based on how 'similar' they are in terms of their distances from each other. However, a range of techniques exist for assessing these similarities. For example, if the data we have are already similar (there are many observations with values close together), we may not want to use a linkage strategy that is based on the two observations in different clusters that are the closest, since this will quickly produce one very large cluster with a small number of outlying minor clusters or individuals. Of the various methods for calculating the linkage between clusters, the following are the most important:

- Single linkage – as noted above, this method is based on the minimum distance between an observation in one cluster and that of another. Also termed 'nearest neighbour', this method is useful if observations have a clear definition or space between each other.

- Average linkage – this method examines not only the distances between two observations in different clusters but also the distance between the cluster centres.

- Centroid linkage – this uses another averaging technique that attempts to link clusters according to the cluster means.

- Complete linkage – this offers a means by which to examine the *maximum* possible distance between an observation in one cluster and that of another. By this method, the clusters identified tend to be of a relatively similar size and uniformity. This method can mean that outliers are of more significance, *pulling* the maximum limits of any given cluster and skewing the result.

- Median linkage – median linkage ensures that the median, and not the mean, distance between two clusters provides the distance measure.

Depending on the distance measure and linkage method adopted, a process of *agglomeration* or *pairing* will take place by adding observations to clusters until just one cluster remains that contains all the individual observations. This pairing process is based on the assumption that distances are calculated using the same scales and orders of measurement. However, this may cause problems when data scales vary and, for example, one wishes to examine the similarity of observations when using quite different measures such as income in pounds sterling and distance travelled to work in kilometres. In this case, standardisation of the variables would be more appropriate. This can easily be undertaken in SPSS and MINITAB using the methods described in section 5.8, and is strongly recommended where magnitude ranges over the measurement variables are different. If data have been standardised, it is usually recommended that the Pearson distance measure is used (see above).

The pairing process begins with the two most similar cases. Other pairs may then be grouped if they are now the most similar, or this new cluster (at present with only two cases in it) can be compared with other observations and paired to the next most similar and so on. By this means individuals are progressively drawn into clusters, and those clusters gradually drawn together, all in an order dictated by their distances and the selected linkage method. At crucial stages in the *amalgamation* process, there will be instances where large clusters will join each other to form very large groupings. On the other hand, it is often the case that there are individuals that are significantly different from others in the dataset and will be left out of the amalgamation process until late in the pairing procedure. This can often result in a near-final solution that has two or three very large clusters and one small one. The pairing process continues until one 'cluster' has been formulated from the cases in the dataset. This is not to imply that all cases are equal, but rather that the logical end of the process necessitates the final joining of the two penultimate clusters, which might be very different from each other.

The process of pairing according to similarity (whichever method is used) is conceptually a simple one. However, the technique of cluster analysis can only provide a framework for showing how similar one set of clusters are to another. What it cannot do is to provide a means by which to examine the most effective or efficient linkage sequence, and some monitoring of the procedure is advisable. During the pairing process, SPSS and MINITAB will, helpfully, give an account of how many clusters there are in each step of the amalgamation process, and when new cases join the cluster or another cluster itself merges. This is normally specified according to the similarity level or to the distance between clusters. The similarity level is defined by:

$$s(ij) = \frac{100\,(1 - d(ij))}{d(max)} \tag{12.2}$$

Equation 12.2

$s(ij)$ = similarity between two clusters or observations

d = distance measure

$d(max)$ = maximum value in the distance matrix

As the distance between centres of the developing clusters increases, the similarity used to link them decreases. The development of these linkages is a key feature of cluster analysis, and to examine how we can interpret them more effectively, we can use a diagrammatic representation of the pairing process known as a *dendrogram*.

12.3 Dendrograms in cluster analysis

Most computer packages that offer cluster analysis will provide a diagrammatic representation of the pairing process indicating how many clusters existed at any particular part of the process, and when these were radically changed to formulate a further cluster. Figure 12.1 is a typical example of a dendrogram, with the X axis presenting the original observations ordered by their measurement scales, and the Y axis representing the degree of similarity (equally we could have plotted distance as a measure on the Y axis) as the grouping takes place.

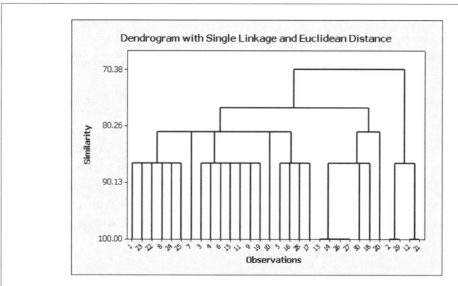

FIGURE 12.1   MINITAB Dendrogram based on degrees of similarity and showing the amalgamation process

You will note that in the first instance, every observation is represented as an individual, thereafter clusters and individuals not found to be identical at the first stage are represented by vertical lines. The process begins by questioning whether any of the cases are identical according to the measurements used. The current dendrogram shows, for example, that observations 13, 14, 26 & 27 immediately form a cluster, as do observations 2 & 29 and 12 & 21. As the pairing process or amalgamation continues, the vertical lines are connected by horizontal links that indicate the point at which the two smaller clusters reach a point of similarity. In Figure 12.1, there are several discernable levels of similarity at which a large number of pairs or clusters are joined to form larger clusters. One relatively small cluster (2, 29, 12, 21) remains and is only integrated at the final step. The key stage in cluster analysis is not the amalgamation of clusters to the end product of one, but rather knowing at what point to cease amalgamation and extract a specific number of clusters for further analysis. This process is commonly referred to as *cutting* the dendrogram.

Cutting is a subjective and somewhat difficult process as the number of clusters one wants to retain for further analysis may depend on the research objectives. The decision may also depend on whether the work is explanatory or confirmatory. In the former case, where no underlying assumptions have been made about the pattern of clusters that should appear, it is a question of the level of similarity that one wants to accept that will guide the cutting point. Again, there are no rules about what constitutes an 'acceptable' level of similarity. Where there is a confirmatory element in the research, the dendrogram might be cut according to the relevant number of clusters sought. However, in reality, one normally enters into such work with an open mind, seeking to identify particular clusters of individuals or cases that can provide the most effective means of classifying data. To this extent, cluster analysis is normally based on the very subjective selection of clusters following a close examination of the dendrogram. To provide a useful example of the cutting process, we can examine Figure 12.1 in more detail. These data are taken from a study of travel-to-work attitudes and behaviour. Four attitudes were used in this example to examine whether there were specific groups that could be identified. The four attitudes (of the six in the original questionnaire) that were analysed related to the agreement of respondents to the following statements:

Travel attitude 1: 'I value my quality of life over my job.'

Travel attitude 2: 'I like to live as near to work as I can.'

Travel attitude 5: 'I like to have a clear distance between work and home.'

Travel attitude 6: 'I'd rather be earning money than relaxing.'

Responses could vary between 'strongly agree' (5) to 'strongly disagree' (1). The research was interested in examining whether different types of individuals could be identified according to these attitudes. For example, were there types of individual who valued quality of life and, perhaps, wished to live closer to work, or other types who wished to earn more money and perhaps sacrifice quality of life? Indeed, and going one stage further, if such groups did exist, what were their demographic profiles and how did such groupings relate to other variables in the research?

No assumptions were made beforehand concerning how many clusters there ought to be and during the amalgamation process, the scores of each individual for every attitude were compared. The two individuals with the most similar pattern of scores were paired first. In fact, and as noted earlier, there were three clusters that could be formed of individuals with 100 per cent similarity. These were 13, 14, 26 & 27; 2 & 29; and, finally, 12 & 21. It is difficult to interpret the character of the amalgamation process until the later stages of the analysis. This is an important point that is dealt with relatively easily in this example as there are only 30 cases, but in projects with many more individuals the problem of dendrogram interpretation quickly becomes a challenging exercise. However, some clear trends emerge, and there appear to be two major clusters that are joined at the same point of similarity in the left-hand part of the dendrogram. It is not until the final stage of the process that the cases on the right-hand side of the dendrogram enter the main stream and cease to exist as a third, very distinctive, cluster. This process offers some insight into the data we are examining, since these individuals are quite different in their attitudinal elements to others in the sample. But before we can identify these individuals, we still have to decide where to cut the dendrogram. If we accept that there are three distinct clusters, then we would cut it at around 80 per cent similarity and thereby confirm that we want to retain three clusters. Very helpfully, these clusters can then be retained for further analysis by asking the computer package to store the cluster membership of each individual case in the dataset.

12.4 Cluster analysis in MINITAB and SPSS

The means of undertaking a cluster analysis in the two computer packages focused on here differ significantly. We will deal with MINITAB in the text, while SPSS is dealt with on the CD. MINITAB provides a robust cluster analysis, in the sense that the researcher is able to enter a large number of observations and variables into the analysis and be provided with a comprehensive output. SPSS provides an equally comprehensive output, but the dendrogram produced of the amalgamation process can be somewhat unwieldy. The final choice depends, however, on the needs of the researcher, who will have to decide which program offers the most advantages.

In MINITAB, there are many options concerning both the distance and the linkage methods that can be used. For a practical example of cluster analysis we will return to our example in section 12.3 and in which we have data on the attitudes and behaviour of 30 individuals towards travel to work in Britain. We might want to examine whether there were particular types of individuals that held specific travel attitudes and the extent to which these related to other attributes of the sample, such as gender, the distance travelled to work or income level. We might hypothesise, for example, that there are at least two groups of individuals within our sample – those who like travelling a lot and don't mind separating work from home and those who prefer to be closer to their place of work and have a preference for a higher quality of life. But do these types actually exist in reality? Using the dataset TRAVEL_DATA.MTW, we can look for the existence of these hypothesised groups. The four attitudes of interest relate to those outlined in section 12.3. In the case of travel attitudes 5 and 6 the data were reverse coded so that those that disagreed with the final two statements (having a longer distance to go to work, and earning more money) were in the same conceptual direction as the first two statements.

The question of concern, therefore, relates to the extent to which different groups or individuals can be identified according to their attitudes towards travelling to work and quality of life. As noted in section 12.2, had the statements been on different scales (some 1 to 5, but others 1 to 10 for example) or other variables been imported, then we would have to standardise the measures (see below). In this case this was not necessary as all four variables used the same 1 to 5 point scale. To perform a cluster analysis in MINITAB, use the commands **Stat > Multivariate > Cluster Observations**. This will bring up the dialogue box in Figure 12.2. In the dialogue box, the variables that contain the observations that you want to examine are transferred into the **Variables** box. For the purposes of this example, we will transfer the four 'Travel attitude' variables of 'quality of life', 'live near work', 'separate work' and 'enjoy work'. These are held in columns C8, C9, C12 and C13 of the data file. If the variables need to be standardised (not the case here), the **Standardize variables** option in the dialogue box needs to be

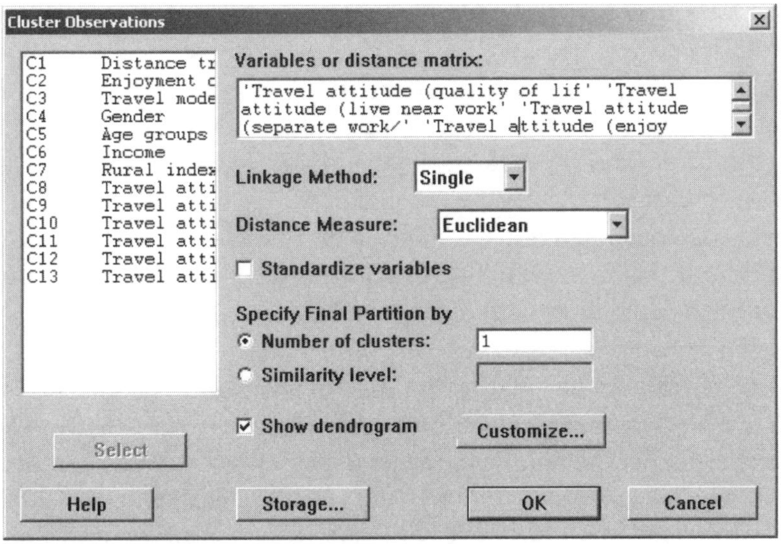

FIGURE 12.2 MINITAB **Cluster Observations** dialogue box

checked. The **Distance Measure** in the dialogue box is used to define which mathematical operation willbe used to measure the distance between observations and clusters. There are threeoptions, relating directly to the choices outlined in section 12.2 above, and we willselect to use the **Euclidean** option. In part this choice is made because we are not using standardised data and because the nature of our measurement scale (1 to 5 only) means that we need not be concerned with outlying observations. The **Linkage Method** refers to the way in which individual clusters are joined together (section 12.2). There are a number of options, dependent on the type of data in the analysis and, as we have noted above, the choice depends on how you want to conceptualise similarity. In the case of our analysis, we are interested in examining the *minimum* distance between two cases. On that basis we would use the single linkage method, more commonly termed the 'nearest neighbour' method. In addition we suspect that the observations may contain quite different groups and are unlikely to amalgamate too quickly into large clusters even with this nearest neighbour option.

Once the various options have been decided upon, we need to ensure we have a view of the linkage process, which requires the selection of a dendrogram. This can be undertaken by checking the **Show dendrogram** box. There is also the option (not used here) of clicking the **Customize . . .** button, which allows the dendrogram to be enhanced by the addition of titles, case labels and so on. Returning to the main dialogue box, we are asked to specify how the **Final Partition** of the analysis is to be specified. This is essentially a function of the second stage of analysis, undertaken only after the dendrogram and linkage process have been interrogated. In many cases it is advisable to leave the default option of 1, producing one final cluster. After pressing **OK**, there will be considerable output in the Session window, but the more important output comes in the form of the dendrogram, as shown in Figure 12.1.

The dendrogram demonstrates the linkage of the alternative clusters, which at the beginning of the process are individual cases. Each case is paired to another and so on, until there is one final cluster. You will note that the dendrogram has re-ordered the cases on the X axis from 1 to 30 to an apparently random sequence. This ordering reflects, however, the similarity of adjacent individuals prior to pairing, so we begin with 1, but its closest other individual is number 23, which is placed next in sequence, and so on. This is not, importantly, to suggest that observations on the left of the dendrogram are 'more' similar to those on the right; the ordering simply reflects MINITAB's ordering procedure.

The Y axis of the dendrogram indicates the numerical value of similarity measure – as defined in Equation 12.2. However, we could also have opted to examine the relative distances between the observations in the clusters. To view this on the Y axis, we could have pressed the **Customize . . .** button in the **Cluster Observations** dialogue box (Figure 12.2). This brings up the dialogue box in Figure 12.3. Here we can select to give the dendrogram a title and whether to label the Y axis with the similarity level or distance measure. In addition, if the number of cases is large, you may also select to

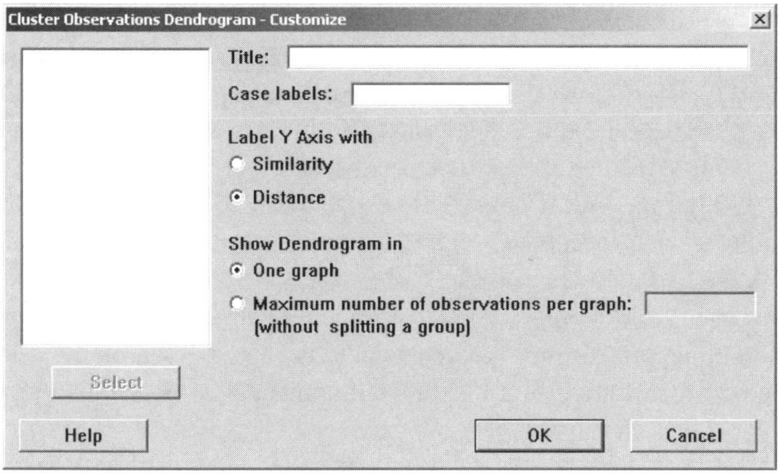

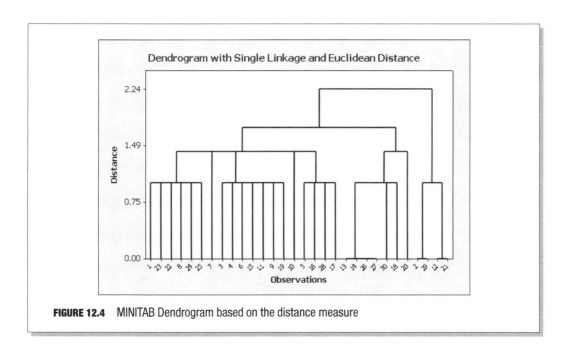

FIGURE 12.3   MINITAB **Customize** dendrogram dialogue box

FIGURE 12.4   MINITAB Dendrogram based on the distance measure

have the dendrogram appear on sequential graphs. One useful aspect of this dialogue box is that it enables cases to be labelled. If we had case labels in a text column, we could tell MINITAB to use these to label the *X* axis instead of numbers. By pressing **OK**, we return to the main dialogue box and press **OK** again to undertake the cluster analysis once again with the amended dendrogram. This can be seen in Figure 12.4 in which the 'distance' scaling of the Y axis should be noted and contrasted with percentage 'similarity' scale of Figure 12.1.

In this case, Figure 12.4 shows that using the Euclidean distance measure, and with a view to abstracting three clusters, we should cut the dendrogram at 1·49 or thereabouts. Where to cut the dendrogram is a key issue and in this case it is more a question of whether one wants to retain two or three clusters for further analysis. In most cases, as noted above, this is a question of subjectivity and there are no hard and fast rules.

An alternative way of examining the linkage process is to scrutinise the extensive output that MINITAB generates in the Session window. The results for the current example are presented in Figure 12.5, where we can see how the three clusters were derived. The output plots the linkage process in terms of the observations paired, the number of new clusters formed and the different number clusters and their properties

Cluster Analysis of Observations: Travel attit, Travel attit, Travel attit, ...

Euclidean Distance, Single Linkage
Amalgamation Steps

Step	Number of clusters	Similarity level	Distance level	Clusters joined		New cluster	Number of obs. in new cluster
1	29	100.000	0.00000	2	29	2	2
2	28	100.000	0.00000	26	27	26	2
3	27	100.000	0.00000	14	26	14	3
4	26	100.000	0.00000	12	21	12	2
5	25	100.000	0.00000	13	14	13	4
6	24	86.755	1.00000	13	30	13	5
7	23	86.755	1.00000	16	28	16	2
8	22	86.755	1.00000	24	25	24	2
9	21	86.755	1.00000	8	24	8	3
10	20	86.755	1.00000	1	23	1	2
11	19	86.755	1.00000	1	22	1	3
12	18	86.755	1.00000	9	19	9	2
13	17	86.755	1.00000	13	18	13	6
14	16	86.755	1.00000	16	17	16	3
15	15	86.755	1.00000	5	16	5	4
16	14	86.755	1.00000	6	15	6	2
17	13	86.755	1.00000	2	12	2	4
18	12	86.755	1.00000	6	11	6	3
19	11	86.755	1.00000	6	9	6	5
20	10	86.755	1.00000	1	8	1	6
21	9	86.755	1.00000	4	6	4	6
22	8	86.755	1.00000	3	4	3	7
23	7	81.268	1.41421	13	20	13	7
24	6	81.268	1.41421	3	10	3	8
25	5	81.268	1.41421	1	7	1	7
26	4	81.268	1.41421	3	5	3	12
27	3	81.268	1.41421	1	3	1	19
28	2	77.058	1.73205	1	13	1	26
29	1	70.383	2.23607	1	2	1	30

Final Partition
Number of clusters: 1

	Number of observations	Within cluster sum of squares	Average distance from centroid	Maximum distance from centroid
Cluster1	30	178.167	2.25058	3.91933

FIGURE 12.5 MINITAB output from the cluster analysis option

joined in sequence, from top (30 individual cases) to bottom (one cluster with 30 observations).

The linkage process reveals that at the 81·3 per cent similarity level there are a large number of observations that simultaneously form a small number of clusters. In one case the cluster has 19 members, although the outlying small cluster of four (individuals 2, 29, 12 & 21) was formed earlier in the sequence at step 17. The elements of Figure 12.5 can be summarised as follows:

- **Step** – the stage in the agglomeration process
- **Number of clusters** – a running record of the amalgamation of observations into clusters
- **Similarity level** – the calculation of the similarity based on Equation 12.2
- **Distance level** – corresponds to the similarity level, but is based on the distance between clusters (see above)
- **Clusters joined** – the identifying numbers of the observations and latterly the clusters as they are joined
- **New cluster** – the identifying number of the new cluster, which is always the lowest number among the members of the new group
- **Number of obs. in new cluster** – the number of individuals in each new cluster.

We can plot the progression of the development of the three clusters through the process of agglomeration. From the final column in Figure 12.5, it can be seen that the last cluster to join the final solution in Step 29 is cluster 2, which joins cluster 1. Cluster 2 developed early in the agglomeration process, at step 1 and then step 17. This is a small cluster with only four cases in it, whereas clusters 1 and 13 do not develop until later but are larger. In deciding on the final number of clusters to retain by using Figure 12.5, we might consider examining the change in the number of observations at various similarity or distance stages in the procedure, and we would note that similarity between the clusters is high until the final couple of steps, where the last four observations are included. We might on the basis of this tabulated output cut the process at 81 per cent similarity, which is the same as we had decided for the dendrogram. The number of clusters retained for further analysis is normally termed the *final partition*.

The next step is to ensure that cluster membership is stored so that further analyses can be undertaken on the data. Examples of these analyses are given in section 12.5 of this chapter as a worked example. Cluster membership can be stored in MINITAB by use of the original dialogue box (Figure 12.2) in which there are two options. One is to select a particular similarity level that can be interpreted from either the output or the dendrogram (**Specify Final Partition by . . . Similarity level**), or more commonly, one can choose to select a number of clusters to store (**Specify Final Partition by . . . Number of clusters**). This seems quite simple, but it must always be remembered that the number of clusters to be retained may include a one-item cluster, which should be excluded from further analyses. In any case these should be stored in a new column to which MINITAB should be directed using the **Storage . . .** button at the bottom of the original dialogue box to bring up Figure 12.6. In this example we will specify C16 for storage of the results. The empty column for cluster membership to be placed is selected and typed into the **Cluster membership column**. The column will then be filled with cluster membership numbers at the selected level of similarity or group membership, enabling the properties of each cluster to be examined. In this case we have specified a three group partitioning of the data. This three group partitioning and the group compositions can be seen in Figure 12.1 at the cut-off' similarity' level of 80·26 in which group 1 contains items 1 to 17 (in the order imposed by the system), group 3 contains items 13 to 20 and group 2 items 2 to 21. The evolution of these groups and their numbering (1, 2 and 3) is described in Figure 12.5. Note that group 2 forms early in the process, but groups 1 and 3 undergo more continual evolution as other clusters are added at each stage.

12.5 Using cluster solutions in research

Applying cluster analysis to geographical research can have many potential benefits. A useful example of this approach can be given using the data and results already included in this chapter. We posed a question in section 12.4 regarding what the overall properties and character of the derived clusters would be in terms of the range of variables in the initial study. We might, therefore, be interested in examining the properties of the three clusters identified according to some of the following variables included in the travel study but not forming part of the clustering process. These might usefully include:

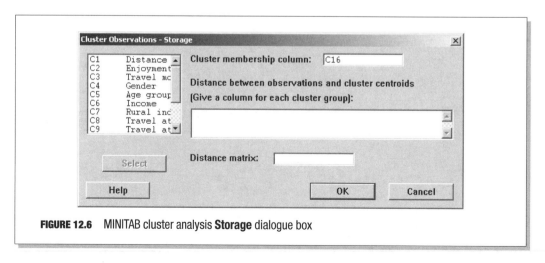

FIGURE 12.6 MINITAB cluster analysis **Storage** dialogue box

- travel mode used to get to work;

- distance travelled to work each day in kilometres;

- gender.

We can examine how the three groups differ in terms of these other variables, remembering of course, that there may be no contrasts and that these variables were not used to discriminate the original clusters.

One way to examine the nature of the clusters is to use MINITAB's **Stat > Tables > Cross Tabulation and Chi-Square** option to examine the distribution of cases in each of the clusters. In this example, we can place the attitudinal trait of interest ('quality of life') into the **For rows** section of the dialogue box and the newly-stored cluster membership elements (column C16) into the **For columns** section (see Figure 12.7). Press **OK** and the output from this is provided in the Session window, given in Figure 12.8. Here the three clusters form the columns, in each of which the number of responses over the five possible (1 to 5) are given.

The results in Figure 12.8 provide a pattern that can guide our further analysis. Remembering that the rows refer to the agreement with the attitude statements provided in section 12.3 (with 1 being 'strongly disagree' and 5 being 'strongly agree') and that the columns refer to cluster membership, we can see that there are distinct properties for each of the three clusters:

- Cluster 1 – these individuals tend to disagree that quality of life is more important and score mostly 2 and 3 on that response.

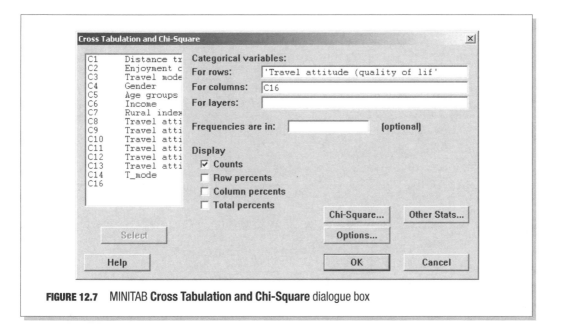

FIGURE 12.7 MINITAB **Cross Tabulation and Chi-Square** dialogue box

```
              Tabulated statistics: Travel attitude (quality of lif, C16

         Rows: Travel attitude (quality of lif   Columns: C16

                   1   2   3   All

         1         1   0   0    1
         2        10   0   0   10
         3         8   0   0    8
         4         0   0   5    5
         5         0   4   2    6
         All      19   4   7   30

         Cell Contents:       Count
```

FIGURE 12.8   MINITAB output of frequency statistics for travel attitudes and cluster membership. The rows represent the five responses to the 'quality of life' question, and the three columns the different clusters of individuals

- Cluster 2 – these individuals are very keen to preserve their quality of life, and all score on response 5 ('strongly agree' that quality of life is important).

- Cluster 3 – tends to comprise individuals who do appreciate a good quality of life, but are not as strongly persuaded by this aspect of travel as those of cluster 2, and score mostly 4 with two 5s.

This exercise can be repeated across other questionnaire responses to provide a more detailed, and complex, picture of the attitudinal composition of the three clusters.

We might consider providing each of these clusters with names, which are evidently subjective. However, the focus here is on how we might examine further properties of these clusters. We could, for example, enquire into the extent to which there are differences between the distances travelled to work by members of the different clusters. Given the attitudes outlined above to quality of life, we might expect that those in cluster 1 might be more willing to travel further, while those in cluster 2 travel the least. To examine this, we can use MINITAB's **Display Descriptive Statistics** command by using **Stat > Basic Statistics > Display Descriptive Statistics**, which brings up the dialogue box in Figure 12.9 in which we place the variable to be examined (in this case the 'Distance travelled 2001') into the **Variables** box, and place the column with the cluster membership numbers in (C16) into the **By variables** box and press **OK**. The output in Figure 12.10 is generated in the Session window. In this case we requested (using the **Statistics . . .** option in the dialogue box) only a small range of descriptive statistics.

The means and other measures are provided according to the three clusters, and it is evident immediately that the hypothesis that cluster 1 members are the most prepared to travel longer distances to work, and those of cluster 2 the least, is supported by the mean distance of 39·1 km for the former but only 15·5 km for the latter.

As a final example of this approach we might examine the extent to which there is a gender difference between the three clusters. For example, we might ask whether there

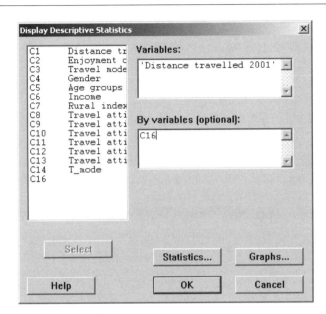

FIGURE 12.9 MINITAB **Display Descriptive Statistics** dialogue box

Descriptive Statistics: Distance travelled 2001

Variable	C16	Mean	StDev	Minimum	Median	Maximum
Distance travell	1	39.05	8.72	21.00	41.00	53.00
	2	15.50	4.51	10.00	15.50	21.00
	3	28.14	6.84	20.00	27.00	41.00

FIGURE 12.10 MINITAB output of summary statistics for the distance travelled to work by the three clusters of individuals identified in the grouping procedure

is a greater probability that females would prefer to live closer to home and have a better quality of life than males. To examine this (note, we are not testing this hypothesis, merely examining the descriptive data), we can rerun the **Stat > Tables > Cross Tabulation and Chi-Square** procedure but now place 'gender' in the **For rows** box and leave our cluster membership column (C16) in the **For columns** box. The output provided in the Session window is given in Figure 12.11.

As many as 14 males in the sample (gender coded 1: male, 2: female) fell within cluster 1, none in cluster 2 and only two in cluster 3. In contrast, the female respondents are spread much more evenly between the clusters. We might choose to test this imbalance statistically using a chi-square test (section 7. 15), but for the moment it is sufficient to state that there is reasonable evidence that males do tend to place less emphasis on quality of life and may prefer to live further from work, while the position with regard to females is much less clear in respect of this variable.

```
                    Tabulated statistics: Gender, C16

            Rows: Gender    Columns: C16

                    1  2  3  All

            1      14  0  2   16
            2       5  4  5   14
            All    19  4  7   30

            Cell Contents:      Count
```

FIGURE 12.11   MINITAB output for cross-tabulation of gender (rows) and cluster membership (columns)

12.6 Cluster analysis: observations and evaluation

Cluster analysis is a useful analytical tool and can be a powerful way to identify complex groupings in data that cannot readily be examined by simpler methods. However, we must be careful not to become too complacent about the results we generate. Cluster analysis is more subjective than many methods, and the point at which we cut the dendrogram is always a questionable and major issue. In the above example, we might have decided to cut the dendrogram and just retain two clusters for analysis. Would this have been more appropriate as clusters 2 and 3 do seem fairly similar in their characteristics? Or indeed, would it be wrong to eliminate the third and smallest cluster?

Cluster analysis is also problematic for some researchers given the evident stipulation that no missing data can be permitted as the technique relies on calculating the distance between observations for a range of values all of which must be included for the technique to be effective. It is also the case that with data that are heavily skewed, there are difficulties in identifying clusters given the likelihood that many observations will group into one cluster very quickly. Accordingly, the choice of linkage method becomes even more important.

Finally, we must also note that as with most other statistical techniques, the absence of any identifiable or apparently useful groupings does not mean that they do not exist nor indeed that finding no groups is unimportant. On many occasions we may need to experiment with linkage methods to find out which one provides us with an acceptable solution. Only after such experimentation with no satisfactory outcome may we have to accept that there are no clearly identifiable patterns in our data. But even this may be an important finding, and reflect on either our data collection methods or the structure of the sample drawn.

13

Spatial indices and pattern analysis

13.1 Introduction

MANY OF THE STATISTICAL techniques that geographers commonly use tend to be of a non-spatial type that can just as easily be applied to any other scientific discipline. Indeed, the majority of the techniques mentioned so far in this book fall into this category, where location is but one of many variables under examination. However, there also exists a set of spatial statistics which allow the geographer to summarise and describe numerically a variety of spatial patterns ranging from simple dot distributions through to contour maps. It is possible to recognise a typology of maps that loosely correspond to the nominal, ordinal, interval and ratio scales of measurement that we discussed in Chapter 4. In this way a picture can be built up of the types of data we are likely to want to analyse using different spatial statistics. To carry out such spatial analysis three major groups of techniques are available, namely: centrographic techniques, spatial indices and point pattern analysis. It has, however, to be observed that while such methods may fall clearly within the realm of geographical research, they are poorly served by commercially available packages such as MINITAB and SPSS that are designed for a wide range of discipline-based uses.

13.2 Centrographic techniques

Centrographic techniques are an extension of the descriptive statistics discussed in Chapter 4, but applied to data in two-dimensional space. Such techniques, also termed geostatistics, have been used for some considerable time, with the concept of the mean centre being introduced in the USA Census of population as early as 1870. Similarly, a school of so-called centrography, based on these methods, was developed in Russia in the early part of the twentieth century. The main measures used within these studies were those concerned with central tendency, in particular the arithmetic mean centre. Geographers have used such spatial statistics since the 1950s, and extended the techniques over the following years.

The mean centre can be most easily used to summarise a spatial distribution of point patterns. In this case the data must first be identified by grid co-ordinates. If the mean centre of a point distribution is to be calculated, then the first step is to derive the mean of the X and Y co-ordinates for the point distribution, using Equation 13.1:

$$\bar{X} = \frac{\Sigma X_i}{N} \qquad \bar{Y} = \frac{\Sigma Y_i}{N}$$

(13.1)

Equation 13.1

X_i and Y_i = co-ordinates of individual points

N = total number of points

These calculations are demonstrated for a simple, hypothetical example in Table 13.1; while Figure 13.1 shows how the mean centre of this dot distribution is represented by the intersection of $\bar{X}$ and $\bar{Y}$. It is also possible to calculate the weighted mean centre of a distribution where each dot represents a different value. For example, each dot on the map may represent a factory of different size, and we may want to work out the mean centre of factory floor space. In this case, we could weight out calculations in terms of the size of each factory. The mean centre is then found by multiplying the weights of

TABLE 13.1 Calculation of the mean centre for a simple distribution of points

X	Y	Point
1	5	1
2	6	2
2	4	3
2	3	4
3	7	5
3	5	6
3	4	7
4	6	8
4	3	9
5	5	10
29	48	Total
$\bar{X}$ = 29/10 = 2·9	$\bar{Y}$ = 48/10 = 4·8	

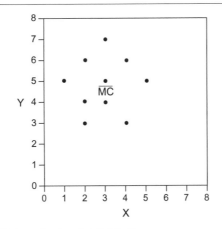

FIGURE 13.1 Mean centre (MC) for a simple point distribution

each occurrence by its X and Y co-ordinate values, and dividing by the sum of the weights, as in Equation 13.2:

$$\overline{X}_w = \frac{\Sigma(X_i W_i)}{\Sigma W_i} \qquad \overline{Y}_w = \frac{\Sigma(Y_i W_i)}{\Sigma W_i} \tag{13.2}$$

where W are the weighted values.

As with conventional measures of central tendency, geostatistics can also make use of the median centre and the modal centre. The former is unfortunately described in quite different ways by a number of standard statistical texts. Some define the median centre as the point of intersection of two orthogonal lines from the X and Y axes, which have an equal number of points on each side (Figure 13.2a). Others refer to the median centre as the point in a distribution at which the sum of the absolute deviations of each point is minimised. That is, statistical distances between the median centre and each point are at a minimum. It therefore represents the point of theoretical 'minimum aggregate travel', and its position can be found by the use of grid overlays. There are three basic steps involved in an iterative process that can be fairly lengthy without the aid of specifically written computer programs. The first stage is to overlay a co-ordinate grid on the map, the limits of which are set by the four most extreme points in the pattern. Second, for each new grid co-ordinate point (X_0, Y_0), the square root of the sum of the squared distances to the n points (X_i, Y_i), of the original pattern is calculated (Figure 13.2b). The point having the lowest value, using Equation 13.3, is then identified:

$$M_c = \sqrt{\Sigma[(X_0 - X_i)^2 + (Y_0 - Y_i)^2]} \tag{13.3}$$

Equation 13.3

X_0, Y_0 = grid co-ordinates

X_i, Y_i = co-ordinates of individual points

M_c = median centre

In the third stage, this point of minimum value is now taken as the centre of a new, finer grid overlay determined in a subjective manner. At this point, step two is repeated using Equation 13.3. A new, more accurate, point of minimum distance is thus established. Such iterations can be carried out as deemed necessary to determine more accurately the 'median centre'. The concept of the median centre as the point of minimum aggregate travel is of considerable use within the study of economic geography and has done much to extend analysis in the area of spatial modelling.

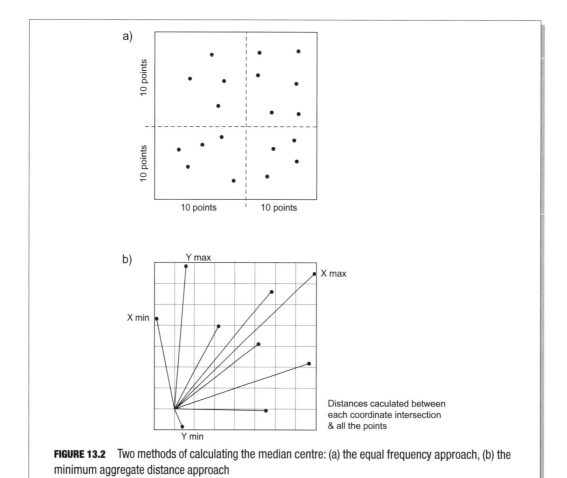

FIGURE 13.2 Two methods of calculating the median centre: (a) the equal frequency approach, (b) the minimum aggregate distance approach

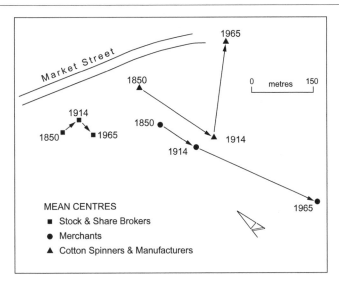

FIGURE 13.3 Use of the spatial mean to indicate functional change in central Manchester (modified from Varley 1968)

At a simpler, but nevertheless effective, level of analysis the concept of the mean centre has proved extremely useful in studying the changing pattern of distributions over time. These changes can be described by calculating the mean centre of a distribution at different time periods and by plotting such changes, as shown in Figure 13.3. Considerable work has also been carried out by Russian economic geographers during the 1920s and 1930s; when they calculated the mean centre for a variety of economic activities and constructed so-called centrograms.

As was shown in Chapter 4, measures of central tendency were only one way of describing a distribution, since use could also be made of statistics measuring dispersion. In geostatistics, a commonly used measure of dispersion is the standard distance, which is analogous to the standard deviation in simple, descriptive statistics. The simplest method of calculating the standard distance of a distribution is shown in Equation 13.4:

$$SD = \sqrt{\left[\frac{\sum (X - \bar{X})^2}{N} + \frac{\sum (Y - \bar{Y})^2}{N} \right]}$$

(13.4)

Equation 13.4

N = number of points

$\bar{X}$ and $\bar{Y}$ = means of X and Y

SD = standard distance

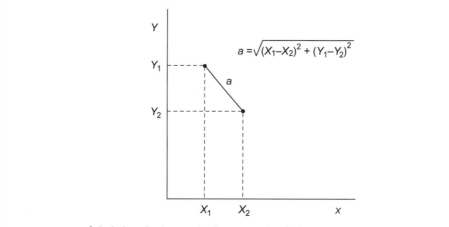

FIGURE 13.4 Calculation of point to point distances using Pythagoras' theorem

TABLE 13.2 Calculation of the standard distance of a point pattern

X	Y	$X-\bar{X}$	$(X-\bar{X})^2$	$Y-\bar{Y}$	$(Y-\bar{Y})^2$
1	5	−1·9	3·61	0·2	0·04
2	6	−0·9	0·81	1·2	1·44
2	4	−0·9	0·81	−0·8	0·64
2	3	−0·9	0·81	−1·8	3·24
3	7	0·1	0·01	2·2	4·84
3	5	0·1	0·01	0·2	0·04
3	4	0·1	0·01	−0·8	0·64
4	6	1·1	1·21	1·2	1·44
4	3	1·1	1·21	−1·8	3·24
5	5	2·1	4·41	0·2	0·04
Total			12·90		15·60
Standard distance			1·29		1·56

Means of X and Y were taken from Table 13.1.

This measure of distance is based on Pythagoras' theorem, where linear distances between points can be calculated from their X and Y co-ordinates (Figure 13.4). The method of calculation is shown in Table 13.2 for the same data as in Table 13.1. Very often it is useful to use the mean centre and the standard distance together in order to describe adequately a spatial distribution. However, few studies have used both measures.

Measures of standard distance are useful, but absolute standard distance is affected by the shape and size of the area under study. For example, standard distances are usually greater for larger spatial areas of study (cities, towns etc.). To overcome this problem use needs to be made of relative standard distance measures. There are a number of ways of calculating such relative measures, depending on the phenomena under investigation. For example, in some studies commercial functions have been related to the population distribution, and the relative dispersion was calculated by dividing the standard distance of the function by that for the population. Other studies have used a relative measure based on the radius of the area of each country, which was assumed to be circular.

13.3 Spatial indices and the Lorenz curve

Apart from the centrographic techniques discussed in the previous section, distributions can also be compared using spatial indices that relate to the *Lorenz curve*. The latter is a simple, but effective, means of illustrating graphically the difference between spatial patterns, and in many texts it is introduced as a technique of map comparison. A number of stages are involved in the calculation and construction of the Lorenz curve, as can be illustrated in a simple example which compares the distributions of black people and white people in the USA (Table 13.3). First, the ratio between blacks and whites needs to be calculated for each area (in our example census regions). Second, these areal units are then ranked on the basis of these ratios, from the smallest to the largest. Next, each observation is converted into a percentage of the total for its own area. Thus, in our example, for each census region of the USA the numbers of black and white people are

TABLE 13.3 Calculation of Lorenz curve for ethnic segregation in the USA (1981)

| Region | Number (000s) of: | | X/Y | Rank | X (%) | Y (%) | Cum. X (%) | Cum. Y (%) |
	White	Black						
N England	11,586	475	24·4	8	6·2	1·8	94·7	99·0
Mid-Atlantic	30,743	4,374	7·0	4	16·3	16·5	47·6	69·5
EN Central	36,139	4,548	7·9	5	19·2	17·2	66·8	86·7
WN Central	16,045	789	20·3	7	8·5	3·0	88·5	97·2
S Atlantic	28,648	7,648	3·7	1	15·2	28·9	15·2	28·9
EC Central	11,700	2,868	4·1	2	6·2	10·8	21·4	39·7
WS Central	18,597	3,525	5·3	3	9·9	13·3	31·3	53·0
Mountain	9,957	269	37·0	9	5·3	1·0	100·0	100·0
Pacific	24,926	1,993	12·5	6	13·2	7·5	80·0	94·2
Total	188,341	26,489						

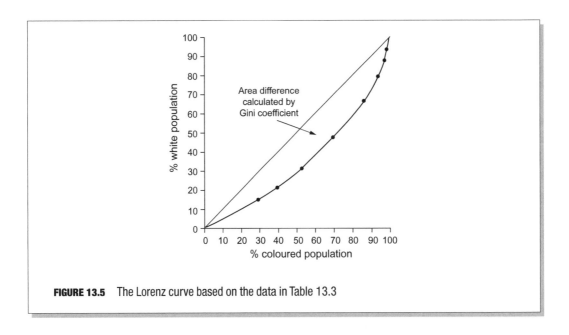

FIGURE 13.5 The Lorenz curve based on the data in Table 13.3

expressed as percentages. Finally, as Table 13.3 shows, these percentage values are accumulated, maintaining the ranks, from 1 upwards. These values can then be plotted out as a graph, or Lorenz curve, as shown in Figure 13.5.

In general terms, the Lorenz curve has a number of obvious features; one being that if the distributions are proportionally identical in each area, then the plot will be a straight line (Figure 13.5). Differences between the distributions will be shown in the form of deviations away from this diagonal line. The extreme case is one of complete separation between two distributions, where the line would follow the X axis and then the vertical boundary of the graph when the value of X reached 100 per cent. In the example given in Figure 13.5 it can be seen that a degree of difference does exist between the two distributions, representing in this case some measure of racial separation at a fairly broad, regional scale within the USA.

One method of measuring the differences revealed by the Lorenz curve is to calculate the *index of dissimilarity* (D_s). This may be defined as the maximum vertical distances between the diagonal line and the Lorenz curve (Figure 13.5). In fact, there are three different ways of obtaining this index. First, it can be calculated from the data, as the maximum difference in the cumulative percentages of the two distributions. Thus, in Table 13.3 D_s would be given by $69.5 - 47.6$, and has the value 21.9. A second method of calculating the index is by measuring it from the Lorenz curve in Figure 13.5, since the area between the two curves is a measure of how poor the fit is. Finally, D_s can be calculated using Equation 13.5, which has the advantage that it deals with percentages that have not been cumulated and therefore avoids some of the work in Table 13.3:

$$D_s = \frac{\sum |X_i - Y_i|}{2} \tag{13.5}$$

where X_i and Y_i are the individual percentages of each variable and D_s has a range of 0 to 100. This statistic is also known as the *Gini coefficient*.

A glance through the literature shows that owing to the flexibility of the index of dissimilarity, it has been applied to a variety of studies. Thus, in our example the index was used as a measure of ethnic segregation, indicating that at a regional scale segregation was not particularly high, with an index of 21.9. Indeed, it is within the context of segregation studies that the index has been widely used.

A second type of use for Lorenz curve analysis is within the area of economic geography. In this instance, the measure of dissimilarity from the Lorenz curve is known as the *coefficient of geographical association*. This produces a measure of the extent to which economic activities are concentrated spatially relative to some other form of activity.

A further use of the index would be to compare population or employment with land area. Thus, population would be plotted on the Y axis and the size of each areal unit as values of X. A perfectly even distribution of population would therefore have an index of zero, with values approaching 100 (or 1, depending on whether percentages are used) indicating greater degrees of population concentration. Such measures of dispersal or concentration based on the Lorenz curve can obviously be applied to a variety of activities other than population.

In addition to the measures based on the Lorenz curve, geographers have also used a variety of spatial indices, or coefficients. The most extensively used is probably the *location quotient* (*LQ*), which measures the extent to which different areas depart from some norm, for example the national average. The quotient can be calculated using Equation 13.6 or, if the data are expressed as percentages, Equation 13.7:

$$LQ = \frac{(X_i / X)}{(Y_i / Y)} \tag{13.6}$$

Equation 13.6

X_i = employment in a given activity *i*, in an area

X = total employment in an area

Y_i = national employment in activity *i*

Y = total national employment

$$LQ_j = \frac{X_j}{k} \tag{13.7}$$

In Equation 13.6 the location quotient indicates the degree of concentration, with higher values of *LQ* representing high concentrations, and values of 1 indicating equal distributions. Table 13.4 illustrates how such measures can be derived for two different types of economic activity. Geographical variations in employment concentrations based on the location quotient can be illustrated by mapping the quotients (Figure 13.6).

One of the problems with the location quotient, and indeed with a number of these spatial indices, is that, statistically, nothing is known about their sampling distributions. Furthermore, as the scale for the quotient is arranged around unity, values below the national norm are compressed between 0 and 1; but above unity the quotient can rise to any value. One coefficient that does not suffer from these disadvantages is the Gini coefficient of concentration, which can be calculated using Equation 13.5, and which varies on a scale of 0 to 100. It is widely supposed that if the sampling is done without replacement from an infinite population then the sampling distribution will approximate to normal.

Finally, some mention must be made of the problems associated with using the Lorenz curve. First, there are data restrictions since variables must be expressed as frequencies

TABLE 13.4 Calculation of location quotients for employment in engineering and textile manufacturing in England (1976), employment numbers are in thousands

Region	Engineering	LQ	Textiles	LQ	Total manufacturing
North	192	0·94	52	0·97	438
Yorkshire and Humberside	242	0·74	149	1·71	711
East Midlands	210	0·77	171	2·38	587
East Anglia	82	0·91	14	0·58	195
South East	943	1·10	108	0·47	1,851
South West	215	1·10	36	0·70	420
West Midlands	577	1·28	42	0·36	976
North West	399	0·86	190	1·53	1,005
Total	2,860		762		6,183

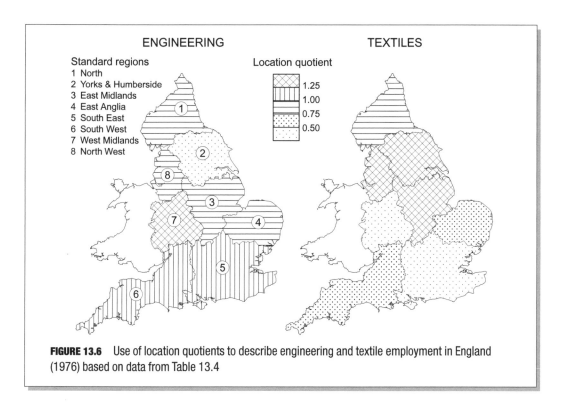

FIGURE 13.6 Use of location quotients to describe engineering and textile employment in England (1976) based on data from Table 13.4

for each areal unit, and negative values cannot be included. This therefore makes it rather more difficult to apply the technique to a study of a continuous variable. Second, the index is affected by changes in the spatial boundaries of the study units, and changes in spatial scale. This can be partly illustrated by the example of previous studies of ethnic segregation that tend to indicate very high levels of segregation at smaller spatial scales. Indeed, there are predictable variations in the index D_s with changes in spatial scale, and lower values of D_s are to be expected in a study with only a few areal units.

Leading on from these difficulties, commonly associated with changing boundaries and scale, is a third problem relating to the fact that the Lorenz curve is insensitive to spatial arrangement or pattern. Thus, the Lorenz curve and its related indices are an effective way of describing the relationships between distributions, but offer no indication or measure of spatial pattern.

13.4 Pattern analysis

In the earlier sections of this chapter, the techniques we discussed were concerned with either measuring spatial distributions or providing summary statistics to describe such distributions. However, in many circumstances geographers may be interested in the locations of individuals relative to each other, often expressed as points on a map. Such work is concerned with the techniques of point pattern analysis. Early approaches to this type of study were subjective and merely involved the mapping of individuals to produce a simple dot map. Very often the interpretation of these patterns lacked objectivity, making accurate description difficult and comparative studies impossible.

The first attempts to study point patterns in an objective fashion were made by ecologists in the analysis of plant communities. These studies were soon adapted and used by geographers. All these studies have one important feature in common – they make use of some type of probability distribution as a means of describing spatial patterns. Thus, a link is established between an observed distribution of points on a map and probability theory as explored in Chapter 5.

One of the most widely used measures is the Poisson probability distribution, which has the following assumptions. First, it postulates the condition of equal probability that, in the context of point patterns, refers to the situation where any location on a map has an equal probability of registering a point. For example, if we had a map of a particular woodland, the Poisson theory suggests that any part of the area would have an equal opportunity of having a tree. We may infer from this that the process producing such patterns is therefore a random one. Second, the theory assumes a condition of independence, whereby each of the points located on a map would be independent of one another. Thus, in our woodland example the assumption is made that the location of one tree would neither repel nor attract another. Based on these assumptions and the use of the Poisson probability function, as discussed in section 5.15, it is possible to model a distribution of points on a map. These expected patterns can then be compared with observed or real patterns, and thus used as a standard yardstick, from which we can measure deviations. By applying the Poisson distribution, we are therefore using the concept of randomness as our basic measure.

In the study of point patterns we can recognise two important violations of the assumptions made by the Poisson model, each of which produce non-random processes. The first of these concerns patterns that result from competitive processes. This may be illustrated by the example of food stores competing with each other in a city. Over time, those located close to other food stores may be driven out of business by more powerful competitors, thereby reducing store clusters and producing a regular pattern. The best example of such competitive processes in the geographical literature is that of the evolution of market centres and described by central place theory. A second deviation from the Poisson model is the situation where the locations of existing activities attract others. This is termed a contagious process, and tends to produce a clustered pattern as points are attracted to one another.

Given this background it is possible to recognise three basic types of point patterns, namely regular, random, and clustered, each of which can be modelled by a particular

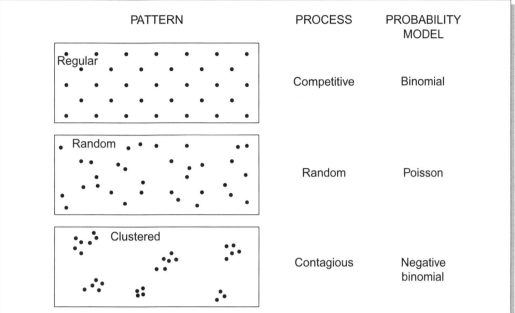

FIGURE 13.7   Types of point patterns and their probability distributions (Note: the binomial and Poisson distributions have already been discussed in Chapter 5, but no formal examination of the negative binomial distribution is attempted here.)

probability distribution (Figure 13.7). These distributions provide the geographer with some basic yardsticks with which to compare observed point patterns, and also provide a conceptual framework to account for some of the possible variations from randomness.

13.5 Measurement of point patterns

At the start of this section it is important to make clear the distinction that statisticians draw between 'pattern' and 'dispersion'. By operational definition, 'pattern' should be taken to mean the distances between and arrangements of points in space, and 'dispersion' refers, by contrast, to the areal extent of a collection of points. Failure to bear these distinctions in mind can lead to meaningless and misleading expressions, such as, 'random dispersion'. Attention in this section is devoted to patterns in the sense that they are defined above.

There are a number of ways in which geographers have studied point patterns. Later in this section we shall look at 'nearest neighbour analysis', but we shall start with *quadrat analysis.* The latter has been popular with both geographers and botanists but has recently been less widely adopted as an appreciation of some of its problems has grown. Nevertheless it remains an important part of geographical methodology.

In quadrat analysis the study area is overlaid by a grid of lines forming units of equal size, and the number of points in each cell are counted. We have already used this method in section 5.15 when the spatial distribution of grocers' shops in Sunderland was examined. Traditionally, the grid systems are based on squares although other shapes, such as hexagons, could be used provided that they combine to form a complete cover. Irregular shapes, rectangles or units of different areas should not be used. Squares are clearly the easiest units to construct and measure and will form the basis of what follows, although the theoretical implications apply to all suitable shapes.

The points that can be studied and counted using the quadrat method can consist of any spatially distributed 'point' phenomenon. Shops have already been cited, and there is a substantial literature on their study in this way. But plant species, cases of disease, industrial locations and even settlement patterns are equally amenable to this approach. The points, or events, must be spatially discrete, and continuous variables such as rainfall or altitude are not suitable. We hope that by counting the numbers of point events within each square we can derive a measure of the points' pattern. The guiding principle underlying these attempts is that point patterns can be described according to their location along a continuum which varies from perfectly regular (all points equidistant) at one end to perfectly clustered (all points touching) at the other. The random distribution lies mid-way between these extremes. Figure 13.7 conveys something of the form of these patterns, and later in this section we shall see how the distances between points can be used to describe them, but another method of description is to compare the quadrat counts with a hypothesised probability distribution. The Poisson distribution has already been examined and has a particular, though limited, application to this problem.

In the earlier example of Sunderland shops we hypothesised that their spatial distribution was random. If that hypothesis was correct then the observed distribution should approximate to the Poisson which is, as we explained in Chapter 5, a random distribution in which events are independent and located without spatial preference. Section 7.9 demonstrated how the differences between observed and hypothesised observations were tested. The distributions are described by the number of quadrats which contain 0, 1, 2, 3, etc. points, and in the latter example the observed data differed so little from that expected from a Poisson distribution that the pattern was concluded to be random.

Another approach to this problem of pattern analysis would have been to use the variance to mean ratio of the observed distribution. The mean, denoted by λ, is given by the observed density of points, which in the earlier example was 0·407 shops per quadrat. The variance of the observed distribution is given by:

$$\sigma^2 = \frac{\sum X^2}{\sum X} - \frac{\sum X}{N} \tag{13.8}$$

where X is the number of points in each of the quadrats taken in turn and N the number of quadrats.

One of the hallmarks of the Poisson distribution is the equality of mean and variance. Thus, if the variance-mean ratio is unity or close to it, we may conclude the distribution to be Poisson and, consequently, spatially random. Departures from unity in the ratio reflect tendencies towards either clustering or regularity. Regularly located points yield very low variances because most quadrats record a similar number of points, with the result that the variance-mean ratio is less than 1·0. On the other hand, clustered point patterns give variances that are very high, because a few quadrats have many points and the majority have very few or none, and the resulting variance-mean ratios are greater than 1·0. The degree of departure from 1·0 can be converted to a z-score after calculating the standard error of the difference (SE_x) from:

$$SE_x = \sqrt{[2/(N-1)]} \qquad (13.9)$$

in which N is the total number of quadrats, and:

$$z = \frac{observed\ ratio - expected\ ratio}{standard\ error} \qquad (13.10)$$

Given this information, we can rework the shops example. The mean of the spatial pattern we have already established to be 0·407 shops per quadrat, and its variance we estimate from Equation 13.8. The constituent observations (X) consist of the number of shops counted in each of the 135 quadrats. In this case, there were 96 quadrats with zero shops, 27 with one, nine with two, two with three and only one with four. We may prepare our data for Equation 13.8 in the form shown in Table 13.5, taking care to keep the distinction between N (the number of quadrats) and ΣX (the total number of shops) clearly in mind. We find that $\sigma^2 = 1·356$ and the variance-mean ratio is therefore $1·357/0·407 = 3·332$.

We can move on to examine the degree to which the variance-mean ratio of the shop pattern differs from the hypothesised value of 1·0. The first step is to calculate the standard error of the difference from Equation 13.9:

TABLE 13.5 Method of calculating the variance of spatial patterns using quadrant counts of grocers' shops in Sunderland (see also section 5.15)

Number of shops per quadrant (N)	Number of quadrants with N shops (q)	Number of shops by quadrants ($X = Nq$)	$X^2 = NX$
0	96	0	0
1	27	27	27
2	9	18	36
3	2	6	18
4	1	4	16
Totals	135	55	97

$$SE_x = \sqrt{[2/(135-1)]}$$
$$= \sqrt{0.01493} = 0.1222$$

From this the z-value (t-value if ΣX is less than 30) is calculated by dividing the standard error into the difference between the observed and expected variance-mean ratios:

$$z = \frac{3.334-1.0}{0.1222} = 19.08$$

Thus, at the 0.01 significance level, for which the critical z-values are ± 2.58, the differences are sufficiently great for us to conclude that the distribution is, by this method, non-random. Moreover, if we pay attention to the sign of the z-value we can see, because of the nature of Equation 13.10, that positive results show a tendency towards clustering while negative values arise from a tendency towards regularity. The positive result here suggests a degree of clustering of the points.

Hence we come, by different routes, to contradictory conclusions concerning this distribution. Such difficulties are not uncommon in point pattern analysis and warn us to be on our guard. There are, unfortunately, further problems that have to be considered. Most importantly, both the observed and the hypothesised (Poisson) distributions are density-dependent and by varying the grid-size placed over the study area or its limits, the measured density can be drastically altered. Figure 5.20 has shown the effect that variations in density (which provides the Poisson mean λ) can have on the character of the distribution. It is unfortunate that pattern is completely independent of density, yet the distributions used here to analyse them are strongly density-dependent. Equally, patterns are independent of scale, and those shown in Figure 13.7 are as likely to be encountered on a scale of kilometres as a scale of centimetres. Nevertheless, variations in quadrat size can still lead to unrepresentative contrasts between the observed distributions that they generate.

Clearly we need to select the boundaries of the study areas with care. Less easy to accomplish is the choice of a suitable quadrat size, and the injudicious selection of quadrat size can simulate a Poisson distribution where none exists. The effect of quadrat size has been widely examined by plant scientists whose work has shown that, in visually clustered patterns such as that in Figure 13.7, very small quadrats usually produce results suggesting randomness; since it is likely that quadrats would only contain small numbers of points and not measure the clusters. Similarly, very large quadrats in such circumstances produce result that seem to indicate a regular pattern, as most quadrats would contain similar numbers of points. If, on the other hand, we are examining a pattern that appears to be visually regular, then this characteristic will be shown as quadrat size increases.

There are two ways in which this problem of quadrat size can be tackled. The first is to derive some method of determining an ideal quadrat size for particular point distributions. Ecologists have examined such a notion and define quadrat size as $2A/N$, where A is the area of study and N is the number of points, i.e. twice the mean area around each point. Taylor (1977), however, suggests that such quadrats are probably too large for geographical studies, particularly where spatial competition is important. In these conditions he recommends the use of quadrats determined by the area of the map divided by the number of points (A/N).

A further, though time-consuming, solution is to test for Poisson randomness over a range of quadrat sizes. If it is present throughout, we might be confident in claiming its existence. The problem of appropriate quadrat size has yet to be resolved and the final choice may well be determined by the nature of the project rather than the character of the data.

Fortunately, we can use the effect of quadrat size variations in a more positive fashion. Thus, by using quadrats of different sizes to examine the same pattern, we can explore variations in the scale or 'grain' of point distributions.

There is, however, nothing intrinsically sacred about the Poisson distribution and its applicability of spatial observations. Scatters of points in space can be described by other distributions, for example the negative binomial, whose exclusion from this text should not be interpreted as a relegation of their importance. Most of these distributions make allowances for a 'contagion' effect in which occurrences influence the probability of other events. The Poisson distribution specifically forbids any such effect and requires the events to be wholly independent. Contagion effects can often be very important in describing point patterns. Some urban retail functions tend, by their nature, to be randomly located over wide areas of towns and cities. On the other hand, there are other functions, such as banks and department stores that tend to cluster together in city centres; it would be inappropriate to attempt to describe their patterns in the urban field by the Poisson distribution.

There are some probability distributions that can take specific account of contagion effects, and they can be applied to cases in which the Poisson distribution is theoretically imprecise, i.e. if it is thought that the point pattern is not random. These distributions possess rather exotic titles such as 'Neyman's type A' and the 'Polya-Aeppli' distributions. They are less widely known than those reviewed in Chapter 5, but are particularly useful when studying patterns generated by clustering and contagion. A good example might be the pattern of locations created by car component factories, which tend to cluster around the car factories themselves. However, the equations describing these probability distributions are not easy to evaluate. The interested reader is referred to more detailed discussions (e.g. Rogers 1974).

Despite the mathematical elegance of these distributions, they remain, like the simpler Poisson distribution, highly dependent on quadrat size. As a result, the failure of a point pattern to conform to one of them does not imply that the pattern is not one of contagion. Neither does a correspondence provide irrefutable proof that contagion is present. Indeed, any point pattern may be approximated by two or three different probability distributions. Here, then, is another reason why quadrat analysis is now less popular, because different theoretical interpretations, based on approximations to different distributions, can be made for each case. Nevertheless, the thoughtful use of quadrat analysis for point pattern description or for testing a priori assumptions against real-world observations remains a valuable geographical tool.

An alternative method to quadrat analysis is to use measures based on the spacing between points, by taking the distance of each point to its nearest neighbour. These procedures require a knowledge of the population density, and the analysis involves a comparison between an observed spacing of a point distribution and the spacing expected in a random pattern. The average expected distances are calculated using Equation 13.11:

$$\bar{r}_e = 0.5 \sqrt{(A/N)} \tag{13.11}$$

Equation 13.11

$\bar{r}_e$ = average expected distance

A = area of study region

N = number of points

Once again, such expected values are described by the Poisson function. The nearest neighbour statistic (R) is derived by dividing the observed by the expected distances, the results of which must fall within a range of values from 0 to 2·1491:

$$R = \bar{r}_a / \bar{r}_e \tag{13.12}$$

Equation 13.12

$\bar{r}_a$ = average observed distance

$\bar{r}_e$ = average expected distance

This index shows how more, or less, spaced the observed distribution is compared with a random one.

Under conditions of maximum aggregation all the individuals in a point distribution occupy the same locus and the distance to the nearest neighbour is therefore zero. At the other extreme, conditions of maximum spacing, the individuals will be distributed in an even hexagonal pattern (Figure 13.7). Consequently, every point will be equidistant from six other individuals, so that the mean distance to the nearest neighbour is maximised and $R = 2·1491$. If $R = 1$, then the observed and expected distances are equal, thus indicating a random pattern. Therefore, when values of R are less than 1 this suggests distributions tending towards a clustered pattern, while values above 1 describe tendencies towards dispersion.

The concept of randomness has traditionally been applied as the base measure in point pattern analysis. In theory, a random pattern is one in which the location of each point is totally uninfluenced by the remaining points. However, in practice it is much more useful to view patterns as deviating from clustered or regular, with the results falling on a continuum between the two. In reality, locational forces are unlikely to operate randomly, but are more often capable of transforming either of the extreme conditions towards a random pattern. The applicability of this approach can be improved with the application of a test assessing the significance of the R-value, which takes into account possible variations in the random processes. Thus, the probability that an R-value could have arisen by chance can be established, using its standard error and consequent z-scores (see Chapter 6). The standard error of the expected average nearest neighbour distance can be calculated using Equation 13.13:

$$SE_{re} = \frac{0 \cdot 26136}{\sqrt{[N(N/A)]}}$$ (13.13)

Equation 13.13

N = number of points

A = area of study

SE_{re} = standard error of expected average distance

This standard error can then be used in the normal fashion, with 95 per cent of the expected values falling within $\pm 1 \cdot 96 \times SE_{\bar{r}_e}$ of the average computed distance. It follows that the z-value of the difference between observed and expected R-value is derived using Equation 13.14:

$$Z_R = \frac{|\bar{r}_e - \bar{r}_a|}{SE_{\bar{r}e}}$$ (13.14)

Equation 13.14

$\bar{r}_e$ = average expected distance

$\bar{r}_a$ = average observed distance

$SE_{\bar{r}e}$ = standard error of expected average distance

The implication of the nearest neighbour technique is that the area under study is an isotropic (perfectly uniform) surface. Attention therefore needs to be given to defining the actual study area in terms of a *biotope space*, which, for example, in an urban environment involves measuring the extent of the built-up area. In addition, consideration needs to be given to the definition of any study area, since both the size and the shape of the area may influence the results. As a general rule, the study area should be defined relative to the problem under investigation, but some have gone so far as to suggest circular built-up areas.

The nearest neighbour technique can be extended to take into account the scale elements in a point pattern. This can be achieved by measuring order neighbour distances up to the nth value, and by calculating the corresponding values of R. We are not thereby restricted to the 'nearest' neighbour, but could consider the second or third nearest neighbours. The formula for such measures is:

$$\text{Expected distance to } n\text{th neighbour} = \frac{1}{\sqrt{M}} \frac{(2n)! \, n}{(2^n \, n!)^2} \qquad (13.15)$$

Equation 13.15

M = density of points per unit area

n = order of nearest neighbour

If measurements are taken to the nth order neighbour, then clearly some idea of the scale at which point patterns are occurring can be gained. In theory, by plotting rank order of the nearest neighbour against the corresponding R-values, a measure of the 'grain' or scale of pattern intensity can be achieved. Thus, in terms of mean distance between points, if the pattern were of a 'fine-grained' nature, then a plot of order neighbour against mean distance would give a curve of only gradual increase, with a smooth profile. Conversely, in a 'coarse-grained' pattern, such a curve would be less smooth with sharp increases, as distance measurements become of an inter-group type. One problem in applying this extension concerns the number of neighbours to which measurements should be taken. However, in the few attempts at this type of analysis, the number selected has been at least of the order of three. The calculations are obviously time consuming by hand, especially for large numbers of points, and in such circumstances the measurement and calculations can be speeded up using a computer program and it is regrettable therefore that most standard software does not offer scope for this type of analysis.

The technique can, however, be illustrated by an examination of patterns of retail change, which has seen a frequent use of such spatial statistics (Kivell and Shaw 1980). The example presented here relates specifically to changes in the pattern of footwear retailers in Kingston-upon-Hull from 1880 to 1950. For the purposes of the analysis, two distinct retail organisational types were recognised, multiples and independents, that had different locational requirements. The former refers to those firms that had five or more branch shops, and they were often controlled by national companies.

An analysis of first-order neighbours using Equation 13.12 gives an indication of pattern intensity, and clear differences can be recognised between the two shop types

TABLE 13.6   Trends in the patterns of footwear retailers in Kingston-upon-Hull

Time	Independents			Multiples		
	Nearest neighbour value	Pattern type	Shops	Nearest neighbour value	Pattern type	Shops
1880	1·053	Regular	256	Nil	Nil	Nil
1890	1·264	Regular	275	0·915	Random	16
1900	0·975	Random	235	0·630	Clustered	19
1910	0·919	Random	189	0·684	Clustered	22
1920	0·991	Random	124	0·873	Clustered	25
1930	0·923	Random	100	0·640	Clustered	32
1940	0·863	Clustered	52	0·426	Clustered	29
1950	0·781	Clustered	22	0·591	Clustered	19

(Table 13.6). Despite differences in basic patterns, the overall trend for both types was towards a clustered state, a condition that took the independents longer to achieve. Such results essentially represent the local variations in the retail pattern, and the spatial scale of the analysis can be extended using higher-order neighbours. In this case, calculations were also made to the tenth-order neighbour to measure the grain of the pattern. An example of a graph, plotting rank order neighbour against corresponding values of R, is illustrated in Figure 13.8.

The independent retailers exhibited a fine-grained pattern and the resultant curves decrease in a monotonic fashion towards a general clustered pattern. At high-order neighbours, the R-value is low, indicating a high degree of large-scale clustering. In contrast, the multiples had a more complex pattern with a much stronger element of localised clustering. The step-like nature of the rank order curves suggests that the multiples occurred in loosely associated groups of stores, probably at points of relatively high accessibility.

13.6 Problems in the interpretation of point patterns

Point pattern analysis, in addition to having a number of methodological problems, also suffers from difficulties in the interpretation of results. From the previous two sections in this chapter, it is clear that the analysis of point patterns is based on a comparison of the observed distribution with some known theoretical one. If there is a close fit between the two, then we may describe a pattern as random, clustered or dispersed. However, we should be very cautious about inferring processes from point patterns. First there may be a number of different probability models that fit our

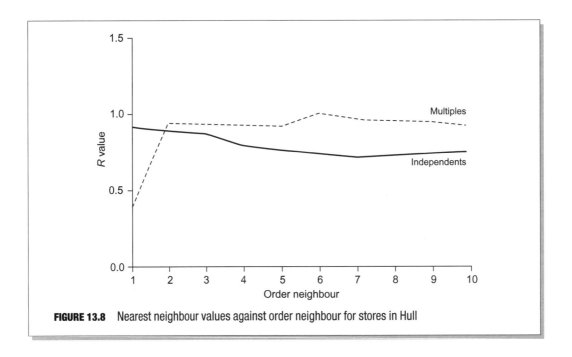

FIGURE 13.8   Nearest neighbour values against order neighbour for stores in Hull

observed points and we therefore must, in some cases, use other background evidence to discriminate between them. Second, even if we only have one clear model that fits our data, this is not sufficient evidence to infer conclusively that a specific process produced the pattern. It is because of such inferential problems that, since the mid-1970s, point pattern analysis has fallen from favour in many areas of geographical research. Thus, while the technique can help us objectively to describe and classify point patterns, it fails to provide the necessary information about spatial processes. This is especially the case in human geography with its increasing emphasis on the study of behavioural processes.

Areas beneath the standard normal curve

z	p	z	p	z	p	z	p	z	p
0·00	0·00000	0·30	0·11791	0·60	0·22575	0·90	0·31594		
0·01	0·00399	0·31	0·12172	0·61	0·22907	0·91	0·31859		
0·02	0·00798	0·32	0·12552	0·62	0·23237	0·92	0·32121		
0·03	0·01197	0·33	0·12930	0·63	0·23565	0·93	0·32381		
0·04	0·01595	0·34	0·13307	0·64	0·23891	0·94	0·32639		
0·05	0·01994	0·35	0·13683	0·65	0·24215	0·95	0·32894		
0·06	0·02392	0·36	0·14058	0·66	0·24537	0·96	0·33147		
0·07	0·02790	0·37	0·14431	0·67	0·24857	0·97	0·33398		
0·08	0·03188	0·38	0·14803	0·68	0·25175	0·98	0·33646		
0·09	0·03586	0·39	0·15173	0·69	0·26490	0·99	0·33891		
0·10	0·03983	0·40	0·15542	0·70	0·25805	1·00	0·34134		
0·11	0·04380	0·41	0·15910	0·71	0·26115	1·01	0·34375		
0·12	0·04776	0·42	0·16276	0·72	0·26424	1·02	0·34614		
0·13	0·05172	0·43	0·16640	0·73	0·26730	1·03	0·34849		
0·14	0·05567	0·44	0·17003	0·74	0·27035	1·04	0·35083		
0·15	0·05962	0·45	0·17364	0·75	0·27337	1·05	0·35314		
0·16	0·06356	0·46	0·17724	0·76	0·27637	1·06	0·35543		
0·17	0·06750	0·47	0·18082	0·77	0·27935	1·07	0·35769		
0·18	0·07142	0·48	0·18439	0·78	0·28230	1·08	0·35993		
0·19	0·07535	0·49	0·18793	0·79	0·28524	1·09	0·36214		
0·20	0·07926	0·50	0·19146	0·80	0·28815	1·10	0·36433		
0·21	0·08317	0·51	0·19497	0·81	0·29103	1·11	0·36650		
0·22	0·08706	0·52	0·19847	0·82	0·29389	1·12	0·36864		
0·23	0·09095	0·53	0·20194	0·83	0·29673	1·13	0·37076		
0·24	0·09483	0·54	0·20540	0·84	0·29955	1·14	0·37286		
0·25	0·09871	0·55	0·20884	0·85	0·30234	1·15	0·37493		
0·26	0·10257	0·56	0·21226	0·86	0·30511	1·16	0·37698		
0·27	0·10642	0·57	0·21566	0·87	0·30785	1·17	0·37900		
0·28	0·11026	0·58	0·21904	0·88	0·31057	1·18	0·38100		
0·29	0·11409	0·59	0·22240	0·89	0·31327	1·19	0·38298		

z	p	z	p	z	p	z	p
1·20	0·38493	1·50	0·43319	1·80	0·46407	2·50	0·49379
1·21	0·38686	1·51	0·43448	1·81	0·46485	2·55	0·49461
1·22	0·38877	1·52	0·43574	1·82	0·46562	2·60	0·49534
1·23	0·39065	1·53	0·43699	1·83	0·46638	2·65	0·49598
1·24	0·39251	1·54	0·43822	1·84	0·46712	2·70	0·49653
1·25	0·39435	1·55	0·43943	1·85	0·46784	2·75	0·49702
1·26	0·39617	1·56	0·44062	1·86	0·46856	2·80	0·49744
1·27	0·39796	1·57	0·44179	1·87	0·46936	2·85	0·49781
1·28	0·39973	1·58	0·44295	1·88	0·46995	2·90	0·49813
1·29	0·40147	1·59	0·44408	1·89	0·47062	2·95	0·49841
1·30	0·40320	1·60	0·44520	1·90	0·47128	3·00	0·49865
1·31	0·40490	1·61	0·44630	1·91	0·47193	3·05	0·49886
1·32	0·40658	1·62	0·44738	1·92	0·47257	3·10	0·49903
1·33	0·40824	1·63	0·44835	1·93	0·47320	3·15	0·49918
1·34	0·40988	1·64	0·44950	1·94	0·47381	3·20	0·49931
1·35	0·41149	1·65	0·45053	1·95	0·47441	3·25	0·49942
1·36	0·41309	1·66	0·45154	1·96	0·47500	3·30	0·49952
1·37	0·41466	1·67	0·45254	1·97	0·47558	3·35	0·49960
1·38	0·41621	1·68	0·45352	1·98	0·47615	3·40	0·49966
1·39	0·41774	1·69	0·45449	1·99	0·47670	3·45	0·49972
1·40	0·41924	1·70	0·45543	2·00	0·47725	3·50	0·49977
1·41	0·42073	1·71	0·45637	2·05	0·47982	3·55	0·49981
1·42	0·42220	1·72	0·45728	2·10	0·48214	3·60	0·49984
1·43	0·42364	1·73	0·45818	2·15	0·48422	3·65	0·49987
1·44	0·42507	1·74	0·45907	2·20	0·48610	3·70	0·49989
1·45	0·42647	1·75	0·45994	2·25	0·48778	3·75	0·49991
1·46	0·42785	1·76	0·46080	2·30	0·48928	3·80	0·49993
1·47	0·42922	1·77	0·46164	2·35	0·49061	3·85	0·49994
1·48	0·43056	1·78	0·46246	2·40	0·49180	3·90	0·49995
1·49	0·43189	1·79	0·46327	2·45	0·49286	4·00	0·49997

Columns headed p give the probabilities of an event with the range of $z = 0·0$ to the selected z-value. Because the normal distribution is symmetrical about $z = 0·0$, the table applies equally to negative values of z.

To estimate the probability of an event exceeding the selected z-value, subtract the tabled probability from 0·50000.

Critical values on student's *t*-distribution

	Confidence limits				
	0·90	0·95	0·98	0·99	0·999
	Two-tailed significance levels (one-tailed levels in brackets)				
v	0·10 (0·05)	0·05 (0·025)	0·02 (0·01)	0·01 (0·005)	0·001 (0·0005)
1	6·31	12·71	31·81	63·66	636·6
2	2·92	4·30	6·97	9·93	31·60
3	2·35	3·18	4·54	5·84	12·92
4	2·13	2·78	3·75	4·60	8·61
5	2·02	2·57	3·37	4·03	6·86
6	1·94	2·45	3·14	3·71	5·96
7	1·90	2·37	3·00	3·50	5·41
8	1·86	2·31	2·90	3·36	5·04
9	1·83	2·26	2·82	3·25	4·78
10	1·81	2·25	2·76	3·17	4·59
11	1·80	2·20	2·72	3·11	4·44
12	1·78	2·18	2·68	3·06	4·32
13	1·77	2·16	2·65	3·01	4·23
14	1·76	2·15	2·62	2·98	4·14
15	1·75	2·13	2·60	2·95	4·07
16	1·75	2·12	2·58	2·92	4·02
17	1·74	2·11	2·57	2·90	3·97
18	1·73	2·10	2·55	2·88	3·92
19	1·73	2·09	2·54	2·86	3·88
20	1·73	2·09	2·53	2·85	3·85
21	1·72	2·08	2·52	2·83	3·82
22	1·72	2·07	2·51	2·82	3·79
23	1·71	2·07	2·50	2·81	3·77

		Confidence limits			
	0·90	0·95	0·98	0·99	0·999
	Two-tailed significance levels (one-tailed levels in brackets)				
v	0·10 (0·05)	0·05 (0·025)	0·02 (0·01)	0·01 (0·005)	0·001 (0·0005)
24	1·71	2·06	2·49	2·80	3·75
25	1·71	2·06	2·49	2·79	3·73
26	1·71	2·06	2·48	2·79	3·71
27	1·70	2·05	2·47	2·77	3·69
28	1·70	2·05	2·47	2·76	3·67
29	1·70	2·05	2·46	2·76	3·66
30	1·70	2·04	2·46	2·75	3·65
40	1·68	2·02	2·42	2·70	3·55
60	1·67	2·00	2·39	2·66	3·46
Over 60	approximates to the normal distribution				
z	1·64	1·96	2·35	2·58	3·29

The critical t-value is found by reference to the appropriate degrees of freedom (v) and the selected significance level or confidence limits. In the former case the values for the two-tailed test should be read as + or $-t$. Equivalent one-tailed critical values are found under the bracketed column headings and be assigned to either + or $-t$.

Adapted from Fisher, R. A. and Yates, F. (1948) *Statistical Tables for Biological, Agricultural and Medical Research*. Edinburgh: Oliver and Boyd.

Critical values on the χ^2 distribution

	Significance level				
v	0·10	0·05	0·01	0·005	0·001
1	2·71	3·84	6·64	7·88	10·83
2	4·60	5·99	9·21	10·60	13·82
3	6·25	7·82	11·34	12·84	16·27
4	7·78	9·49	13·28	14·86	18·46
5	9·24	11·07	15·09	16·75	20·52
6	10·64	12·59	16·81	18·55	22·46
7	12·02	14·07	18·48	20·28	24·32
8	13·36	15·51	20·29	21·96	26·12
9	14·68	16·92	21·67	23·59	27·86
10	15·99	18·31	23·21	25·19	29·59
11	17·28	19·68	24·72	26·76	31·26
12	18·55	21·03	26·22	28·30	32·91
13	19·81	22·36	27·69	30·82	34·55
14	21·06	23·68	29·14	31·32	36·12
15	22·31	25·00	30·58	32·80	37·70
16	23·54	26·30	32·00	34·27	39·29
17	24·77	27·59	33·41	35·72	40·75
18	25·99	28·87	34·80	37·16	42·31
19	27·20	30·14	36·19	38·58	43·82
20	28·41	31·41	37·57	40·00	45·32
21	29·62	32·67	38·93	41·40	46·80
22	30·81	33·92	40·29	42·80	48·27
23	32·01	35·17	41·64	44·16	49·73
24	33·20	36·42	42·98	45·56	51·18
25	34·38	37·65	44·31	46·93	52·62
26	35·56	35·88	45·64	48·29	54·05

	Significance level				
v	**0·10**	**0·05**	**0·01**	**0·005**	**0·001**
27	36·74	40·11	46·96	49·65	55·48
28	37·92	41·34	48·28	50·99	56·89
29	39·09	42·56	49·59	52·34	58·30
30	40·26	43·77	50·89	53·67	59·70
40	51·81	55·76	63·69	66·77	73·40
50	63·17	67·51	76·15	79·49	86·66
60	74·40	79·08	88·38	91·95	99·61
70	85·53	90·53	100·43	104·22	112·32
80	96·58	101·88	112·33	116·32	124·84
90	105·57	113·15	124·12	128·30	137·21
100	118·30	124·34	135·81	140·17	149·45

The critical values are determined by reference to the degrees of freedom (v) and the selected significance level. If the test statistics equals or exceeds the critical (table) value, the null hypothesis is rejected.

Adapted from Fisher, R. A. and Yates, F. (1948) *Statistical Tables for Biological, Agricultural and Medical Research*. Edinburgh: Oliver and Boyd.

Critical values on the Kolmogorov-Smirnov (*D*) distribution

			Significance level		
n	0·20	0·15	0·10	0·05	0·01
1	0·900	0·925	0·950	0·975	0·995
2	0·684	0·726	0·776	0·842	0·929
3	0·565	0·597	0·642	0·708	0·828
4	0·494	0·525	0·564	0·624	0·733
5	0·446	0·474	0·510	0·565	0·669
6	0·410	0·436	0·470	0·521	0·618
7	0·381	0·405	0·438	0·486	0·577
8	0·358	0·381	0·411	0·457	0·543
9	0·339	0·360	0·388	0·432	0·514
10	0·322	0·342	0·368	0·410	0·490
11	0·307	0·326	0·352	0·391	0·468
12	0·295	0·313	0·338	0·375	0·450
13	0·284	0·302	0·325	0·361	0·433
14	0·274	0·292	0·314	0·349	0·418
15	0·266	0·283	0·304	0·338	0·404
16	0·258	0·274	0·295	0·328	0·392
17	0·250	0·266	0·286	0·318	0·381
18	0·244	0·259	0·276	0·309	0·371
19	0·237	0·252	0·272	0·301	0·363
20	0·231	0·246	0·264	0·294	0·356
25	0·210	0·220	0·240	0·270	0·320
30	0·190	0·200	0·220	0·240	0·290
35	0·180	0·190	0·210	0·230	0·270

	Significance level				
n	0·20	0·15	0·10	0·05	0·01
over 35	$\dfrac{1 \cdot 07}{\sqrt{n}}$	$\dfrac{1 \cdot 14}{\sqrt{n}}$	$\dfrac{1 \cdot 22}{\sqrt{n}}$	$\dfrac{1 \cdot 36}{\sqrt{n}}$	$\dfrac{1 \cdot 63}{\sqrt{n}}$

The null hypothesis is rejected if the test D-statistic exceeds the critical value for that sample size (n) at the selected significance level.

When n is greater than 35 the appropriate equation (determined by choice of significance level) should be used to calculate the critical value of D.

Adapted from Massey, F. J. (1951) 'The Kolmogorov-Smirnov test for goodness of fit', *Journal of the American Statistical Association* **46**, 126–7.

Probabilities and critical values of the Mann-Whitney statistic (U)

(a) Probabilities of the Mann-Whitney statistic (U)

	$n_2 = 3$		
n_1	1	2	3
U			
0	0·250	0·100	0·050
1	0·500	0·200	0·100
2	0·750	0·400	0·200
3		0·600	0·350
4			0·500
5			0·650

	$n_2 = 4$			
n_1	1	2	3	4
U				
0	0·200	0·067	0·028	0·014
1	0·400	0·133	0·057	0·029
2	0·600	0·267	0·114	0·057
3		0·400	0·200	0·100
4		0·600	0·314	0·171
5			0·429	0·243
6			0·571	0·343
7				0·443

$n_2 = 5$

n_1	1	2	3	4	5
U					
0	0·167	0·047	0·018	0·008	0·004
1	0·333	0·095	0·036	0·016	0·008
2	0·500	0·190	0·071	0·032	0·016
3	0·667	0·286	0·125	0·056	0·028
4		0·429	0·196	0·095	0·048
5		0·571	0·286	0·143	0·075
6			0·393	0·206	0·111
7			0·500	0·278	0·155
8			0·607	0·365	0·210
9				0·452	0·274
10				0·548	0·345
11					0·421
12					0·500
13					0·579

$n_2 = 6$

n_1	1	2	3	4	5	6
U						
0	0·143	0·036	0·012	0·005	0·002	0·001
1	0·286	0·071	0·024	0·010	0·004	0·002
2	0·428	0·143	0·048	0·019	0·009	0·004
3	0·571	0·214	0·083	0·033	0·015	0·008
4		0·321	0·131	0·057	0·026	0·013
5		0·429	0·190	0·086	0·041	0·021
6		0·571	0·275	0·129	0·063	0·032
7			0·357	0·176	0·089	0·047
8			0·452	0·238	0·123	0·066
9			0·548	0·305	0·165	0·090
10				0·381	0·214	0·120
11				0·457	0·268	0·155
12				0·545	0·331	0·197
13					0·396	0·242
14					0·465	0·294
15					0·535	0·350
16						0·409
17						0·469

The notes at the foot of Appendix V(c) provide details on the use of these tables.

(b) Probabilities of the Mann-Whitney statistic (U)

$n_2 = 7$

n_1	1	2	3	4	5	6	7
U							
0	0·125	0·028	0·008	0·003	0·001	0·001	0·000
1	0·250	0·056	0·017	0·006	0·003	0·001	0·001
2	0·375	0·111	0·033	0·012	0·005	0·002	0·001
3	0·500	0·167	0·058	0·021	0·009	0·004	0·002
4	0·625	0·250	0·092	0·036	0·015	0·007	0·003
5		0·333	0·133	0·055	0·024	0·011	0·006
6		0·444	0·192	0·082	0·037	0·017	0·009
7		0·556	0·258	0·115	0·053	0·026	0·013
8			0·333	0·158	0·074	0·037	0·019
9			0·417	0·206	0·101	0·051	0·027
10			0·500	0·264	0·134	0·069	0·036
11			0·583	0·324	0·172	0·090	0·049
12				0·394	0·216	0·117	0·064
13				0·464	0·265	0·147	0·082
14				0·538	0·319	0·183	0·104
15					0·378	0·223	0·130
16					0·438	0·267	0·159
17					0·500	0·314	0·191
18					0·562	0·365	0·228
19						0·418	0·267
20						0·473	0·310
21						0·527	0·355
22							0·402
23							0·451
24							0·500

The notes at the foot of Appendix V(c) provide details on the use of these tables.

(c) Probabilities of the Mann-Whitney statistic (*U*)

$n_2 = 8$

n_1	1	2	3	4	5	6	7	8
U								
0	0·111	0·022	0·006	0·002	0·001	0·000	0·000	0·000
1	0·222	0·044	0·012	0·004	0·002	0·001	0·000	0·000
2	0·333	0·089	0·024	0·008	0·003	0·001	0·001	0·000
3	0·444	0·135	0·042	0·014	0·005	0·002	0·001	0·001
4	0·556	0·200	0·067	0·024	0·009	0·004	0·002	0·001
5		0·257	0·097	0·036	0·015	0·006	0·003	0·001
6		0·356	0·139	0·055	0·023	0·010	0·005	0·002
7		0·444	0·188	0·077	0·033	0·015	0·007	0·003
8		0·556	0·248	0·107	0·047	0·021	0·010	0·005
9			0·315	0·141	0·064	0·030	0·014	0·007
10			0·387	0·184	0·085	0·041	0·020	0·010
11			0·461	0·230	0·111	0·054	0·027	0·014
12			0·539	0·285	0·142	0·071	0·036	0·019
13				0·341	0·177	0·091	0·047	0·025
14				0·404	0·217	0·114	0·060	0·032
15				0·467	0·262	0·141	0·076	0·041
16				0·533	0·311	0·172	0·095	0·052
17					0·362	0·207	0·116	0·065
18					0·416	0·245	0·140	0·080
19					0·472	0·286	0·168	0·097
20					0·528	0·331	0·198	0·117
21						0·377	0·232	0·139
22						0·426	0·268	0·164
23						0·475	0·306	0·191
24						0·525	0·347	0·221
25							0·389	0·253
26							0·433	0·287
27							0·478	0·323
28							0·522	0·360
29								0·399
30								0·439
31								0·480
32								0·520

Appendices V(a) to (c) are arranged to give probabilities for each U statistic. These are determined by reference to the larger and smaller sizes (n_1 and n_2 respectively). The null hypothesis is rejected if the tabled probability of U is less than the selected significance level. The probabilities are calculated for one-tailed tests (the usual condition in Mann-Whitney procedures). The two-tailed equivalent values are found by doubling the tabled value. Where $p > 0.5$, the two-tailed value can be taken only to approximate to 1.0.

Appendices V(a) to (c) are adapted from Mann, H. B. and Whitney, D. R. (1947) 'On a test of whether one of two random variables is stochastically larger than the other', *Annals of Mathematical Statistics* **18**, 50–60.

(d) Critical values of the Mann-Whitney statistic (U)

Significance level = 0·10 (two-tailed) or 0·05 (one-tailed)

n_1	9	10	11	12	13	14	15	16	17	18	19	20
n_2												
2	1	1	1	2	2	2	3	3	4	4	4	4
3	3	4	5	5	6	7	7	8	9	9	10	11
4	6	7	8	9	10	11	12	14	15	16	17	18
5	9	11	12	13	15	16	18	19	20	22	23	25
6	12	14	16	17	19	21	23	25	26	28	30	32
7	15	17	19	21	24	26	28	30	33	35	37	39
8	18	20	23	26	28	31	33	36	39	41	44	47
9	21	24	27	30	33	36	39	42	45	48	51	54
10	24	27	31	34	37	41	44	48	51	55	58	62
11	27	31	34	38	42	46	50	54	57	61	65	69
12	30	34	38	42	47	51	55	60	64	68	72	77
13	33	37	42	47	51	56	61	65	70	75	80	84
14	36	41	46	51	56	61	66	71	77	82	87	92
15	39	44	50	55	61	66	72	77	83	88	94	100
16	42	48	54	60	65	71	77	83	89	93	101	107
17	45	51	57	64	70	77	83	89	96	102	109	115
18	48	55	61	68	75	82	88	93	102	109	116	123
19	51	58	65	72	80	87	94	101	109	116	123	130
20	54	62	69	77	84	92	100	107	115	123	130	138

The null hypothesis is rejected if the test statistic (U) is LESS than or equal to the tabled critical value for the larger and smaller group sizes (n_1 and n_2 respectively) at the selected significance level.

(e) Critical values of the Mann-Whitney statistic (U)

Significance level = 0·05 (two-tailed) or 0·025 (one-tailed)

n_1	9	10	11	12	13	14	15	16	17	18	19	20
n_2												
2	0	0	0	1	1	1	1	1	2	2	2	2
3	2	3	3	4	4	5	5	6	6	7	7	8
4	4	5	6	7	8	9	10	11	11	12	13	13
5	7	8	9	11	12	13	14	15	17	18	19	20
6	10	11	13	14	16	17	19	21	22	24	25	27
7	12	14	16	18	20	22	24	26	28	30	32	34
8	15	17	19	22	24	26	29	31	34	36	38	41
9	17	20	23	26	28	31	34	37	39	42	45	48
10	20	23	26	29	33	36	39	42	45	48	52	55
11	23	26	30	33	37	40	44	47	51	55	58	62
12	26	29	33	37	41	45	49	53	57	61	65	69
13	28	33	37	41	45	50	54	59	63	67	72	76
14	31	36	40	45	50	55	59	64	67	74	78	83
15	34	39	44	49	54	59	64	70	75	80	85	90
16	37	42	47	53	59	64	70	75	81	86	92	98
17	39	45	51	57	63	67	75	81	87	93	99	105
18	42	48	55	61	67	74	80	86	93	99	106	112
19	45	52	58	65	72	78	85	92	99	106	113	119
20	48	55	62	69	76	85	90	98	105	112	119	127

The null hypothesis is rejected if the test statistic (U) is LESS than or equal to the tabled critical value for the larger and smaller group sizes (n_1 and n_2 respectively) at the selected significance level.

(f) Critical values of the Mann-Whitney statistic (U)

Significance level = 0·02 (two-tailed) or 0·01 (one-tailed)

n_1	9	10	11	12	13	14	15	16	17	18	19	20
n_2												
2					0	0	0	0	0	0	1	1
3	1	1	1	2	2	2	3	3	4	4	4	5
4	3	3	4	5	5	6	7	7	8	9	9	10
5	5	6	7	8	9	10	11	12	13	14	15	16
6	7	8	9	11	12	13	15	16	18	19	20	22
7	9	11	12	14	16	17	19	21	23	24	26	28
8	11	13	15	17	20	22	24	26	28	30	32	34
9	14	16	18	21	23	26	28	31	33	36	38	40
10	16	19	22	24	27	30	33	36	38	41	44	47
11	18	22	25	28	31	34	37	41	44	47	50	53
12	21	24	28	31	35	38	42	46	49	53	56	60
13	23	27	31	35	39	43	47	51	55	59	63	67
14	26	30	34	38	43	47	51	56	60	65	69	75
15	28	33	37	42	47	51	56	61	66	70	75	80
16	31	36	41	46	51	56	61	66	71	76	82	87
17	33	38	44	49	55	60	66	71	77	82	88	93
18	36	41	47	53	59	65	70	76	82	88	94	100
19	38	44	50	56	63	69	75	82	88	94	101	107
20	40	47	53	60	67	73	80	87	93	100	107	114

The null hypothesis is rejected if the test statistic (U) is LESS than or equal to the tabled critical value for the larger and smaller group sizes (n_1 and n_2 respectively) at the selected significance level.

Appendices V(d) to (f) are adapted from Auble, D. (1953) 'Extended tables for the Mann-Whitney statistic', *Bulletin of the Institute of Educational Research at Indiana University* **1**(2).

Critical values on the *F*-distribution

(a) At significance level 0·10

Significance level = 0·10										
ν_1	1	2	3	4	5	6	8	12	24	inf
ν_2										
1	39·86	49·50	53·59	55·83	57·24	58·20	59·44	60·71	62·00	63·23
2	8·52	9·00	9·16	9·24	9·29	9·33	9·37	9·41	9·45	9·49
3	5·54	5·46	5·39	5·34	5·31	5·28	5·25	5·22	5·18	5·13
4	4·54	4·32	4·19	4·11	4·05	4·01	3·95	3·90	3·83	3·76
5	4·06	3·78	3·62	3·52	3·45	3·40	3·34	3·27	3·19	3·10
6	3·78	3·46	3·29	3·18	3·11	3·05	2·98	2·90	2·80	2·72
7	3·59	3·26	3·07	2·96	2·88	2·83	2·75	2·67	2·58	2·47
8	3·46	3·11	2·92	2·81	2·73	2·67	2·59	2·50	2·40	2·29
9	3·36	3·01	2·81	2·69	2·61	2·55	2·47	2·38	2·28	2·16
10	3·29	2·92	2·73	2·61	2·52	2·46	2·38	2·28	2·18	2·06
11	3·23	2·86	2·66	2·54	2·45	2·39	2·30	2·21	2·10	1·97
12	3·18	2·81	2·61	2·48	2·39	2·33	2·24	2·15	2·04	1·90
13	3·14	2·76	2·56	2·43	2·35	2·28	2·20	2·10	1·98	1·85
14	3·10	2·73	2·52	2·39	2·31	2·24	2·15	2·05	1·94	1·80
15	3·07	2·70	2·49	2·36	2·27	2·21	2·12	2·02	1·90	1·76
16	3·05	2·67	2·46	2·33	2·24	2·18	2·09	1·99	1·87	1·72
17	3·03	2·64	2·44	2·31	2·22	2·15	2·06	1·96	1·84	1·69
18	3·01	2·62	2·42	2·29	2·20	2·13	2·04	1·93	1·81	1·66
19	2·99	2·61	2·40	2·27	2·18	2·11	2·02	1·91	1·79	1·63
20	2·97	2·59	2·38	2·25	2·16	2·09	2·00	1·89	1·78	1·61
21	2·96	2·57	2·36	2·23	2·14	2·08	1·98	1·87	1·76	1·59
22	2·95	2·56	2·35	2·22	2·13	2·06	1·97	1·86	1·74	1·57
23	2·94	2·55	2·34	2·21	2·11	2·05	1·95	1·84	1·72	1·55
24	2·93	2·54	2·33	2·19	2·10	2·04	1·94	1·83	1·70	1·53

Significance level = 0·10

v_1	1	2	3	4	5	6	8	12	24	inf
v_2										
25	2·92	2·53	2·32	2·18	2·09	2·02	1·93	1·82	1·69	1·52
26	2·91	2·52	2·31	2·17	2·08	2·01	1·92	1·81	1·68	1·50
27	2·90	2·51	2·30	2·17	2·07	2·00	1·91	1·80	1·67	1·49
28	2·89	2·50	2·29	2·16	2·06	2·00	1·90	1·79	1·67	1·48
29	2·89	2·50	2·28	2·15	2·06	1·99	1·89	1·78	1·65	1·47
30	2·88	2·49	2·28	2·14	2·05	1·98	1·88	1·77	1·64	1·46
40	2·84	2·44	2·23	2·09	2·00	1·93	1·83	1·71	1·57	1·36
60	2·79	2·39	2·18	2·04	1·95	1·87	1·77	1·66	1·51	1·29
120	2·75	2·35	2·13	1·99	1·90	1·82	1·72	1·60	1·45	1·19
inf	2·71	2·30	2·08	1·94	1·85	1·77	1·67	1·55	1·38	1·00

The critical F-value is determined by reference to the degrees of freedom associated with the greater and the lesser variances (v_1 and v_2 respectively). The observed variance ratio is significant if it equals or exceeds the critical (tabled) value. Intermediate values should be estimated by interpolation.

(b) At significance level 0·05

Significance level = 0·05

v_1	1	2	3	4	5	6	8	12	24	inf
v_2										
1	161·4	199·7	215·7	224·6	230·2	234·0	238·0	243·9	249·0	254·3
2	18·51	19·00	19·16	19·25	19·30	19·33	19·37	19·41	19·45	19·59
3	10·13	9·55	9·28	9·12	9·01	8·94	8·84	8·74	8·64	8·53
4	7·71	6·94	6·39	6·39	6·26	6·16	6·04	5·91	5·77	5·65
5	6·61	5·79	5·41	5·19	5·05	4·95	4·81	4·68	4·53	4·36
6	5·99	5·14	4·76	4·53	4·39	4·28	4·15	4·00	3·84	3·67
7	5·59	4·74	4·35	4·12	3·97	3·87	3·73	3·37	3·41	3·23
8	5·32	4·46	4·07	3·84	3·69	3·58	3·44	3·28	3·12	2·93
9	5·12	4·26	3·86	3·63	3·48	3·37	3·23	3·07	2·90	2·71
10	4·96	4·10	3·71	3·48	3·33	3·22	3·07	2·91	2·74	2·54
11	4·84	3·98	3·59	3·36	3·20	3·09	2·95	2·79	2·61	2·40
12	4·75	3·88	3·49	3·26	3·11	3·00	2·85	2·69	2·50	2·30
13	4·67	3·80	3·41	3·18	3·02	2·92	2·77	2·60	2·42	2·21
14	4·60	3·74	3·34	3·11	2·96	2·85	2·70	2·53	2·35	2·13
15	4·54	3·68	3·29	3·06	2·90	2·79	2·64	2·48	2·29	2·07
16	4·49	3·63	3·24	3·01	2·85	2·74	2·59	2·42	2·24	2·01
17	4·45	3·59	3·20	2·96	2·81	2·70	2·55	2·38	2·19	1·96
18	4·41	3·55	3·16	2·93	2·77	2·66	2·51	2·34	2·15	1·92
19	4·38	3·52	3·13	2·90	2·74	2·63	2·48	2·31	2·11	1·88
20	4·35	3·49	3·10	2·87	2·71	2·60	2·45	2·28	2·08	1·84
21	4·32	3·47	3·07	2·84	2·68	2·57	2·42	2·25	2·05	1·81
22	4·30	3·44	3·05	2·82	2·66	2·55	2·40	2·23	2·03	1·78
23	4·28	3·42	3·03	2·80	2·64	2·53	2·38	2·20	2·00	1·76
24	4·26	3·40	3·01	2·78	2·62	2·51	2·36	2·18	1·98	1·73
25	4·24	3·38	2·99	2·76	2·60	2·49	2·34	2·16	1·96	1·71
26	4·22	3·37	2·98	2·74	2·59	2·47	2·32	2·15	1·95	1·69
27	4·21	3·35	2·96	2·72	2·57	2·46	2·30	2·13	1·93	1·67
28	4·20	3·34	2·95	2·71	2·56	2·44	2·29	2·12	1·91	1·65
29	4·18	3·33	2·93	2·70	2·54	2·43	2·28	2·10	1·90	1·64
30	4·17	3·32	2·92	2·69	2·53	2·42	2·27	2·09	1·89	1·62
40	4·08	3·23	2·84	2·61	2·45	2·34	2·18	2·08	1·79	1·51
60	4·00	3·15	2·76	2·52	2·37	2·25	2·10	1·92	1·70	1·39
120	3·93	3·07	2·68	2·45	2·29	2·17	2·02	1·83	1·61	1·25
inf	3·84	2·99	2·60	2·37	2·21	2·09	1·94	1·75	1·52	1·00

The critical *F*-value is determined by reference to the degrees of freedom associated with the greater and the lesser variances (v_1 and v_2 respectively). The observed variance ratio is significant if it equals or exceeds the critical (tabled) value. Intermediate values should be estimated by interpolation.

(c) At significance level 0·01

Significance level = 0·01

v_1	1	2	3	4	5	6	8	12	24	inf
v_2										
1	4,052	4,999	5,403	5,625	5,764	5,859	5,981	6,106	6,234	6,366
2	98·49	99·01	99·17	99·25	99·30	99·33	99·36	99·42	99·46	99·50
3	34·12	30·81	29·46	28·71	28·24	27·91	27·49	27·05	26·60	26·12
4	21·20	18·00	16·69	15·98	15·52	15·21	14·80	14·37	13·93	13·46
5	16·26	13·27	12·06	11·39	10·97	10·67	10·27	9·89	9·47	9·02
6	13·74	10·92	9·78	9·15	8·75	8·47	8·10	7·72	7·31	6·88
7	12·25	9·55	8·45	7·85	7·46	7·19	6·84	6·47	6·07	5·65
8	11·26	8·65	7·59	7·01	6·63	6·37	6·03	5·67	5·28	4·86
9	10·56	8·02	6·99	6·42	6·06	5·80	5·47	5·11	4·73	4·31
10	10·04	7·56	6·55	5·99	5·64	5·39	5·06	4·71	4·33	3·91
11	9·65	7·20	6·22	5·67	5·32	5·07	4·74	4·40	4·02	3·60
12	9·33	6·93	5·95	5·41	5·06	4·82	4·50	4·16	3·78	3·36
13	9·07	6·70	5·74	5·20	4·86	4·62	4·30	3·96	3·59	3·16
14	8·88	6·51	5·56	5·03	4·69	4·46	4·14	3·80	3·43	3·00
15	8·68	6·36	5·42	4·99	4·56	4·32	4·00	3·67	3·29	2·87
16	8·53	6·23	5·29	4·77	4·44	4·20	3·89	3·55	3·18	2·75
17	8·40	6·11	5·18	4·67	4·34	4·10	3·79	3·45	3·08	2·65
18	8·28	6·01	5·09	4·58	4·25	4·01	3·71	3·37	3·00	2·57
19	8·18	5·93	5·01	4·50	4·17	3·94	3·63	3·30	2·92	2·49
20	8·10	5·85	4·94	4·43	4·10	3·87	3·56	3·23	2·86	2·42
21	8·02	5·78	4·87	4·37	4·04	3·81	3·51	3·17	2·80	2·36
22	7·94	5·72	4·83	4·31	3·99	3·76	3·45	3·12	2·75	2·31
23	7·88	5·66	4·76	4·26	3·94	3·71	3·41	3·07	2·70	2·26
24	7·82	5·61	4·72	4·22	3·90	3·67	3·36	3·03	2·66	2·21
25	7·77	5·57	4·68	4·18	3·86	3·63	3·32	2·99	2·62	2·17
26	7·72	5·53	4·64	4·14	3·82	3·59	3·29	2·96	2·58	2·13
27	7·68	5·49	4·60	4·11	3·78	3·56	3·26	2·93	2·55	2·10
28	7·64	5·45	4·57	4·07	3·75	3·53	3·23	2·90	2·52	2·06
29	7·60	5·42	4·54	4·04	3·73	3·50	3·20	2·87	2·49	2·03
30	7·56	5·39	4·51	4·02	3·70	3·47	3·17	2·84	2·47	2·01
40	7·31	5·18	4·31	3·83	3·51	3·29	2·99	2·66	2·29	1·80
60	7·08	4·98	4·13	3·65	3·34	3·12	2·82	2·50	2·12	1·60
120	6·85	4·79	3·95	3·48	3·17	2·96	2·66	2·34	1·95	1·38
inf	6·64	4·60	3·78	3·32	3·02	2·80	2·51	2·18	1·79	1·00

The critical *F*-value is determined by reference to the degrees of freedom associated with the greater and the lesser variances (v_1 and v_2 respectively). The observed variance ratio is significant if it equals or exceeds the critical (tabled) value. Intermediate values should be estimated by interpolation.

Appendix VI is adapted from Fisher, R. A. and Yates, F. (1948) *Statistical Tables for Biological, Agricultural and Medical Research*. Edinburgh: Oliver and Boyd.

Critical values of the Kruskal-Wallis statistic (*H*)

Sample sizes			Significance level		
n_1	n_2	n_3	0·10	0·05	0·01
2	2	2	4·571		
3	2	1	4·286		
3	2	2	4·470	4·714	
3	3	1	4·571	5·143	
3	3	2	4·556	5·710	
3	3	3	4·622	5·600	6·489
4	2	1	4·199	4·822	
4	2	2	4·458	5·125	6·000
4	3	2	4·444	5·400	6·300
4	3	3	4·700	5·727	6·746
4	4	1	4·066	4·966	6·667
4	4	2	4·555	5·300	6·875
4	4	3	4·477	5·586	7·144
4	4	4	4·581	5·692	7·490
5	2	1	4·170	5·000	
5	2	2	4·342	5·071	6·373
5	3	1	3·982	4·915	6·400
5	3	2	4·495	5·205	6·822
5	3	3	4·503	5·580	7·030
5	4	1	3·974	4·923	6·885
5	4	2	4·522	5·268	7·118
5	4	3	4·542	5·631	7·440
5	4	4	4·619	5·618	7·752
5	5	1	4·056	5·018	7·073
5	5	2	4·508	5·339	7·269
5	5	3	4·545	5·642	7·543

Sample sizes			Significance level		
n_1	n_2	n_3	0·10	0·05	0·01
5	5	4	4·521	5·643	7·791
5	5	5	4·560	5·720	7·980

The null hypothesis is rejected if the calculated H-value equals or exceeds the critical (tabled) value. The latter is determined by reference to the three sample sizes n_1, n_2 and n_3 and the significance level, although for some combinations there are no reliable values.

Reprinted from the Kruskal, W. H. and Wallis, W. A. (1952) 'Use of ranks in one-criterion variance analysis', *Journal of the American Statistical Association* **47**, 614–7. (Copyright 1952 by the American Statistical Association. All rights reserved.)

Critical values of the Pearson product-moment correlation coefficient

	Two-tailed significance levels (one-tailed in brackets)			
n	0·10 (0·05)	0·05 (0·025)	0·02 (0·01)	0·01 (0·005)
3	0·988	0·997	1·000	1·000
4	0·900	0·950	0·980	0·990
5	0·805	0·878	0·934	0·959
6	0·729	0·811	0·882	0·917
7	0·669	0·754	0·833	0·875
8	0·621	0·707	0·789	0·834
9	0·582	0·666	0·750	0·798
10	0·549	0·632	0·715	0·765
11	0·521	0·602	0·685	0·735
12	0·497	0·576	0·658	0·708
13	0·476	0·553	0·634	0·684
14	0·458	0·532	0·612	0·661
15	0·441	0·514	0·592	0·641
16	0·426	0·497	0·574	0·623
17	0·412	0·482	0·558	0·606
18	0·400	0·468	0·543	0·590
19	0·389	0·456	0·529	0·575
20	0·378	0·444	0·516	0·561
21	0·369	0·433	0·503	0·549
22	0·360	0·423	0·492	0·537
23	0·352	0·413	0·482	0·526
24	0·344	0·404	0·472	0·515
25	0·337	0·396	0·462	0·505
26	0·330	0·388	0·453	0·496

	Two-tailed significance levels (one-tailed in brackets)			
n	0·10 (0·05)	0·05 (0·025)	0·02 (0·01)	0·01 (0·005)
27	0·323	0·381	0·445	0·487
28	0·317	0·374	0·437	0·479
29	0·311	0·367	0·430	0·471
30	0·306	0·361	0·423	0·463
31	0·301	0·355	0·416	0·456
32	0·296	0·349	0·409	0·449
33	0·291	0·344	0·403	0·443
34	0·287	0·339	0·397	0·436
35	0·283	0·334	0·391	0·430
40	0·264	0·312	0·367	0·403
45	0·249	0·294	0·346	0·380
50	0·235	0·279	0·328	0·361
55	0·224	0·266	0·313	0·345
60	0·214	0·254	0·300	0·330
65	0·206	0·244	0·288	0·317
70	0·198	0·235	0·278	0·306
75	0·191	0·227	0·268	0·296
80	0·185	0·220	0·260	0·286
85	0·180	0·213	0·252	0·278
90	0·174	0·207	0·245	0·270
95	0·170	0·202	0·238	0·263
100	0·165	0·197	0·232	0·256
150	0·135	0·160	0·190	0·210
200	0·117	0·139	0·164	0·182

The observed correlation coefficient is significant if it equals or exceeds the tabled value at the selected significance level with sample size *n*.

Reproduced from Table 6.2 in Neave, H. R. (1978) *Statistical Tables*. London: George Allen and Unwin.

Critical values of the Spearman's rank correlation coefficient

	Two-tailed significance levels (one-tailed in brackets)			
n	0·10 (0·05)	0·05 (0·025)	0·02 (0·01)	0·01 (0·005)
5	0·900	1·000	1·000	1·000
6	0·829	0·886	0·943	1·000
7	0·714	0·786	0·893	0·929
8	0·643	0·738	0·833	0·881
9	0·600	0·700	0·783	0·833
10	0·564	0·648	0·745	0·794
11	0·536	0·618	0·709	0·755
12	0·503	0·587	0·678	0·727
13	0·484	0·560	0·648	0·703
14	0·464	0·538	0·626	0·679
15	0·446	0·521	0·604	0·654
16	0·429	0·503	0·582	0·635
17	0·414	0·488	0·566	0·618
18	0·401	0·472	0·550	0·600
19	0·391	0·460	0·535	0·584
20	0·380	0·447	0·522	0·570
21	0·370	0·436	0·509	0·556
22	0·361	0·425	0·497	0·544
23	0·353	0·416	0·486	0·532
24	0·344	0·407	0·476	0·521
25	0·337	0·398	0·466	0·511
26	0·331	0·390	0·457	0·501
27	0·324	0·383	0·449	0·492
28	0·318	0·375	0·441	0·483

Two-tailed significance levels (one-tailed in brackets)

n	0·10 (0·05)	0·05 (0·025)	0·02 (0·01)	0·01 (0·005)
29	0·312	0·368	0·433	0·475
30	0·306	0·362	0·425	0·467
31	0·301	0·356	0·419	0·459
32	0·296	0·350	0·412	0·452
33	0·291	0·345	0·405	0·446
34	0·287	0·340	0·400	0·439
35	0·283	0·335	0·394	0·433
40	0·264	0·313	0·368	0·405
45	0·248	0·294	0·347	0·382
50	0·235	0·279	0·329	0·363
55	0·224	0·266	0·314	0·346
60	0·214	0·255	0·301	0·331
65	0·206	0·245	0·291	0·322
70	0·198	0·236	0·280	0·310
80	0·185	0·221	0·262	0·290
90	0·174	0·208	0·247	0·273
100	0·165	0·197	0·234	0·259

The observed correlation coefficient is significant if it equals or exceeds the tabled value at the selected significance level with sample size n.

Reproduced from Table 6.4 in Neave, H. R. (1978) *Statistical Tables*. London: George Allen and Unwin.

Critical bounds on the Durbin-Watson distribution (*d*)

(a) At significance level 0·05

	Significance level = 0·05									
	$k = 1$		$k = 2$		$k = 3$		$k = 4$		$k = 5$	
n	d_l	d_u	d_l	d_u	d_l	d_u	d_l	d_u	d_l	d_u
15	1·077	1·361	0·946	1·543	0·814	1·750	0·685	1·977	0·562	2·220
16	1·106	1·371	0·982	1·539	0·857	1·728	0·734	1·935	0·615	2·157
17	1·133	1·381	1·015	1·536	0·897	1·710	0·779	1·900	0·664	2·104
18	1·158	1·391	1·046	1·535	0·933	1·696	0·820	1·872	0·710	2·060
19	1·180	1·401	1·074	1·536	0·967	1·685	0·859	1·848	0·752	2·023
20	1·201	1·411	1·100	1·537	0·998	1·676	0·894	1·828	0·792	1·991
21	1·221	1·420	1·125	1·538	1·026	1·669	0·927	1·812	0·829	1·964
22	1·239	1·429	1·147	1·541	1·053	1·664	0·958	1·797	0·863	1·940
23	1·257	1·437	1·168	1·543	1·078	1·660	0·986	1·785	0·895	1·920
24	1·273	1·446	1·188	1·546	1·101	1·656	1·013	1·775	0·925	1·902
25	1·288	1·454	1·206	1·550	1·123	1·654	1·038	1·767	0·953	1·886
26	1·302	1·461	1·224	1·553	1·143	1·652	1·062	1·759	0·979	1·873
27	1·316	1·469	1·240	1·556	1·162	1·651	1·084	1·753	1·004	1·861
28	1·328	1·476	1·255	1·560	1·181	1·650	1·104	1·747	1·028	1·850
29	1·341	1·483	1·270	1·563	1·198	1·650	1·124	1·743	1·050	1·841
30	1·352	1·489	1·284	1·567	1·214	1·650	1·143	1·739	1·071	1·833
31	1·363	1·496	1·297	1·570	1·229	1·650	1·160	1·735	1·090	1·825
32	1·373	1·502	1·309	1·574	1·244	1·650	1·177	1·732	1·109	1·819
33	1·383	1·508	1·321	1·577	1·258	1·651	1·193	1·730	1·127	1·813
34	1·393	1·514	1·333	1·580	1·271	1·652	1·208	1·728	1·144	1·808
35	1·402	1·519	1·343	1·584	1·283	1·653	1·222	1·726	1·160	1·803

Significance level = 0·05

n	k = 1 d_l	k = 1 d_u	k = 2 d_l	k = 2 d_u	k = 3 d_l	k = 3 d_u	k = 4 d_l	k = 4 d_u	k = 5 d_l	k = 5 d_u
36	1·411	1·525	1·354	1·587	1·295	1·654	1·236	1·724	1·175	1·799
37	1·419	1·530	1·364	1·590	1·307	1·655	1·249	1·723	1·190	1·795
38	1·427	1·535	1·373	1·594	1·318	1·656	1·261	1·722	1·204	1·792
39	1·435	1·540	1·382	1·597	1·328	1·658	1·273	1·722	1·218	1·789
40	1·442	1·544	1·391	1·600	1·338	1·659	1·285	1·721	1·230	1·786
45	1·475	1·566	1·430	1·615	1·383	1·666	1·336	1·720	1·287	1·776
50	1·503	1·585	1·462	1·628	1·421	1·674	1·378	1·721	1·335	1·771
55	1·528	1·601	1·490	1·641	1·452	1·681	1·414	1·724	1·374	1·768
60	1·549	1·616	1·514	1·652	1·480	1·689	1·444	1·727	1·408	1·767
65	1·567	1·629	1·536	1·662	1·503	1·696	1·471	1·731	1·438	1·767
70	1·583	1·641	1·554	1·672	1·525	1·703	1·494	1·735	1·464	1·768
75	1·598	1·652	1·571	1·680	1·543	1·709	1·515	1·739	1·487	1·770
80	1·611	1·662	1·586	1·688	1·560	1·715	1·534	1·743	1·507	1·772
85	1·624	1·671	1·600	1·696	1·575	1·721	1·550	1·747	1·525	1·774
90	1·635	1·679	1·612	1·703	1·589	1·726	1·566	1·751	1·542	1·776
95	1·645	1·687	1·623	1·709	1·602	1·732	1·579	1·755	1·557	1·778
100	1·654	1·694	1·634	1·715	1·613	1·736	1·592	1·758	1·571	1·780

The upper (d_u) and the lower (d_l) bounds are determined by reference to the number of observations (n) and the number of independent terms (k).

(b) At significance level 0·01

	Significance level = 0·01									
	k = 1		k = 2		k = 3		k = 4		k = 5	
n	d_l	d_u	d_l	d_u	d_l	d_u	d_l	d_u	d_l	d_u
15	0·811	1·070	0·700	1·252	0·591	1·464	0·488	1·704	0·391	1·967
16	0·844	1·086	0·737	1·252	0·633	1·446	0·532	1·663	0·437	1·900
17	0·874	1·102	0·772	1·255	0·672	1·432	0·574	1·630	0·480	1·847
18	0·902	1·118	0·805	1·259	0·708	1·422	0·613	1·604	0·522	1·803
19	0·928	1·132	0·835	1·265	0·742	1·415	0·650	1·584	0·561	1·767
20	0·952	1·147	0·863	1·271	0·773	1·411	0·685	1·567	0·598	1·737
21	0·975	1·161	0·890	1·277	0·803	1·408	0·718	1·554	0·633	1·712
22	0·997	1·174	0·914	1·284	0·831	1·407	0·748	1·543	0·667	1·691
23	1·018	1·187	0·938	1·291	0·858	1·407	0·777	1·534	0·698	1·673
24	1·037	1·199	0·960	1·298	0·882	1·407	0·805	1·528	0·728	1·658
25	1·055	1·211	0·981	1·305	0·906	1·409	0·831	1·523	0·756	1·645
26	1·072	1·222	1·001	1·312	0·928	1·411	0·855	1·518	0·783	1·635
27	1·089	1·233	1·019	1·319	0·949	1·413	0·878	1·515	0·808	1·626
28	1·104	1·244	1·037	1·325	0·969	1·415	0·900	1·513	0·832	1·618
29	1·119	1·254	1·054	1·332	0·988	1·418	0·921	1·512	0·855	1·611
30	1·133	1·263	1·070	1·339	1·006	1·421	0·941	1·511	0·877	1·606
31	1·147	1·273	1·085	1·345	1·023	1·425	0·960	1·510	0·897	1·601
32	1·160	1·282	1·100	1·352	1·040	1·428	0·979	1·510	0·917	1·597
33	1·172	1·291	1·114	1·358	1·055	1·432	0·996	1·510	0·936	1·594
34	1·184	1·299	1·128	1·364	1·070	1·435	1·012	1·511	0·954	1·591
35	1·195	1·307	1·140	1·370	1·085	1·439	1·028	1·512	0·971	1·589
36	1·206	1·315	1·153	1·376	1·098	1·442	1·043	1·513	0·988	1·588
37	1·217	1·323	1·165	1·382	1·112	1·446	1·058	1·514	1·004	1·586
38	1·227	1·330	1·176	1·388	1·124	1·449	1·072	1·515	1·019	1·585
39	1·237	1·337	1·187	1·393	1·137	1·453	1·085	1·517	1·034	1·584
40	1·246	1·344	1·198	1·398	1·148	1·457	1·098	1·518	1·048	1·584
45	1·288	1·376	1·245	1·423	1·201	1·474	1·156	1·528	1·111	1·584
50	1·324	1·403	1·285	1·446	1·245	1·491	1·205	1·528	1·164	1·587
55	1·356	1·427	1·320	1·466	1·284	1·506	1·247	1·548	1·209	1·592
60	1·383	1·449	1·350	1·484	1·317	1·520	1·283	1·558	1·249	1·598
65	1·407	1·468	1·377	1·500	1·346	1·534	1·315	1·568	1·283	1·604
70	1·429	1·485	1·400	1·515	1·372	1·546	1·343	1·578	1·313	1·611
75	1·448	1·501	1·422	1·529	1·395	1·557	1·368	1·587	1·340	1·617

	Significance level = 0·01									
	k = 1		k = 2		k = 3		k = 4		k = 5	
n	d_l	d_u	d_l	d_u	d_l	d_u	d_l	d_u	d_l	d_u
80	1·466	1·515	1·441	1·541	1·416	1·568	1·390	1·595	1·364	1·624
85	1·482	1·528	1·458	1·553	1·435	1·578	1·411	1·603	1·386	1·630
90	1·496	1·540	1·474	1·563	1·452	1·587	1·429	1·611	1·406	1·636
95	1·510	1·552	1·489	1·573	1·468	1·596	1·446	1·618	1·425	1·642
100	1·522	1·562	1·503	1·583	1·482	1·604	1·462	1·625	1·441	1·647

The upper (d_u) and the lower (d_l) bounds are determined by reference to the number of observations (n) and the number of independent terms (k).

Appendix X (a and b) is adapted from original material in Koerts, J. and Abrahamse, A. P. J. (1969) *On the Theory and Application of the General Linear Model*. Rotterdam: University of Rotterdam Press.

Table of random numbers

19223	95034	05756	27813	96409	12351	42544	82853
73676	47150	98400	01927	27764	42468	84225	36290
45467	71709	77588	00095	32863	29485	82226	90056
52711	38889	93074	60227	40011	85848	48767	52573
95592	94007	69971	91481	60779	53971	17297	59335
68417	35013	15829	72765	85089	56067	50211	47487
82739	57890	20807	47511	81767	55330	94383	14983
60940	72042	17868	24943	61790	90565	87964	18885
36009	19365	15412	39368	85453	46816	84385	41979
39448	49789	18338	24697	39364	42006	76688	08708
81486	69487	60513	09297	000412	71238	27499	39950
59636	88804	04643	71197	18352	73089	84898	45785
62568	70206	40235	03699	71080	22553	11486	11776
45159	32992	73750	66280	03819	56202	02938	70915
61041	77684	94322	24709	73689	14526	31893	32593
38162	98532	61283	70632	23417	26185	41448	75532
73190	32533	04470	29669	84407	90785	65496	86382
95857	07718	87664	92099	58806	66979	96624	84826
35476	55975	39421	65850	04266	35435	43742	11937
71487	00984	29077	14863	61683	47052	62224	51025
13875	81598	95052	90908	73592	75186	87136	95761
54580	81507	27102	56027	55893	33063	41842	81868
71035	09001	43367	49427	72719	96758	27611	91965
96927	19931	36089	74192	77567	88741	48409	41903
43909	99477	25330	64359	40085	16925	85117	36071
15689	14227	06565	14374	13352	49367	81982	87209
36759	58984	68288	22913	18638	54303	00795	07827
69051	64817	87174	09751	84534	06489	87201	97245

05007	16332	81194	14873	04197	85576	45195	96505
68732	55259	84292	08796	43456	93739	31865	97150
45740	41807	65561	33302	07051	93623	18132	09547
66925	55685	39100	78458	11206	19876	87151	31260
08421	44753	77377	28744	75592	08563	79140	95254
53645	66812	61421	47836	12609	15374	98481	14592
66831	68908	40772	21558	47781	33856	79117	06928
55588	99404	70708	41098	43563	56934	48394	51719
12975	13258	13048	45114	72321	81940	00360	02428
96767	35964	23822	96012	94591	65194	50842	53372
72829	50232	97892	63408	77919	44575	24870	04178
88565	42628	17787	49376	61762	16593	88604	12724
62974	88145	83083	69543	46109	59505	69680	00900
19687	12633	57857	95806	09931	02150	43163	58636
37609	59057	66979	83401	60705	02384	90597	93600
54973	86278	88737	74351	47500	84552	19909	67181
00694	05877	19664	65441	20903	62371	22725	53340

References

Alpin, P. (2003) 'Using remotely sensed data', in Clifford, N. J. and Valentine, G. (eds) *Key Methods in Geography*. London: Sage.

Auble, D. (1953) 'Extended tables for the Mann-Whitney statistic', *Bulletin of the Institute of Educational Research at Indiana University* **1**(2).

Babbie, E. (2001) *The Practice of Social Research*, 9th edn. Belmont, California: Wadsworth.

Barr, S., Gilg, A. W. and Ford, N. J. (2003) 'Who are the environmentalists? Part 1: environmentalism in Britain today', *Town and Country Planning* **72**(6), 185–6.

Beresford, M. and Hurst, J. G. (1971) *Deserted Medieval Villages*. London: Lutterworth.

Borchert, J. R. (1987) 'Maps, geography and geographers', *The Professional Geographer* **39**, 387–9.

Central Statistical Office (1971–   ) *Regional Trends*. London: HMSO.

Central Statistical Office (1980) *Guide to Official Statistics*. London: HMSO.

Central Statistical Office (1981) *Regional Trends 1981*. London: HMSO.

Central Statistical Office (1991) *Regional Trends 1991*. London: HMSO.

Clifford, N. J. and Valentine, G. (2003) *Key Methods in Geography*. London: Sage.

Dunn, K. (2000) 'Interviewing', in Hay, I. (ed.) *Qualitative Research Methods in Human Geography*. Melbourne: Oxford University Press.

Fink, A. and Kosecoff, J. (1999) *How to Conduct Surveys: A Step-by-Step Guide*. Thousand Oaks: Sage.

Fisher, R. A. and Yates, F. (1948) *Statistical Tables for Biological, Agricultural and Medical Research*. Edinburgh: Oliver and Boyd.

Fowler, F. (2002) *Survey Research Methods*, 3rd edn. Thousand Oaks: Sage.

Gibson, P. J. (2000) *Introductory Remote Sensing: Principles and Concepts*. London: Routledge.

Gibson, P. J. and Power, C. H. (2000) *Introductory Remote Sensing: Digital Image Processing and Applications*. London: Routledge.

Goudie, A. S. (ed.) (1990) *Geomorphological Techniques*, 2nd edn. London: Unwin & Hyman.

Harvey, D. (1969) *Explanation in Geography*. London: Arnold.

Heywood, I., Cornelius, S. and Carver, S. (1998) *An Introduction to Geographical Information Systems*. Harlow: Prentice Hall.

Institute of Hydrology (1991) *Hydrological Data UK 1990 Yearbook*. Wallingford, Oxon: Institute of Hydrology.

Kitchin, R. and Tate, N. J. (2000) *Conducting Research into Human Geography*. Harlow: Prentice Hall.

Kivell, P. T. and Shaw, G. (1980) 'The study of retail location', in Dawson, J. A. (ed.) *Retail Geography*. London: Croom Helm.

Koerts, J. and Abrahamse, A. P. J. (1969) *On the Theory and Application of the General Linear Model*. Rotterdam: University of Rotterdam Press.

Kruskal, W. H. and Wallis, W. A. (1952) 'Use of ranks in one-criterion variance analysis', *Journal of the American Statistical Association* **47**, 614–17.

Lillesand, T. M. and Kiefer, R. W. (2000) *Remote Sensing and Image Interpretation*, 4th edn. New York: Wiley.

Madge, C. H. and Willmott, P. (1981) *Inner City Poverty in Paris and London*. London: Routledge.

Maguire, D. J. (1989) *Computers in Geography*. Harlow: Longman.

Mann, H. B. and Whitney, D. R. (1947) 'On a test of whether one of two random variables is stochastically larger than the other', *Annals of Mathematical Statistics* **18**, 50–60.

Massey, F. J. (1951) 'The Kolmogorov-Smirnov test for goodness of fit', *Journal of the American Statistical Association* **46**, 126–7.

McLafferty, S. L. (2003) 'Conducting questionnaire surveys', in Clifford, N. J. and Valentine, G. (eds) *Key Methods in Geography*. London: Sage.

Meteorological Office (1991) *British Rainfall 1990*. Bracknell, Berks: Meteorological Office.

Neave, H. R. (1978) *Statistical Tables*. London: George Allen and Unwin.

Noelle-Newman, E. (1970) 'Wanted: rules for wording structured questionnaires', *Public Opinions Quarterly* **34**, 200–10.

Office of Population Censuses and Surveys (1973) *Census 1971 England and Wales County Report: Yorkshire – East Riding*. London: HMSO.

Office of Population Censuses and Surveys (1984) *Census 1981 (10% sample) – Workplace and Transport to Work*. London: HMSO.

Openshaw, S. (1995) *Census Users' Handbook*. Cambridge: GeoInformation International.

Oppenheim, A. N. (1992) *Questionnaire Design, Interviewing and Attitude Measurement*. London: Pinter.

Reid, I. (2003) 'Making observations and measurements in the field: an overview', in Clifford, N. J. and Valentine, G. (eds) *Key Methods in Geography*. London: Sage.

Rice, S. (2003) 'Sampling in geography', in Clifford, N. J. and Valentine, G. (eds) *Key Methods in Geography*. London: Sage.

Rogers, A. (1974) *Statistical Analysis of Spatial Dispersion: the Quadrat Method*. London: Pion.

Rose, D. and O'Reilly, K. (1998) *ESRC Review of Government Social Classifications*. London: Office for National Statistics.

Siegel, S. (1956) *Nonparametric Statistics for the Behavioral Sciences*. New York: McGraw-Hill.

Smith, D. M. (1975) *Patterns in Human Geography*. Harmondsworth: Penguin.

Taylor, P. J. (1977) *Quantitative Methods in Geography*. Boston: Houghton-Mifflin.

United Nations (1969) *Growth of the World's Urban and Rural Population 1920–2000*. New York: United Nations.

Varley, R. (1968) *Land Use Analysis in the City Centre with Special Reference to Manchester*. Univ. of Wales unpublished MA thesis.

Walford, N. (2002) *Geographical Data: Characteristics and Sources*. Chichester: Wiley.

Wiltshire County Council (1979) *West Wiltshire Structure Plan 1979*. Swindon: Wiltshire County Council.

Websites

BBC Vote 2001
http://newssearch.bbc.co.uk/vote2001/

British Atmospheric Data Centre (BADC)
http://badc.nerc.ac.uk/help/query.html

Climatic Research Unit (CRU), University of East Anglia
http://www.cru.uea.ac.uk/

Joint Institute for the Study of the Atmosphere and Ocean (JISAO)
http://tao.atmos.washington.edu/jisao_sitemap.html

Minitab Inc.
http://www.minitab.com

National Oceanographic and Atmospheric Administration (NOAA)
http://www.ngdc.noaa.gov/paleo/paleo.html

National Statistics Online
www.statistics.gov.uk

SPSS plc
http://www.spss.com

UK Met Office
http://metoffice.com

Free downloadable data files at:
http://www.metoffice.com/climate/uk/stationdata/index.html

Met Office's research unit at the Hadley Centre (for long time series climatic data):
http://www.met-office.gov.uk/research/hadleycentre/CR_data/

UK National River Flow Archive (NRFA)
http://www.nwl.ac.uk/ih/nrfa/index.htm

US Federal statistics
www.fedstats.gov

Index